"Many good books have been written on healthy building, but until now there has no[t been a] manual that covers everything from theory to specification language in a way that can be applied t[o any] construction type. *Prescriptions for a Healthy House* is introductory enough to be used by someone new to the field, yet detailed and practical enough to be a valuable reference for the more experienced.
The best thing about this book is that it is laid out to be used. The graphic design allows for easy perusal to find the charts, case studies, specification language, resources, details, or supporting text. In fact, I made use of *Prescriptions* the first day I got it: a client called with a question, and I turned straight to the relevant page and read her a concise list of practical suggestions. I was relieved not to have to comb my mental or physical database!
The backgrounds of the authors—experienced architect, M.D., and healthy building consultant—combine to give the book a breadth and depth rarely found in one place. More than an admonition to go nontoxic or a list of materials, the book includes practical strategies and procedures, clearly gained from experience, to ensure that the finished home is a haven, not a nightmare. The case studies bring home the authors' points. When you read that a cleanup product caused a nearly finished house to be uninhabitable, you know why you need to specify everything that is used on the site. In fact, it makes me want to specify that every contractor read this book!"
Carol Venolia, publisher of *Building with Nature* newsletter and author of *Healing Environments*, Santa Rosa, CA

"*Prescriptions for a Healthy House* really is a practical guide. It is easy to follow, enlightening, and incorporates materials and methods that are reasonable to apply to normal construction.
I would highly recommend this book to Architects, Owners, and Contractors."
Richard Skinner, Architect, Jacksonville, FL

"Having read the first edition of *Prescriptions for a Healthy House*, I was so impressed that I asked the architect designing our house in Florida to use these concepts throughout. We're very pleased with the results."
Mathias B. Bowman, Chief Investment Officer of a very large venture capital fund, New York, NY

"Thank you for giving me and my builder access to a healthier way of building my home.
Your book has been our bible!"
Hope Connors Brown, *Hope Connors Interiors*, LLC, Denver, CO

"As a chemically sensitive individual, I would not want to be without this essential guide book because it is extraordinarily helpful, bridges the gap between the theory and the practice of building a healthy home, and even includes special comprehensive lists of healthy building products and where to find them. I would highly recommend this book to anyone interested in building a healthy home. There's no other book like it."
Gina Block, Iowa City, IA

Prescriptions
for
A Healthy House

Prescriptions
for
A Healthy
House

A PRACTICAL GUIDE FOR
Architects, Builders, & Homeowners

REVISED & EXPANDED
SECOND EDITION

Paula Baker-Laporte, A.I.A.
Erica Elliott, M.D.
John Banta, B.A.

Illustrations by Lisa Flynn

NEW SOCIETY PUBLISHERS

Cataloguing in Publication Data: A catalog record for this publication is available from the National Library of Canada.

Cover design by Diane McIntosh. Book and page layout by Jeremy Drought
Second printing June, 2002. Third printing March, 2005.
Printed in Canada by Friesens.

New Society Publishers acknowledges the support of the Government of Canada through the Book Publishing Industry Development Program (BPIDP) for our publishing activities, and the assistance of the Province of British Columbia through the British Columbia Arts Council.

BRITISH
COLUMBIA
ARTS COUNCIL
Supported by the Province of British Columbia

Paperback ISBN: 0-86571-434-7.

Inquiries regarding requests to reprint all or part of *Prescriptions for a Healthy House* should be addressed to New Society Publishers at the address below.

To order directly from the publishers, please call toll-free (North America) 1-800-567-6772, or order online at www.newsociety.com.

Any other inquiries can be directed by mail to:

New Society Publishers
P.O. Box 189, Gabriola Island, British Columbia V0R 1X0, Canada

New Society Publishers' mission is to publish books that contribute in fundamental wys to building an ecologically sustainable and just society, and to do so with the least possible impact on the environment, in a manner that models this vision. We are committed to doing this not just through education, but through action. We are acting on our commitment to the world's remaining ancient forests by phasing out our paper supply from ancient forests worldwide. This book is one step towards ending global reforestation and climate change. It is printed on acid-free paper that is **100% old growth forest-free** (100% post-consumer recycled), processed chlorine free, and printed with vegetable based, low VOC inks. For further information, or to browse our full list of books and purchase securely, visit our website at www.newsociety.com

Dedication

This book is dedicated to the millions of people

who are chronically ill from chemical exposures.

May we be forewarned and learn from your suffering.

Table of Contents

Acknowledgments

THE authors wish to thank the many people who have offered their guidance, expertise, and encouragement in the completion of this book. Special thanks go to Pauline Kenny for her tireless efforts and computer wizardry, which helped to transform the data into something that resembled a book. Our gratitude goes to Will and Louise Pape, who graciously offered their ranch as a working retreat center and offered practical advice and inspiration each step of the way. Thanks are due to Santa Fe consultants Greg Friedman of the Good Water Company and Carl Rosenberg of Sunspot Design, who provided useful information about water filtration and mechanical systems respectively. And thanks to members of the Healthy Housing Coalition, as well as to friends, family, patients, and clients, who prodded us along with the refrain, "Is it finished yet?"

We wish to offer special acknowledgment to Helmut Ziehe, founder of the Institute for Bau-biologie and Ecology in Clearwater, Florida, teacher and mentor of many of us who are concerned about healthy homes.

Paula and John would like to thank the following individuals for their valuable contributions to this second revised and expanded edition: Tony Fuge of Plaza Hardwoods for sharing her knowledge on issues of wood sustainability and flooring; Pauline Kenny, once again, for her computer wizardry; and James Holland of Restoration Consultants. Paula would like to acknowledge her husband Robert Laporte, not only for his patience in living with a "writing" partner, but also for the teaching and inspiration he has shared with her in the field of natural building.

June 2001
Paula Baker-Laporte, AIA
John Banta, BA
Erica Elliott, MD

About the Authors

PAULA BAKER-LAPORTE is the primary author of this book. As an architect, Paula is intimately familiar with the materials and methods of standard construction. As a bau-biologist (see Introduction, p. 1), she also knows where these practices are in conflict with human health. Having designed and supervised the construction of many healthy homes, both for the well and those with multiple chemical sensitivities, she is well-versed in the available alternatives for healthier construction and in the challenges presented when one deviates from accepted construction norms. It was her vision to bring diverse information together into a practical reference book. Her collaboration with Erica and John has enabled this vision to become a reality.

As a physician trained in both family practice and environmental medicine, **Erica Elliott** has extensive clinical experience in the medical consequences of exposure to pollutants in the home and workplace. In this book she has interpreted the world of medicine and chemistry so that the reader can begin to understand the complex relationship between chemical exposure in the indoor environment and human health. As a talented linguist, she has lent her skills to this book by editing and clarifying a rather technical subject matter.

John Banta brings invaluable insight to the topics covered in this book, gained in the course of over a decade of experience in troubleshooting indoor environmental problems. His expertise covers many aspects of indoor air quality, including the detection and reduction of electromagnetic fields, and the recognition and remediation of mold problems. John holds a degree in Environmental Health Science.

Preface

IT has been said that we shape our buildings, and then our buildings shape us. When we consider that the average North American spends at least 90% of life indoors, the significance of this statement becomes apparent. In this era of unprecedented technological advancement, it stands to reason that we would use our knowledge to create indoor environments with exceptional vitality, which could enhance our health and sense of well-being. Yet this has not been the case. The U.S. Environmental Protection Agency (EPA) has recently stated that "indoor air pollution in residences, offices, schools, and other buildings is widely recognized as one of the most serious potential environmental risks to human health" and is, in fact, many times more of a health threat than outdoor air pollution.

How has this sad state of affairs developed? Since the oil embargo of 1973, we have placed a high priority on energy efficiency, creating buildings that are increasingly airtight. Concurrently, the building industry has promoted inexpensive synthetic building products and furnishings that are mass-produced and require little maintenance. Until recently, minimal attention has been paid to the toxicity of these products, allowing consumers to remain largely ignorant of the health threat that they pose.

The average person lacks a background in chemistry and has a false assumption that in order for building products to be allowed on the market, they must be reasonably safe. The disturbing truth is that, according to the EPA, of the more than 80,000 chemicals common in commercial use today, fewer than 1,000 have been tested for toxic effects on the human nervous system. The limited testing that has been implemented rarely takes into consideration the ongoing, low-level exposure to hundreds of chemicals we inhale or absorb simultaneously throughout our daily lives.

The toll on human health resulting from exposure to the chemical soup surrounding us is finally becoming clear. In 1986 the National Academy of Science estimated that 15% of the population suffered from chemical sensitivities. Based on current unofficial reports by physicians specializing in environmental medicine, that number is rising rapidly. These figures do not include people who unknowingly suffer from problems either directly or indirectly related to chronic, low-level toxic exposure. All too often symptoms are falsely attributed to the normal aging process.

Exposure to toxins in the indoor environment, even at low levels, has been linked to a vast spectrum of illnesses ranging from chronic sinus infections, headaches, insomnia, anxiety, and joint pain to full-blown multiple chemical sensitivity (MCS) and other immune system disorders.

In spite of overwhelming evidence of the health risks, most new construction in North America continues to create environments that harm human health.

There is, in fact, nothing complicated about creating a healthy building. The process is composed of many simple, but important steps. Safer alternative materials and methods of design and building are becoming readily available. Nevertheless, the homeowner who desires to create a healthy building or remodel an existing one is still a pioneer facing the following major obstacles.

1. Building for health is not the current standard of the construction industry. Although most architects and builders are now aware that health problems are associated with standard building practices, the industry in general has not responded with appropriate changes to these standards. There are no set and sanctioned prescriptions to follow for healthy building.

2. The homeowner receives false information. Most building professionals are uninformed about the details of healthful design and building. The prospective client who has heard about healthy building is often ill advised by professionals, who state either that there is no need for concern or that the cost of healthy building is prohibitive.

3. There is a dearth of concise information. If homeowners are still committed to creating a healthy house and have managed to find an architect and builder who are receptive to working with them, then they must together undertake the daunting task of educating themselves and others. Distilling enough information to create a set of specifications for a project requires extensive time and dedication.

4. Even if healthy materials and practices are specified, a lack of quality control may result in a major degradation of the building, which in turn can lead to occupant health problems, decline of energy efficiency, and structural damage. These damages may be especially difficult to discover and costly to repair when they are hidden in wall cavities or other inaccessible spaces.

The purpose of this book is to take the mystery out of healthy house building by walking the owner/architect/builder team through the construction process. It explains where and why standard building practices are not healthful, what to do differently, and how to obtain alternative materials and expertise.

The authors hope that you will find *Prescriptions for a Healthy House* a useful tool in your quest for healthier living.

Part I: Overview

Introduction

Until about 25 years ago, indoor air pollution was a limited phenomenon. Since that time, two basic things have changed in the way that buildings are constructed. First, thousands of chemicals have been incorporated into building materials. Second, buildings are sealed so tightly that the chemicals remain trapped inside, where the inhabitants inhale them into the lungs and absorb them into the skin. Prior to the energy crisis of the 1970s, the typical home averaged approximately one air exchange per hour. Now, in a well sealed home, the air is often exchanged only once every five hours or even less frequently, and that is not enough to ensure healthful air quality.

There are two basic schools of thought about to how to solve the indoor pollution problem. The first approach eliminates as many pollutants as possible from within the building envelope and seals it tightly on the inside so that there is less need to worry about the chemical composition of the structure or insulation. Clean filtered air is then mechanically pumped in, keeping the house under a slightly positive pressure so that air infiltration is controlled. Thus, the residents isolate themselves from a toxic world. If you do not have the luxury of clean, vital, and refreshing natural surroundings, then a certain amount of isolation and filtering may be essential.

The second school of thought involves building the structure out of natural or nontoxic materials that "breathe." (A further explanation of this concept, and examples of natural building alternatives, can be found in *Division 4* of this book.) The building is seen as a third skin (our clothes are the second), as a permeable organism interacting with the natural world and facilitating a balanced exchange of air and humidity. This approach is based on the precepts of *bau-biologie*. Bau-biologie (which combines the German words for building and life) is a holistic study of the interaction between human and other life forms and the environment, including the impact of the building environment on human health and the application of this knowledge to the construction or modification of homes and workplaces. On a philosophical level, we find this approach more appealing because it is based on an interactive relationship with the surrounding environment and considers the environmental impact of the building process in addition to its impact on human health.

In the first approach to reducing indoor pollution, the home is isolated from a toxic world, while in the second approach the home interacts with the surrounding environment. One approach strives to create a healthy environment through technology, and the other through a return to nature. Much of the information in this book applies to either approach because the purpose is to identify and eliminate the causes of environmental pollution commonly found in the home. As well, although our emphasis is on home construction, many of the same problems and solutions apply to schools and workplaces.

How Much More Will It Cost to Build a Healthy Home?

Frequently the first question posed to Paula by her clients is "How much more will it cost to build a healthy home?" The answer is usually that it will cost somewhere between zero and 25% more than standard construction.

Assume for a moment that you are house hunting. Your real estate agent contacts you and is very excited about having found a real bargain, a house going for 20% less than market value. Upon further inquiry, you learn that the house contains lead paint and asbestos insulation, and that it sits on a bed of radon-emitting granite. If your reaction would be to snatch it up, then read no further because this book will be of little interest to you. This book is about how to avoid substances like lead, asbestos, or radon, which are harmful to your health but which are commonly used in construction today.

In some cases, it costs little or no extra money to use less toxic substances and methods to build and maintain a healthy home. A few examples are listed below.

- Additive-free concrete costs no more than concrete with toxic admixtures, provided that climatic conditions are appropriate for the project.
- Circuit-breaker panels with reduced field configurations are the same price as other panels.
- Using careful planning to shorten wiring runs will not only reduce exposure to electromagnetic fields, but will also save money.
- Unscented and nonchlorinated cleaning products cost no more than, and can be just as effective as, compounds containing harsh chemicals.

In other cases, healthier alternatives are more expensive initially, but are more economical in the long run. For example:

- The most inexpensive types of roofing to install are tar-and-gravel or asphalt shingles, but the useful life of these products is much shorter than that of many of the less-toxic roofing systems specified in *Division 7, Roofing*.
- Although forced air is less expensive to install, a properly designed gas-fired, hydronic, radiant floor heating system is not only more comfortable and healthier, but is also virtually maintenance-free. Higher initial installation costs will be outweighed over time by lower heating bills.

In some areas your decision to "go healthy" will cost more, and you will be faced with some difficult choices. We will try to offer you facts and a range of alternatives so that your choices can be well informed. There is no right answer in many instances. Sometimes your decision will come down to a trade-off between luxury and health. But then, what is luxury without health? You could ultimately spend a fortune on medical bills and lose quality of life, as have the people who shared their stories with us. Furthermore, the environmental cost of many current building practices is astronomical. Our children and grandchildren will ultimately pay the heaviest price.

Sources of Indoor Pollution

Indoor air pollutants can be classified into five main categories: volatile organic compounds (VOCs), toxic by-products of combustion, pesticides, electromagnetic field pollution, and naturally occurring pollutants. We describe each category of pollutant in the following sections.

Volatile Organic Compounds (VOCs)

Organic compounds are chemicals containing carbon-hydrogen bonds at the molecular level. They can occur naturally or be manufactured. Most synthetic organic compounds are petrochemicals, that is, derived from oil, gas, or coal.

Organic compounds can exist in the form of a gas, liquid, or solid particles. Substances that readily release vapors at room temperature are called volatile organic compounds. This evaporation of volatile compounds contained in solid material is called outgassing and results in a slow release of chemicals into the air.

Organic compounds can be classified into three categories based on how far removed they are from the original petroleum products. The primary organic compounds include components directly derived from gas, oil, and coal and include propane, butane, benzene, xylene, paraffins, toluene, and styrene. These products are then used to derive the intermediate substances such as formaldehyde, phenols, acetone, isopropanol, and acetaldehyde. The end products produced from crude oil and natural gas include solvents, waxes, lacquers, synthetic detergents, synthetic fibers, and paints. Common sources of volatile organic compounds occurring in the indoor environment include:

- plywood
- particleboard
- wood paneling
- carpets and carpet pads
- insulation

- paints
- finishes
- solvents
- adhesives
- synthetic fabrics

Sources of indoor pollution

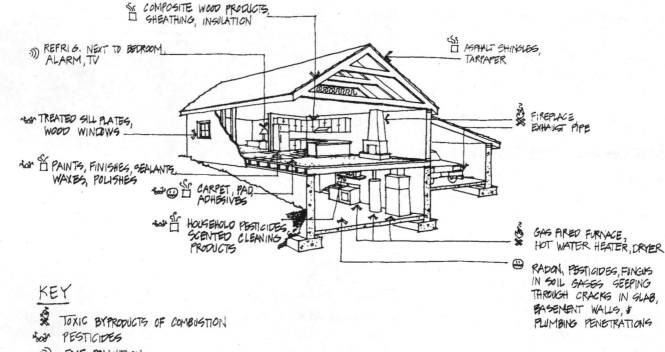

COMPOSITE WOOD PRODUCTS, SHEATHING, INSULATION

REFRIG. NEXT TO BEDROOM, ALARM, TV

ASPHALT SHINGLES, TARPAPER

TREATED SILL PLATES, WOOD WINDOWS

FIREPLACE EXHAUST PIPE

PAINTS, FINISHES, SEALANTS, WAXES, POLISHES

CARPET, PAD, ADHESIVES

HOUSEHOLD PESTICIDES, SCENTED CLEANING PRODUCTS

GAS FIRED FURNACE, HOT WATER HEATER, DRYER

RADON, PESTICIDES, FUNGUS IN SOIL GASES SEEPING THROUGH CRACKS IN SLAB, BASEMENT WALLS, & PLUMBING PENETRATIONS

KEY

TOXIC BYPRODUCTS OF COMBUSTION

PESTICIDES

EMF POLLUTION

VOLATILE ORGANIC COMPOUNDS

NATURALLY OCCURING POLLUTANTS (MOLDS, BACTERIA, RADON)

- cleaning products
- body care products
- mothballs
- insecticides

- aerosol products
- art and hobby materials
- dry-cleaned garments
- air-fresheners

At present, about 80,000 synthetic organic compounds are commercially available, and thousands more are produced annually by the chemical industry.[1] VOCs constitute a major source of toxic overload and can threaten individual health. Any organ of the body can be affected. Some of the more common symptoms include rashes, headaches, eye irritation, chronic cough, chronic sinus infections, joint and muscle pain, memory loss, inability to concentrate, irritability, fatigue, anxiety, depression, and increasing numbers of allergies.

Some of the more chemically sensitive individuals also react to naturally occurring VOCs, such as terpenes, which outgas from wood products. These individuals should test their reactions to each product before making a major purchase, even if the product is derived from a natural source.

You are undoubtedly familiar with the distinctive smell of a new house. The odor is composed primarily of outgassing chemicals from toxic volatile organic compounds. The makers of some building products now report the parts per million (PPM) of VOCs on labels, but this information can be misleading. Yes, it is true that the fewer parts per million the better, but certain chemicals, such as

Plastered walls, recycled wood flooring over radiant floor heating and specialty finishes are used in this straw bale home in New Mexico. Interior view shows deep window seat in the country kitchen. Architect: Baker-Laporte and Associates; Builder: Prull and Associates; Photo: Julie Dean.

dioxin, are not safe in any detectable amount.[2] One of the goals in constructing a healthy house is to reduce the use of toxic VOCs.

Toxic By-products of Combustion

Gas, oil, coal, wood, and other fuels burned indoors consume valuable indoor oxygen unless air for combustion is supplied from the outdoors. In tight, energy-efficient buildings, these fumes can cause serious health consequences.

Indoor combustion is found in fireplaces, woodstoves, gas-fired appliances (such as ranges, clothes dryers, water heaters, and furnaces), gas- and kerosene-fired space heaters, and oil and kerosene lamps. Some of the potentially harmful emissions include nitrogen dioxide, nitrous oxide, sulfur oxides, hydrogen cyanide, carbon monoxide, carbon dioxide, formaldehyde, particulate matter, and hydrocarbons from natural gas fumes such as butane, propane, pentane, methyl pentane, benzene, and xylene. The amount of fuel burned and the rate of exchange with outdoor air determine the indoor levels of these gases.

In a study of 47,000 chemically sensitive patients, the most important sources of indoor air pollution responsible for generating illness were the gas stove, the improperly vented water heater, and the furnace.[3] Hazardous fumes can leak at the pipe joints and remain undetected, especially if they occur under flooring. In addition, every pilot light adds fumes, and the burning process itself releases fumes into the air.

What are some of the potential health effects of combustion by-product gases? Exposure to gas fumes primarily affects the cardiovascular and nervous system, but it can harm any organ of the body. Some of the earliest symptoms include depression, fatigue, irritability, and inability to concentrate.

Carbon monoxide is commonly produced during incomplete combustion, especially from gas-fueled appliances, and quickly diffuses throughout the entire house. Typically, these appliances must be removed from the homes of chemically sensitive patients to restore their health. Chronic exposure can result in multiple chemical sensitivities because carbon monoxide has the ability to interfere with the detoxification pathways in the liver. This allows toxic substances to accumulate in the body. Other effects of chronic carbon monoxide exposure include heart arrhythmia, decreased cognitive abilities, confusion, and fatigue.

Carbon dioxide is produced when natural gas burns. Elevated levels result in decreased mental acuity, loss of vigor, and fatigue. Nitrogen oxides are also released from gas appliances. A major source of contamination is the gas stove, particularly older models with pilot lights. These gases are known to affect the nervous and reproductive systems.

Coal, gas, and wood-burning fireplaces that are not equipped with sealed doors emit particulate matter as well as toxic fumes. They also consume indoor oxygen unless fresh outdoor air is supplied to them. Particles not expelled by blowing or sneezing can find their way into the lungs, where they might remain for years.

It is important to mention that when you park or operate an automobile in an attached garage, gas, oil, and other VOCs can diffuse into the building structure and affect the home's indoor air quality. Garages must be properly isolated from the main structure.

Pesticides

Although some pesticides may technically be considered VOCs, these often odorless and invisible substances have become such a health threat that they warrant a separate discussion. Pesticides, or biocides, are poisons designed to kill a variety of plants and animals such as insects (insecticides), weeds (herbicides), and mold or fungus (fungicides). They were first developed as offshoots of nerve gas used during World War II. Most pesticides are synthetic chemicals made from petroleum. They are composed of active ingredients—the chemical compounds designed to kill the target organism—and and inert ingredients-the chemicals that deliver the active ingredients to the target, preserve them, or make them easier to apply.

Many people assume that the pesticides they buy, or those used by lawn and pest control companies, are "safe." They assume the government is protecting them; that pesticides are scientifically tested; that if they are used according to the instructions on the label, no harm will be done; and that the products would not be on the market if they were unsafe. All of these assumptions are incorrect.

EPA registration does not signify pesticide safety.[4] The EPA approves pesticides based on efficacy, not safety. Efficacy means the pesticide will kill the targeted pest. Out of the hundreds of active ingredients registered with the EPA, less than a dozen have been adequately tested for safety.[5] In fact, it is a violation of federal law to state or imply that the use of a pesticide is "safe when used as directed." When the EPA, in the face of overwhelming evidence of negative human health effects, does decide to ban a pesticide, the process is a slow one fraught with compromise. For example, on June 8, 2000, the EPA agreed to phase out home and garden uses of chlorpyrifos.[6] Chlorpyrifos, the active ingredient in Dursban™ and Lorsban™, is a known neurotoxin. Between 1991 and 1996 more than 17,000 cases of unintentional chlorpyrifos exposure were reported to poison control centers. Although less toxic and nontoxic alternatives are available

Case Study 1:

Acute exposure to pesticides with long-term consequences

Louise Pape is a 59-year-old woman whose life changed drastically in 1993. On a warm spring day, she and her husband were slowly driving home with the windows rolled down so they could enjoy the cool breeze. At the roadside she spotted a man from a tree-care company wearing a gas mask and spraying pesticides on the trees with a large hose. Louise suddenly felt a shower of chemicals on her face, in her eyes, nose, and mouth, as the sprayer overshot his target. She later learned that the pesticide was a mixture of Malathion and Sevin.

The incident was the beginning of a nightmare illness for Louise, an environmental planner who, ironically, had just finished developing a safe pesticide plan for her employer, a transnational corporation. She was disabled for several months with flu-like symptoms: aching joints and muscles, severe headaches, dizziness, thyroid problems, insomnia, and shortness of breath. She was often bedridden and sometimes lapsed into a near comatose state when she was re-exposed to even minute amounts of pesticides. Louise eventually developed full-blown multiple chemical sensitivity disorder. Since the incident she has been virtually homebound, still unable to tolerate the trace amounts of pesticides and other chemical exposures that occur during routine activities when out in the world.

Her illness notwithstanding, Louise and her husband have become articulate spokespeople, educating the public regarding the hazards of pesticides and other chemicals. The ranch home they recently built has become a model for nontoxic living.

Discussion

Many of the most harmful pesticides fall into three categories: organochlorines, organophosphates, and carbamates. In Louise Pape's case, the onset of illness was associated with a single large exposure to an organophosphate-and-carbamate mixture. The cause of the prolonged illness was obvious. In most cases, however, the cause is not so obvious. Many people are exposed to repeated, low-dose applications of pesticides, which can result in general malaise with flu-like symptoms, chronic fatigue, and subtle neurological deficits. When patients complain of such symptoms to the doctor, they are rarely questioned about exposures to chemicals such as pesticides. Most emergency room doctors are familiar with acute pesticide poisoning, but few physicians have knowledge regarding long-term, chronic effects.

for all chlorpyrifos applications, more than 11 million pounds of the ingredient have been applied annually. The phase-out will allow:

- home- and garden-use sales to continue through December 2001;
- existing stock to be sold in retail outlets until depleted;

Case Study 2:

Chronic illness from "harmless" pesticide

Barbara Adler is a 47-year-old woman who was in good health until March 1996, when she suddenly began to have severe migraine headaches, loss of energy, frequent dizzy spells, and difficulty concentrating. Barbara consulted with a neurologist and many other health care practitioners over the ensuing months. None were able to help relieve her symptoms or shed light on the cause of her deteriorating health.

At some point in her search for wellness, Barbara reviewed the journal she had been keeping in which she recorded certain events in her life. She noted that around the time of the onset of her symptoms, her husband had purchased a bug spray from one of the local nurseries. He was told that the insecticide would be appropriate for the bugs on his houseplants. Barbara remembers that the bug spray smelled noxious to her, which prompted her to put some of the sprayed plants in the garage. She looked at the label on the bottle and saw that it contained Diazinon, a potent organophosphate known to have toxic effects on the nervous system. Barbara returned to the nursery to register a complaint and was told that Diazinon was not harmful.

Discussion

Although it is illegal for manufacturers to claim their pesticides are "safe," Dr. Elliott notes that in her experience local nurseries and other establishments selling pesticides frequently tell customers that organophosphates such as Sevin, Dursban, and Diazinon are harmless when applied according to instructions. In fact, many people with multiple chemical sensitivity disorder attribute the onset of their illness to pesticide exposure. While the patient in the above case became ill after an acute exposure to which she reacted immediately, the majority of cases occur after repeated, low-level exposures that can cause a gradual decline in health and vitality.

+ continued use on food crops (except tomatoes), golf courses, and for mosquito and fire ant control;
+ continued spot and local use for termite control until December 31, 2002;
+ use in new home pretreatment until December 31, 2005; and
+ unrestricted export.

Inert ingredients, which can account for up to 99% of a pesticide, are not usually identified on the label. The Trade Secrets Act protects manufacturers from being required to fully disclose ingredients, even if the inert ingredients are potentially hazardous to human health. No studies of any kind are required on the inert ingredients. Many inert ingredients can be more toxic than the active

Case Study 3:

Chronic illness from repeated low-level exposure to pesticides

E. Merriam is a 52-year-old woman who complained of frequent flu-like symptoms after beginning employment at a new location. The symptoms seemed to recur every month and were especially severe over the winter. Conventional medications were of no benefit. After two years of watching her health decline, the patient discovered that the building in which she worked was being treated prophylactically one weekend a month with a pesticide that contained an organophosphate called Dursban. She then associated her flu-like symptoms with the monthly pesticide applications. The patient felt she could no longer continue to jeopardize her health and left her job. Three years later she finally regained her health, but continues to remain sensitive to petrochemicals.

ingredients, yet warning labels only apply to the active ingredients. In a Freedom of Information Act lawsuit, the Northwest Coalition for Alternatives to Pesticides (NCAP) obtained from the EPA a list of 1,400 of the 2,000 substances being used as inert ingredients in pesticides. These ingredients included Chicago sludge and other hazardous waste, asbestos, and some banned chemicals such as DDT.[7]

A recent study found that combining pesticides can make them up to 1,600 times more potent.[8] A good illustration of this synergy is found in a class of pesticides called pyrethroids, which are mistakenly thought to be harmless because they are plant-derived. The unlabeled inert ingredient commonly mixed with the pyrethroids is PBO (piperonyl butoxide). Alone, each substance has limited toxicity to insect species; when combined, the mixture is extremely toxic. PBO makes the pyrethroid more toxic by destroying one of the enzymes in the detoxification pathway that deactivates the pesticide in the insect. When humans are exposed to this mixture, their livers become less able to metabolize toxins in the environment.

Pesticides can drift a long distance from the site of application, leaving residues throughout the surrounding community and contaminating everything and everyone they contact. Residues are found in rain, fog, snow, food, water, livestock, wildlife, newborn babies, and even in the Arctic ice pack. People and pets may track pesticide residues into the house. An EPA study in Florida found the highest household pesticide residues in carpet dust.[9] As well, many building products and household furnishings such as carpets, paints, and wood products are treated with biocides.

Pesticides and biocides can be absorbed through the skin, inhaled, or swallowed. Infants and small children are more likely to be harmed by pesticides because they are more sensitive and more likely to come into direct contact with treated carpets and lawns.

Pesticides may cause both acute and chronic health effects. Acute health effects appear shortly after exposure. Chronic health effects may not be apparent until months or years after exposure. Chronic effects generally result from long-term exposure to low levels of toxic chemicals, but may also arise from short-term exposure. A tragic misconception about pesticides is that the potential for harm is primarily the result of acute or immediate poisoning. In fact, delayed effects pose the greatest problems to human health. Many pesticides are fat-soluble and bioaccumulate in tissues, where they can exert prolonged effects on the immune, endocrine, and nervous systems. Children are most susceptible because their developing organs and nervous systems are more easily damaged.

Pesticide Facts

+ A National Cancer Institute study indicated that the likelihood of a child contracting leukemia was more than six times greater in households where herbicides were used for lawn care.[10]
+ According to a report in the *American Journal of Epidemiology*, more children with brain tumors and other cancers were found to have had exposure to insecticides than children without cancer.[11]
+ According to the New York State Attorney General's office, 95% of the pesticides used on residential lawns are considered probable carcinogens by the EPA.[12]
+ 2,4-D was a component of Agent Orange and is used in about 1,500 lawn care products.[13]
+ Pesticides have been linked to the alarming rise in the rate of breast cancer.[14]
+ Besides causing cancer, pesticides have the potential to cause infertility, birth defects, learning disorders, neurological disorders, allergies, and multiple chemical sensitivities, among other disorders of the immune system.

When building or remodeling a healthy home, you can lower your pesticide exposure by not treating the soil under the building and by eliminating or sealing standard building products that contain biocides. *Division 10* includes a discussion of pest management that emphasizes preventing pest invasions through the use of physical barriers and the control of moisture, which eliminates potential food sources.

Electromagnetic Field Pollution

Electromagnetic energy is ubiquitous. Some electromagnetic (EM) waves are natural, such as sunlight. Others are generated by human activity, such as radio and television waves, microwaves, and electrical waves carried by power lines. Scientists classify EM waves according to frequency, which corresponds to the wavelength. At one end of the spectrum are the infinitesimally short, high-frequency gamma rays. At the other end are long, extremely low-frequency vibrating waves, used by submarines for underwater communication that may cover thousands of miles.

The magnetic field that envelops the Earth produces a steady, nonoscillating direct current at 7.83 cycles per second, or 7.83 Hertz, similar to that of the human body. This current pulsates on and off, but the electrons producing the electricity always move in a single direction. Each cell in the body has a pulsating vibration with an associated electromagnetic field. Communication between cells in the body is a function of electrical charges. These charges generate electrical currents that govern many of the body's major functions, such as heart beat, nerve conduction, and transport across cell membranes. These natural fields pulse on and off, but do not oscillate.

Manufactured fields oscillate back and forth. Unlike those in natural current, the electrons creating the fields change direction, and it is thus called alternating current (AC). The electrical power grid operates at 60 Hertz and simultaneously produces an electric and a magnetic field. Each field, electric and

A poor choice for a home site in an area of elevated electromagnetic fields.
Photo: Reinhart, Kanuka, Fuchs.

magnetic, has distinct properties and is measured separately using different meters. Common sources of 60-Hertz electromagnetic fields (EMFs) include power lines, electrical wires, electric blankets, fluorescent lights, televisions, and other household appliances.

Radio waves are a form of EMF. On a typical radio receiver, you will find a dial used to change stations, known as the frequency tuner. As you move the dial to the higher numbers, you are increasing the frequency of the radio EMF you are seeking; when you move the dial to lower numbers, you are reducing the frequency. AM radio stations are found between 550 and 1600 kiloHertz (550,000 and 1,600,000 Hertz). If the radio could be tuned all the way down the dial to 60 Hertz, you would be listening to the (very noisy) sound of electrical equipment.

There are major differences between radio waves and the electrical waves used to power electrical equipment. One difference is that radio waves are broadcast through the air; they are wireless and can travel for extended distances. Electricity, on the other hand, is transported through wires. It would be ideal if the fields from wiring systems stayed in the wires while the electricity was transported from one place to another. The problem is that wires "leak," broadcasting electromagnetic fields. The distance the fields are broadcast depends on their amperage. Amperage is analogous to the volume at which electric fields are being transmitted through the wires.

Assume that a radio receiver could be tuned to radio stations operating between 40 and 80 Hertz. As mentioned previously, if you were to tune the dial to 60 Hertz, you would hear a lot of noise because electricity in North America operates at 60 Hertz. Next, assume that you take the same radio receiver to Europe. Upon tuning the radio to 60 Hertz, you would hear nothing because the European power system operates at 50 Hertz.

To experiment with the sound of electricity, take a cheap AM transistor radio and tune it between stations at the low end of the dial. Then hold the radio near an operating electrical appliance or a dimmer switch. You will pick up static or a buzzing noise. The noise you hear is not the 60-Hertz frequency but, rather, higher-frequency interference created by the 60-Hertz frequency.

Before meters for measuring elevated EMFs were readily available, some people would use an AM radio to obtain a rough approximation of whether an area contained elevated manufactured EMFs. The method is far from foolproof, but it was certainly better than nothing. Several models of inexpensive meters are available today to provide more accurate assessments.

Many scientists agree that electromagnetic fields have biological effects, but they disagree on the exact effects and whether they are harmful. Research has indicated that magnetic fields can induce a small electrical field inside the body, which in turn creates an electric current in and around the cells.[15] Some scientists think this current alters the function of cell chemistry and can inhibit or enhance cell growth. Although there is no consistent dose/response relationship between magnetic fields and cancer, experiments on laboratory animals have shown that magnetic fields cause changes in protein synthesis and hormone levels.

Studies in Europe have indicated that exposure to varying levels of electric fields can contribute to nervous disorders such as insomnia, depression, and anxiety. One U.S. study found an increase in aggressive behavior among baboons exposed to electric fields.[16] Other studies have indicated that magnetic and electric field exposures may have a synergistic influence, making the combination more harmful than exposure to either field alone.

Over the past 50 years, people have been exposed to ever-increasing amounts of manufactured radiation. The long-term consequences of this exposure are not clearly understood. Millions of Americans are now unwittingly engaged in long-term experiments on themselves.

While Sweden has set limits for certain types of electric and magnetic field exposure, the U.S. government has not. From time to time the government has officially recommended "prudent avoidance" (without defining the EMF levels that it would be prudent to avoid). Yet recent epidemiological studies have linked elevated risk of childhood leukemia to exposures as low as 4 milligauss.[17] Given the potentially dangerous (albeit controversial) consequences of EMF exposures, coupled with the ease of reducing these exposures in new construction, it makes sense to explore strategies for EMF reduction when planning and building a new home. Several simple and inexpensive measures to reduce EMF exposures are explained in *Division 11, Appliances and Magnetic or Electric Fields,* and *Division 16.*

Curiously, the magnetic portion of the electromagnetic field is indirectly prohibited by the National Electric Code of the U.S. The code specifically prohibits net current (current that is uncancelled) because it creates heat and is a potential fire hazard. Net current is also what creates magnetic fields, although most electricians are not aware of this. When magnetic fields are found in wiring it is usually the result of a wiring error that violates code. Preventing magnetic fields caused by wiring is simply a matter of introducing protocol on the job site that ensures that a building has been wired per code. This may include tests to verify there is no uncancelled current creating magnetic fields.

Naturally Occurring Pollutants

Not all toxins are manufactured. Some naturally occurring substances in homes can have harmful effects on humans. Some of these pollutants include radon and radioactive contaminants, trace metals, house dust, molds, and pollens.

Radioactive Contaminants

Radioactive contaminants such as radium and uranium occur naturally within the Earth's crust. During the decay or breakdown of uranium, radon is produced. Radon is an invisible, odorless, radioactive gas that seeps from the ground into homes, commonly through cracks in the foundation or basement slab, or through mechanical openings. Radon can also enter into the groundwater and affect water supplies.

Closed spaces present a hazard because radon levels can build up to values thousands of times higher than outdoor levels. High radon levels can cause radiation exposure equivalent to what a person would receive from thousands of chest x-rays per year. Information on detecting and preventing radon contamination in homes is provided in *Division 7*.

Heavy Metals

Trace amounts of heavy metals can often be found in drinking water. These metals—including aluminum, copper, and lead—can accumulate over time in human tissues and are known to damage the brain, liver, and kidneys. It's a good

The Problem: Gypsum board was glued directly to concrete block below floor level. Ground moisture passing through the block wall and condensation has resulted in mold growth on the gypsum board. Recommendation: Proper drainage design would have prevented moisture movement through the wall. Gypsum board is particularly vulnerable to mold growth when damp. If the block had been furred out prior to installation of gypboard then there would have been more opportunity for drying to occur.
Photo: Restoration Consultants.

Case Study 4:

Chronic illness due to acute exposure to virulent mold species

Tomasita Gallegos is a 41-year-old woman who first consulted Dr. Elliott in 1993. At that time she was frightened, in a state of severe agitation, and somewhat disoriented. Her face was bright red, her mouth showed increased salivation, her eyes were watery with constricted pupils, and her skin was warm to the touch. She was referred to Dr. Elliott by another physician who felt she might have experienced a pesticide exposure.

Ms. Gallegos was employed as a housekeeper in a private home. The morning of the day she became ill, Ms. Gallegos was instructed to clean the guest house, which had recently been occupied. Shortly after she entered the guest house, she became acutely ill with the above-mentioned symptoms. After the acute symptoms subsided, Ms. Gallegos was left with multiple problems, including chronic fatigue, panic attacks, chest pains, headaches, memory loss, and extreme chemical sensitivity. Her constellation of symptoms were baffling since it was determined that no harmful chemicals had been used on the premises.

An environmental engineering company was consulted to evaluate the guest house. Upon removing the furnace and cooling coils to allow access for a thorough cleaning of the ductwork system, the consultant found approximately two inches of water with green slime at the bottom of the supply plenum. Because the area was dark and cool and in the direct airstream of the house ductwork, it was likely that microorganisms had spread from this source. Close inspection revealed that a defective humidification system was the source of the leaking water. Most of the microbial agents were fungi that, although found widely in nature, were highly concentrated in the interior environment. Many fungi produce toxic compounds called "mycotoxins." The intense microbial exposure had the effect of sensitizing the patient, leaving her with an overreactive immune system, known as "environmental illness."

At present, with diligent avoidance of molds, toxic chemicals, and allergens, Ms. Gallegos is slowly beginning to regain her health. Why was she so severely affected from such a brief exposure? The type of mold was a particularly virulent species. In addition, some individuals are more susceptible to fungal contaminants than others due to their own biochemical individuality. If the detoxification pathway in the liver is already at maximum capacity, then it might take only a relatively small exposure to overwhelm the system. This theory is called the "rain barrel effect" and refers to total toxic load. When more toxins enter the "barrel" than the body can excrete, the barrel overflows and symptoms develop.

idea to have drinking water tested for contaminants in order to determine if you need a water purification device. Refer to *Division 11, Water Treatment Equipment,* for further information.

Case Study 5:

Asthma related to mold exposure

Dori Bennett is a 50-year-old woman who consulted with Dr. Elliott after the sudden onset of severe asthma. She had apparently been in good health until she moved into a new home. A leak in the home was repaired prior to the move, and the house had passed inspection. After her asthma progressed to the point that she required hospitalization, suspicion fell on her home as the source of her problem. An environmental consulting firm noted heavy mold growth in the crawl space, including aspergillus, actinomycetes, bacillus, cladosporium fusarium, mucor, penicillium, phoma, and ulocladium. Several strains of virulent molds, including some known to cause asthma, pneumonia, hypersensitivity pneumonitis, and immune dysfunction, grew on culture plates.

Ms. Bennett hired an environmental cleanup crew to rid the house of the mold in order to prepare it for resale. An outdoor unit was constructed to house a large heater fan to blow air under the house, while a unit on the opposite side of the house removed moisture-laden air. It took six weeks to dry out the earth under the house. A detailed mold remediation of the house and contents followed. The cost of the cleanup was $40,000. When further testing showed that the house was fully remediated, it was sold. Ms. Bennett now lives in a mold-free home and her health is slowly improving.

Biological Pollutants

Biological pollutants include pollen, house dust, and mold spores. Pollens from weeds, grasses, flowers, bushes, and trees enter the house through the doors and windows. They can be problematic for people with allergies. Air-filtration methods are addressed in *Division 15*.

House dust is composed of much more than simply soils. It is a complex mixture of dust mites, animal dander, mold spores, textile particles, heavy metals from car exhaust, skin cells, and more. Mites are a major culprit in causing allergies from house dust. They feed on skin cells and breed in mattresses, pillows, carpets, and upholstered furniture. Although generally harmless, their skeletal parts and fecal matter, which stick to dust, can elicit allergic reactions in sensitive people.

Mold plays a significant role in triggering allergies, asthma, and chemical sensitivities. Mold can produce by-products as toxic as some of the most hazardous manufactured chemicals that affect the nervous and immune systems. Mold is commonly assumed to be a problem only in older homes, but it can be found wherever moisture accumulates, such as in basements, bathrooms, windowsills, laundry rooms, or wherever leaks and flooding occur. Moist building

Case Study 6:

The relationship between allergies and chemical exposure

In the 1950s it was estimated that about 14% of the population suffered from allergies. According to some estimates, the proportion at present is estimated at between 40 and 75%. Why the dramatic increase? Allergists in Japan pondered the question and put forward the hypothesis that certain chemicals act as sensitizing agents. To test the hypothesis, two groups of mice were exposed to high levels of the Japanese equivalent of juniper pollen, and then tested for an allergic response. In both the study and the control group, about 5% of the mice developed allergies to the pollen. The study group was then exposed to benzene fumes from car exhaust. Upon retesting, there was a significant increase in the study group's allergic response to the pollen, while the control group remained at 5%. The experiment is described by M. Muranaka, et al., in "Adjutant activity of diesel exhaust particulates for the production of IgE antibody in mice," in the *Journal of Allergy and Clinical Immunology* (Vol. 77, April 1986, 616–623).

Discussion

Although there is clearly a link between chemical exposures and allergies, the exact mechanism has not yet been elucidated. Most people who have acquired multiple chemical sensitivities also suffer from traditional allergies to pollens, dust, dander, and mold.

Benzene is only one of many pollutants known to damage the immune system. These chemicals are found in thousands of modern products for home and industrial use, so millions of people are constantly exposed to low levels of these chemicals at work and at home.

materials, including new materials, can become breeding grounds for mold and bacteria within a few days. Many of the materials used in standard construction of new homes are susceptible to water damage and fungal growth. A moldy home is frequently a sign of a home with deteriorating building materials. Even when molds are contained inside walls or other building cavities such as attics and crawl spaces, the slightest air current can send fungal spores swirling through the air, where they can easily be inhaled.

Carpets act as large reservoirs for dust, bacteria, and mold. Microbes commonly grow within the ductwork of forced-air heating systems, which can result in mold and dust spread throughout the house. Unless kept spotlessly clean, toilets and many modern appliances that use water reservoirs, such as vaporizers and humidifiers, can breed microbes. Methods for preventing and controlling mold infestation are discussed throughout the specifications.

A Summary of Strategies for Creating a Healthy Home

The use of toxic substances in construction is standard. Furthermore, certain prevalent construction practices inadvertently lead to destructive moisture conditions, pest invasions, or unsafe combustion, all of which can cause even the most chemically inert home to become an unhealthy one over time. Finally, the occupants will greatly influence the longevity and healthfulness of any home through their day-to-day interaction with it.

In *Part II*, we will explain the many instances, some obvious and others less so, where undesirable materials and practices might be found in standard construction. We list healthier options for materials selection, and specify quality control measures for the construction phase.

Following is a brief overview of the strategies behind the specifications found in *Part II*. These five strategies are:

1. Designing for health
2. Employing a climate-based understanding for construction detailing
3. Reducing toxic emissions through careful choice of building materials
4. Introducing quality control measures during the construction process
5. Providing for an ongoing healthy home environment through occupant education

This entryway is designed for "tracking off" dirt and for shoe removal. It features a covered paved entry way and a sunken vestibule with easily mopped stone floors, that effectively keeps outside mud and dirt from finding its way into the home. Photo: Paula Baker-Laporte.

Deep roof overhangs and a covered entry help protect the natural wall elements of this straw-clay timberframe home. Architect: Paula Baker-Laporte; Builder: Econest Building Co.; Photo: Paula Baker-Laporte.

Designing for Health

All homes should be designed to support health, yet healthy housing is unfortunately considered to be a specialized field of residential design. There are basic design features that should be included in all homes, but they are often overlooked. These features, described below, are essential to our health, life, safety, and sense of well being.

Design for Responsiveness to the Natural Climate

In all but the most hostile environments, a home that is designed to be responsive to its surroundings will provide a fuller range of opportunities for the residents to reap the health benefits of nature while reducing dependency on energy-consuming mechanical space conditioning.

- Good window design can greatly reduce dependence on mechanical heating and cooling. If windows are placed so they prevent overheating and allow cross ventilation and solar gain when needed, the result will be energy savings and a higher level of comfort. Proper window placement, the right type of window design, and glass coating, used in conjunction with overhangs and trellises, can contribute to a successful home design.
- Proper room layout and window placement can also provide good natural lighting and a sense of well being while reducing dependence on electrical lighting.

Adobe interior walls and stone flooring store heat in the winter and remain cool in the summer while the straw bale walls of this home (not shown) provide a high degree of insulation. These natural materials provide an energy efficient solution for the cold winters and hot summers of Northern New Mexico. Architect: Baker-Laporte and Associates; Builder: Living Structures; Photo: Eric Swanson.

+ Screened porches, overhangs, trellises, and patios can provide opportunities for extended outdoor living while acting as climatic buffer zones around the home.
+ A paved entry path, covered entry porch, and foyer will reduce the amount of tracked-in dirt and provide a convenient place for shoe removal or cleaning. This will result in a cleaner home.
+ Extending the design process to include surrounding landscaping lets you incorporate vegetation to provide shade, allow in sun, block harsh winds, or funnel helpful breezes. Edible vegetation can also double as an organic food source.

Design for Combustion Source Management and Safety

Introducing harmful combustion by-products into the home poses a serious health threat that can be entirely avoided through proper design and equipment specification. The measures described here are not required by code, nor are they commonly found in standard construction:

+ The mechanical room and mechanical equipment should be designed so that no exchange of air takes place between the mechanical room and living space.
+ All gas appliances for occupant use should be properly vented to the outside.

+ The garage should be separated from the living space so that air exchange does not occur between the two.
+ Any home with gas or other combustion appliances should be equipped with carbon monoxide (CO) monitors.
+ There should be a source of fresh air to make up for air consumed in combustion processes.

Design for Water Management

Many health problems begin when buildings become moldy. Throughout this book we suggest strategies for the proper control of water and water vapor. Moisture control begins with good design that includes:

+ Sufficient roof overhangs and protection over doors and windows that will help keep rain and melting snow away from the building and its openings.
+ A well-designed and detailed perimeter drainage system that will keep basements, crawl spaces, and floor slabs dry.
+ Sufficient means for evacuating moisture generated by human activity within the building.
+ Placement of floor drains and detailing so that when water disasters occur due to equipment failure (and equipment often eventually fails!) this will not result in costly and health-threatening situations.

Design for Durability and Serviceability

+ A large part of design involves issues of cost and quality. If the owner is informed about costs over the life of materials and systems, rather than just initial costs, then he or she will be much more likely to make choices favoring durable and easily maintained materials. For example, a tar-and-gravel roof is less expensive than a single-ply membrane roof, but the first roof may come with only a two-year warranty, while the second one bears a ten-year warranty. The first roof will offgass for several weeks each time it is replaced, and the home will become filled with the carcinogenic tar fumes. The second roof may be a "torched down" application that causes little pollution when patched or replaced. If the owner plans to stay in the home for more than five years, then the second roof, although more expensive initially, will in the long run be a healthier and cost-effective choice.

+ Every homeowner has specific needs that will affect the indoor environmental quality, and these needs should be fully considered in the design phase. For example, there may be a need for extra ventilation in hobby areas, or it may be important to have a locked closet so that inappropriate materials are kept away from small children.
+ Family sizes grow and shrink. As people age they require greater ease of accessibility. Small children require constant surveillance. As children grow they require more autonomy. More and more people are choosing to work at home. A flexible design can more easily accommodate these lifestyle changes and allow a family to stay in the home as they occur. This sense of permanence can promote initial choices based on quality and longevity. Anyone who has ever moved can relate to the extreme stress caused by the process of relocation.

Employing a Climate-based Understanding in Construction Detailing

The building industry in the United States, a country with vast climatic variations, is primarily regulated by a handful of building codes. These codes do not sufficiently address the fact that each climatic zone carries particular concerns about how moisture, temperature, wind, vegetation, and wildlife will affect the building envelope. Historically, regional building types evolved throughout the world over time, with local materials fashioned into a perfect response to the surrounding climatic conditions. Much of this indigenous wisdom has been cast aside in our lifetime. Residential building techniques have undergone sweeping experimentation since World War II. With the introduction of mass-produced and transported building components and highly mechanized heating and cooling capacity, our homes are for the most part constructed in the same manner regardless of location. The need for energy conservation has lead to tight, highly insulated envelope construction.

As a result of these factors, we have placed greater performance demands on the building envelope than ever before. A new suburban home in Cincinnati may look identical to one built in Los Angeles. In spite of the vastly different climatic conditions in Cincinnati and Los Angeles, the two buildings will be mechanically equipped to provide the occupant with interior conditions of 70 degrees Fahrenheit for 24 hours a day, 365 days a year. However, the interaction between the climate and the building envelope in these cities will be very different. Professionals in the building industry are now discovering that certain assumptions made 20 years ago about how the new products would interact with climate and mechanized space conditioning were shortsighted. As a result, we are experiencing widespread envelope failures. To further complicate matters, similar buildings will fail in different ways in different climates. These failures affect not only the longevity of buildings, but also their ability to support human health.

Architects, builders, and homeowners must become familiar with the specific conditions of the potential home site. It is beneficial to ask about the kinds of problems that have developed in local buildings due to the natural environment. Local building lore can potentially be a rich source of information. Listed below are a few examples (by no means exclusive) of differing regional conditions and respective challenges.

- The air of coastal locations typically has high salt content, which causes metal corrosion.
- Areas experiencing alternating freeze/thaw conditions will be subject to ice damming problems. Buildings will also be much more susceptible to deterioration caused by water seeping into cracks and then expanding as it turns to ice.
- Wood products exposed to the elements in southwestern deserts will suffer from accelerated UV exposure and drying.
- Moisture and mold problems associated with condensation caused by air-conditioning are typical in climates with high temperatures and humidity.
- Fire safety is a major concern in wooded areas.
- Nearly every region has specific insect and vermin problems.

In summary, certain conditions unique to your building location will not be remedied or addressed by building codes, standard building practices, or materials manufacturers. Architects and builders must be jointly responsible for investigating specificities. To this end, we highly recommend the *EEBA Builder's Guides* listed in the bibliography.

Reduction of Toxic Emissions from Building Material

As explained previously, one reason modern building techniques have created sick buildings is because they use materials that outgas toxic emissions. In order to create healthy environments, we must find ways to reduce the pollution generated by these building materials. The following products and materials are common sources of indoor pollution in standard construction:

+ Insecticides, mildewcides, herbicides, and other biocides found in building materials or applied on site.
+ Composite wood products that are bound with formaldehyde-emitting glues, including particleboard, chipboard, plywood, and manufactured sheathing.
+ Building products, finishes, cleaning products, and additives that emit harmful VOCs, including solvent-based paints, sealants, finishes, and adhesives.
+ Asphalt and products containing asphalt, including impregnated sheathing, roofing tars, and asphalt driveways.
+ Building materials containing mold.
+ Materials that are absorbent, that are hard to clean and maintain, and that require frequent replacement (such as carpet).

There are several strategies for reducing the chemical load that we introduce into a newly constructed home. In order of effectiveness these strategies are:

1. Eliminate sources of pollution.
2. Substitute healthier materials.
3. Exercise prudence when using unavoidable toxic substances.
4. Cure materials before they are installed within the building envelope.
5. Seal materials so that they offgas less.

Elimination

If all toxins could simply be eliminated from buildings, we would have the basis for an ideal environment. In many situations this is not only possible, but also cost-effective. For example, countertop materials can often be attached to cabinets with mechanical fasteners, thereby eliminating the need for toxic adhesives.

Substitution

Where chemicals must be used, it is almost always possible to substitute a less-toxic substance in place of a standard one. For example, paint with no harmful emissions, VOCs, or preservatives can be specified in place of a standard paint that contains harmful chemicals such as formaldehyde.

Prudent Use

In a few cases, the use of a toxic substance is unavoidable. For example, there is no acceptable substitute for the solvent-based glues used to join plastic plumbing lines, but the quantity of glue used can be greatly reduced through prudent application.

Curing

In some cases where toxic substances are chosen for reasons such as cost or durability, the impact of the product will be reduced if it is properly cured. For example, the specifications will explain how to cure plywood before application. Many materials can be purchased with factory-applied finishes that have been heat-cured. Such finishes, which may have been quite noxious in their liquid state, are safely applied and cured under controlled conditions. Many factory-applied finishes will have little impact on air quality by the time they are installed in the home.

The Problem: Exterior gypsum board sheathing has been installed on this home during the rain. Building paper is now being installed over the wet sheathing. This will trap thhe moisture and is likely to result in a moldy wall.
Recommendation: Building materials should be protected from the elements and rapidly dried if they do become wet.
Photo: Restoration Consultants.

Sealing

If a toxic building component cannot be eliminated or substituted, then sealing it will help to reduce the rate of offgassing. Although this approach is far from perfect, there are cases where we recommend vapor sealants or barriers for this purpose. For example, premanufactured wood windows are routinely dipped in fungicides. As it is almost always cost-prohibitive to have custom windows made, sealing the windows with a special clear sealer or primer will help limit pesticide exposure.

Throughout the planning of a healthy home, you will be weighing the health risks, cost, time, and aesthetics of the above five strategies to find the solution that is best for you.

The Problem: Construction debris was not properly removed from this site. A wall cavity was used for debris disposal and then covered over. When there was an accidental flood in this building the hidden material became wet and could not dry out quickly. A serious mold problem resulted.

Recommendation: Building cavities should be left clean and free of debris.

Photo: Restoration Consultants.

Quality Control Measures During Construction

Even a home with the finest design and most careful materials selection can become a home that does not support occupant health. Typically, all of the quality control that a homeowner might expect or wish to have performed will not be done unless it is part of the building contract. In order to ensure that the design intent and the written and drawn instructions are properly executed, certain procedures and tests should be agreed upon and required. Quality control measures are discussed throughout this book (particularly in *Division 1* and *Division 13, Environmental Testing*) and include:

+ Clear contractual agreements between the owner and the builder regarding both standard and special project procedures, protocols, materials, and contract close-out.
+ Procedures, inspections, and tests to be performed during construction and upon commissioning of the building, which assure that the building will perform as intended.

Occupant Education

A home that is well conceived and well built will provide a healthy environment initially. However, the home will only continue to nurture the health of its occupants in the most optimum manner if the occupants are fully educated about the healthy maintenance of their home.

Case Study 7:

Fragrant fumes

E.B. had a ten-year history of chronic sinus congestion, hoarseness, and headaches. By the time he consulted with Dr. Elliott, he had tried many forms of treatment including nasal surgery, frequent courses of antibiotics, decongestants, and steroid nasal drops. After removing dairy products from his diet, he noticed only a partial improvement in the congestion. Dr. Elliott then suggested that he try eliminating all scented products from his body, including detergents, soaps, and colognes. Through a process of trial and error, E.B. discovered that his aftershave lotion was a significant cause of his symptoms. His voice has now returned to its former resonance and he is without headaches or sinus congestion.

Discussion

Millions of people are made ill by artificial fragrances. Most people are unaware that fragrances can cause or contribute to health problems. The most common symptoms related to fragrances include asthma, headaches, dizziness, fatigue, mental confusion, memory loss, nausea, irritability, depression, rashes, and muscle and joint pains. With increasing awareness and growing demand, products are now available to the public that are fragrance-free or scented with purely plant-derived substances.

Owners Manual

The contractor should provide the owner with a manual that contains the following information:

+ A description of the building construction materials and components, including updated drawings and specifications with any "as built" changes clearly marked.
+ Maintenance schedules and manuals for household and mechanical appliances
+ A checklist for the regular and periodic maintenance and inspection of the building exterior for which the owner is responsible, including inspection of drainage, roof gutters, roofing, painting, staining, etc.
+ A checklist of regular maintenance requirements for which the owner may call upon outside services, such as chimney sweeping and ductwork cleaning.
+ Warranties and contact numbers of appropriate subcontractors.

Proper Use of Exhaust Fans, Smoke Detectors, and CO Monitors

Smoke detectors and CO (carbon monoxide) monitors will only warn occupants if they are functional. Exhaust fans will only prevent excess moisture or remove pollutants from cooking if the occupant remembers to use them. When exhaust fans are in operation, it may be necessary for the owner to provide make-up air by opening a window or manually turning on a supply switch. Understanding and maintaining such devices is an important part of maintaining a healthy home.

Avoiding the Use of Artificial Fragrance in the Home

The use of toxic fragrances is so prevalent in our culture that many chemically sensitive individuals have a hard time finding a home to rent or buy that is free of acquired odors from scented products. In fact, the use of these common synthetic fragrances poses a health threat to any occupant. They should not be used in a healthy home.

Artificial fragrances are found throughout most homes and workplaces in body and hair care products, household cleaners, detergents, fabric softeners, air fresheners, and even in some magazines. Fragrance is cited as an indoor irritant and pollutant in several major studies, including the EPA's TEAM (Total Exposure Assessment Methodology) Study of June 1987, and *Chemical Sensitivity: A Report to the New Jersey State Department of Health* by Nicholas Ashfor, PhD, and Claudia S. Miller, MD (December 1989).

In the days before "better living through chemistry," fragrances were made from flowers. Now, approximately 95% of all ingredients used by the fragrance industry are synthetic.[18] According to the U.S. Food and Drug Administration (FDA), about 4,000 petroleum-derived chemicals are used in fragrances.[19] These include toluene, formaldehyde, acetone, benzene derivatives, methylene chloride, phenyl ethyl alcohol, methyl ethyl ketone, and benzyl acetate. A single fragrance can contain as many as 600 different chemicals.

In a 1988 study, the National Institute of Occupational Safety and Health found that in a partial list of 2,983 chemicals now being used by the fragrance industry, 884 toxic substances were identified.[20] Many of these substances are capable of causing cancer, birth defects, central nervous system disorders, reproductive disorders, and skin irritation. According to the National Academy of Science, there is minimal or no data on the toxicity of 84% of the ingredients found in fragrances.[21]

Currently there is no agency regulating the fragrance industry. The FDA is aware of the serious nature of the problem but is unable to undertake the astronomical expense of testing each of the hundreds of chemicals found in fragrances. Without such testing, the FDA would be subject to lawsuits by manufacturers if fragrances were banned. Thus, as is often the case, the onus falls on the consumer to make informed choices.

In the resource list we have compiled names of companies that supply fragrance-free products or products with fragrances derived from natural sources.

Avoiding the Use of Biocide in the Home and Garden

It should be unnecessary to use pesticides in a well built home. Similarly, a well-planned and healthy garden with site-appropriate plant selections and careful gardening practices should not require the use of any toxic herbicides.

There are almost always effective benign methods for dealing with house and garden pests. Because of the potentially devastating health consequences of pesticide, one should rigorously pursue these benign solutions when a pest problem arises. We discuss the principles of integrated pest management at greater length in *Division 10*.

Healthful Home Cleaning

Home cleaning substances labeled with skull-and-crossbones abound in our grocery stores, but these highly toxic and caustic substances should not be used for the maintenance of a healthy home. Safe and environmentally friendly cleaning products are readily available. The listing of *Nontoxic Products, Retail Outlets and Catalog Distributors* found at the end of *Part I*, and the section *General Cleanup* in *Division 1*, contain healthy suggestions for every cleaning need.

A Healthy Home Must be a Smoke-free Home

Almost everyone knows of the threat to personal health caused by smoking tobacco. Most people are also well aware of the dangers of inhaling passive smoke. Once smoke is absorbed into the surfaces of a home, it takes extensive renovation to rid the home of it. A no-smoking policy, along with careful design and use of fireplaces, is essential to maintaining good air quality.

Endnotes

[1] National Research Council, Assembly of Life Sciences, *Indoor Pollutants* (National Academy Press, 1986). Cited in Cindy Duehring and Cynthia Wilson, *The Human Consequences of the Chemical Problem* (White Sulphur Springs, MT: Chemical Injury Information Network, 1994), 3.

[2] "Environment 1992," *Science News* 142:25–26 (December 17 and 26, 1992), 436.

[3] William Rea, *Chemical Sensitivity*, Vol. 2 (Lewis Publishers, 1994), 706.

[4] Marion Moses, *Designer Poisons* (San Francisco, CA: Pesticide Education Center, 1995), 309.

[5] U.S. General Accounting Office, "Lawn Care Pesticides: Risks Remain Uncertain While Prohibited Safety Claims Continue" (Washington, DC: U.S. Government Printing Office, March 1990), 4–5.

[6] Jay Feldman, Press Release from Beyond Pesticides/National Coalition Against the Misuse of Pesticides, June 8, 2000.

[7] Michael H. Surgan, "EPA Pesticide Registration: Our Safety in the Balance?" *NYCAP News* 4:3 (Fall 1993), 21–23.

[8] Steven Arnold, et al., "Synergistic Activation of Estrogen Receptor with Combinations of Environmental Chemicals," *Science*, 272 (June 7, 1996), 1489–1492.

[9] Marcia Nishioka, et al., "Measuring Transport of Lawn-applied Herbicides from Turf to Home: Correlation of Dislodgeable 2,4-D Turf Residues with Carpet Dust and Carpet Surfaces Residues," *Environmental Science Technology* 30(1):3313–3320.

[10] Jack Leiss and David Savitz, "Home Pesticide Use and Childhood Cancer: A Case-control Study," *American Journal of Public Health* (February 1995), 249–252.

[11] E. Gold, et al., "Risk Factors for Brain Tumors in Children," *American Journal of Epidemiology* 109 (1979), 309–319.

[12] American Cancer Society, "Drug-free Lawns" (Pamphlet), 1993.

[13] Rea, *Chemical Sensitivity*, 880.

[14] D.J. Hunter and K.T. Kelsey, "Pesticide Residues and Breast Cancer: The Harvest of a Silent Spring?" *Journal of the National Cancer Institute*, 85 (April 21, 1993), 598–599.

[15] Robert Becker, *Body Electric* (Tarcher Press, Inc., 1985).

[16] Research conducted by Anthony Coehlo and Steve Easley of Southwest Research Institute, San Antonio, TX. Cited in *Sacramento Bee* (July 14, 1990).

[17] "Leading Epidemiologists See Childhood Leukemia Risk at 4 mG," *Microwave News* (September-October 2000).

[18] Report by the Committee on Science and Technology, U.S. House of Representatives (Report 98-821, September 16, 1986). Cited in Duehring and Wilson, *The Human Consequences of the Chemical Problem*, 5.

[19] "Neurotoxins: At Home and the Workplace," Report by the Committee on Science and Technology, U.S. House of Representatives (Report 99-827, September 16, 1986). Cited in Duehring and Wilson.

[20] Ibid.

[21] Ibid.

Further Reading and Resources

Publications

Anderson, Nina, et al. *Your Health and Your House*. Keats Publishing, 1995. A resource guide to health symptoms and the indoor air pollutants that aggravate them.

Bower, John. *Healthy House Building: A Design and Construction Guide*. The Healthy House Institute, 1993. Step-by-step guide of author's construction of a model healthy house.

Bower, John. *The Healthy House: How to Buy One, How to Build One, How to Cure a 'Sick' One*. Lyle Stuart, 1989. Describes in great depth a three-step approach consisting of elimination, isolation, and ventilation. As many toxins as possible are identified and eliminated; a tight air barrier isolates occupants from infiltration; and air is exchanged and purified by means of mechanical ventilation. The author speaks from firsthand experience in successfully creating a chemical-free sanctuary for his spouse.

Breecher, Maury M. and Shirley Linde. *Healthy Homes in a Toxic World*. John Wiley and Sons, 1992. The authors identify household health hazards, the human health conditions associated with them, and solutions for healthier environments.

Colburn, Theo, Dianne Dumanoski, and John Peterson Myers. *Our Stolen Future*. Plume, 1997. A gripping account of the scientific research linking reproductive failures, birth defects, and sexual abnormalities to synthetic chemicals that mimic natural hormones, causing disruption of the endocrine system.

Dadd, Debra. *Non-toxic, Natural, and Earthwise*. J.P. Tarcher, 1990. A practical, easy-to-use guide to nontoxic alternatives for cleaning products, personal care products, lawn and garden supplies, baby care items, pet care, and household furnishings.

The Green Guide. Available from: 40–West 20th Steet, New York, NY 10011-4211. Phone: (888) ECO•INFO. This newsletter discusses various relevant topics and promotes safe and ecologically sound consumer choices.

Green, Nancy Sokol. *Poisoning Our Children*. The Noble Press, 1991. The contemporary pesticide problem comes alive as the author relates the nightmare she endured after unwittingly poisoning herself in her own home with repeated pesticide exposures.

Institute for Bau-biologie and Ecology correspondence course. Available through Helmut Ziehe, IBE, Box 387, Clearwater, FL 33757. Phone: (727) 461·4371; Internet: www.bau-biologieusa.com. This certified home-study course has been translated into English from the original work of Dr. Anton Schneider, who is the driving force behind the bau-biologie movement in Europe. The course provides a comprehensive discussion of the interrelationship between the built environment, human health, and planetary ecology.

Lawson, Lynn. *Staying Well in a Toxic World: Understanding Environmental Illness, Multiple Chemical Sensitivities, Chemical Injuries, and Sick Building Syndrome.* Lynnword Press, 1994. Highly readable, informative, and comprehensive overview of the devastating effect of toxic surroundings, authored by a former medical writer with a thorough understanding of the contemporary chemical problem.

LeClaire, Kim and David Rousseau. *Environmental by Design: Interiors, A Sourcebook of Environmentally Aware Choices.* Hartley and Marks, 1993. Provides a "cradle to grave" environmental analysis of common building materials.

Lstibureck, Joe. *EEBA Builder's Guides.* Available through the Energy Efficient Building Association, 10740 Lyndale Avenue South, Suite 10W, Bloomington, MN 55420. Phone: (952) 881·3048; Internet: www.eeba.org. A series of climate-based field guides with explanations, details, and techniques to effectively implement energy- and resource-efficient residential construction.

Our Toxic Times. Published by the Chemical Injury Information Network, P.O. Box 301, White Sulphur Springs, MT 59645. Phone: (406) 547·2255. A useful newsletter for people interested in understanding how chemicals impact human health.

Pearson, David. *The Natural House Book: Creating a Healthy, Harmonious, and Ecologically Sound Home Environment.* Fireside, 1989. The author gives a thoughtful explanation of the problems associated with standard building practices in terms of human health and environmental impacts. He then shows an inspiring array of natural building materials and systems from around the world.

Rogers, Sherry A., M.D. *Tired or Toxic.* Prestige Publishing, 1990. Detailed and comprehensive medical explanations about how chemicals are impacting human health.

Roodman, David Malin and Nicholas K. Lenssen. *A Building Revolution: How Ecology and Health Concerns are Transforming Construction.* Washington, DC: Worldwatch Paper 124-5, March 1995.

Schoemaker, Joyce and Cherity Vitale. *Healthy Homes, Healthy Kids.* Island Press, 1991. The authors discuss ways to protect children from everyday environmental hazards found in the home.

Thrasher, Jack and Alan Broughton. *The Poisoning of Our Homes and Workplaces: The Indoor Formaldehyde Crisis*. Seadora, Inc., 1989. Detailed analysis of the indoor formaldehyde crisis in the United States.

Venolia, Carol. *Healing Environments: Your Guide to Indoor Well-being*. Celestial Arts, 1988. The author takes the reader through a series of environmental-awareness-raising exercises, expanding a holistic approach to health and the built environment that includes the wellness of body, mind, and spirit.

Wilson, Cynthia. *Chemical Exposure and Human Health*. McFarland & Company, 1993. A reference guide to 314 chemicals, with a list of symptoms they can produce, and a directory of environmentally concerned health and public interest organizations.

Zamm, Alfred and Robert Gannon. *Why Your Home May Endanger Your Health*. Simon and Schuster, 1982. Based on a ten-year scientific study, this book explains how millions of Americans may be suffering ill health because their homes have become toxic chambers. The author discusses remedies for many of the major health hazards found in the home.

Nontoxic Products, Retail Outlets, and Catalog Distributors

The Allergy Relief Shop, 3360 Andersonville Highway, Andersonville, TN 37705. Phone: (865) 494•4100; Toll-free: (800) 626•2810; Internet: www.allergyreliefshop.com. Mail-order catalog offering supplies and building products for the allergy-free home.

Allergy Resources, 301, East 57th Avenue, Unit D, Denver, CO 80216. Toll-free: (800) 873•3529; Phone: (303) 438•0600; Internet: www.catalogcity.com (under allergy related catalogs). Internet: allergyresources@hotmail.com. Nontoxic cleaning compounds and body care products.

American Environmental Health Foundation, 8345 Walnut Hill Lane, Suite 225, Dallas, TX 75231. Toll-free: (800) 428•2343; Phone: (214) 361•9515; Internet: www.aehf.com. Sells a wide range of household, building, personal care, and medical products as well as organic clothing, books, and vitamins.

Aubreys Organics, 4419, N. Manhattan Avenue, Tampa, FL 33614. Toll-free: (800) 282•7394; Internet: www.aubrey-organics.com. Over 200 hair, skin, and body care products made from herbs and vitamins, without synthetic chemicals.

Building for Health—Materials Center, P.O. Box 113, Carbondale, CO 81623. Phone: (970) 963•0437; For orders only, Toll-free: (800) 292•4838; Internet: www.buildingfor health.com. Distributor of a wide variety of healthy building products. The owner, Cedar Rose, is also a building contractor who has practical experience with most products sold by the center.

Dasun Company, P.O. Box 668, Escondido, CA 92033. Toll-free: (800) 433•8929. Catalog sales of air- and water-purification products.

Eco Products, Inc., 3655 Frontier Avenue, Boulder, CO 80301. Phone: (303) 449•1876; Internet: www.ecoproducts.com. Supplier of ecologically sound building products.

Environmental Home Center, 1724, 4th Avenue South, Seattle, WA 98134. Toll-free: (800) 281•9785; Phone: (206) 682•7332; Internet: www.enviresource.com.

Healthy Interiors, P.O. Box 9001, Santa Fe, NM 87504. Phone: (505) 820•7634; Internet: www.healthyhomeinteriors.com.

Janice Corporation, 198, Route 46, Budd Lake, NJ 07828. Toll-free: (800) 526•4237; Internet: www.janices.com. Supplier of natural and organic bedding and linens, as well as hypoallergenic and unscented personal care products.

The Living Source, P.O. Box 20155, Waco, TX 76702. Phone: (254) 776•4878; Voice mail order line, Toll-free: (800) 662•8787; Internet: www.living source.com. Catalog sales of "products for the environmentally aware and chemically sensitive."

The Natural Choice, 1365 Rufina Circle, Santa Fe, NM 87505. Toll-free: (800) 621•2591; Internet: www.bioshieldpaint.com. Catalog sales of natural paints, stains, and healthy home products.

NEEDS, 6010 Drott Drive, East Syracuse, NY 13057. Toll-free: (800) 634•1380; Internet: www.needs.com or www.needs4u.com. Mail-order service offering a wide array of personal care products for the chemically sensitive.

The Nontoxic Hot Line. For consultations, Phone: (510) 472•8868. Line for orders only, Toll-free: (800) 968•9355; Internet: www.nontoxic.com. Catalog sales of products for achieving and maintaining indoor air quality and safety for homes, offices, and automobiles.

Planetary Solutions, 2030, 17th Street, P.O. Box 1049, Boulder, CO 80302. Phone: (303) 442•6228; Internet: www.planetearth.com. Environmentally sound materials for interiors.

Part II: Specification

Introduction

CONSTRUCTION specifications are the detailed written instructions that support architectural drawings. Together the "specs" and drawings make up the construction documents.

The drawings explain the physical layout and appearance of the building, how it will be structured, and the choice of general construction materials. Specifications contain instructions that cannot be shown easily on the drawings. They indicate how materials are to be handled and installed, and prescribe brand names of products and performance requirements. Detailed specifications are not often included in the construction documents for residential construction, but if you want to build a healthy home, detailed specifications are essential because many standard practices and materials are unacceptable.

The specifications in this book are designed as a guideline for homeowners, architects, and builders to use in building a healthy home. We have used the *16-Division Master Format* list, developed by the Construction Specification Institute and widely recognized as the standard for organizing construction specifications. The Master Format covers all aspects of construction in a sequence familiar to architects and builders. *Part II* therefore comprises *16 Divisions* rather than standard chapters or sections.

Construction specifications contain information about standards that ensure the structural integrity and quality of construction. The guidelines in this book are not intended as a substitute for standard specifications, but as an addition to them. For example, standard concrete specifications will set out the strength of concrete to be used, how it is to be mixed and poured, and procedures for testing its strength. The specifications in this book do not include such basic information. Instead, the information appearing in the following *16 Divisions* focuses on the health of home occupants as well as the health of home builders and component installers.

Where appropriate, we explain the differences between healthy and standard construction. We also list products, manufacturers, tradespeople, and consultants involved in healthy building, and include toll-free numbers and websites in the

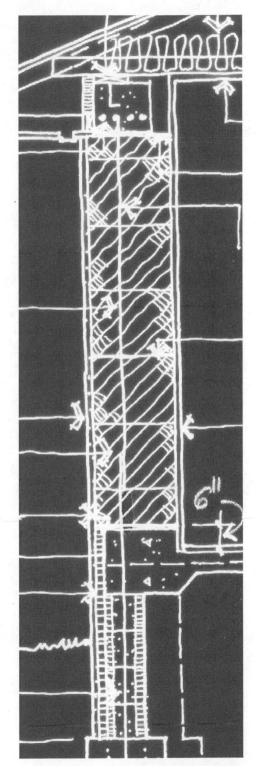

resource list, when they are available, so that you may conveniently locate the closest distributors.

Dispersed throughout the specifications are relevant medical and building case studies, the stories of real people from different walks of life with whom the authors have come in contact over the past few years. What they all have in common is their firsthand experience of the consequences of living in unhealthy environments. They have agreed to share their stories with you.

Division 1: General Requirements

Statement of Intent

Clear communication between contractor, owner, and architect is a key factor in the success of any building project. When creating a healthy home, there are many special project procedures that must be communicated with even greater clarity than in standard construction. The owner's intentions and instructions for special projects can be formally transmitted in *Division 1* of the specifications, thus making them part of the construction contract.

In the box below is a sample of specifications language that succinctly states what the owner wishes to create in a special project.

> This house is being constructed as a healthy house. The products specified herein are intended to be as free of harmful chemicals as are presently available and reasonably attainable. In using these products, we are safeguarding, to the best of our ability, the health of future inhabitants, as well as the workers involved in this construction. Our concern extends also to the workers involved in the manufacture of these products.

Coordination

Building a healthy home can be a pioneering endeavor. Choosing the right architect and contractor for this task is of paramount importance. Creativity, intelligence, common sense, and acceptance of the ideals of healthy house building are essential characteristics. At times you and your team will be experimenting with products that have not been on the market long enough to have a performance history or wide distribution. At other times you may find yourself participating in a revival of materials and techniques that were used successfully for centuries but have been replaced in standard construction by commercialized products containing harmful chemicals.

The contractor will need to allow more time for locating special materials, scheduling their use, and supervising their installation. You may encounter initial resistance from subcontractors who are reluctant to do things that are unfamiliar.

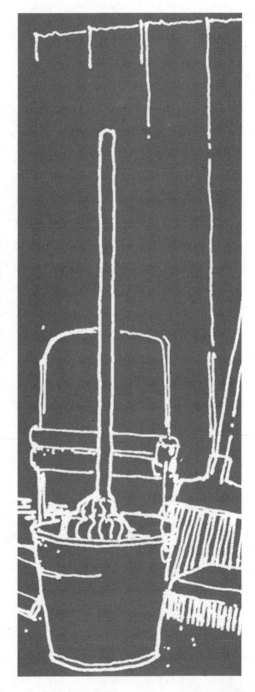

Some of the healthier products might be harder to work with as they do not contain certain additives that make application easy. For these reasons the general contractor will need to supervise the project more closely than in standard construction.

During the construction of a healthy building, the owner may wish to hire subcontractors to carry out specific environmentally related testing, quality control inspections, procedures, or installations. Included in standard contracts from the American Institute for Architecture (AIA) is document A201, "General Conditions for Construction," which acknowledges the owner's right to hire his or her own subcontractors. Careful coordination with the contractor is necessary, however, because any delays and associated expenses incurred by the contractor due to this work will be the responsibility of the owner. Some of the additional testing and inspections are described in *Division 13*. Other quality control procedures will be outlined where appropriate throughout the text.

In summary, a healthy home can take more time and effort to build, which may be reflected in the contractor's scheduling and pricing. Once committed to the project, however, the contractor's role is like that of the symphony conductor, who must lead all players to a successful performance regardless of the difficulty of the piece. You will wish to state this expectation clearly in your specification document. An example of such language follows.

> • The contractor shall be responsible for obtaining all specified materials or approved substitutes and for performing all special project procedures within the contract time, as stated within the construction contract.
> • The contractor shall be responsible for the general performance of the subcontractors and tradespeople, and for any necessary training, specifically with regards to the special project procedures, materials, and prohibitions as outlined in these specifications.

Special Project Procedures

Healthy home building does not permit many behaviors and practices that are commonly accepted at standard job sites. The procedural expectations must be clearly stated by the owner and upheld by the contractor. Below are some basic rules that you may wish to include and expand upon in your specifications.

The following special project procedures must be obeyed at all times:
- Smoking is prohibited within or near any structure on the job site.
- The use of gas-generated machinery and gas- or kerosene-fired heaters is prohibited within or near the building.
- No insecticides, herbicides, or chemicals other than those specified may be used on the job site without prior approval by architect or owner.
- All materials are to be protected from contamination and moisture damage during storage and after installation.

Procedures to Prevent Insect and Rodent Infestation

Some simple measures can be applied from the outset of construction that will prevent infestation by rodents and insects. Consider adding the following requirements to the above list.

- All foodstuffs shall be disposed of in containers, which will be removed from the job site and emptied at the end of each workday.
- All debris shall be removed from under and around the building premises and properly disposed of in a dumpster. The dumpster shall be removed when full on a regular basis so that piles of debris do not accumulate on the ground around it.

Quality Control

There may be some instances where you will be asked by your contractor to share in the responsibility for application of an experimental material. You may choose to accept this responsibility on a case-by-case basis. However, aside from any agreed-upon exceptions, the contractor must be willing to provide the same warranty for your finished home that she or he would when using standard products. The contractor should have no problem doing so as long as he or she carefully follows the manufacturer's instructions for materials.

Manufacturers will specify the conditions required for the proper application of their products, such as proper curing times, acceptable temperature ranges, or specific preparation of substrates. Because the materials contain fewer chemical additives, the manufacturer's specifications may be both

Case Study 1.1:

Quality Control: A mishandled spill

Early in his career as an environmental consultant, John Banta received a frantic call from a woman with chemical sensitivities who was in the process of having a home built. The client had painstakingly detailed plans and specifications with the help of John and her architect. The project had proceeded virtually without problems and was entering the final interior-painting-and-sealing phase when a worker for the subcontracting painter accidentally kicked over a bucket of nontoxic paint, spilling it on the unfinished floor. The worker ran to his truck and grabbed a can of mineral spirits, which he used to clean up the spill. The solvent soaked into the floor and the fumes filled the house. John's client became distraught because her new house was making her feel sick.

Many methods were used in an attempt to remove the noxious mineral spirit odor from the home, but the solvent had been absorbed by the construction materials. Even pulling up the contaminated portion of the floor was insufficient to fix the problem. The cleaning substance used by the painter was clearly in violation of the job contract and it appeared that a lawsuit was imminent. Fortunately, the house was quickly sold to a less-sensitive person who wanted an ecologically constructed home and who was not affected by the residual odor of mineral spirits.

Discussion

In spite of all the best efforts, accidents still happen. The subcontractor failed to educate his worker. The spilled paint was water based, which meant that the use of mineral spirits was unnecessary and inappropriate. The painter should have wiped up as much as possible using clean rags, then scrubbed the rest with water. Since the floor was unfinished, any remaining paint could have been removed with sanding.

different and more stringent than those tradespeople are accustomed to. Consequently, the contractor may need to supervise them closely to maintain a high quality standard.

Another area requiring special vigilance on the contractor's part is the careful screening of materials as they arrive on site to ensure that no spoilage, adsorption of odors, mold, or other forms of contamination have occurred.

We know of a case where batt insulation was shipped to the job site in a truck that was also used to transport fertilizer. Once the insulation was installed, the home took on a distinctly unpleasant odor due to the adsorbent nature of the batt insulation. In another case the painter, who was unfamiliar with milk-based paints, did not realize that the products he was using had spoiled. As a result, the finished home smelled like rancid milk.

Subcontractors may be unfamiliar with some of the healthier products we recommend and thus may not recognize a problem when it arises. These products typically have little odor. If a product emits a strong odor, that may be cause for concern. The contractor's nose becomes an important quality control mechanism. (Exceptions include products such as silicone caulks and vapor-barrier sealants; they have a strong odor upon application, but quickly dissipate and become neutral.) A call to the architect or manufacturer may provide reassurance when questions arise.

It is important to have a clear agreement from the outset about your expectations concerning quality. This agreement can be formalized in the specifications using language similar to the following.

- The contractor shall perform and maintain the special project procedures with the same quality of workmanship as would be expected with standard materials and methods.
- The contractor shall maintain a quality control program that ensures full protection of work against exposure to prohibited materials and practices.
- Except as otherwise approved by the architect or owner, the contractor shall determine and comply with the manufacturer's recommendations on product handling, storage, installation, and protection.
- The contractor shall verify that, prior to installation, all materials are undamaged, uncontaminated, and free of acquired odors. Any products found to be defective shall not be used unless approved by the owner or architect.

Signage

Even if your contractor is well aware of your intentions, he probably will not have the chance to speak personally to the dozens of people who will work at your site during the course of construction. It is important that the special rules that apply to your home be posted in a prominent spot where all who enter will read them. You can specify that a job sign be made and posted. You can indicate in your specifications the kind of signage you want, using this sample wording.

A sign, posted in a prominent place on the job site, alerts everyone as to the special project procedures.
Photo: Paula Baker-Laporte

The following sign is to be made and prominently posted on the job site. It is the responsibility of the general contractor to ensure that his labor force, all subcontractors and their labor forces, all suppliers, and other visitors be made aware of these rules and follow them at all times.

Sign to be Posted:

- This house is being constructed as a healthy home. Only specified products and procedures may be used. If in doubt, contact the general contractor.

- The use of any toxic substances such as insecticides, fungicides, or noxious cleaning products is prohibited anywhere on this site.

- Smoking within or near the building and its garage or outbuildings is strictly prohibited.

- No gasoline-generated machines or open combustion heaters shall be used inside or near the house after the foundation is completed.

- Spills of fuels, solvents, or chemicals must be avoided. If a spill occurs, report it to the general contractor immediately.

- Alternatives to specified materials must be approved in writing by the owner and/or architect prior to use.

Prohibited Products

Because it is difficult to foresee every single product application that will be required in a project, it is prudent to list the major categories of prohibited materials that are the worst health offenders. This gives the general contractor and subcontractor the "big picture" in terms of materials. Sample language containing such a list follows.

The use of substances listed below is prohibited:

• Herbicides, fungicides, insecticides, and other pesticides, except as specified
• Composite wood products containing urea-formaldehyde binders
• Asphalt or products containing asphalt or bitumen
• Commercial cleaning products other than those specified
• Adhesives, paints, sealers, stains, and other finishes except as specified
• Any building materials contaminated by mold or mildew
• Any building materials or components that have been contaminated while in storage or during shipment

Contact the architect for further instructions about any application where these substances would normally be used if information for a substitution is not in this document.

Product Substitution Procedure

Contractors will often ask if they can substitute a product that is different from the one that you have specified. The specified product may be unavailable, too expensive, or too difficult to apply, or contractors may have a similar product that they have used before and prefer. New and healthier products continue to be developed; it may be worth your while to consider certain substitutions. The first step in researching alternatives is to examine the product's Materials Safety Data Sheet (MSDS). You may also request a physical sample. In order to ensure that no substitutions are made without your consent or that of your architect, you may wish to add the following language to your agreement.

• No products may be substituted for the specified product unless agreed upon in writing by the owner or architect.
• An MSDS and product literature must be provided on any substitution in order for it to be considered.
• Submit a physical sample to the owner or architect whenever possible.

The Material Safety Data Sheet (MSDS)

The Material Safety Data Sheet (MSDS) provides information about the chemical substances in a product, its handling precautions, and known health effects. The responsibility for preparing the MSDS lies with the chemical manufacturer. All manufacturers are required to create an MSDS for every chemical compound they offer. It must include the following information:

- With the exception of trade secrets, the specific chemical name and common names for hazardous ingredients
- Physical and chemical characteristics
- Physical hazards
- Health hazards
- Primary routes of entry to the body
- Occupational Safety and Health Administration (OSHA) Permissible Exposure Limit (PEL) and any other recommended exposure limit
- Whether the chemical is a confirmed or potential carcinogen
- Precautions for safe handling and use
- Emergency and first aid procedures
- Name, address, and telephone number of manufacturer or other responsible party. MSDSs can be obtained from either the distributor or the manufacturer of the product in question.

What an MSDS Will Not Tell You

There is important information an MSDS does not reveal. Due to the *Trade Secrets Act*, companies are not required to list ingredients that they define as trade secrets. The OSHA Hazard Communication Standard requires that an MSDS list all health effects, yet health effects of trade secret ingredients can be exempted.[1] Furthermore hazardous ingredients that are present in amounts of less than 1% and carcinogens present in amounts less than 0.1% need not be listed.

The consumer is not allowed access to this information. However, one of the codes under the same law (OSHA Hazard Communication Standard 29, Code of Federal Regulation 1910.1200) permits physicians and other health care providers to access all product ingredient information for diagnostic and treatment purposes. Most doctors are unaware of their right to know.

Another significant omission is the lack of disclosure of the "inert" ingredients, which can account for up to 99% of product volume. Some of these so-called inert ingredients are more hazardous than the active ingredient(s).[2]

The permissible exposure levels (PELs) set by OSHA, and the threshold limit values (TLVs) established by the American Conference of Governmental Industrial Hygienists (ACGIH) are misleading. Industry interests have played a major role in establishing these exposure limits, and most of them were established without prior testing.[3]

The small amount of testing that has been carried out was based on exposing rats to a single dose of a single chemical with cancer or death as the end point. In reality, people are exposed to hundreds of chemicals at a time, the effects of which can be synergistic and accumulate in the body tissues over months and years. Monitoring for cancer or death does not take into account the many noncarcinogenic effects of chemicals, such as damage to the nervous, endocrine, and immune systems. It is also important to recognize that workplace standards are not set according to the safety of the worker, but rather according to what is considered feasible for industry.

Health effects listed in the MSDS are often vague and misleading. They are most accurate when listing the acute, short-term effects of chemicals, such as eye and nose irritation, rashes, and asthma. The data on chronic, long-term exposure is often lacking and does not take into account cumulative effects over time as well as synergistic effects with other chemicals.

How an MSDS Can Be a Useful Tool

Although the MSDS has shortcomings, it is still an important tool for people involved in construction. If you are not working with a physician/architect team knowledgeable about chemicals, the MSDS can be confusing to interpret, but you can apply certain rules of thumb to evaluate a chemical listed in the MSDS. For example, if no special precautions are required when using the chemical, there are no known health effects, and cleanup involves only water, then you might assume that the chemical in question has relatively low toxicity. On the other hand, if it is recommended that you wear gloves and goggles and use a respirator in a well-ventilated area, the product is likely a health hazard while it is being applied. This does not indicate with certainty that the product will have detrimental health effects once it is fully cured. Certain chemicals should pique your concern, such as chlorinated or fluorinated compounds, and chemicals that contain toxins such as toluene, phenol, benzene, xylene, styrene, formaldehyde, and the heavy metals, to name just a few.

With more than 80,000 chemicals in common use, and no toxicity data on most of them, our evaluation can only be partial at best. The U.S. Environmental

Protection Agency has published a list of 53 chemicals that ranked highest as persistent, bioaccumulative, and toxic compounds or PBTs.[4] The California Office of Environmental Health Hazard Assessment has published a list of chronic exposure levels that it has adopted for 41 common chemicals.[5] Lists such as these are far from comprehensive, and they cannot help us choose products with certainty. They can, however, help us to identify known hazardous chemicals and exposure levels and to reject products that contain these.

In summary, although you cannot base your decisions solely on information from the MSDS, it is nevertheless useful. In the following sections we give examples of two MSDSs to show how they are interpreted. Product and manufacturer names have been omitted. Because MSDSs do not always follow a consistent format, comparisons can be difficult. Section numbers will vary, but the information covered remains the same. While the MSDS for **Product #1** describes a product that may be safe to use and in fact is a product that we recommend to our clients, the MSDS for **Product #2** provides cause for concern.

Product Identification

This section includes the name of the product, the manufacturer, the date the MSDS was prepared, and by whom. In the first sample MSDS, the product is a wood preservative. The second sample involves a foam insulation material. As suggested in the examples, product identity information may range from very little to substantial.

Product #1

Material Safety Data Sheet	
Section I: Product Identity	*Manufacturer's Name:*
Date Prepared:	
Preparer's Name:	
Chemical Name: Water-based wood preservative	*Product:*
Chemical Formula: N/A (Product is a mixture)	*Product Identification No.:*
DOT Shipping Class: Not regulated	
Emergency Telephone Number:	

Product #2

Material Safety Data Sheet	
Manufacturer:	Date Prepared:
Telephone Numbers:	
Emergency Number:	
Technical Information:	
(Regular Business Hours):	

Material Identification and Hazardous Components

This section lists the chemical names of all ingredients in the product found to be reportable health hazards. Exposure limits in some instances are established by government agencies. OSHA PEL refers to the permissible exposure limits set by the Occupational Safety and Health Administration. ACGIH TLV refers to the threshold limit values set by the American Conference of Governmental Industrial Hygienists. These values are updated on an annual basis.

If you are not familiar with the toxicity of the chemicals listed and you have no references available on the subject, then you can infer this information by examining the limits set by the government. When the limit is in parts per million (PPM), then you can be sure that the product is highly toxic. NE stands for no established limit and could mean either that adequate testing has not been performed or that the product is not considered highly toxic.

Product #1

Section II: Hazardous Ingredients				
Hazardous Components: *(Special Chemical Identity/Common Name(s))*:*	CAS #	Wt. %	OSHA PEL	ACGIH TLV
Propylene Glycol	57-55-6	30–50	None established	None established
Polyethylene Glycol	25322-68-3	30–50	None established	None established
Disodium Octoborate Tetrahydrate	12008-91-2	20–30	15 mg/m3 (dust)	10 mg/m3 (dust)
* Denotes a toxic chemical reportable under SARA Title 111 Section 313, Supplier Notification provision *HMIS Information*: Health 1; Flammability 0; Reactivity 0				

With a health rating of 1, flammability and reactivity levels of 0, and no established exposure limits, we can assume that the ingredients in this product are relatively safe.

Product #2

Section II: Hazardous Ingredients/Identity Information				
CHEMICAL NAME	CAS NO.	OSHA PEL	ACGIH TLV	PERCENTAGE
Polyurethane Resin	NE*	NE*	NE*	50–85
4,4-Diphenylmethane Diisocynate	101-68-8	0.02 ppm CEIL	0.005 ppm TWA	5–15
Chlorodifluoromethane (HCFC-22)	75-45-8	1,000 ppm TWA	1,000 ppm TWA	15–25
* Not established				
Hazard Rating: Health 3; Flammability 0; Reactivity 1				

In the second sample MSDS, recommended exposure levels for the chemicals 4,4-diphenylmethane diisocyanate and chlorodifluoromethane (HCFC-22) are limited to parts per million. Both chemicals are in fact known to be extremely toxic. Prolonged or repeated exposure to diisocyanates and halogenated hydrocarbons can damage the nervous, immune, and endocrime systems. Note that the Health Hazard Rating is 3 out of a possible 4.

Physical and Chemical Characteristics

This section describes how the material behaves. The information is useful for the design of ventilation systems and for providing adequate equipment and procedures for fire and spill containment.

- *Vapor pressure* tells you how much vapor the material may give off. A high vapor pressure indicates that a liquid will easily evaporate.
- *Vapor density* refers to the weight of the pure gaseous form of the material in relation to air. The weight of a given volume of a vapor (with no air present) is compared to the weight of an equal volume of air.
- *Specific gravity* tells you how heavy the material is compared to water and whether it will float or sink.
- *Evaporation rate* refers to the rate at which a material changes from a liquid or solid state to its gaseous form.
- *Volatile organic content* provides you with an idea of the degree to which the substance will outgas. If the material is toxic, the degree of volatility would be an important point to consider.

- *Solubility* indicates whether the chemical reacts with water to release a gas that is flammable or presents a health hazard.
- *Appearance and odor* indicates how a product is supposed to look and smell. For example, if the product is supposed to be clear and odorless but arrives on site with an acrid smell and/or appears cloudy, the product may be contaminated.

Product #1

Section III: Physical Characteristics			
Boiling Range:	>369°F	Vapor Pressure (mm Hg.):	125 mm Hg @ 100°F
Specific Gravity (H₂O = 1):	1.1–1.3	Vapor Density (Air = 1):	> 1
% Volatile (Volume):	< 1%	Evaporation Rate (Bu) Ac = 1:	> 1
Volatile Organic Content (VOC):	3.8 lb./gal.		
Solubility (specify solvents):	Miscible in water, alcohol, acetone, some glycol ethers, insoluble in petroleum hydrocarbons		
Appearance and Odor:	Clear, odorless liquid		

NOTE: In the above MSDS, the evaporation rate is compared to the rate of evaporation for butyl acetate. With this particular product, the evaporation rate is less than that of butyl acetate.

Product #2

Section III: Physical/Chemical Characteristics	
Boiling Point HCFC-22:	-41.4°F at 1 ATM
Polyurethane Resin NE*	
Vapor Pressure HCFC-22:	136 psia at 70°F
Vapor Density (AIR = 1) HCFC-22:	2.98 at 1 ATM
Specific Gravity (H₂O = 1):	Polyurethane Resin 1.1
Solubility in Water:	Insoluble, reacts with water
Appearance and Odor:	Gel under pressure. Faint ether-like odor.

NOTE: Hydrochlorofluorocarbons or HCFCs are fluorinated carbons that are harmful to the ozone layer.

Fire and Explosion Hazard Data

The flash point tells you the minimum temperature at which a liquid will give off enough flammable vapors to ignite. Obviously, the more stable the product, the safer it will be.

Reactivity Hazard Data

This section can provide you with clues regarding the toxicity of a product.

Product #1

Section IV: Fire and Explosion Hazard Data			
Flash Point (Method Used):	Nonflammable	Flammable Limits (% in air):	Nonflammable
Extinguishing Media:	Nonflammable		
Special Fire Fighting Procedures:	Nonflammable		
Unusual Fire and Explosion Hazards:	None known		
Reactivity:	Stable	Conditions to Avoid:	Avoid extreme heat
Hazardous Polymerization:	May Not Occur	Conditions to Avoid:	None known
Incompatibility (Materials to Avoid):	None known		
Hazardous Decomposition or By-products:	None known		

Product #1 is stable, with no incompatibility with other products and without hazardous decomposition or by-products.

Product #2

Section IV: Fire and Explosion Hazard Data
Flash Point Polyurethane Resin: >400°F
Extinguishing Media: Water fog, foam, CO_2, or dry chemical
Fire Fighting Procedure: Wear self-contained breathing apparatus and turnout gear. Hazardous decomposition products include CO, CO2, NO, and traces of HCl. *Cured Foam:* Wear self-contained breathing apparatus. Hazardous decomposition products include CO, CO_2, NO, and traces of HCl.
Usual Hazards: Temperatures above 120°F will increase the pressure in the can, which may lead to rupturing. *Cured Foam:* This product will burn. Do not expose to heat, sparks, or open flame. This product is not intended for use in applications above 250°F (121°C). Always protect foam with approved facings. This product is not a FIRE STOP or FIRE BARRIER penetration sealant.

Product #2 – continued:

Section V: Reactivity Data
Stability: Stable under normal storage and handling conditions. Do not store above 120˚F. Cured foam will deteriorate when exposed to UV light.
Incompatibility: Water, alcohols, strong bases, finely powdered metal such as aluminum, magnesium or zinc, and strong oxidizers.
Conditions/Hazards to Avoid: Contamination with water may form CO_2. Avoid high heat, i.e., flames, extremely hot metal surfaces, heating elements, combustion engines, etc. Do not store in auto or direct sunlight.

Product #2 is unstable when exposed to ultraviolet light and high heat, and is incompatible with many substances.

Health Hazard Data

This section provides useful information that will help you to determine the toxicity of the product in question.

Product #1

Section V: Health Hazard Data
Route(s) of Entry: Eye contact, inhalation, ingestion
Acute Health Effects: **Eye Contact**: May cause redness or irritation; **Inhalation**: N/A; **Ingestion**: In sufficient doses may cause gastrointestinal irritation; **Skin Contact**: N/A
Chronic Health Effects: Not listed as a carcinogen by the NTP, IARC, or OSHA; no adverse long-term effects are known. Medical Conditions Generally Aggravated by Exposure: No adverse long-term effects are known
Emergency & First Aid: **Eye Contact**: Wash with clean water for at least 15 minutes. If irritation persists, get medical attention; **Inhalation**: N/A; **Ingestion**: If irritation persists, get medical attention; **Skin Contact**: N/A.

Examining the health hazard section for **Product #1** would provide reassurance. The product appears to be only an irritant, with no known long-term health effects. Of course an edible product would be the ultimate assurance of product safety!

In contrast, the information on **Product #2** is not at all reassuring. This product is known to be carcinogenic, mutagenic, and teratogenic. It also may cause irreversible asthma, allergies, and other damage to the immune system. Although this product evaporates quickly, the workers who install the product are exposed to an extreme health hazard.

Product #2

Section VI: Health Hazard Data		
Toxicology Test Data	MDI:	Rat, 4 hr inhalation LC50 – Aerosol 490 mg/m^3 – Highly Toxic
		Rat, 4 hr inhalation LC 50 – Vapor 11 mg/l – Toxic
		Rat, oral LD 50 – > 10,000 mg/kg – Practically Nontoxic
		Rat, inhalation oncogenicity study – @ ~0.2, 1, 6 mg/m^3; URT irritant; Carcinogenic @ 6 mg/m^3
	HCFC-22:	Rat, 2 hr inhalation LC50 – 200,000ppm

Acute Overexposure Effects: Eye contact with MDI may result in conjunctival irritation and mild corneal opacity. Skin contact may result in dermatitis, either irritative or allergic. Inhalation of MDI vapors may cause irritation of the mucous membranes of the nose, throat, or trachea, breathlessness, chest discomfort, difficult breathing and reduced pulmonary function. Airborne overexposure well above the PEL may result additionally in eye irritation, headache, chemical bronchitis, asthma-like findings or pulmonary edema. Isocyanates have also been reported to cause hypersensitivity pneumonitis, which is characterized by flu-like symptoms, the onset of which may be delayed. Gastrointestinal symptoms include nausea, vomiting and abdominal pain.

HCFC-22 vapor is irritating to eyes. Liquid is irritating to eyes and may cause tissues to freeze. Contact of liquid with skin may cause tissue to freeze (frostbite). Dense vapor displaces breathing air in confined or unventilated areas. Inhaling concentrated vapors can cause drowsiness, unconsciousness, respiratory depression and death due to asphyxiation. This compound also increases the sensitivity of the heart to adrenalin, possibly resulting in rapid heartbeat (tachycardia), irregular heartbeat (cardiac arrhythmias), and depression of cardiac function. Persons with preexisting heart disease may be at increased risk from exposure.

Polyurethane resin forms a quick bond with skin. Cured foam is hard to remove from skin. May cause eye damage.

Chronic Overexposure Effects: Acute or chronic overexposure to isocyanates may cause sensitization in some individuals, resulting in allergic symptoms of the lower respiratory tract (asthma-like), including wheezing, shortness of breath and difficulty breathing. Subsequent reactions may occur at or substantially below the PEL and TLV. Asthma caused by isocyanates, including MDI, may persist in some individuals after removal from exposure and may be irreversible. Some isocyanate-sensitized persons may experience asthma reactions upon exposure to nonisocyanate containing dusts or irritants. Cross sensitization to different isocyanates may occur. Long-term overexposure to isocyanates has also been reported to cause lung damage, including reduced lung function, which may be permanent. An animal study indicated that MDI may induce respiratory hypersensitivity following dermal exposure.

Carcinogenicity: Results from a lifetime inhalation study in rats indicate that MDI aerosol was carcinogenic at 6 mg/m3, the highest dose tested. This is well above the recommended TLV of 5 ppb (0.05 mg/m3). Only irritation was noted at the lower concentration of 0.2 and 1 mg/m3 .

Lifetime exposure of rats to 5% HCFC-22 in air resulted in a slightly higher incidence of fibrosarcomas (a malignant connective tissue tumor) in male rats compared to controls. Some of these tumors involved the salivary glands. This effect was not seen in female rats at the same dose level or in rats of either sex at the lower dose level of 1%. Rats given HCFC-22 orally also showed no increased incidence of tumors. In addition, mice exposed to 5 and 1% HCFC-22 in a similar fashion showed no increased incidence of tumors. Spontaneously occurring fibrosarcomas are not uncommon in aging rats, and the increase seen in male rats may have been due to a weak tumor-promoting effect or other nonspecific effect (stress, etc.) of HCFC-22.

Mutagenicity: HCFC-22 has been shown to cause mutations in the bacterium salmonella. This may be due to the unusual metabolic capabilities of this organism. HCFC-22 is not mutagenic in yeast cell, hamster cell, or in vivo mouse and rat cell assays (dominant lethal and bone marrow cytogenic toxicity tests).
Teratogenicity: Offspring born to rats exposed to 5% of HCFC-22 for six hours per day during pregnancy showed stunted growth and a small, but statistically significant, incidence of absent eyes. However, this dose level also caused maternal toxicity. An increased incidence of absent eyes did not occur in rabbits exposed at 5% of HCFC-22 and below, or in rats at 1% of HCFC-22 and below, where maternal toxicity was not observed.
Medical Conditions Generally Aggravated by Exposure: Breathing difficulties, chest discomfort, headache, eye and nose membrane irritation.
Emergency and First Aid Procedures: **Inhalation**: Remove to fresh air. Give oxygen. If not breathing, give artificial respiration. Keep victim quiet. Do not give stimulants. Get immediate medical attention; **Skin**: If frostbitten, warm skin slowly with water; otherwise, wash affected areas with soap and water. Remove contaminated clothing and launder before reuse. Remove wet foam immediately from skin with acetone or nail polish remover. Dried foam is hard to remove from skin. If foam dries on skin, apply generous amounts of petroleum jelly or lanolin, leave on for one hour, wash thoroughly, and repeat process until foam is removed. Do not attempt to remove dried foam with solvents; **Eye**: In case of eye contact, flush with water for 15 minutes. Get immediate medical attention; **Ingestion**: In case of ingestion, get immediate medical attention.

Safe Handling Precautions and Leak Procedures

This section offers more clues regarding the safety of the product. The fewer the precautions given, the more reassuring the information.

Product #1

Section VI: Spill or Leak Procedures
Should be taken in case material is released or spilled: Soak up spill with absorbent material.
Waste Disposal Method: Dispose of in accordance with all local, state, and federal regulations.

Product #2

Section VII: Precautions for Safe Handling and Use
Allow form to cure (harden).
Waste Disposal: Dispose according to federal, state, and local regulations.
Container Disposal: Dispose according to federal, state, and local regulations.
Storage: Store in cool, dry place. Ideal storage temperature is 60°F to 80°F. Storage above 90°F will shorten the shelf life. Do not store above 120°F (49°C). Protect containers from physical abuse. Do not store in auto or in direct sunlight. Store upright.

Control and Preventive Measures

This section lists the personal protective equipment that must be used, the type of ventilation to be used, and precautions to be taken when using the material for its intended purpose.

Product #1

Section VII: Special Protection Data
Respiratory Protection: None normally required
Ventilation: None normally required
Protective Gloves: None normally required
Other Protective Clothing or Equipment: None normally required

Section VIII: Storage and Handling Data
Precautions to be Taken in Handling and Usage: Store in original container; keep tightly closed. Do not reuse container for other purposes. KEEP OUT OF REACH OF CHILDREN.
Other Precautions: Read and observe all precautions on product label.

Product #2

Section VIII: Personal Protection
Respiratory Protection: None required if in well-ventilated area.
Clothing: Wear gloves, coveralls, long-sleeve shirt, and head covering to avoid skin contact. Contaminated equipment or clothing should be cleaned after each use or disposed of.
Eye Protection: Wear face shield, goggles, or safety glasses.
Ventilation: If ventilation is not enough to maintain P.E.L. exhaust area.

Product #1 requires no special protective clothing or equipment, which is an indication of product safety. For **Product #2**, good ventilation and protective clothing over the entire body, including a face shield or goggles, are necessary.

The above MSDS examples demonstrate that the information supplied in the MSDS, although incomplete, is nevertheless useful. An MSDS allows you to obtain a general impression about the level of toxicity of many products you may consider using in home construction.

General Cleanup

Household cleaning products are among the most toxic substances we encounter on a daily basis. It is ironic that our efforts to clean up often produce further contamination by spreading noxious fumes throughout the house. Moreover, these products end up down the drain, where they pollute air, soil, and water.

Case Study 1.2:

General Cleanup: Toxic fumes from cleaning products

L.G., a 53-year-old woman, was in reasonably good health until two years after she began working for a hotel as a housekeeper. At that time she consulted with Dr. Elliott, complaining of rashes, headaches, joint pain, and fatigue. After extensive questioning, Dr. Elliott concluded that the source of her symptoms was probably found at her place of employment. Through a process of elimination, it became apparent that she had become sensitized to the pine-scented product she used to disinfect bathrooms. Although this woman was unable to convince her employer to switch to less-toxic cleaning products, her symptoms improved when she was transferred to a different job within the same building.

Discussion

Certain strong-smelling cleaning products and disinfectants contain phenol, which is known to sensitize the immune system in some people, as happened to the unfortunate woman described in this case study. When checking to see if phenol is an ingredient in a product, a general rule of thumb is to look for any ingredient ending in "ol" or including phenol in its name.

Most commercial cleaning products are made from synthetic chemicals derived from crude oil. Labeling laws and the *Trade Secrets Act* make it difficult to know exactly what is in any particular product. The product may contain highly toxic substances, but consumers have no way of knowing.

Some of the harmful ingredients found in commercial cleaning products include phenol, toluene, naphthalene, penta-chlorophenol, xylene, trichloro-ethylene, formaldehyde, benzene, perchlorethylene, other petroleum distillates, chlorinated substances, ethanol, fluorescent brighteners, artificial dyes, detergents, aerosol propellants, and artificial fragrances.

Commercial Cleaning Products

Professional-strength formulas, which are even more dangerous than household cleaning products, are often used on residential construction cleanup when this work is contracted out to janitorial service providers.

Green Seal is an independent not-for-profit organization that has created environmental and health standards for industrial and institutional cleaners. Based on information provided by the manufacturers, Green Seal has recommended industrial and institutional cleaners that meet the following criteria:[6]

- Are not toxic to human or aquatic life
- Contain VOC levels under 10% by weight when diluted for use
- Are readily biodegradable
- Are not made of petrochemical compounds or petroleum
- Do not contain chlorine bleach
- Are free of phosphates and derivatives
- Do not contain phenolic compounds or glycol ethers
- Are free of arsenic, cadmium, chromium, lead, mercury, nickel, and selenium
- Have acceptable pH levels
- Work optimally at room temperature

The following institutional/industrial-strength cleaners are among those recommended by Green Seal[7] and are ones we have found to be reasonably available for use by contractors:

- **Earth Friendly Products**: A complete line of floor care, all-purpose, and specialty cleaners.
- **ECO 2000**: A multipurpose cleaner and degreaser derived from naturally occurring, renewable, rapidly biodegradable resources. It can be used at a 1:5 dilution as a degreaser and stripper, and all the way down to a 1:64 dilution as a window cleaner.
- **Enviro Care**: Cleaning products for all washable surfaces.
- **EnviroSmart**: Makers of Natural Wonder Heavy Duty Degreaser and Natural Wonder Ultra Dilutable Cleaner.
- **Formula G-510**: A multipurpose concentrated colloidal cleaner/degreaser.
- **Green Unikleen**: An industrial-strength degreaser/cleaner.
- **The Natural**: A complete line of naturally derived, fragrance-free cleaning products that include all-purpose cleaners, degreasers, furniture polish, carpet shampoo, wax stripper, lime and scale remover, tub cleaner, and glass cleaner.

Household Cleaning Products

For normal household cleaning, several effective alternatives to harsh chemical cleaning compounds are available. The following brand-name cleaning products do not contain harsh chemicals.

- **AFM SafeChoice Safety Clean**: Industrial strength cleaner/degreaser and disinfectant.

- **AFM SafeChoice Superclean**: All-purpose cleaner and degreaser.
- **AFM SafeChoice X158 Mildew Control**: Low-odor, antifungal, antibacterial treatment.
- **Bio Shield**: A complete line of biodegradable, soap-based household cleaners containing natural and mostly organic ingredients.
- **Bon Ami Polishing Cleanser**: Non-chloride, all-purpose scouring powder.
- **Mystical**: Odorless cleaner and deodorizer.
- **Naturally Yours**: A complete line of "economological" household and personal cleaning products.
- **SDA 1600**: Spectracidal disinfectant agent, a benign germicide.

Common Household Products That Clean

The following common household products may also be used for cleaning.

- **Baking soda** cleans, deodorizes, scours, and softens water. It is noncorrosive and slightly abrasive and is effective for light cleaning.
- **Borax** cleans, deodorizes, disinfects, and softens water. It is also effective for light cleaning, soiled laundry in the washing machine, and for preventing mold growth.
- **Hydrogen peroxide** (H_2O_2) is effective in removing mold. Purchase a 10% food grade solution. (The solution most commonly sold off the shelf is only 3%.) Use protective gloves to apply. A 10% solution will bleach many types of surfaces.
- **Soap** (as opposed to detergents) biodegrades safely and completely. It is an effective and gentle cleaner with many uses. For hands, dishes, laundry, and light cleaning, use the pure bar or soap flakes without perfume additives.
- **T.S.P.** (trisodium phosphate) can be used, as per manufacturer's instructions, for grease removal. It is available in hardware stores. Surfaces cleaned with T.S.P. should be neutralized with baking soda before finishes are applied. Note: Fluids containing T.S.P. should not be disposed of in septic systems or sewer systems due to high phosphate content.
- **Vodka** is effective for dissolving alcohol-soluble finishes. Use a high proof (alcohol content) product.
- **Washing soda** (sodium carbonate) cuts grease, removes stains, disinfects, and softens water. It is effective for heavily soiled laundry and general cleaning purposes.

• **White vinegar** cuts grease and removes lime deposits. You can make a safe and useful all-purpose cleaning solution with distilled white vinegar and plain water in a 50/50 ratio. For window cleaning, add 5 tablespoons of white vinegar to 2 cups of water. The solution should be placed in a glass spray bottle. Glass is preferred because plastics are known to release hormone-disrupting chemicals into bottle contents. Vinegar can be used to clean and control mold growth, but the thin film of residue left on the surface supplies nutrients for new growth.

Contract Close-Out

Once construction is complete, and before the home is handed over from the contractor to the owner, various tests should be run on the building. This provides the opportunity for tuning and adjusting various systems and either assures that the building is operating as intended, or detects errors and omissions in the building system so that the contractor or appropriate subcontractor can correct them prior to occupation. This also provides an opportunity for the contractor to do a "walk through" with the owner in order to explain how the systems work and how the owner needs to maintain and monitor them.

Throughout this book we suggest various tests that the owner may wish to include as part of the contract, to be conducted either by the contractor and his subcontractors or by a third party as part of the building contract. (Refer to *Division 13* for more specifics.) Some of these include:

• Testing for air leakage in the heating, ventilation, and air conditioning (HVAC) system (if there is one)
• Pressure balancing of HVAC, or start up and balancing of radiant floor heating
• Cycling all appliances
• Testing for magnetic fields
• Air and water quality tests

We also suggest that the owner request various documentation from the contractor, such as an owners manual and "as-built" drawings, which are marked-up copies of the original drawings and specifications that indicate any changes made in the course of construction and that locate any pertinent information not on the original documents. (Refer to *Occupant Education* in *Division 1*.)

Endnotes

[1] Elizabeth Kersten and Bruce Jennings, *Pesticides and Regulation: The Myth of Safety* (California Senate Office of Research, Senate Reprographics, April 1991), 41 pages.

[2] Robert Abrams (Attorney General), "The Secret Hazards of Pesticides" (New York Department of Law, June 1991), 5 pages.

[3] B.I. Castleman and G.E. Ziem, "Corporate Influence on Threshold Limit Values," *American Journal of Industrial Medicine* 13 (1988): 531–559.

[4] "EPA Releases RCRA Waste Minimization PBT Chemical List," EPA Environmental Fact Sheet 530-F-98-028, November 1998 (www.EPA.gov/ epaoswer/hazwaste/minimize/chemlist/index.htm).

[5] Office of Environmental Health Hazard Assessment (OEHHA), All Chronic Reference Exposure Levels Adopted by OEHHA as of May 2000 (www.oehha.ca. gov/air/chronic_rels/AllChrels.htm1).

[6] Green Seal, Green Report on Industrial and Institutional Cleaners, September-October 1999.

[7] The complete list is available through Green Seal, 1001 Connecticut Avenue NW, Suite 827, Washington, DC 20036-5525. Phone: (202) 872•6400; Internet: www.greenseal.org.

Further Reading

Ashford, Nicholas and Claudia Miller. *Chemical Exposures: Low Levels and High Stakes.* Van Nostrand Reinhold, 1991. A scientific discussion of the mechanisms underlying chemical sensitivities.

Bower, Lynn Marie. *The Healthy Household.* Healthy House Institute, 1995. This book contains a useful section on household cleansers.

Dadd, Debra Lynn. *Nontoxic, Natural and Earthwise.* J.P. Tarcher, 1990. This book contains a good selection of alternatives to toxic cleaning products.

Lab Safety Supply, Inc. *Preparing, Understanding, and Using Material Safety Data Sheets.* This booklet can be obtained from Lab Safety Supply, Inc. at Toll Free: (800) 356•0783.

Wilson, Cynthia. *Chemical Exposure and Human Health*. McFarland and Company, Inc., 1993. A reference to 314 chemicals with a guide to symptoms. We use this handy guide to supplement information from the MSDS.

Resource List

Product	Description	Manufacturer/Distributor
AFM SafeChoice Safety Clean	Industrial strength biodegradable cleaner and degreaser for high-moisture areas.	AFM (American Formulating and Manufacturing) 3251–3rd Avenue San Diego, CA 92103 (800) 239•0321, (619) 239•0321 www.afmsafecoat.com
AFM SafeChoice Superclean	All-purpose, biodegradable cleaner/ degreaser.	Same
AFM SafeChoice X158 Mildew Control	Low-odor liquid surfactant coating for prophylactic use where mold and mildew are likely to appear.	Same
Bio Shield Cleaners	A complete line of biodegradable, soap-based, household cleaning products.	Bio Shield Paint Co. 1365 Rufina Circle Santa Fe, NM 87505 (800) 621•2591, (505) 438•0199 www.bioshieldpaint.com
Bon Ami Polishing Cleanser	Kitchen and bath scouring cleanser without perfumes, dyes, chlorines, or phosphates. A complete line of domestic and institutional cleaning products.	Faultless Starch/Bon Ami Company Kansas City, MO 64101-1200. Available in grocery, health food stores.
Earth Friendly Products	Multipurpose cleaner/ degreaser meeting Green Seal standards.	Native Solutions P.O. Box 3274 Lacey, WA 98509-3274 (888) 281•3524, (360) 491•0992 www.ecos.com
ECO 2000	Cleaning products for all washable surfaces: nontoxic, biodegradable, noncorrosive, and nonreactive.	KC Products 707 N.E. Broadway, Suite 210 Portland, OR 97232 (503) 287•4608, (800) 927•9442
Enviro Care	"Natural Wonder" line of heavy-duty cleaner, degreaser, and other household cleaning products.	Rochester Midland 1015 North Street Omaha, NE 68102 (800) 283•4248, (402) 342•4248
EnviroSmart	Multipurpose cleaner meeting Green Seal standards.	EnviroSmart Products Company 555 West Arlington Place, Suite 502 Chicago, IL 60614 (773) 248•7089, (888) 655•3772 www.espesp.com
Formula G-510	An industrial strength, bio-degradable, water-soluble degreaser/cleaner which removes grease, oil, dirt, graphite, and carbon and leaves a residue-free surface for welding or painting.	20-10 Products, Inc. P.O. Box 7609 Salem, OR 97303 www.2010products.com
Green Unikleen	An industrial-strength degreaser/cleaner.	IPAX Cleanogel, Inc. 8301 Lyndon Avenue Detroit, MI 48238 (800) 930•4729, (313) 933•4211 www.ipax.com
Mystical	Odorless cleaner and deodorizer.	The Nontoxic Hot Line 3441 Golden Rain Road #3 Walnut Creek, CA 94595 (800) 968•9355 (orders only), (510) 472•8868 www.nontoxic.com
Naturally Yours	A complete line of household cleaning products derived from pure, natural ingredients.	Naturally Yours 1926 South Glenstone Avenue #406 Springfield, MO 65804 (417) 889•3995, (888) 801•7347

Product	Description	Manufacturer/Distributor
SDA 1600	Spectracidal disinfectant agent; EPA-approved, nontoxic germicide.	Apothecure, Inc. 13720 Midway Road, Suite 109 Dallas, TX 75244 (800) 969•6601 www.apothecure.com
The Natural	A complete line of cleaning and homecare products. Degreaser; Bath, Tub & Tile Cleaner; and all-purpose products meet Green Seal standards.	The Clean Environment Co., Inc. P.O. Box 4444 Lincoln NE 68504 (402) 464•0988

Division 2: Site Work

Introduction

This Division contains information on site selection and site maintenance and restoration during the construction process.

Site Selection

Long before construction begins, you will choose the appropriate site. When the ancient Romans selected a site for housing, they paid careful attention to the health-giving qualities of the land. To test the potential home site, cattle were confined to graze in the area for a specific period of time, after which they were slaughtered and the innards examined. If the animals had unhealthy livers, the site was abandoned.

Unfortunately, the natural health hazards of almost any site pale in comparison to potential hazards created by humans. Keep the following guidelines in mind when choosing a site.

- Choose a location where the air is relatively unpolluted.
- Evaluate levels of light and noise pollution.
- Determine the direction that prevailing winds blow and how they change seasonally. Consider what is upwind from you.
- Avoid industrial areas, power plants, agricultural lands with heavy pesticide use, and other major pollution producers.
- Avoid proximity to high-voltage power lines, microwave relay stations, and cellular phone and broadcast towers. In general, a distance of one-tenth mile from high voltage power lines and one-half mile from microwave cellular and broadcast towers is adequate. Many public utilities will provide free site measurements for background magnetic field levels. Ensure that measurements are taken at a time when power lines in the area are operating at peak load, or have the magnetic field calculated based on peak-load projections. Utility companies should provide this information in writing.
- Avoid sites adjacent to parking lots and traffic corridors.

+ Crest locations generally have better air quality and more air movement than valley sites.
+ If you are considering a site in a populated area, analyze your neighborhood in terms of present use and future development. How are nearby empty lots zoned? Do the neighbors use pesticides? Is there wood smoke from woodstoves and fireplaces in the winter?
+ Investigate water quality in the area.

Professional Assistance in Site Selection

You may require assistance in selecting your site, especially when remedies to suspected problems may be costly. Industrial toxins in the soil, poor percolation for installing a septic system, or unstable soils are examples of conditions that might cause concern. We recommend that you make your offer to purchase contingent on inspections by professional consultants. In this way, you can avoid being obligated to purchase a contaminated or unacceptable site. The following sections describe some of the more common consultant specialties.

Phase I Environmental Inspector

If you are considering a property that was used for industry or agriculture in the past, or that contains underground fuel tanks, or if you suspect that old buildings may contain lead or asbestos, then a Phase I environmental audit should be conducted to identify the risks. Remember that up-front costs are minor compared to the cost of a hazardous waste cleanup, which may far exceed property value.

Geotechnical Consultant

If you are concerned about the geological structure of the site, then you should consult a geotechnical engineer. This person will be able to troubleshoot problems such as high water tables, unstable soils, expansive soils, earthquake faults, and sink holes. Engineering solutions can be devised for many of these problems so that the costs of development can be determined before you purchase the land.

Septic Engineer

In many locations where municipal sewers are not available, an engineered septic system plan is required before a building permit will be issued. The septic engineer, who is often a geotechnical engineer as well, will study the land formation and perform percolation tests to determine how the sewage waste projected for your development can best be handled. In areas with limited percolation, steep slopes, or high water tables, the installation of a proper septic system could be costly or even impossible. If such conditions exist, it is best to be informed prior to purchasing the land.

Water Quality Specialist

In the event that a site lacks water, it is important to determine the cost of obtaining it. If the local municipality serves the site, then the water company may be able to give you an estimate. If the site is rocky, you may need to excavate trenches by blasting the surrounding rock. If you must drill a well, the neighbors or the local well driller can inform you of the depth of surrounding wells and also give you information about water quality. If the site already contains a well, ensure that the submersible pump was manufactured after 1979 or that it is safe. The oils in some older pumps contain polychlorinated biphenyls (PCBs) and represent a serious health threat should a rupture occur.

Whatever the source of potable water, it should be tested by a professional and filtered or purified as required. Water quality will be discussed further in *Division 11*.

Site Clearing

Although it is more convenient for a contractor to build on a site without obstacles such as trees, native vegetation, and boulders, some, but not all contractors will go to great lengths to preserve as much natural vegetation and other landscape features as possible. Do not assume that the preservation of your site will be a priority of the same magnitude for a contractor as it will be for you. To clarify your desires and the contractual obligations of the contractor in this regard, you can formalize site preservation intentions by stating them as part of your contract. Following is an example of site specifications created for the purpose of preserving the natural features of the site and preventing bug infestations as a result of the clearing process.

- The owner and architect shall approve the site layout prior to digging the footings.
- Topsoil and large boulders shall be stockpiled for future use by the owner.
- All trees designated for removal from the building site are to be marked for review by the owner or architect.
- Tree stumps and all dead foliage should be fully removed from around and under the building site and disposed of offsite so that they do not attract termites and other pests.
- The owner and architect shall determine which trees are to be transplanted or maintained during construction.
- The construction area and access to the construction area shall be as small as is reasonable to facilitate construction of the home. This area is to be clearly demarcated and roped off to prevent any destruction of natural terrain outside it by construction vehicles.

Grading

Many mold problems originate with poor drainage around the building perimeter, which can cause water to puddle against the building and sometimes to seep inside. Although less prevalent in dry climates, mold is still a serious health threat, especially in flat roof construction where canales or scuppers are used for roof drainage, and erosion around the discharge is common. An adequate roof overhang will be the first line of defense in keeping water away from the building envelope. Good site grading will be the second line of defense, and a perimeter drainage system in combination with stem wall dampproofing (as described in *Division 7, Perimeter Drainage*) constitutes the third component to a comprehensive rainwater management plan. The following specification for surface water run-off management is recommended.

- Water shall have positive drainage away from the building at all points along its perimeter. Ground shall slope away at a minimum of 5%, and soil used to grade around the building shall be of an impervious nature with high clay content.

> • All canales, scuppers, and downspouts shall have splash blocks and an adequate drainage path away from the building.

Soil Treatment

Sometimes the soils under brick walkways or interior brick pavers surrounding the structure or under the structure itself are treated with insecticides or herbicides. This practice should be avoided. Many people have become sensitive to very low levels of pesticide exposure. Children are especially vulnerable. Some harmful agents will remain potent long after the building is gone. Where soil treatment is mandated or otherwise unavoidable we recommend the use of boric acid, diatomaceous soil, or other least-toxic measures. (Refer to the section on integrated pest management in *Division 10*.). You may wish to specify the following.

> • Do not treat soil with manufactured chemical treatments.
> • Treat sand surfaces under floors and brick or stone walkways with diatomaceous soil. Inhaling dust from diatomaceous soil is hazardous, and proper precaution should be used during application.
> • Use barrier cloth under exterior walkways to prevent weed overgrowth.

Pavement

Petroleum tar, which is the main component of asphalt or "black top" paving, is carcinogenic and should be avoided. Not only does it emit harmful vapors during installation, but it will also volatilize when heated by the sun. More healthful options include concrete slab, concrete or brick pavers, and paving stone or gravel over a well-drained and compacted base. The following products are innovative alternatives to asphalt paving.

> • **Perma-Zyme:** A biodegradable and environmentally safe road stabilization enzyme that works by lowering the surface tension of water, promoting penetration and dispersal of moisture. This causes hydrated clay particles to fill voids in soil so that it forms a tight, dense, and permanent stratum.

+ **Road Oyl:** An emulsion of natural tree resin that is combined with earth materials to create a high-strength pavement.
+ **Stabilizer:** A colorless, odorless, psylium-based, concentrated powder soil additive for dirt or crushed stone surfaces. Stabilizer binds and flocks aggregate screenings to provide a firm natural surface for pathways, trails, and driveways.

Further Reading

International Institute for Bau-Biologie and Ecology. Home Study Courses and Seminars. P.O. Box 387, Clearwater, FL 33757. Phone: (727) 461·4371.

Resource List

Product	Description	Manufacturer/Distributor
Perma-Zyme	A biodegradable and environmentally safe road stabilization enzyme that can be used in place of asphalt paving.	Idaho Enzymes, Inc. 1010 West Main Jerome, ID 83338 (208) 324·3642
Road Oyl	An emulsion of natural tree resin that is combined with earth materials to create pavement.	Soil Stabilization Products Co., Inc P.O. Box 2779 Merced, CA 95344-0779 (800) 523·9992 www.sspco.org
Stabilizer	A colorless, odorless, psylium-based additive for pathways, trails, and driveways.	Stabilizer Solutions, Inc. 205 South 28th Street Phoenix, AZ 85034 (800) 336·2468, (602) 225·5900 www.stabilizersolutions.com

Division 3: Concrete

Introduction

Concrete is widely used in residential construction for footings, stem walls, exposed basement flooring, as a subfloor for slab on grade construction, and as a finished floor material.

Concrete consists of cement (usually Portland cement), aggregate, and water. It is high in embodied energy due to the tremendous heat required to make cement. Toxic industrial waste products are sometimes burned in order to provide these high temperatures. We believe that cement products that are produced through the burning of toxic wastes should be boycotted, not necessarily because the cement is inferior, but because the use of toxic waste as fuel is an environmentally destructive practice.

Once cured, concrete becomes an inert product and is not usually associated with health problems. However, certain practices can make concrete harmful to human health and should be avoided. These practices are discussed in the following sections.

Aggregate

The aggregate component accounts for 60 to 80% of concrete volume. The size and characteristics of the aggregate will affect the quantities of cement and water required, as well as the compressive strength, weight, and surface character of the finished concrete. Aggregate materials range in size from fine sand to crushed rock pieces. Sometimes recycled materials are used as aggregate and these may be a source of contamination. Recycled industrial waste products such as fly ash may contain hydrocarbons and sulfur. If the source of the fly ash is an industrial process with residual heavy metals or toxic compounds, the fly ash can have toxic properties.

Other recycled materials such as crushed brick are highly absorbent and may have been exposed to atmospheric pollutants prior to being used in concrete. You should specify that you want aggregate free of toxins and acquired odors to be used in your construction, using language similar to the following.

> - Only clean, natural mineral aggregates are acceptable. The following are unacceptable aggregates: crushed brick, crushed sandstone, crushed concrete slag, fly ash (unless it is possible to verify that it contains no heavy metals or toxic substances), cinder, and volcanic material (other than pumice).
> - The contractor shall verify the aggregate content with the concrete supplier prior to pouring.

Water

You should specify that you want only clean potable water used in the concrete.

> - Water shall be of potable quality, free of taste, color, and odor. It should not foam or fizzle.

Admixtures

Many different types of admixtures may be added to the concrete mix to modify various properties. For example, air-entrainment admixtures disperse air bubbles throughout the concrete to improve resistance to freezing and thawing. Water-reducing admixtures decrease the amount of water required. Retarders and accelerators modify the setting time of concrete.

Super plasticizers allow for lower water-to-cement ratios. They frequently contain sulfonated melamine, formaldehyde condensates, sulfonated napthalene, and other potentially harmful ingredients.

Water-reducing agents and air-entrainment admixtures are frequently added to concrete mixtures even when not specifically requested. The exact ingredients of an admixture are usually proprietary. Although admixtures generally make up a very small portion of the concrete and do not pose a significant problem to any but the most sensitive individuals, they can be completely eliminated if concrete work is scheduled for warm weather and if the concrete supplier is aware of this requirement. Even with admixtures, concrete must never be poured on frozen soil or when there is a risk that frost may penetrate under the slab while it cures. If you wish to avoid additives, you must specify this.

> • No admixtures shall be used in the concrete. It is the contractor's responsibility to comply with the necessary climatic parameters so that required strengths and finishes are obtained without additives. Verify with supplier that all concrete is free of admixtures, including air-entrainment and water-reducing agents, accelerants, and retardants.

Slab Reinforcement

It is common practice to place a mesh of welded wire fabric within a concrete slab to help prevent cracking, but the presence of metal throughout a structure may contribute to electro-pollution, and this practice can distribute unwanted voltage throughout the home. Several types of approved nonmetallic reinforcing fibers are now readily available to do the same job at very little or no increase in cost. Check with local code officials to determine their acceptability in your jurisdiction. If wire mesh reinforcing is being excluded for reasons of electromagnetic considerations, then you should add the following specification (and refer to *Division 16, Electric Fields*).

> • Slab reinforcing shall be 1/2" fiberglass or polypropylene fibers as manufactured by **Fibermesh** or **Fiber-Lock** or equal.

Stem Wall Reinforcement

Steel bars are placed in footings and stem walls to reinforce the concrete. In situations where the ground is higher than the floor level, such as in a basement or behind a retaining wall, steel reinforcing is also present, often at horizontal and vertical intervals of 12 inches or less.

In cases where an owner wishes to eliminate large amounts of conductive metal from structures, it is possible to use fiberglass reinforcing bars. These rebars were originally designed for bridge construction because they do not rust, corrode, or dissolve from galvanic action. Because the fiberglass rebar cannot be bent on site and must be preordered, you should carefully think out your use of this product in advance. Fiberglass rebar can be ordered through **Kodiak FRP**. If you plan to use fiberglass rebar, verify with local code enforcement officials that they will accept a particular product before you purchase it. We have used fiberglass rebar successfully on a few homes, but have found it to be expensive and inconvenient. You can reduce electric fields by grounding metal rebar, but the presence of the metal still provides a potential pathway for stray magnetic fields.

Form Release Agents

Concrete formwork is usually coated with release agents so that it can be easily removed and reused once concrete has cured. Although many inert products may be used for this purpose, diesel fuel and other equally noxious substances are commonly used because they are least expensive and readily available. These practices should not be allowed in a healthy house and we suggest the following be specified.

> The use of petroleum-based form oil as a release agent is prohibited. The following are acceptable for use as form release agents:
> • Non-rancid vegetable oil or an acceptable paint as specified in *Division 9: Finishes*.
> • **Bio-Form:** A very low-odor, nontoxic, spray-on application specifically designed as a concrete form release agent or approved equal.

Concrete Curing

After pouring, concrete can only cure and gain strength if it remains nearly saturated with water for a minimum of 28 days. The curing process stops if the relative humidity of the concrete drops below 80%. Improperly cured concrete will develop structural weaknesses and cracks that can become pathways for unwanted moisture and soil gases to creep into the building. Rushing the drying process may also weaken the surface so that concrete dust continually sloughs from the surface into the home. Pouring slabs in cold weather is also risky since cold temperatures impede the curing process. The use of propane heaters to keep the slab warm may cause the concrete surface to become weak and cracked as combustion gases enter the material and interfere with its chemical composition.

Improperly cured concrete will have high alkalinity levels that can cause certain substrates and finishing materials to break down or rot. pH testing can help to determine whether a concrete surface has been properly cured and whether problems will develop with certain finish applications. A simple test is described in *Division 13, pH Testing for Concrete*.

Concrete Finishes

The simplicity, durability, and ease of cleaning of an exposed concrete slab can make it a good choice for an attractive finished flooring surface in a healthy home. Usually when a slab is used as the finished floor it must be trowelled to a smoother finish than a slab slated for use as a subfloor would be.

Smooth-surfaced concrete requires the expertise of an experienced tradesperson. When it is first poured, the concrete will contain more water than it needs to complete the setting reaction. Some of this extra water will come to the surface. If the concrete is finished before the extra water has fully migrated upward, the moisture will become trapped in the upper layer of concrete, resulting in a weakened surface that will release concrete dust into the indoor environment. The window of opportunity for properly smoothing the surface is short. If too much time has elapsed, the surface will have set and will remain rough.

For exposed finished slabs, control joint locations must be carefully planned for their esthetics, and often more joints are added to minimize random cracking. Color is often added, either integrally mixed into the wet concrete or applied after the concrete sets. Because the slab is usually poured near the beginning of the construction, it must be kept covered during the course of construction to ensure that it is not damaged or stained. All of these factors will add to the price of the concrete work, but will still make the process cost-effective when the price of covering the concrete with another material is considered. Both the coloring agents and the surface treatment must be selected carefully to achieve a healthy finish. Acceptable sealers are listed in the *Slab and Stem Wall Treatment and Detailing* section below. The following are specifications for slab coloring.

> * No aniline-based coloring agents are to be used.
> * Use only high-quality mineral pigments such as **Chromix Admixture** and **Lithochrome Color Hardener** or **Davis Colors**. Verify with the manufacturer that the selected color is free of chromium and other heavy metals.

Slab and Stem Wall Treatment and Detailing

Concrete can act as a wick for ground moisture, thereby promoting water damage and fungal growth in other materials due to moisture transfer. A layer of coarse gravel under the slab, with no fines (fine pieces) smaller than half an inch, will break capillary action. A layer of continuous, unpunctured polyethylene directly under the slab will help prevent water vapor and soil gases such as radon from finding their way through cracks in the slab. A fully cured slab can also be sealed to block moisture and soil gases from entering the building and to create a more finished floor surface. Some sealers are solvent based and should be avoided. The following sealers are more benign:

- **AFM Safecoat Paver Seal .003, AFM Safecoat MexeSeal, AFM Safecoat Penetrating Waterstop**: Water-based sealers and finish coats.
- **Sodium Silicate**: A clear sealer supplied by various manufacturers. Avoid inhaling powdered sodium silicate because it can cause silicosis. This product is suitable for use on a finished exposed slab.
- **Weather-Bos Masonry Boss Formula 9**: A water-reducible sealer for all above-grade concrete and masonry surfaces. Helps reduce dusting, powdering, efflorescence, spalling, cracking, and freeze-thaw damage.
- **Vocomp-25**: A solvent-reduced, water-based sealer.
- **Xypex**: A nontoxic (according to manufacturer), zero-VOC, chemical treatment for the waterproofing and protection of concrete. It creates a nonsoluble crystalline structure that permanently plugs the pores and capillary tracts of concrete. Xypex concentrates DS-1 and DS-2 are dry-shake formulations designed for horizontal surfaces.

Further Reading

Timusk, John, National Building Envelope Council. "Slabs on Grade." Building Science Treatise. Construction Canada 92-07.

Resource List

Product	Description	Manufacturer/Distributor
AFM Safecoat Paver Seal .003	A low-odor, water-based sealer for previously unsealed concrete that fills up pores and preps slab for topcoat.	AFM (American Formulating and Manufacturing) 3251 3rd Avenue San Diego, CA 92103 (800) 239•0321, (619) 239•0321 www.afmsafecoat.com
AFM Safecoat MexeSeal	A satin-finish topcoat to be used over Paver Seal .003.	Same
AFM Safecoat Penetrating Waterstop	A satin-finish final coat that may be used over MexeSeal to further improve water repellency.	Same
Bio-Form	An environmentally friendly vegetable-based, spray-on, concrete release agent.	Leahy-Wolf Company 1951 North 25th Avenue Franklin Park, IL 60131 (888) 873•5327 www.leahywolf.com
Chromix Admixture	Mineral pigment containing no chromium or other heavy metals; for use in concrete.	L.M. Scofield Company P.O. Box 1525 Los Angeles, CA 90040 (800) 222•4100 www.scofield.com
Davis Colors	Mineral-based pigments for concrete.	Laporte Pigments/Davis Colors 3700 E. Olympic Blvd. Los Angeles, CA 90023 (800) 356•4848, (323) 269•7311 www.daviscolors.com
Fiber-Lock	Polypropylene fiber additive reinforcement for concrete slabs.	Fiber-Lock Company 4308 Garland Drive Fort Worth, TX 76117 (800) 852•8889, (817) 498•0042
Fibermesh	Fiberglass reinforcing for concrete slabs.	SI Geosolutions P.O. Box 22788 Chattanooga, TN 37416 (800) 621•0444, (423) 899•0444 www.sixsoil.com
Kodiak FRP Rebar	Fiberglass reinforcing bars.	Seasafe, Inc. 209 Glaser Drive Lafayette, LA 70508 (800) 326•8842, (337) 406•2345 www.seasafe.com
Lithochrome Color Hardener	Mineral pigment containing no chromium or other heavy metals; for use in concrete.	L.M. Scofield Company P.O. Box 1525 Los Angeles, CA 90040 (800) 222•4100 www.scofield.com
Sodium Silicate	Clear sealer for concrete floors. Widely distributed in hardware and ceramic supply stores.	Ashland Chemical, Inc. 5200 Blazer Parkway. Dublin, OH 43017 (800) 258•0711, (614) 889•3333 www.gotoashland.com
Vocomp-25	Water-based acrylic concrete sealer.	W.R. Meadows P.O. Box 543 Elgin, IL 60121 (800) 342-5976 www.wrmeadows.com

Product	Description	Manufacturer/Distributor
Weather-Bos Masonry Boss Formula 9	A water-reducible sealer for all above-grade concrete and masonry surfaces. Helps reduce dusting, powdering, efflorescence, spalling, cracking, and freeze-thaw damage.	Weather-Bos International 316 California Avenue, Suite 1082 Reno, NV 89509 (800) 664·3978 www.weatherbos.com
Xypex Concrete Waterproofing	EPA-approved for concrete potable water containers. Protects concrete against spalling, efflorescence, and other damage caused by weathering and bleeding of salt.	Xypex Chemical Corporation 13731 Mayfield Place Richmond, BC, Canada V6V 2G9 (800) 961·4477, (604) 273·5265 www.xypex.com

Division 4: Earth Masonry and Other Alternatives to Frame Construction

Introduction

Code-approved building materials in North America are for the most part manufactured in industrialized processes that create components of uniform size and form, with predictable performance characteristics such as fire resistance, permeability ratings, insulation value, structural properties, etc. The process of testing such materials for code approval is extremely expensive. Only large manufacturers who intend to produce, package, and sell a product for wide distribution can afford it. This makes product approval an exclusive process that is independent of product merit. This approval process is not geared towards the analysis and acceptance of nonproprietary, unprocessed natural building materials and it has all but closed the door on 9,000 years of preindustrial building technology.

There is at least one exception to this trend that perhaps serves as a model for future code approval of other natural building materials. Wood is a naturally occurring, minimally processed building material that has universal code acceptance even though it is flammable, subject to shrinkage, comes with inconsistent structural properties, and will rapidly deteriorate through rot and insect infestation if left unprotected. In spite of its embarrassingly "preindustrial" nature, it remains the dominant building material in residential construction, and building codes have succeeded in creating safe guidelines for its classification and use.

Why consider alternative natural materials such as earth and straw as an option for healthy housing? Because these historically derived methods of construction differ from standard cavity wall construction techniques in that manufactured vapor and air barriers are not installed to retard the flow of air and vapor through the walls. Instead, vapor and air are allowed to flow naturally through the massive walls. Because temperature change occurs very slowly in the flow-through process, and because dried mud has the ability to absorb and desorb large amounts of moisture without deteriorating,[1] accumulation from condensation is insignificant. When a home is properly constructed using these

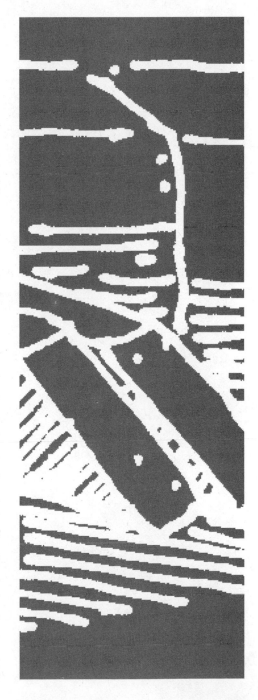

mass wall techniques, it will be an extremely comfortable environment with a high degree of temperature and humidity stability. Furthermore, because the solid walls themselves provide insulation and can be finished with a covering of plaster or furred-out wood applied directly to them, the need for synthetic exterior sheathing, batt insulation, gypsum board, joint fillers, and paint is eliminated. Many volatile organic compound (VOC) contamination sources are thereby eliminated as well.

A wall made of unprocessed materials through which the flow of air and vapor is unhindered is called a "breathing wall" in the philosophy of bau-biologie and is central to the bau-biologie concept of creating a healthy dwelling. (Actually, the term "breathing wall" is a misnomer because the walls are not the primary ventilation source for the building. The term "permeable wall" would perhaps be more accurate.) Another bau-biologie analogy is that of the building envelope being a "third skin" (our clothing being our second skin). This analogy is a more useful one in describing how a "breathing wall" actually works. Our skin is the organ of contact with the outer environment, and it regulates the balance of moisture and temperature of the body in relation to the environment. Skin must remain permeable to facilitate a healthy interaction between the natural environment and the human organism. So too, according to bau-biologie, must our third skin; the walls of our dwellings remain permeable in order to achieve an optimal environment for health.

There is an intimate connection between the health of individuals and the health of their environment. All building processes involve the extraction of raw materials from nature and the disruption of the natural ecosystem. The alternative materials and methods described below use these materials in a minimally processed state with far less environmental impact than the highly refined and processed materials prevalent in conventional construction techniques. When one considers that 40% of material resources entering the global economy are related to the building industry,[2] it becomes clear that the building material choices that we make have a global impact on the health of the ecosystem, the ultimate determinant of human health.

In recent years, with renewed interest in environmental concerns and energy efficiency, several alternative methods of building have enjoyed a limited renaissance, sparking the interest of environmentally concerned homeowners, designers, and builders.

Methods of Earth Construction

Earth is widely available at little or no cost; it is inflammable, infinitely recyclable, is not subject to insect infestation, is a natural preservative, has excellent thermal mass storage capacity,[3] has the ability to handle large amounts of water vapor diffusion and to stabilize humidity without mechanical augmentation and, unlike postindustrial manufactured building materials, it has a proven record of longevity, with intact examples dating back more than 7,000 years.

Earth is the predominant preindustrial building material. Earth construction, in all of its various forms, has not been codified on a national level in this country, and in spite of the fact that it is the wall-building material for more than a third of the world's residences, its use is considered by most building departments to be "experimental." In Germany, simple standardized tests for measuring various structural properties of mud have been developed and codified. The work done there could pave the way for wider acceptance here if more performance-based criteria for code compliance are permitted in the future. For the most part, approval is currently at the discretion of the local building authority.

Earth Block Construction

Earth block construction is used in every hot, dry, subtropical climate throughout the world. Examples have been found in Turkistan dating back as far as 6000 B.C. The historical core of Shibam in Yemen, where eight-storey buildings date back to the 15th century, is constructed entirely of adobe.

Earth blocks are primarily used in modern construction in three forms. Adobes are mixed wet, poured into formwork, and then sun dried. Pressed blocks are made from moist soil that is compacted by a mechanical or hand press. Green bricks are extruded in a brick-making plant and used in the unfired state.

In the U.S. Southwest, adobe is a traditional building material that has remained in continuous use and is the material of choice for some of the most exclusive residences being built today. It has been jokingly called the building material for "the idle rich" or "the idle poor" because stacking the heavy blocks is labor intensive.

Because the R-value of earth blocks is fairly low, walls require additional insulation in order to meet energy requirements in all but the warmest portions of North America.[4] A higher R-value is usually obtained by adding foam insulation to the exterior of the building, which affects the "breathability" of the wall and creates a dubious marriage between natural and synthetic materials. A company in Germany has developed an insulating spray plaster of natural

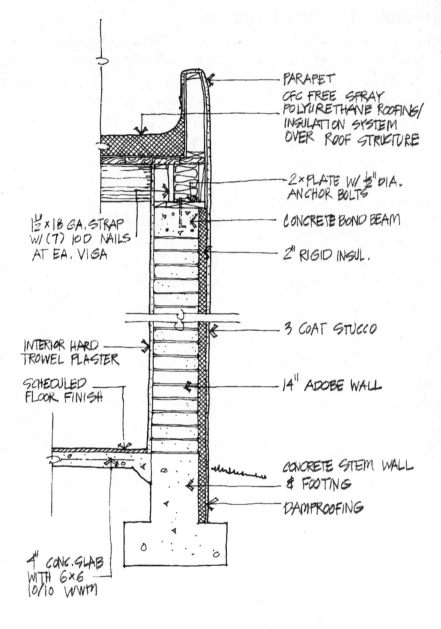

PARAPET

CFC FREE SPRAY POLYURETHANE ROOFING/ INSULATION SYSTEM OVER ROOF STRUCTURE

2× PLATE W/ $\frac{1}{2}$" DIA. ANCHOR BOLTS

CONCRETE BOND BEAM

2" RIGID INSUL.

3 COAT STUCCO

14" ADOBE WALL

CONCRETE STEM WALL & FOOTING

DAMPROOFING

$1\frac{1}{2}$ × 18 GA. STRAP W/ (7) 10D NAILS AT EA. VIGA

INTERIOR HARD TROWEL PLASTER

SCHEDULED FLOOR FINISH

4" CONC. SLAB WITH 6×6 10/10 WWM

Section through adobe wall

materials including cork, straw, and diatomite, which holds promise for future solutions in this country.[5]

Although most earth block is currently used in desert climates and for exterior wall construction, its excellent mass and acoustic properties make it a superb product for interior mass wall construction in any climate where it is available or can be produced.

Adobe blocks are frequently "stabilized" by adding chemicals to the wet mud mixture, mainly to make them more water-resistant and to prevent breakage during transport. The most common stabilizer is asphalt, a carcinogenic material that should be avoided in the healthy home. Unstabilized adobes can be purchased from some adobe yards. Compressed earth blocks can also be made onsite with an adobe press, thereby eliminating the need to protect blocks during transportation. Earth blocks that are not stabilized must be protected from groundwater damage. This can be accomplished by holding the first course of blocks off the floor, usually by installing a layer of concrete block.

The State of New Mexico has developed its own comprehensive code for load-bearing adobe construction, which has served as a model for parts of Colorado and Arizona.

Cob and Other Wet Clay Techniques

Throughout history, several methods for mud construction have evolved, using wet mud that is fashioned into various shapes and stacked onto the wall while still plastic. It is then fused with the layers below it in order to create a monolithic wall. This type of construction has lent itself to laybuilders because it requires no formwork or special equipment and no processing other than onsite mixing. Two modern innovations in this building method are of note.

In Germany, Gernot Minke has developed a method called "Stranglehm" for building with extruded clay profiles. Casein or whey is added to the clay mixture to make the clay more water-resistant. Minke has created a mechanized extrusion apparatus for use at the building site that can produce about 6 feet of material per minute. The uniformly extruded profiles, which are 3" × 6" and just over 2 feet long, are stacked one on top of another and pressed to adhere to the layer below. Construction joints are placed vertically between the ribbons and "caulked" with a mud mixture after the ribbons are dry so that shrinkage is controlled and air infiltration can be blocked. The system is non-load bearing and is being used as infill between wooden structural members. Insulation must be added to the exterior to make it suitable for colder climates.

In North America, the Cob Cottage Company has been responsible for the revival of cob or wet mud construction. Founders Ianto Evans and Linda Smiley have developed a stronger mix using a more controlled formulation process than their predecessors. The Oregon Cobb method that they have developed is characterized by small, free-flowing, sculpturally shaped homes with arched windows and doors and a strong solar orientation. Their designs emphasize

Home of Professor Gernot Minke showing the "stranglehm" wall components. Photo: Robert Laporte

maximum use of space through curvilinear formations and built-in benches and platforms.

Cob construction uses moistened earth containing suitable clay and sand content that is mixed with straw and formed into stiff loaves of a size that can be moved, person to person, from the mix site to the building site. The loaves are then piled onto a wall and blended with the previous layers. The result is a monolithic, load-bearing mud wall.

Cob has comparable R-values to adobe construction and is best suited to warmer climates where less insulation is required and high thermal mass is effective. Cob is also valuable for adding thermal mass in the interior of buildings, especially for heat storage in passive solar designs. Anecdotal evidence has indicated that it exhibits better seismic performance than adobe because the walls are monolithic.[6]

Rammed Earth

Historically, rammed earth construction has been found not only in hot arid climates, but throughout the cold wet regions of Europe as well. Thousands of rammed earth structures, some dating back 400 years, can be found in the Rhone River valley.

Earth containing the proper moisture, sand, gravel, and clay content is rammed into formwork in 6" to 8" layers. When the formwork is full, it can immediately be removed and reused for the next section of wall. Due to their low moisture content,

5-storey rammed earth and compressed earth block in Multiple Housing complex in Lyon France by Craterre. Photo: Robert Laporte.

Rammed Earth or "pise" multi-storey houseing complex by Craterre in Lyon, France.
Photo: Robert Laporte.

the walls, if properly constructed, will not shrink or crack. No curing time is required and construction can continue without any delay in sequencing.

The finished walls are thick, precise, and beautiful. Different colors of earth can be used to create decorative effects. Rammed earth walls are usually left exposed without any further finishing. Unlike adobe or stone masonry, where the joints are weakened when water expands and contracts as it freezes and melts, the monolithic surface of rammed earth has proven to hold up extremely well to freeze and thaw cycles.

With modern comfort and energy demands, this technique is most suitable in arid climates, however innovations—such as placing a 2" board of rigid insulation at the center of the wall—have been used to adapt this method for cold climate use.

Of all the earth-building techniques described in this chapter, rammed earth technology has advanced the most through the use of modernized machinery. It has been calculated that the historic homes of rammed earth took as many as 30 worker-hours per cubic meter of wall construction, whereas highly mechanized techniques can take as few as 2 worker-hours per cubic meter of wall.[7] Adaptation to mechanization, improvements in formwork, high compressive strength, and short curing time make this type of earth construction suitable for large projects. Highly refined, multi-storey buildings have been created using this technique, including the five-star Kooralbyn Hotel and Resort in Australia.

With more and more test data being accumulated on the structural properties of rammed earth, both in North America and Europe, it is becoming easier for professional engineers to create reliable structural designs and predict how the material will act under extreme conditions. In earthquake zones, some concrete has been added to the mix, and steel reinforcement has been used in much the same way it would be in concrete structures, thus allowing permits to be granted throughout earthquake-prone California where David Easton, a pioneer and innovator in the rammed earth revival, lives and works.

Light Clay Construction

For construction in colder climates, where required insulation values are higher than can be provided by mud alone, several methods that combine earth with

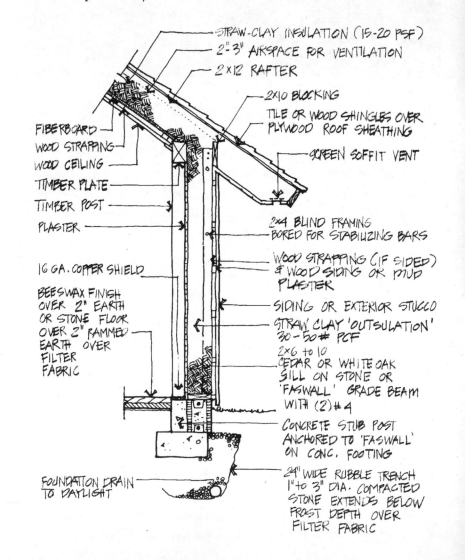

Section through light clay wall

lightweight natural aggregates have evolved. These include mixing mud with pumice, volcanic rock, straw, wood chips, expanded clay, vermiculite etc. In the U.S., "straw-clay" construction has become the most well-known of these methods due to the work of Robert Laporte of the Econest Building Company, who has taught workshops and built straw-clay structures in 17 states. The Laporte technique uses a lightweight mixture of straw and clay as an "outsulating" wall around a timber-frame structure. Straw-clay can also be used as an infill material between deep structural members.

Straw is mixed with a clay slurry so that each strand is coated. The wet material is then compacted into a 12" wide formwork. The formwork is removed the same day. The result is a precise wall that has enough texture to accept mud plaster without any further wall preparation or lathing.

The walls must be allowed to dry thoroughly. Because clay has the capacity to wick water away from the straw that it encases, mold growth has not posed any problem in this wall system, provided that initial full curing of the wall takes place in a timely manner. A completed wall that accidentally becomes wet will dry out without molding, but the walls must be finished with materials that will allow for sufficient vapor diffusion. Earth plasters are ideal for this.

A straw-clay wall weighs approximately 50 lbs/ft^3. The density can be varied to provide more mass on the south side of a building and more insulation on the north side, with weights of 60 lbs/ft^3 and 40 lbs/ft^3 respectively. The R-value of

Right: The timberframe structure and light-clay walls of the Baker-Laporte Residence. Builder: Econest Building Co.; Photo: Lisl Dennis.

Left: One of many 800 year old structures in Germany. Composed of timberframe and earthen and straw wall materials it stands as a testimonial to the beauty and longevity of natural building materials. Photo: Robert Laporte.

a 12" thick, plastered, straw-clay wall is approximately R-24,[8] making it thermally acceptable in all but the coldest regions of North America. The high thermal mass also makes it an excellent material for use in hot dry regions. In areas with rainfall of more than 30 inches a year, an exterior sheathing of wood with a vented air space between the wood and straw-clay is advised.

Straw-clay is less suitable for locations that do not have a predictable dry season of at least four months duration, when proper curing can occur. However many examples of straw-clay buildings, including some that are several hundred years old, can be found in Germany, which has an extremely damp climate. The older examples of mud-and-straw wall construction found in Europe are denser and contain a higher clay content than our modern formulas, which are designed to have higher insulation values. As with all natural systems, a good above-grade stem wall or plinth and large roof overhang will help protect the walls and provide for greater longevity.

Because the straw-clay is non-load bearing, permits have been readily granted in many localities. If you are interested in building with straw-clay, check with your local building department to determine whether approval will be forthcoming. The State of New Mexico has passed official guidelines for straw-clay construction, and this information, which is available on the Econest website, may be helpful for obtaining approval from code officials elsewhere.

Other Alternative Building Systems

Straw Bale

Although straw has been an important component of natural building for centuries, straw bale is a relatively new form of alternative construction that appears to be an innovation of the early settlers of the Nebraska plains, where little wood and unsuitable soils made necessity the mother of invention. The high insulative value of straw bale (between R-57 and R-33 depending on the type of bale and the testing facility) and the aesthetics of the thick walls have quickly made it a popular alternative building material.

Because much of the straw grown in the United States is heavily sprayed with pesticides, we recommend looking for straw that has been organically grown. The Last Straw, listed in the bibliography of this chapter, has published a list of organic straw sources.

Straw bale residence in Santa Fe, New Mexico. Metal roof, wide roof overhangs and rain gutter system protect the stucco finishes from the occasional high desert rains.
Architect: Baker-Laporte and Associates;
Builder: Prull and Associates;
Photo: Julie Dean.

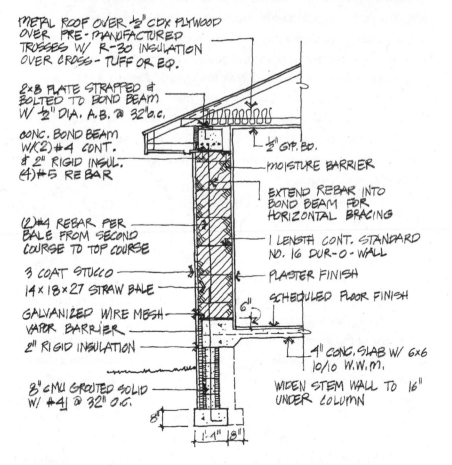

METAL ROOF OVER ½" CDX PLYWOOD OVER PRE-MANUFACTURED TRUSSES W/ R-30 INSULATION OVER CROSS-TUFF OR EQ.

2×8 PLATE STRAPPED & BOLTED TO BOND BEAM W/ ½" DIA. A.B. @ 32" o.c.

CONC. BOND BEAM W/(2)#4 CONT. & 2" RIGID INSUL. (4)#5 REBAR

(2)#4 REBAR PER BALE FROM SECOND COURSE TO TOP COURSE

3 COAT STUCCO

14×18×27 STRAW BALE

GALVANIZED WIRE MESH

VAPOR BARRIER

2" RIGID INSULATION

8" CMU GROUTED SOLID W/ #4 @ 32" O.C.

8"

1'-1" 8"

½" GYP. BD.

MOISTURE BARRIER

EXTEND REBAR INTO BOND BEAM FOR HORIZONTAL BRACING

1 LENGTH CONT. STANDARD NO. 16 DUR-O-WALL

PLASTER FINISH

SCHEDULED FLOOR FINISH

6"

4" CONC. SLAB W/ 6×6 10/10 W.W.M.

WIDEN STEM WALL TO 16" UNDER COLUMN

Section through straw bale wall

Because cellulose is a perfect food for mold, bales of straw often contain mold. This means it is even more important with straw bale building to incorporate rigorous water and moisture management strategies into the design. The walls are allowed to breathe so, in theory, the bales will always remain dry enough that mold will not be a problem. Using earth-based plasters instead of cement-based plasters on interior walls will help keep water away from the bales and allow them to dry out more readily when they do get wet. On the exterior of the building, earth-based plasters that are augmented to prevent water penetration may prove to be more desirable from a moisture movement standpoint than cement-based plasters, which are less flexible, tend to crack more, and are less permeable to vapor diffusion. Should water become trapped in the wall due to roof failure, plumbing leaks, poor drainage, or other building systems failures, then mold can become a problem.

Many techniques have evolved for straw bale construction. Building permit approval is greatly simplified when structures are non-load bearing, and most straw bale construction relies on a variety of structural systems including exposed and buried post and beam, steel posts, and poured or masonry concrete peers. Load-bearing straw bale houses have been built in Colorado, Arizona, and Canada.

Several jurisdictions have adopted straw bale codes, including the States of New Mexico and California; Pima County and Guadalupe, Arizona; Austin, Texas; and Boulder and Cortez, Colorado. Whereas some jurisdictions will permit load-bearing straw bale construction, others will permit it only as a non-load-bearing wall system.

Pumice-Crete

In this method, mixing pumice, a very porous volcanic rock, with a light soupy concrete, creates 14" to 24" thick walls. The mixture is poured into formwork. The resulting walls have both thermal mass and a high insulation value, and are ready to accept plaster without further preparation. When used with a concrete bond beam at the top, the walls are load bearing.

Because of the simplicity of this system and the absence of organic matter in the wall construction, pumice-crete is very suitable for persons with chemical sensitivity who are often also highly sensitive to wood terpines, mold, and pesticides that may be found in small quantities when other building techniques are used.

Since the wall uses a certain amount of concrete, the rules for concrete formwork and aggregate composition, outlined in *Division 3*, must be followed.

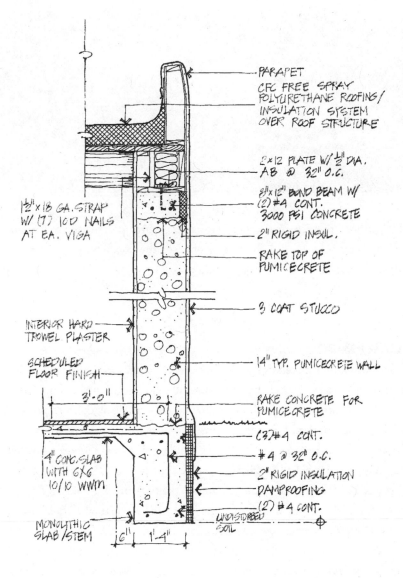

PARAPET

CFC FREE SPRAY POLYURETHANE ROOFING/ INSULATION SYSTEM OVER ROOF STRUCTURE

2×12 PLATE W/ $\frac{1}{2}$" DIA. AB @ 32" O.C.

8"×12" BOND BEAM W/ (2) #4 CONT. 3000 PSI CONCRETE

2" RIGID INSUL.

RAKE TOP OF PUMICECRETE

$1\frac{1}{2}$"×18 GA. STRAP W/ (7) 10D NAILS AT EA. VIGA

3 COAT STUCCO

INTERIOR HARD TROWEL PLASTER

SCHEDULED FLOOR FINISH

14" TYP. PUMICECRETE WALL

3'-0"

RAKE CONCRETE FOR PUMICECRETE

(3) #4 CONT.

#4 @ 32" O.C.

2" RIGID INSULATION

DAMPROOFING

(2) #4 CONT.

4" CONC. SLAB WITH 6×6 10/10 WWM

UNDISTURBED SOIL

MONOLITHIC SLAB/STEM

6" 1'-4"

Section through pumice-crete wall

Pumice can be radioactive. Test samples with a Geiger counter to be sure they are free of radioactive material (refer to *Division 13* for testing methods). Because pumice is highly porous it can readily absorb odors, so it is prudent to specify that pumice be free of acquired odors when it arrives on site and to protect it onsite and in-situ from pollution sources. Once the walls are plastered, this should no longer be a concern.

In order to help stabilize indoor humidity levels and create further thermal mass storage capacity, mud plasters can be applied to interior surfaces and will adhere well without the use of lathing.

This "Santa Fe Style" residence features pumicecrete walls, hard trowelled plaster interior wall finishes, sustainably harvested maple flooring, central air filtration and specialty finishes throughout. Architect: Baker-Laporte and Associates; Builder: Prull and Associates; Photo: Lisl Dennis.

In Europe, pumice and other naturally occurring lightweight volcanic aggregates have been used with mud in place of the concrete. However, these walls are not used in a load-bearing situation.

In Conclusion

A variety of natural materials can be used to create heirloom quality buildings that are ecologically sound, promote health, and have outstanding energy efficiency. In short, natural building materials may, in all of these respects, be superior to the standard building systems prevalent in industrial countries. An owner choosing to use a natural alternative building system is a pioneer who may be well rewarded for his or her adventuresome spirit.

Regional factors such as drainage, rainfall, temperature, humidity, freeze and thaw cycles, and the availability of natural materials will make some natural building systems more suitable for certain locations than others.

When planning to build with alternative materials, make careful inquiry to determine the status of these materials with local building authorities and to ensure that the alternative you have chosen will be permitted in your jurisdiction. Each of the model building codes used in the United States has a provision for alternative methods and materials. Building officials of the jurisdiction in which a project is located have the authority to approve any building that they deem adequately meets the intentions and provisions of the code. It may be necessary to educate a building official about the materials you intend to use, and it is worthwhile to gather information about code approvals for the same materials that have been granted elsewhere. If a building official is unable to make a determination about the alternative material you are presenting, it may be possible to move forward with approvals by creating a legal document holding the building department harmless.

Earlier in this century it was incumbent upon industrial manufacturers to prove to code officials that their products performed as well as their preindustrial counterparts. The powerful forces of industry, with their financial capability to test manufactured products, have now completely reversed this situation, to the point where nonproprietary materials and methods of construction are viewed as inferior. Ironically, this is so in spite of thousands of years of research and development that have gone into the refinement of natural building techniques. In order to gain more widespread acceptance in mainstream building, each example of natural building must be well conceived, well documented, and based on a sound knowledge of the laws of nature. In fact, a thorough understanding of building science is even more important for designers and builders using these alternative systems because of the high degree of experimentation involved when adapting ancient techniques to modern comfort and performance demands.

We would like to emphasize that the use of natural construction materials does not automatically create a healthy home. The material used in the building's walls is only one of many components that go into creating a home environment. However, when the alternative systems described in this chapter are used in conjunction with the other principles of healthy building outlined in this book, it is possible to produce buildings of exceptional vitality.

Endnotes

[1] Gernot Minke, *Earth Construction Handbook* (WIT Press, 2000), 17. Test results show that the surface 1.5 cm-thick layer of mud brick is able to absorb 300 grams of water per m^2 and that when ambient humidity levels drop, this moisture is released back into the room, causing a stability in ambient humidity levels.

[2] David Malin Roodman and Nicholas K. Lenssen, *A Building Revolution: How Ecology and Health Concerns are Transforming Construction*. Washington, DC: Worldwatch Paper 124-5, March 1995.

3 Gernot Minke, *Earth Construction Handbook*, 35.

4 R-value, a measurement of thermal insulation, indicates resistance to heat flow. The U.S. Department of Energy has recommended R-values for every area of the United States. Higher R-values are recommended for colder climates.

5 Gernot Minke, *Earth Construction Handbook*, 55.

6 Lynne Elizabeth and Cassandra Wilson, *Alternative Construction: Contemporary Natural Building Methods* (John Wiley and Sons, 2000), 126.

7 Gernot Minke, *Earth Construction Handbook*, 67.

8 R-values for straw-clay construction were derived from mass and thermal values published for straw and for clay by SIA. SIA is the government organization in Switzerland responsible for the licensing of architects, engineers, and builders and for granting building permits. The organization has codified performance standards for all building materials, including nonproprietary materials such as straw and clay.

Further Reading

Chiras, Daniel D. *The Natural House*. White River Junction, VT: Chelsea Green, 2000.

Cob Cottage Company. *Earth Building and Cob Revival: A Reader*. Third Edition. Cottage Grove, OR: Cob Cottage Company, 1996.

Easton, David. *The Rammed Earth House*. White River Junction, VT: Chelsea Green Publishing Company, 1996.

Elizabeth, Lynne and Cassandra Wilson. *Alternative Construction: Contemporary Natural Building Methods*. John Wiley and Sons, 2000.

The Last Straw. A quarterly journal about straw bale and other natural building. HC 66, Box 119, Hillsboro, NM 88042. Phone: (505) 895·5400; Internet: www.straw homes.com.

Laporte, Robert. *Mooseprints: A Holistic Home Building Guide*. Santa Fe, NM: Econest Building Company, 1993. Phone: (505) 984·2928; Internet: www.econests.com.

MacDonald, S.O. and Matt Myhrman. *Build It with Bales: A Step-by-step Guide to Straw Bale Construction*. Treasure Chest Publications, 1997.

McHenry, Paul G. *Adobe: Build it Yourself*. University of Arizona Press, 1985.

Minke, Gernot. *Earth Construction Handbook*. Southhampton, UK: WIT Press, 2000. Internet: www.witpress.com.

Roodman, David Malin and Nicholas K. Lenssen. *A Building Revolution: How Ecology and Health Concerns are Transforming Construction*. Washington, DC: Worldwatch Paper 124-5, March 1995.

Steen, Athena Swentzell, Bill Steen, and David Bainbridge. *The Straw Bale House*. White River Junction, VT: Chelsea Green Publishing, 1994.

Division 5: Metals

Oil Residue on Metals

Expanded metal lath and other metal goods are often shipped to sites coated in rancid oil residues left over from the manufacturing process. Such residue will be odorous for a pro-longed period of time unless the metal is cleaned. When these oils are left in metal ductwork, hot air blown through the ductwork distributes these odors throughout the house. In order to avoid this unwanted pollution source, consider adding the following to your specifications.

> • Remove oil residue from all coated metal products using a high-pressure hose and one of the acceptable cleaning products listed in these specifications.
> • **TIP:** Some builders have found that the high-pressure hoses at self-service car washes are effective for removing oil residues.

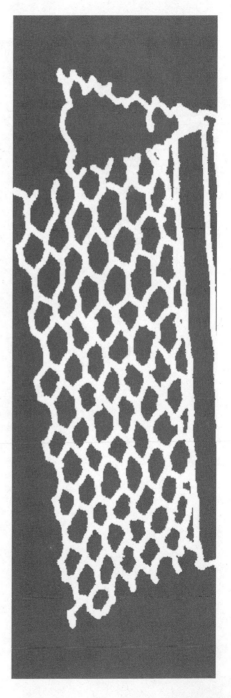

Metals and Conductivity

The role that metals play in the electroclimate of a building, along with proper grounding considerations, will be discussed in *Division 16*.

Metal Termite Shielding

Where floors are joisted, the proper application of metal termite shielding, as illustrated over, will create a physical barrier that is effective against subterranean termites.

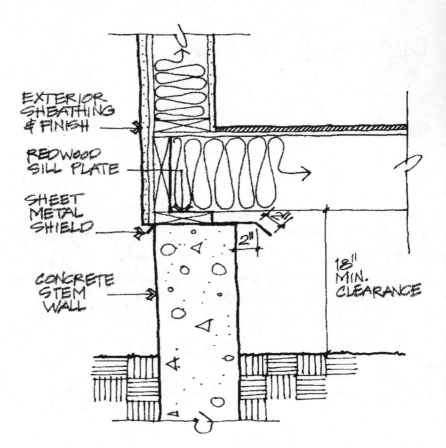

EXTERIOR
SHEATHING
& FINISH

REDWOOD
SILL PLATE

SHEET
METAL
SHIELD

CONCRETE
STEM
WALL

2"

18"
MIN.
CLEARANCE

Termite Shield Detail

Division 6: Wood and Plastics

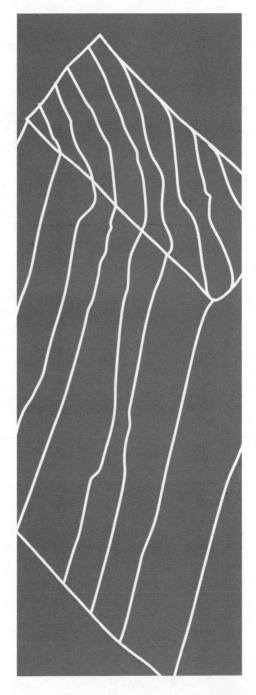

Use of Sustainably Harvested Wood

The history of forest mismanagement in the United States is a very long one and beyond the scope of this book. Suffice to say that wood can be used in an ecologically conscious manner through sustainable harvesting and replanting, along with a commitment to building methods that produce structures with a greater longevity than the growth period of the trees from which they are built. A sustainably harvested forest is one in which the forestry practices are monitored to ensure the present and future quality of both the wood resource and the forest itself. This requires an awareness of the economic and social impact on all communities involved and the protection of regional biological diversity.

Sustainably harvested wood can often be obtained for the same price as lumber harvested by environmentally damaging methods, such as clear cutting. By specifying the use of sustainably harvested woods for a building project, you are helping to raise awareness and increase market demand. You can specify the use of sustainably harvested wood by describing the standards that the wood must meet in order to be classified as sustainable, or more simply by listing local suppliers of wood that has been certified by a reputable certifier. In residential construction, where the builder may not have a sizeable research and purchasing department, the second method is most effective.

The Forest Stewardship Council (FSC) is a leading international organization that sets standards for sustainability and accredits third-party, independent certifiers. In the United States there are currently nine organizations that are FSC-accredited. These include the **Smart Wood Certification Program** and **Scientific Certifications Systems** (SCS). The **Certified Forest Products Council** is a nonprofit organization that provides information on sources for purchasing FSC-certified wood, with state-by-state listings available at its website. It also provides sample specification language that is tailored for use in the CSI Master Format.

Two major building supply outlets, Home Depot and Lows, are committed to stocking mostly FSC-certified wood products by 2002.

Health Concerns with Wood Frame Construction

Wood has historically been used as a component of a "breathing wall" system, whether it be the half-timber, waddle, and daub constructions of medieval Europe or the log cabins of our ancestors in North America (see the introduction of *Division 4* for an explanation of the "breathing wall" concept). Wood is an advantageous material in a healthy home because it has the property of "hygroscoposity." This means that it has the ability to absorb and release moisture, thus helping to balance humidity levels and the electroclimate. However, for many chemically sensitive individuals the natural turpenes found in wood, especially soft or aromatic woods such as pine or cedar, are intolerable. Certain woods may need to be eliminated from, or sealed when used in, a home for a chemically sensitive person.

In standard home construction, the air space between the wood studs may be filled with insulation laden with chemicals. The exterior sheathing often contains formaldehyde-based glue or asphalt backing. The gypsum board applied to the inside face of the studs may be finished with harmful joint compounds. The studs sit on a sill plate that is most often pressure-treated with a pesticide to prevent rot and insect infestation. When standard construction is the only option, we recommend that the most benign wall construction materials available be used and that a barrier be installed between the wall construction and living space. Refer to *Division 7, Air Barrier,* for product and installation information.

Note that in some instances, creating a barrier for the purpose of blocking fumes can cause hidden problems when moisture from condensation is trapped inside the wall. Applying gypsum board in an airtight manner will help block fumes but will not in itself block the normal movement of water vapor. Refer to *Division 9, Creating an Air Barrier With Gypsum Board,* for more specific details on creating a barrier using gypsum board.

Construction lumber is at risk of contamination by pesticides when farmed, when milled, during transportation, and in storage. Certified wood producers and processors are encouraged to use the least-toxic pest management system, while some regional certification organizations have mandated a ban of pesticides for sustainably harvested wood in their jurisdictions. Certain imported woods may be dipped in pesticides that are now banned in this country. For those who have severe sensitivities to pesticides, it is important to locate a source for uncontaminated wood. Woods that are sustainably harvested can be traced from source to sawmill to distributor, and their pesticide history can be determined. In some cases, uncontaminated lumber can be picked up directly from a local mill,

---

Case Study 6.1:

Wood Treatments: Pesticide-treated lumber

Although Germany has been a leader in the bau-biologie and healthy housing movement, it was only during the last decade that the general public became aware of multiple chemical sensitivity disorder. This awareness followed the revelation that hundreds of people who were exposed to lumber treated with both the preservative pentachlorophenol and the pesticide lindane had developed chronic neurological complaints, chronic fatigue, and an unusually heightened sensitivity to chemicals that were previously tolerated. Lindane has subsequently been banned in Germany as a wood treatment.

---

where the sawyer will be closer to the source of the lumber and will know whether or not pesticides are used where the wood is grown.

Wood Selection and Storage

Kiln-dried framing lumber is drier than air-dried lumber. It is therefore more true to size and less susceptible to shrinkage and mold infestation. Certified, sustainably harvested, kiln-dried framing lumber is now becoming widely available. Framing lumber of this type is currently slightly more expensive than standard lumber, which is often logged using unsustainable practices.

Wood may occasionally be delivered to the site containing mold. It can also become moldy while stacked on site if it is unprotected. You should include the following instructions in your specifications to avoid these problems.

- Framing lumber shall be kiln dried.
- Fir, spruce, and hemlock are preferred over pine where available at no additional cost to owner.
- Only wood that is free of mold is acceptable.
- Wood stored on site shall be protected from moisture damage by raising it off the ground and covering it with a tarp during precipitation.
- Wood that becomes wet must be quickly dried by cross stacking to promote aeration. It should have less than 17% moisture content, as tested by a moisture meter, and be free of all signs of mold in order to be acceptable. See *Division 13: Special Construction* for moisture meter testing.

Wood Treatment

Wood surfaces and edges exposed to the weather will usually be surface treated to make them more weather resistant. Woods that are not naturally rot resistant and that will come in contact with moisture must be treated for rot and mold resistance. Pentachlorophenol and creosote are two commonly used wood preservatives that are quite toxic. Creosote is a dark-colored, oily tar that will outgas harmful vapors long after it has been applied. Pentachlorophenol has been shown to cause liver damage in adults and fetal death, and has been banned in some European countries. These substances should be prohibited for use in a healthy home. The following wood treatment products do not contain these harmful ingredients.

Wood Treatment to Prevent Insect and Mold Infestation

- **Bio Shield**: Wood-preservative oils.
- **Bio-Wash**: "Environmentally friendly" waterborne protective coatings for wood, wood brighteners, and paint and stain strippers.
- **Bora-Care**: Low-toxicity, borate-based, penetrating preservative containing glycol, used for protection against powder post beetles and subterranean termites.
- **Livos Donnos Wood Pitch Impregnation**: Penetrating preservative for wood that is in contact with moisture.
- **Old Growth Aging and Staining Solutions**: A two-part process that provides antimicrobial and antifungal properties and imparts an aged patina to woods.
- **Shellguard and Guardian**: Borate-based wood preservatives for protection against wood-boring insects.
- **Timber-Tek UV**: An oil resin-based, waterborne penetrating oil that stains, seals, and protects. Available in 8 standard and 18 custom transparent wood tones. Provides mildew and algae resistance and UV protection.
- **Timbor**: Low-toxicity, borate-based wood preservative that protects against drywood termites and wood decay fungi.
- **Weather-Bos The Boss**: Four different formulas for protection of exterior wood surfaces.

Wood Treatment to Provide Weather and UV Protection

Many wood-treatment products for exterior use are solvent based and highly volatile. They can continue to outgas for several days or even weeks. Although exterior applications will have far less impact on the indoor air quality than products used inside the home, they will still affect the applicator and sensitive people who are in the vicinity and can be completely avoided due to the wide range of more benign products now available. Some of these lower-impact products are listed here.

- **9400 W Impregnant:** Solvent-free, water-repellant, ultraviolet protective coating for wood interior/exterior. Also effective in minimizing mold and mildew growth.
- **Bio Shield:** Wood-preservative oils.
- **Bio-Wash:** "Environmentally friendly" waterborne protective coatings for wood, wood brighteners, and paint and stain strippers.
- **Hydrocote Polyshield:** Interior and exterior polyurethane wood protection.
- **LifeTime Wood Treatment:** Protects, stains, and beautifies wood products.
- **Livos Donnos Wood Pitch Impregnation:** Penetrating preservative for wood that is in contact with moisture.
- **Livos Dubno Primer Oil:** Undercoat for exterior wood.
- **Old Growth Aging and Staining Solutions:** A two-part process that provides antimicrobial and antifungal properties and imparts an aged patina to woods.
- **OS Wood Protector:** Preserves against water damage, mold, mildew, and fungus.
- **Timber-Tek UV:** An oil resin-based, waterborne penetrating oil that stains, seals, and protects. Available in 8 standard and 18 custom transparent wood tones. Provides mildew and algae resistance and UV protection.
- **Weather-Bos The Boss:** Four different formulas for protection of exterior wood surfaces.
- **Weatherall UV Guard:** Exterior acrylic wood finish that penetrates and seals, forming a protective shield against UV, rot, and decay. Comes in clear and semi-transparent finishes.
- **Weather Pro:** A water-based, water-repellant wood stain.

Wood Maintenance

Common products for stripping, cleaning, and brightening wood often contain harsh solvents. The following products are safer.

- **Bio-Wash Products:** A line of safe products for cleaning, stripping, and protecting wood—includes Mill Glaze Away, Simple Wash, Woodwash, Stripex, Stripex-L, Rinse or Peel, Organic Strip.
- **Dekswood:** Cleaner and brightener for exterior wood.

Wood Adhesives

Wood adhesives commonly contain harmful solvents. However, solvent-free solutions are readily available and may be specified. The following adhesives are healthier choices for various wood-related applications.

- **100% Pure Silicone Caulk:** Can be used as a subfloor adhesive. Specify aquarium grade caulk without additives.
- **AFM Safecoat Almighty Adhesive:** Low-odor, nontoxic, water-based adhesive for gluing wood and wood laminates. Available by special order only.
- **Elmer's Carpenter's Glue:** Low-odor, nontoxic, water-based glue for porous materials.
- **Solvent Free Titebond Construction Adhesive:** For plywood, paneling, and hardboard.
- **Solvent Free Titebond Sub-floor Adhesive:** For subfloors.
- **Timberline 2051 Wood Flooring Adhesive:** For laminated plank and parquet flooring.

Rough Carpentry

Sill Plates

Sill plates or mudsills are decay- and insect-resistant wood members used in frame construction wherever wood comes into contact with concrete or soil. For many centuries builders had devised natural means for avoiding rot and insect infestation. They charred the portions of wood that were to be placed in the ground or else used naturally resistant woods. Today the standard building practice is to use lumber that has been pressure treated so it is impregnated with chromated copper arsenate (CCA) or ammoniacal copper arsenate (ACA). CCA and ACA contain arsenic salts and chromium compounds that can leach out on the site and be absorbed through the skin or ingested by mouth. They are extremely toxic to both humans and the environment. CCA imparts a green tinge to the wood. You have probably observed this toxic wood being used in children's playground equipment!

These substances will most likely be used in your home unless you ask for a substitute. For a healthier installation, consider adding the following specifications.

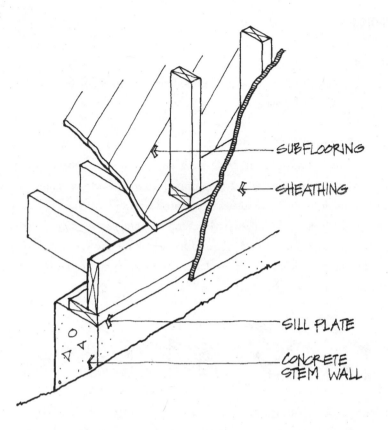

SUBFLOORING

SHEATHING

SILL PLATE

CONCRETE STEM WALL

Wood frame construction showing sill plates

- No wood treated with chromated copper arsenate (CCA) or ammoniacal copper arsenate (ACA) may be used on this job.
- Wood treated with **ACQ** (alkaline/copper/quat) is acceptable. (See **ACQ Preserve** in the *Division 6, Resource List.*)
- The heartwood of untreated farmed cedar or redwood is acceptable for use as sill plates where acceptable by local code officials.
- Where the sill plate is at least 18" above grade, a metal termite shield may be used in lieu of a treated sill plate. Verify acceptability with local code officials.

Framing

Wall Framing

Where wood 2× wall framing is used, follow the guidelines for wood selection and storage in this Division.

Roof and Floor Framing

Solid beams, round logs, or 2× joisting are commonly used for shorter roof spans. Manufactured trusses are commonly used for larger spans. They are typically made up of composite wood products and assembled into profiles engineered for strength. These have several advantages over solid lumber. They are less expensive, use wood more efficiently, have greater span capabilities, provide a deep pocket for roof insulation, and can be fabricated with a built-in slope for flat roof application.

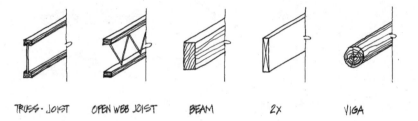

TRUSS·JOIST   OPEN WEB JOIST   BEAM   2×   VIGA

Ceiling framing components

Truss joists, commonly called TJIs, are manufactured components containing either plywood or dimensional lumber for top and bottom chords, and either plywood or pressboard for the webs. Because they are a very cost-effective way to frame large spans, truss joists are widely used in residential construction. The members are subjected to heat during manufacturing, which helps cure them, reducing the quantity of volatile organic compounds (VOCs) that they emit into a new home. A small quantity of formaldehyde still remains. In new home construction, the cumulative effect of several low emissions can add up to unacceptable levels. Where an airtight gypsum board assembly or air barrier is applied between the structure and the living space, these fumes will be fairly insignificant. If there is still concern, however, the TJIs can be sealed. **BIN Primer Sealer** is particularly good for this purpose because the white color allows you to visually inspect the job and make sure everything has been well coated.

Another option is to use open web roof trusses with dimensional lumber for the top and bottom chords and webs, thereby avoiding the use of pressboard entirely.

Sheathing

Sub-flooring

Interior grade plywood and particleboard are typically used for subflooring in standard construction. Urea-formaldehyde glues are used to bond the wood during manufacturing. This is a concentrated, volatile form of formaldehyde that contributes significantly to indoor air pollution. In addition, the subflooring may then be attached to the framing underneath with solvent-based glues that will also contribute to the pollution level.

Solid-wood solutions, as well as the cementitious subfloor sheeting more commonly used in commercial building, can be considerably more expensive. Exterior grade plywood can substitute for interior grade plywood for only a small increase in cost. While exterior grade plywood contains less volatile phenol-based formaldehyde glues, it will still release significant amounts of formaldehyde into the air when new. Airing out the plywood by cross stacking it onsite is better than installing it immediately after delivery. Sealing the plywood after it has been aired out will provide the most protection against toxic fumes, and this extra step may be taken for chemically sensitive individuals. We suggest the following specifications for healthier subfloor installation.

> • The use of subflooring materials such as interior grade plywood, pressboard, or oriented strand board (OSB) containing urea-formaldehyde glues is prohibited.
> • Subfloor adhesive must be solvent-free. (Refer to the *Division 6, Resource List* for suitable subfloor adhesives.)

The following subflooring options are listed in order, starting with the most preferred solutions and also the most expensive.

- Structural cementitous sheeting
- 1× finish floorboards laid parallel to walls over 1× subfloor laid diagonally to walls. (Note: This may be a good solution when a finished wood floor is desired.) Verify for proper span conditions with the architect or engineer.
- Exterior grade plywood that has been aired out and then sealed with **BIN Primer Sealer** or another acceptable sealer on all six sides.
- Exterior grade plywood that has been aired

Exterior Sheathing

Exterior sheathing in wood frame construction is attached to the outside of the frame and makes up the surface to which the exterior finish is applied. Before manufactured sheetgoods such as plywood were available, 1× or 2× material was nailed to the studs for this purpose. In standard wood frame construction today, exterior grade plywood or OSB (oriented strand board, also known as waferboard) is typically used as exterior sheathing at corners where sheer strength is required. These materials contain varying degrees of formaldehyde and isocyanates and do not have the longevity of solid-wood products.

Many problems with the use of OSB in roof and wall sheathing have recently been identified. In fact, one prominent manufacturer has recently been the subject of a class action suit. When the board gets wet it is vulnerable to fungus invasion and rapidly deteriorates. Asphalt-impregnated fiberboard or asphalt-sheathed insulating board are commonly used as infill between the corner shear panels. Since asphalt is a known carcinogen, we believe that any exposure level is too high when other alternatives exist.

When an air barrier or airtight drywall assembly is used on the interior face of the wall section, sheathing material will not have as great an impact on the indoor air quality as will the materials exposed to the interior. Moreover, the sheathing will have had several weeks in place to air out before it is covered up. In a permeable or "breathing" wall system, where vapor barriers are eliminated with the intent of allowing slow air exchange through the wall, the type of exterior sheathing must be more carefully considered both in terms of permeability and harmful chemical content. The following may be included in your specifications to reduce the pollution generated by exterior sheathing.

Roof Sheathing

Roof sheathing is placed on top of roof framing members and under the roofing. As with exterior sheathing, exterior grade plywood or OSB is most commonly used for this purpose. Unlike wall sheathing, roof sheathing will be exposed to higher temperatures and will therefore be subject to more intense offgassing. Roof sheathing usually has less time to air out in-situ since it is roofed over as soon as possible to avoid water damage from precipitation. We therefore recommend that plywood, if used, be stickered and aired on site. We do not recommend OSB because it can develop mold and deteriorate more rapidly if it happens to get wet.

When roofing members are exposed to the interior, as is usual when beams or vigas are used, then solid wood or tongue-and-groove planking is commonly used.

The following products are unacceptable for exterior sheathing:

+ Products containing asphalt.
+ Odorous foam insulation boards.
+ Pressure-treated plywood.

The following products and methods are acceptable for exterior sheathing:

+ 1× recycled lumber laid diagonally, with diagonal metal or wood bracing as structurally required (a more labor-intensive and expensive solution, this option is most suitable for "breathing wall" frame applications).
+ CDX plywood that has been aired out (purchase plywood as far in advance of installation as possible and stack it to allow airflow on all sides of each sheet while protecting it from moisture damage).
+ Non-odorous foam boards such as bead board.

For sloped roofing, when structural conditions permit, purlins or skip sheathing may be acceptable. Purlins are wooden members spaced to receive metal roof panels, while skip sheathing consists of solid wooden members spaced more closely together for shingle and tile roof applications. Both purlins and skip sheathing eliminate the need for sheetgoods and allow ample air movement to ventilate the roof space. However they do not provide the shear strength that plywood provides, and their use must also be weighed from an engineering standpoint.

Where a continuous air barrier is installed between the framing members and living space, the choice of sheathing material is less crucial.

Consider the following guidelines for inclusion in your specifications.

+ The use of solid-wood boards, tongue-and-groove board, solid-wood skip sheathing, or purlins is preferred where structurally acceptable.
+ CDX plywood, when used for roof sheathing, should be purchased as far in advance as possible to allow time for it to air out. Provide protection against moisture damage.
+ Provide a continuous air barrier on the inside face of the ceiling assembly as outlined in *Division 7: Thermal and Moisture Control.*

Finish Carpentry

Many manufactured composite board products designed for interior use contain urea-formaldehyde binders. They offgas formaldehyde for many months and contribute significantly to the indoor pollution level. In standard construction these interior grade composites are used in many finish applications including cabinetry, molding, shelving, and trim. They should not be used in a healthy home. The following may be specified.

- No sheetgoods or trim pieces containing urea-formaldehyde shall be used.
- Exposed interior finish wood shall be solid wood and finished with an acceptably low-VOC finish as specified in *Division 9: Finishes*.
- Where sheetgoods are used, choose one of the low-emission boards listed below under cabinetry carcass options, or exterior grade plywood that has been aired out, then thoroughly sealed on all edges and surfaces with an acceptable vapor barrier sealant, and finished with one of the paints specified in *Division 9: Finishes*.
- Trim pieces shall be milled of solid wood or be made of formaldehyde-free composites as manufactured by **Medite** or equal.

Medium-Density Fiberboards (MDF)

Medium-density fiberboard is sheetgood material used for interior nonstructural applications such as cabinetry carcasses and shelving. Traditionally, MDF has been bound with urea-formaldehyde-based glues, making its use unacceptable in a healthy house. The following products are formaldehyde-free and may be available laminated with plastics or hardwood veneers.

- **Allgreen MDF:** A medium-density fiberboard containing no incremental formaldehyde emissions, made from 100% recovered wood fiber.
- **Isobord:** A medium-density fiberboard containing no incremental formaldehyde emissions, made from straw fiber.
- **Medex or Medite II:** A medium-density fiberboard manufactured without formaldehyde.

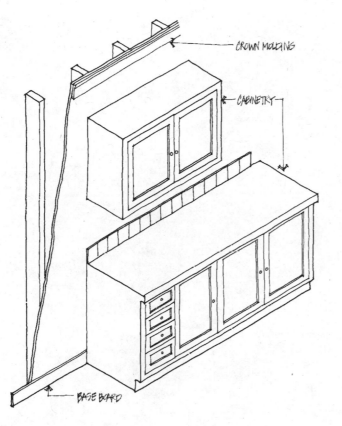

CROWN MOLDING

CABINETRY

BASE BOARD

Typical finish carpentry components

Cabinets

Although the drawers and doors on cabinetry are often made of solid wood, the boxes or cases are usually composed of particleboard, interior grade plywood, or melamine, which has a particleboard core that is exposed where holes have been drilled for adjustable shelving. Cabinets are most often finished with solvent-based finishes that may also outgas high levels of VOCs for several months.

Because standard cabinetry contributes significantly to poor indoor air quality, it is not acceptable in the healthy house. You will pay more for healthier cabinets, but in terms of indoor air quality, this is money well spent. If your budget is tight, we suggest that you explore design strategies that will reduce the amount of cabinetry necessary. For example, you may choose to consolidate a portion of kitchen storage in a pantry area, or you may choose to use attractive solid-wood open shelving for dishes or cookware as a less expensive alternative, replacing some of the upper cabinets.

Finishes on wood cabinet doors and drawers are commonly solvent-based applications that will take many months to fully cure. Some of the lacquer finishes,

Above: This owner chose to have solid wood open shelving, instead of upper cabinets to help offset the higher costs of formaldehyde free cabinets used in the kitchen and bathrooms.
Architect: Baker-Laporte and Associates; Builder: Econest Building Company; Photo: Scott Plunket.

Right: Efficient kitchen storage can obviate the need for some upper cabinets thus helping to offset the higher costs of formaldehyde free cabinetry
Photo: Lisle Dennis.

although odorous when first applied, will completely cure before they are brought to the job site and will provide a very durable finish that will not require refinishing for many years. If these are applied in quality-controlled, well-ventilated shops, they may be worth considering. Ask for a recently applied, dated sample to help make your determination. Other water-based finishes that are more suitable for job-site or factory application are listed in the *Division 9, Resource List*.

As cabinetmakers are becoming more familiar with the need for healthier cabinetry, and as low-VOC finishes and materials become available, the price gap between standard and healthy cabinets is decreasing. The following companies manufacture or provide solutions for cabinetry boxes:

Case Study 6.2:

Countertops: The radioactive countertop

John Banta was called to the home of a woman who was employed as a cook by the television industry. Her task was to prepare samples of the same recipe in various stages of preparation, from raw ingredients to oven-ready mixture to finished product. The prepared foods were then delivered to the television studio so a celebrity on a culinary arts program could demonstrate the recipe.

During the investigation, John discovered that his client was being exposed to an unexpected occupational hazard. The orange-colored tile used for her counter was glazed with uranium oxide, a highly radioactive substance that was making the numbers on the Geiger counter spin too fast to count. For over 30 years this woman had worked at a radioactive counter, slicing, dicing, mixing, and arranging her creations.

When she learned of the radioactivity, the client revealed to John that she had recently had a precancerous lesion removed from her intestines. Her surgical scar was located at the spot where the counter pressed against her while she cooked. The client was advised to have her countertop replaced. Her physician concurred.

- **Architectural Forest Enterprises:** Veneered hardwood products.
- **Cervitor:** Distributors of metal cabinetry with a baked-on enamel finish that may be used with metal or solid-wood doors and drawers.
- **Medex or Medite II:** A medium-density fiberboard manufactured without formaldehyde.
- **Multi-core:** A low-emissions plywood that comes with a variety of hardwood veneers.
- **Neff Cabinets:** Manufactured cabinets with a 98% reduction in formaldehyde content.
- **Neil Kelly Cabinets:** Cabinetry system designed to meet the needs of the chemically sensitive. Cores are wheatboard or Medite II with wood veneers. A wide variety of door and case veneers are available with certified woods. Available prefinished with AFM clear sealers or paints.
- **Panolam:** A company that will laminate melamine or hardwood veneer on to Medex or Medite II. A minimum order of sheets is required.

For all options, specify the use of a solvent-free carpenter's glue in the fabrication process.

Countertops

The ideal countertop material for a healthy home would have a solid, nonporous surface that is stain- and scratch-proof. It would be attached by mechanical means directly to the cabinet boxes, thus avoiding the need for underlay and adhesives. It would be beautiful, inexpensive, and manufactured in a variety of colors. Unfortunately, all of these characteristics are not found in combination in a single countertop option. *Chart 6.1: Countertop Comparisons*, reviews the most common countertop materials and outlines specification concerns for each.

Chart 6.1: Countertop Comparisons

Type	Relative cost	Advantages	Disadvantages	Comments	Specify
High-pressure laminates (e.g., Formica, Wilsonart)	Lowest initial investment	• Wide variety of colors, patterns, textures, and sheens • Low cost • Seamless surface	• Glued to particleboard with toxic glues • Particleboard outgases formaldehyde • Not stain- or acid-resistant • Will scratch • Cannot be resurfaced • Short life; deteriorates quickly if the particleboard gets wet	• Not a good choice for a healthy home	• Fasten to carcass with mechanical fasteners • Seal all exposed edges and surfaces of particleboard with foil or one of the vapor-barrier sealants listed in Division 9
Solid surfaces materials (e.g., Corian, Avonite, Swanstone)	Expensive	• Nonporous • Sanitary; integral bowls and rolled back splashes are easy to clean • No substrate needed for most • Scratches and stains easily sanded	• Color selections are limited • Can be more expensive than granite or marble	• Select a type that does not require substrate	• Fasten to carcass with mechanical fasteners

Type	Relative cost	Advantages	Disadvantages	Comments	Specify
Solid surfaces materials (e.g., Corian, Avonite, Swanstone) – *cont.*		• Attractive marble- and granite-like surfaces • Can be mechanically fastened • Hard, scratch-resistant surfaces			
Tile	Can be moderate	• Large variety of sizes, colors, textures to choose from	• Grout joints are subject to staining and mold and bacteria growth • Glazes may contain heavy metals or be radioactive • Tiles can crack or chip under heavy impact	• Choose the largest tiles available to reduce the number of grout joints • Choose presealed tiles • Choose commercially rated tiles • Choose tiles requiring the narrowest grout joints • Choosing porcelains with integral color will disguise chips	• Follow recommendations in the tile section of Division 9 for underlay, tile setting, and grout sealing
Butcher block	Moderate	• Warm, inviting aesthetics • Natural material • Can be refinished by sanding • Does not require underlayment • Can be mechanically fastened	• Porous surface stains easily and can harbor mold and bacteria growth	• Seams may be glued with formaldehyde-based adhesives	• Finish with odorless, nontoxic oil such as walnut oil • Fasten to carcass with mechanical fasteners

Prescriptions for a Healthy House

Type	Relative cost	Advantages	Disadvantages	Comments	Specify
Solid sheet granite	Expensive	• Wide selection of very beautiful stones • Hard, scratchproof, stain-resistant surface that will last forever • Solid seamless surface • Can be mechanically fastened or glued with silicone • May not require substrate	• May be cost-prohibitive • Surface must be finished with impregnating finish	• Oil or butter left on surface will stain it • Must check for radioactivity	• Adhesives shall be solvent- and formaldehyde-free • Submit MSDS for surface impregnator • Shall be mechanically fastened or fastened with 100% pure silicone caulk (aquarium/food grade)
Granite tile	Moderate	• Can resemble granite but is less expensive than slab • Very thin grout joints can be sealed with transparent silicone • Mar and scratch resistant	• Requires epoxy-type glues to set • Requires underlayment	• Oil or butter left on surface will stain it • Must check for radioactivity	• Submit MSDS for surface impregnator • Shall be mechanically fastened or fastened with 100% pure silicone caulk (aquarium/food grade)
Stainless steel	Expensive	• Nonporous, nonstaining • Easily cleaned continuous surface	• Aesthetically cold • Most suitable for contemporary kitchens • Thinner gauges require underlayment • Noisy • Must be special-ordered	• Conducts electricity • Proper ground fault interruptors are essential to prevent potential electrocution	• Use formaldehyde-free underlayment and mechanical fastening

Resource List

Product	Description	Manufacturer/Distributor
9400 W Impregnant	Solvent-free, water-repellant coating that allows wood to breathe while providing ultraviolet, mildew, and frost protection	Palmer Industries, Inc. 10611 Old Annapolis Road Frederick, MD 21701 (800) 545•7383, (301) 898•7848 www.palmerindustriesinc.com
ACQ Preserve	Pressure treatment for wood that uses alkaline-copper-quat, which contains no known carcinogens or EPA-listed hazardous compounds. Not widely distributed.	Chemical manufactured by: Chemical Specialties, Inc. One Woodlawn Green, Suite 250 Charlotte, NC 28217 (800) 421•8661 www.treatedwood.com Treated wood manufactured by: J.H. Baxter 1700 South El Camino Rael San Mateo, CA 94402 (800) 780•7073, (650) 349•0201 www.jhbaxter.com
AFM Safecoat Almighty Adhesive	A low-odor, nontoxic, water-based adhesive for gluing wood and wood laminates. This product is available only through special order at a 50-gallon minimum.	AFM (American Formulating and Manufacturing) 3251–3rd Avenue San Diego, CA 92103 (800) 239•0321, (619) 239•0321 www.afmsafecoat.com
Allgreen MDF	A medium-density fiberboard made from 100% recovered wood fiber, containing no incremental formaldehyde emissions.	Can Fibre 8 King Street East, Suite 1501 Toronto, Ontario, Canada M5C1B5 (416) 681•9990, (888) 355•4733 www.canfibre.com
Architectural Forest Enterprises	Hardwood plywood veneers from certified sources over a core of Medite II.	Architectural Forest Enterprises 3775 Bayshore Boulevard Brisbane, CA 94005 (800) 483•6337, (415) 467•4800 www.ecoforest.com
BIN Primer Seale	White, paint-on, vapor-barrier sealer for use as prime coat on gypboard and wherever an opaque sealer is desired.	Wm. Zinsser & Company 173 Belmont Drive Somerset, NJ 08875 (732) 469•8100 www.zinsser.com
Bio Shield Hardwood Penetrating Sealer	Same as Penetrating Oil Sealer, but a more dilute solution for use on hardwoods.	Eco Design/Natural Choice 1365 Rufina Circle Santa Fe, NM 87505 (800) 621•2591, (505) 438•3448 www.bioshieldpaint.com
Bio Shield Penetrating Oil Sealer #5	Undercoat for softwood, best used with a finishing stain for UV protection. Free of petroleum distillates and mineral spirits.	Same
Bio Shield Transparent Wood Glaze	Interior/exterior wood finish with ultraviolet protection.	Same
Bio-Wash	"Environmentally friendly" waterborne protective coatings for wood, wood brighteners, and paint and stain strippers.	Bio-Wash Canada 101–7156 Brown Street Delta, BC, Canada V4G 1G8 (800) 858•5011 www.biowash.com
Bora-Care	Designed to penetrate and protect all types of wood from wood-boring insects. Contains disodium octaborate tetrahydrate in ethylene glycol carrier. Water-based solution requiring paint or sealer on top.	Nisus Corporation 215 Dunavunt Drive Rockford, TN 37853 (800) 264•0870, (865) 577•6119 www.nisuscorp.com

Product	Description	Manufacturer/Distributor
Certified Forest Products Council	A nonprofit organization that actively promotes and facilitates the increased purchase, use, and sale of third-party, independently certified forest products.	Certified Forest Products Council 1478 SW Osprey Drive, Suite 285 Beaverton, OR 97007-8424 (503) 590•6600 www.certifiedwood.org
Cervitor	Metal kitchen cabinetry.	Cervitor Kitchens, Inc. 10775 Lower Azusa Road El Monte, CA 91731-1351 (800) 523•2666, (626) 443•0184
Dekswood	Cleaner and brightener for exterior wood.	The Flood Company P.O. Box 2535 Hudson, OH 44236-0035 (800) 321•3444 www.floodco.com
Elmer's Carpenter's Gllue	Solvent-free glue.	Borden, Inc. 180 Broad Street Columbus, OH 43215 (800) 426•7336, (800) 848•9400 www.elmers.com
Fiberock	A reinforced gypsum sheathing used as a backer for exterior finishing.	Available in many retail outlets. U.S. Gypsum-Fiberock 14643 Dallas Parkway, Suite 575, LB#78 Dallas, TX 75240 (800) 527•5193 (Southwest); (800) 274•9778 (East)
Guardian	Borate-based wood preservative.	Perma-Chink Systems, Inc. 1605 Prosser Road Knoxville, TN 37914 (800) 548•3554, (800) 548•1231 www.permachink.com
Hydrocote Polyshield	A tough, super hard, nonyellowing polyurethane that is UV stabilized and UV stable. Use with Hydrocote stains. Can be used with Hydrocote Ultraviolet Light Absorber Blocker to increase UV resistance.	The Hydrocote Company, Inc. 61 Berry Street Somerset, NJ 08873 (800) 229•4937 www.hydrocote.com
Isobord	A medium-density fiberboard made from straw fiber, containing no incremental formaldehyde emissions.	Isobord Global Sales & Marketing Office 1300 SW Fifth Avenue, Suite 3030 Portland, OR 97201 (503) 242•7345 www.isobordenterprises.com
LifeTime Wood Treatment	Wood preservative, wood stain, wood treatment.	Cedar Mountain Wood Products 143A Great Northern Road Sault Ste. Marie, Ontario, Canada P6B 4Y9 (705) 941•9945
Livos Donnos Wood Pitch Impregnation	A penetrating preservative for exterior wood work in contact with moisture. Made of natural ingredients using plant chemistry.	Building for Health-Materials Center P.O. Box 113, Carbondale, CO 81623 (800) 292•4838 (orders only), (970) 963•0437 www.buildingforhealth.com
Livos Dubno Primer Oil	A penetrating oil primer for use as an undercoat on exterior wood.	Same
Medex	Formaldehyde-free, exterior grade, medium-density fiberboard.	Medite Corporation P.O. Box 4040 Medford, OR 97501 (800) 676•3339, (541) 773•2522, (916) 772•3422 www.sierrapine.com
Medite II	Formaldehyde-free, interior grade, medium-density fiberboard.	Same

Product	Description	Manufacturer/Distributor
Multi-core	Hardwood veneered plywood panels with low formaldehyde emissions. Suitable for cabinetry.	Longlac Wood Industries, Inc. 2000 Argentina Road Mississauga, Ontario, Canada L5N 1P7 (905) 542•2700, (888) 566•4522
Neff Cabinets	High-quality manufactured cabinets with low formaldehyde emissions. Boxes are made of phenolic glued plywoods. Solid wood doors can be ordered unfinished.	Neff Kitchen Manufacturers 6 Melanie Drive Brampton, Ontario, Canada L6T 4K9 (800) 268•4527, (905) 791•7770 www.neffweb.com
Neil Kelly Cabinets	Cabinetry system designed to meet the needs of the chemically sensitive.	Neil Kelly Cabinets 804 North Alberta Portland, OR 97217 (503) 335•9275 National Distributor: Building for Health-Materials Center P.O. Box 113 Carbondale, CO 81623 (800) 292•4838, (970) 963•0437 www.buildingforhealth.com
Old Growth Aging and Staining Solutions for Wood	Wood is treated with a nontoxic mineral compound and then with a nontoxic catalyst that binds the natural mineral colors to cellulose, creating an aged patina. It imparts antimicrobial and antifungal properties to the wood while the pigments provide UV protection.	Old Growth Co. P.O. Box 1371 Santa Fe, NM 87504-1371 (505) 983•6877 www.olgrowth.com
OS Wood Protector	A penetrating, natural oil-based wood preservative with zinc oxide. For use on wood exposed to high humidity and moisture to prevent mold and mildew. Does not prevent insect infestation.	Environmental Home Center 1724–4th Avenue South Seattle, WA 98134 (800) 281•9785, (206) 682•7332 www.enviresource.com
Panolam	A melamine board thermally fused to a medex core.	Panolam 3030 SW Calapooia Street Albany, OR 97321 (888) 726•6526, (541) 928•1942, (203) 925•1556 www.panolam.com
Scientific Certification Systems		www.scs1.com
Shellguard	Borate-based wood preservative.	Perma-Chink Systems, Inc. 1605 Prosser Road Knoxville, TN 37914 (800) 548•3554, (800) 548•1231 www.permachink.com
Smart Wood Certification Program		www.smartwood.org
Timberline 2051	Wood flooring adhesive.	W.F. Taylor Company, Inc. 11545 Pacific Avenue Fontana, CA 92337 (800) 397•4583, (909) 360•6677 www.wftaylor.com
Timber-Tek UV	An oil resin-based, waterborne penetrating oil.	Timber-Tek UV 13807 SE McLoughlin Building, Suite 421 Milwaukie, OR 97222 (888) 888•6095 Distributed by: Planetary Solutions 2030–17th Street Boulder, CO 80302 (303) 442•6228 www.planetearth.com

Product	Description	Manufacturer/Distributor
Timbor	Disodium octaborate wood preservative protects against termites, fungus, and wood-boring beetles.	Nisus Corporation 215 Dunavunt Drive Rockford, TN 37853 (800) 264•0870, (865) 577•6119 www.nisuscorp.com
Titebond Solvent Free Construction Adhesive	A multipurpose adhesive for a variety of porous surfaces, including plywood and wood paneling.	Franklin International 2020 Bruck Street Columbus, OH 43207 (800) 347•4583 www.titebond.com
Titebond Solvent Free Sub-floor Adhesive	A multipurpose adhesive for a variety of porous surfaces.	Same
Weatherall UV Guard	Exterior acrylic wood finish that penetrates and seals, forming a protective shield against UV, rot, and decay. Comes in clear and semi-transparent finishes.	Weatherall Co., Inc. 106 Industrial Way Charlestown, IN 47111 (800) 367•7068, (303) 697•1680, FAX (303) 697•1601
Weather-Bos The Boss	Four different formulas for protection of exterior wood surfaces.	Weather-Bos International 316 California Avenue, Suite 1082 Reno, NV 89509 (800) 664•3978 www.weatherbos.com
Weather Pro	A water-based, semi-transparent, water-repellant wood stain.	Okon, Inc. 4725 Leyden Street, Unit A Denver, CO 80216 (800) 237•0565, (303) 377•7800 www.okoninc.com

Divison 7: Thermal and Moisture Control

Foundation Water Management

Dampproofing is used to form a water-resistant barrier on the outside of stem walls where they come into contact with the earth. This treatment is especially important where there is a crawl space or basement below grade. Along with proper grading and perimeter drainage, dampproofing is used as protection against the migration of moisture through the wall. Water migration can result in a damp environment under or inside the home, which can lead to structural deterioration of the building. This is a frequent and serious cause of mold infestation.

Dampproofing of stem walls is only one component in the creation of an effective water barrier. Proper drainage backfilling and final grading are also essential in order to drain unwanted water away from the wall and relieve hydrostatic pressure that, if present, will drive water through any imperfection in the dampproof barrier and the stem wall. Conscientious and thorough workmanship are of the utmost importance. The following sample specifications describe the proper installation of perimeter drainage.

A drain system shall be installed around the perimeter of the foundation footing. The drainage system shall consist of the following items:

- Positive drainage away from the building along the entire perimeter, with a slope of no less than 5% and a top layer of impervious soils.
- Dampproofing of all exterior wall surfaces that are below grade or in contact with soil. (Refer to *Dampproofing and Waterproofing Materials* below for a list of acceptable products.) Dampproofing shall be carefully applied according to the manufacturer's directions to cover all below-grade surfaces to form a watertight barrier. Care shall be taken during backfilling and other construction to prevent damage to the dampproofed surface.
- A free-draining backfill of ³/₄" minimum crushed stone or gravel that is free of smaller particles shall be used to line and fill the excavation for all below-grade walls.

- An engineered drainage system may be substituted for a free-draining backfill. (These systems frequently incorporate perimeter insulation with the drainage.) The engineered drainage system must be installed in strict compliance with manufacturer's specifications.
- A French drain shall be installed so that all perforated pipes are located below the level of the bottom surface of the footing. French drain perforated pipes shall be installed with the holes down to allow water to rise into the pipe. If holes are present in more than one side of the pipe, at least one set of holes shall face downward.
- The perforated pipe shall be surrounded and set in a minimum 2" depth bed consisting of ³/₄" minimum crushed stone free of smaller particles.
- The perforated pipe and crushed stone shall be surrounded by a filter membrane to prevent adjacent soil from washing into and clogging the French drain system.
- French drains shall be sloped downward a minimum ¹/₄" per foot of run and connected to daylight.
- If a French drain cannot be connected to daylight, it may have to be connected to an underground engineered collection pool, a sump pump, or a storm sewer system. The architect or engineer should then provide drawings that explain the exact requirements. This situation is not ideal because sump pumps can fail and storm sewers can back up. If these problems are not quickly corrected, water damage may result. If the storm sewer is connected to the sanitary sewer—a situation that is usually not permitted—any backup may also result in sewage on the exterior side of underground walls.

Dampproofing and Waterproofing Materials

The use of asphaltic and bituminous tar mixtures for dampproofing is standard practice. These materials are known carcinogens. There are several other readily available products made for this purpose that are more healthful choices. The following products may be specified for dampproofing foundation walls or other walls adjacent to soil.

Cementitious Dampproofing/Waterproofing

- **Xypex:** A nontoxic (according to manufacturer), zero-VOC, chemical treatment for the waterproofing and protection of poured concrete. It creates

The Problem: Saturated crawl spaces created perfect conditions for mold growth. Recommendation: Crawl spaces should be dry. Perimeter drainage and detailing should keep water out of the crawl space and a barrier placed over the soil can prevent soil moisture from creating moldy conditions.
Photo: Restoration Consultants.

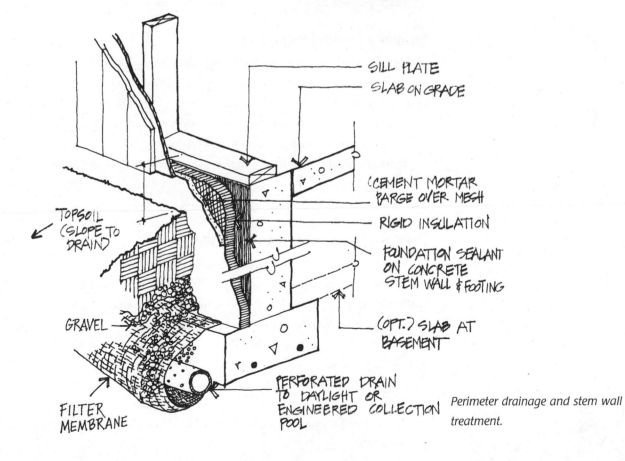

SILL PLATE
SLAB ON GRADE

CEMENT MORTAR PARGE OVER MESH

RIGID INSULATION

FOUNDATION SEALANT ON CONCRETE STEM WALL & FOOTING

(OPT.) SLAB AT BASEMENT

TOPSOIL (SLOPE TO DRAIN)

GRAVEL

FILTER MEMBRANE

PERFORATED DRAIN TO DAYLIGHT OR ENGINEERED COLLECTION POOL

Perimeter drainage and stem wall treatment.

a nonsoluble crystalline structure that permanently plugs the pores and capillary tracts of concrete. Xypex Concentrate can be used as a single-coat waterproof membrane or in a two-coat system with Xypex Modified. Xypex Modified can be used alone where dampproofing is required.

- **Thoroseal Foundation Coating**: A cementitious waterproofing for concrete and CMU (concrete masonry) surfaces.

Fluid Applied Dampproofing

- **AFM Safecoat DynoSeal**: A flexible, vaporproof barrier.
- **AFM Safecoat DynoFlex**: A topcoat for use over DynoSeal.
- **Rub-R-Wall**: Asphalt-free foundation waterproofing membrane products for various foundation applications.

Bentonite Waterproofing

- **Volclay**: A self-healing bentonite-based waterproof panel.

Creating a Capillary Break

Under some conditions, water will move upward through the soil due to capillary action. This type of moisture invasion can be controlled by creating a capillary break. Half-inch minimum gravel, free of smaller fines, placed under a slab will stop capillary action. A dampproofing coating or membrane should also be applied between the footing and stem wall or the stem wall and framing to stop any moisture being carried up through the concrete and entering the framing.

Prevention of Soil Gas Infiltration

There are a variety of natural and man-made soil gases that can infiltrate structures and cause indoor air-quality problems. Soil gases can be sucked into basements, crawl spaces, and floor slabs if negative pressurization exists within or under a structure. You can prevent this by creating a physical barrier between the soil and the home, and by controlling the air-pressure conditions under and within the home

Harmful man-made soil gases are caused by pesticides, herbicides, and gases from nearby landfills or industrial sites. In new construction, most of these problems can be avoided through careful site selection and a no-biocide home and yard policy.

Case Study 7.1:

Radon: How radon first came to the attention of the U.S. public

Stanley Watras had worked as an engineer for 11 years at a nuclear power plant in Pennsylvania. At the end of each workday, a monitor that measured radiation levels checked him and other plant employees. This procedure ensured that unsafe levels of radioactivity had not contaminated them while at work.

In December 1984, Stanley suddenly began setting off the buzzers on the radiation monitors as he walked by the machine on his way out of the building. The readings showed high levels of contamination over Watras's entire body. For several days this scenario was repeated, with Watras subjected to a lengthy decontamination ordeal. Where was Watras picking up this radioactivity and why was the radioactivity only affecting him?

The mystery was solved when Watras decided one morning to go through the monitors at the exit door as he entered the workplace. When the alarms went off, Watras immediately realized that the radiation was coming from somewhere outside the nuclear power plant. The local electric company sent a team of specialists to Watras's house to investigate. The readings on the Geiger counter showed levels 700 times higher than the maximum considered safe for human exposure.

Researchers concluded that the culprit was radon, a naturally occurring radioactive gas derived from underground uranium.

Discussion

At that time, very little was known about radon and its health effects. The Watras house was used as a laboratory for radon researchers who wanted to learn how radon gets into a house and how to get it out. Low-grade uranium ore was discovered beneath the basement of the structure, in direct contact with the house. The foundation of the house was removed, along with the soil underneath, to a depth of four feet. Ventilation fans were installed to pull radon-laden air out from under the house. Watras and his family were eventually able to move back into their home.

Water vapor and radon gas are two naturally occurring soil gases that may infiltrate a structure and result in health problems. The intrusion of water vapor into the home will cause structural damage and mold problems. Radon is an identified cause of lung cancer. These gases are both easily dissipated or blocked from entry by installing appropriate controls during the construction process.

Case Study 7.2:

Radon: A radon control retrofit

John Banta was called to evaluate a home for radon. The owner had received a do-it-yourself radon test kit as a gift from relatives. When he finally got around to performing the test, he could not believe the laboratory results. His daughter's room registered 24 pico-curies, six times higher than the EPA's recommended action level. John's electronic radon equipment confirmed the test results.

John proposed a radon reduction technique called sub-slab suction. It involved sucking radon from under the slab and ventilating it to the outside of the home. Holes would be drilled in the downstairs slab so that pipes could be inserted and connected to an exhaust fan, a method frequently used in unfinished basements. Since the owner had just finished installing an expensive marble floor downstairs, he was not willing to accept this proposal.

After some thought, John suggested that the sub-slab suction technique be modified so that the drilling would take place horizontally under the slab through the outside of the hill on which the first floor rested. A company that drills horizontal wells was contracted for the job. The site was surveyed and the drill set to bore just under the foundation. Six evenly spaced holes were bored horizontally all the way under the house. After the drill was withdrawn from each hole, a perforated pipe was inserted to provide a pathway for gas from radon-contaminated soil to be sucked from under the

home. The owner finished the job by joining all perforated pipes together with solid pipe, which he ran into a small shed a short distance from the home. He connected an exhaust fan to the pipe to suck radon to the outside, where it dissipated. The pipes were then covered with soil and the area landscaped. The home's radon level was reduced to an acceptable level (around 1 pico-curie). If the fan is shut off, however, the radon level again begins to climb.

More radon testing was carried out on other buildings located on the property and in the general neighborhood. No other elevated radon levels were found.

Discussion

Radon can exist in isolated spots, depending on underlying geological formations. Some parts of North America are known to have higher radon levels than others. Homes with basements, cellars, or other subterranean structures are the most susceptible to radon accumulation. Yet even homes with slab foundations and ventilated crawl spaces can have elevated levels. The only way to be certain is through radon testing. In John's experience, radon can almost always be reduced to acceptable levels. When building your home, use appropriate techniques to avoid the possibility of radon accumulation.

Radon Gas Infiltration

Radon is a clear, odorless, gaseous by-product of the natural breakdown of uranium in soil, rock, and water. While radon gas dissipates in open spaces, it tends to cling to particulate matter and accumulates when enclosed. Upon inhalation, radioactive particles become lodged in the mucous membranes of the respiratory system. The U.S. Surgeon General has stated that radon exposure is second only to tobacco smoke as a cause of lung cancer.

It has been estimated that as many as one in 15 homes in the United States contain elevated radon levels. The EPA recommends remediation at levels higher than 4.0pCi/L (pico-curies per liter of air). Even at 4.0pCi/L there is an increased risk of lung cancer; therefore it is prudent to reduce radon to levels between 1.0 and 1.5pCi/L.

Radon mitigation is most effective and least costly when incorporated into the construction of the home. If you are building a new home and there is reason to suspect a radon problem, you'd be well advised to conduct a soil test. Although the test will not tell you definitively what the radon levels will ultimately be in the

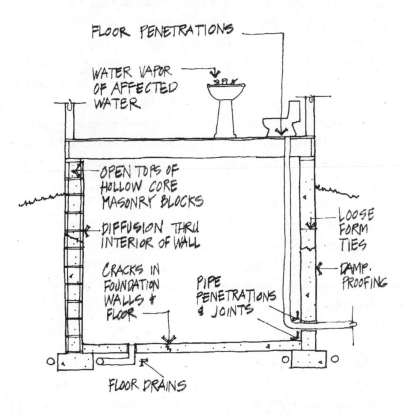

Potential entry points for radon and other soil gases.

finished home, it will be an indicator that will help you decide whether you should include mitigation measures in your construction plans. For more information about this test refer to *Division 13, Radon Soil Testing*.

Water Vapor Infiltration

The infiltration of water vapor as a soil gas is a common problem. It may be due to several conditions including high water tables, underground springs, or hardpan soils that cause excess water to remain at the surface. Certain soils hold moisture so that instead of percolating through the soil, it evaporates and travels upwards. Even with proper perimeter drainage around the building, which will take care of flowing water, this residual water vapor may be sufficient to cause damage.

Soil Gas Mitigation and Prevention

Foundation detailing and design affect the amount of soil gases that will accumulate in a building if they are present in the soil. The basement is most vulnerable to radon and other soil gas seepage because it has the largest surface area in contact with the soil. Crawl spaces under buildings, especially unvented ones, can concentrate these gases. The gas is easily transferred to the living space if there is not an effective air barrier separating the living space from the soil under the crawl space. A slab on grade can form an effective barrier against soil gas, but any cracks, joints, or penetrations in the slab will create routes for soil gas to enter. If you suspect there are elevated soil gas levels on your site, you should not install mud floors or other types of permeable floor systems that come into direct contact with the ground without also applying supplementary controls.

Methods of Soil Gas Mitigation

The EPA conducts radon mitigation training programs for contractors. State offices can provide you with the names of contractors who have been trained under the EPA's Radon Contractor Proficiency (RCP) Program and of those who are RCP qualified. Contractors who understand radon mitigation will have a basis for understanding any type of soil gas mitigation. A good strategy for soil gas mitigation consists of the following three components.

- **Blockage of all potential entry routes:** Concrete slabs and basement walls must be properly reinforced to minimize cracking. (Refer to *Division 3* for information on concrete reinforcement.) Cold joints and expansion joints will help control where inevitable cracking will occur so that the cracks can more easily and reliably be sealed. Plumbing penetrations must be sealed with a flexible caulk. (See the *Division 7, Resource List* for acceptable caulking.) Special barrier sheeting placed under the slab or over the soil in a crawl space will further block soil gas from entering. Basement walls must be thoroughly parged. Concrete floor slabs, and block or poured concrete walls, can be coated with **AFM Safecoat DynoSeal** or another low-emissions flexible membrane to further seal cracks and joints.

+ **Prevention of negative pressurization of the building envelope**: A home that has lower air pressure than the surrounding outside environment is negatively pressurized. This creates a vacuum that will suck air and soil gases into the building wherever there happens to be a route of entry, including tiny cracks in the slab, crawl-space soil barrier, or basement walls. In order to prevent negative pressurization, it is important to provide sources for the controlled supply of outside air into the home to replace the air lost through the operation of various appliances, such as exhaust fans and clothes dryers. Creating a condition where there is a slight positive pressurization can be an effective means of reducing radon and other soil gas infiltration levels. Strategies for providing proper pressurization are discussed in *Division 15*.

+ **Collection of soil gas from under the building envelope and redirection away from the building**: There are several methods for accomplishing this task. **Professional Discount Supply** is a company that specializes in radon mitigation supplies. Many of these same materials are applicable to all soil gas mitigation. You might include the following two collection methods in your specifications, along with instructions for proper installation of barriers and sealants.

+ **Method #1**: A 4" layer of aggregate is placed under the building envelope. A 4" diameter perforated pipe is laid in the aggregate through the center of the envelope. The pipe is connected to an unperforated riser tube that vents to the outside. The vent tube acts as a passive radon removal outlet. If radon levels are still unacceptable once the building is completed, a fan can be attached to the vent pipe to actively suction out the gas.

+ **Method #2**: In place of aggregate and perforated pipe, **Soil Gas Collector Matting** can be laid on the finished grade prior to pouring concrete. The matting, which is covered in filter fabric, is laid around the inside perimeter of the foundation in a swath about 1 foot wide, and the concrete is poured directly on top. The matting is connected to a vertical riser vent that extends through the roof. The natural chimney effect will draw the soil gas upward. If deemed necessary, the system can be adapted for active suction with the addition of a fan once the building is enclosed. Note: In areas with high water tables, consult a geotechnical engineer about proper drainage prior to installing any soil gas removal system.

Acceptable Low-Emissions Barrier Sheeting and Membrane Sealers for Soil Gas Control

You may specify the following products for blocking entry of radon from the ground into the living space.

- **AFM Safecoat DynoSeal**: Water-, vapor- and moisture-proof membrane sealer.
- **Cross-Tuff**: Specify radon-control grade.
- **Tu-Tuf 4**: Cross-linked polyethylene sheeting.

Thermal Protection

Moisture Problems Associated with Building Insulation

The addition of thermal insulation into wall cavities has had a major impact on moisture control in buildings. As buildings have become tighter and better insulated, the opportunity for water vapor to dry out from wall and roof assemblies has been reduced. Trapped water leads to wall assembly failures.

Buildings in cold winter climates will tend to dry to the outside, since moisture flows from the warm interior towards the cold exterior. Under these conditions, water vapor passing through insulated building assemblies will reach a temperature where it will begin to condense. If this condensation occurs before the vapor reaches the exterior of the building, the insulation will start to become wet. Most insulation acts like a sponge, collecting moisture that is unable to escape. If an adverse moisture condition persists, mold and rot will affect the structure, even when inorganic fiberglass insulation has been used.

In hot, humid conditions the situation is reversed but equally problematic. When hot moist air is allowed to enter from the outside, it may condense in the insulation as it approaches the colder, air-conditioned space.

The insulation alone does not create the problem, but because of its absorbent nature it will often augment the problem.

Case Study 7.3:

Moist soil in crawl space causes ceiling damage

A 15-year-old single-family residence was purchased for year-round occupancy in a popular ski area of Idaho. During the first spring in the home, the family noted water dripping from the ceiling of the kitchen. The dripping continued for a couple of days; then the condition appeared to resolve itself. The family forgot about the problem until it reoccurred during the spring of the second year. During the second occurrence they noted a strong musty odor developing inside the kitchen cabinets. Once again the dripping soon stopped, but a few days later mold became visible on the kitchen ceiling and inside the upper and lower cabinetry.

Investigation revealed that the crawl space under the kitchen had damp soil. Due to the high moisture vapor content in the soil under the home, moisture was coming into the home as a soil gas. This was traveling through the ceiling, condensing on the cold underside of the kitchen roof, and freezing. During the spring, the ice block melted into the ceiling space above the kitchen, soaking the gypsum board and insulation. The wet insulation acted like a sponge, holding excess moisture long enough to cause mold growth.

The owner was advised to install a vapor retarder on the soil surface. At this point, the new owner was rather embarrassed and replied that there had been a layer of plastic on the soil when they had purchased the home. He had noticed that it was damp under the plastic, so he had removed it to allow the soil underneath to dry. Unfortunately, the release of the extra moisture was sufficient to cause water damage and mold growth. Had the owner left the soil gas barriers in place, he could have prevented the mold problems from developing.

Discussion

The problem, which led to mold infiltration in his home, originated with excess moisture in the soil and became problematic for the owner due to the cumulative effect of several mistakes and building inadequacies. Better crawl-space ventilation would have helped to remove some of the excess moisture. However, due to the extreme cold in Idaho, large amounts of natural ventilation could freeze pipes. Adequate mechanical ventilation would have been a better solution. The roof also lacked adequate ventilation. Well-built homes will have multiple controls. In this case the vapor barrier worked well enough to prevent noticeable moisture problems for 15 years. The removal of the barrier by the owner was the straw that broke the camel's back.

The type of vapor retarders and air barriers used, and their positioning in relation to the insulation are critical in preventing mold and rot from developing. The general principle is that the vapor retarders and air barriers be installed in such a way that they reduce the amount of moisture able to get into the insulated cavity without impeding the ability of the moisture to escape. The dilemma is that climatic conditions may vary widely on a daily and seasonal basis, creating mixed conditions. This makes the insulation and moisture control procedures more complicated and demands site- and climate-specific design strategies that are beyond the scope of this book. The Energy Efficient Building Association (EEBA) has published design guides for various climates that distinguish and explain design strategies for climate-based moisture control. We highly recommend them.

Fiberglass Batt Insulation

Ninety percent of the homes in the United States are insulated with fiberglass insulation. There has been much debate as to whether or not fiberglass is a human carcinogen, and fiberglass insulation must carry warning labels that it is a "probable human carcinogen." Whatever the case may be, fiberglass is by no means a healthful substance. Fiberglass insulation can release both particulate matter and gaseous contaminants including formaldehyde and asphalt (if asphalt-backed) into the air. There are numerous reports linking fiberglass to pulmonary disease in production workers and installers. Although more healthful alternatives exist, they are generally more expensive and may not be as readily available. The cost of insulation, however, comprises a very small proportion of the overall building cost. Even doubling this figure will not constitute a large increase in cost per square foot for the overall construction of your home.

One of the more reasonably priced alternatives to fiberglass insulation is cellulose spray-in or loose-fill insulation. This product has an R-value of ±3.5 per inch. It can contain corrosive or toxic fire retardants, but many brands are available with more benign borate-based treatment that also protects against mold and insect infestation. Recycled newsprint is often used as a major component of cellulose insulation, which may introduce harmful dioxins into the mix. This type of insulation should not be exposed to the ambient air. Some manufacturers provide virgin or cardboard content instead.

Choosing one of the alternative building systems discussed in *Division 4* is another option. In most of these systems, the more massive walls themselves provide the insulation.

The following brands of fiberglass batt contain fewer harmful chemicals or are encased, thus providing safer installations.

- **CertainTeed**: Manufacturer of undyed, unbacked, fiberglass batt insulation.
- **ComfortTherm**: Fiberglass batts that come prewrapped in polyethelene bags. These have limited application, however, since the bags must be cut open and trimmed wherever spacing is irregular.
- **Miraflex**: An undyed product made without binders and encased in a polywrap. Application is limited as it is currently only available in 16" and 24" wide, R-24 packages.
- **Thermal Shield Free**: An unfaced, white, commercial batt insulation. Fibers are bonded with a formaldehyde-free thermosetting resin. Install in conjunction with an acceptable air barrier as specified below.

Fiberglass Blown-in Blanket System (BIBS)

Loose-fill fiberglass insulation is blown in behind netting or sheeting. The noncombustible fiberglass fibers contain no chemicals and inert binders. The products average R-4 insulation value per inch.

- **Climate Pro** by Johns Manville.
- **InsulSafe III** by CertainTeed Corporation
- **Optima** by CertainTeed

Alternatives to Fiberglass Insulation

The following alternative insulation systems can be cost-effective if applicators with the proper equipment are located in your vicinity.

- **Air Krete***: A cementitious, magnesium oxide foam insulation that is foamed in place.
- **Celbar**: Cellulose insulation treated with a borate compound for fire resistance. Available in loose-fill or spray-in application. The loose fill can be ordered without recycled newspaper content.
- **Icynene Insulation System***: A low-density, sprayed-in-place, modified urethane foam insulation. It is free of formaldehyde, fibers, chloro-fluorocarbons (CFCs), and hydrochlorofluorocarbons (HCFCs), and according to the manufacturer it has no detectable emissions after 30 days. It performs as an air barrier and is vapor permeable. The R-value is 3.6/inch.
- **Ultra-Touch**: A formaldehyde-free, natural fiber insulation made mostly of recycled content. Superior thermal and acoustic performance compared to fiberglass batt. No warning labels and no respirator or protective gear

necessary for installation. Comes unbacked in $5^1/_2$" R-19 batts or $3^1/_2$" R-13 batts.

* Insulation applied wet must be thoroughly dry prior to application of an air barrier in order to avoid trapping excess moisture in the wall cavity.

Insulation over Exposed Beam Ceilings

Where structural members of the ceiling are exposed, the air space between the structural members is not available to receive insulation. Various tapered insulation systems are designed to go over the exposed ceiling decking. The less toxic of such alternatives tend to be expensive. It may be more cost-effective to build in a cavity area over the existing exposed ceiling and insulate with one of the above-mentioned products.

Insulation around Windows and Doors

Regardless of the type of construction, the juncture where windows and doors meet the structure is a potential source of unwanted air infiltration and condensation. The industry standard for sealing this gap is to use an expandable urethane foam product. The foam contains toxic chemicals that will outgas in the wet stage but are believed to completely cure after a short while. These foams may also contain HCFCs, a depleter of the ozone layer. Because polyurethane foams do an excellent job of sealing and insulating these cracks, their efficacy vs. their environmental impact must be weighed. It is possible to lessen the environmental impact by specifying HCFC-free foam. Where the small amount of offgassing from the dried foam is a concern, the foam can be covered, once it has fully cured, with an air barrier material such as **Polyken Tape+337**. This aluminum tape has been used successfully by some chemically sensitive individuals for this purpose.

The following widely distributed polyurethane foams contain no CFCs, HCFCs, or formaldehyde.

+ **Great Stuff**
+ **InstaSeal EcoBlend**
+ **Touch'n Foam**

Those wishing to avoid polyurethane foams may consider the following options.

+ Stuff all of the cracks thoroughly with batting material to provide insulation. Seal inside and outside at the seam with recommended sealants (refer to *Joint Sealants* in this Division) to stop air movement.
+ **Cord Caulk:** This acrylic yarn, saturated in an adhesive wax polymer, is stuffed into the cracks around windows and doors and under sills.

Air Barrier

Impervious sheeting applied to the inside face of stud walls (under finish sheathing such as gypsum board) is often used to block air movement. In fact, it is mandated by building departments in some localities. In a home built with standard frame construction, such an air barrier is also a means of blocking the fumes generated by undesirable building materials in the wall cavity from entering the living space. The barrier itself must be free of undesirable odors and emissions in order to fulfil this function.

This method is not intended for use in hot, humid climates, especially where air-conditioning is in use. The barrier may cause condensation to occur on the insulation side of the barrier, causing hidden water damage and microbial growth. Another more "moisture forgiving" method for applying an air barrier is described in *Division 9, Creating an Air Barrier with Gypsum Board*. When a sheet-type air barrier is to be applied, use only unbacked insulation to avoid creating a double barrier in the wall cavity.

It is almost impossible to avoid punctures, given the complexities of construction and the number of materials that must be mechanically fastened together. However, the ultimate success of the barrier will depend on the quality control that is exercised during installation and, once it is in place, while all finish surfaces are applied. Include the following instructions for the proper installation of sheet-type air barriers in your specifications.

An air barrier shall be applied on the inside face of studs, joists, or rafters (warm side) just prior to the application of the interior facing. After applying the acceptable air barrier (see list below), seal with 100% silicone caulk or foil tape. Staple the barrier in pieces that are as large as possible over the insulation and attach them to the window and door jambs with staples and approved caulk to form a complete seal. Caulk at all wall openings such as plumbing and electrical boxes. Tape or caulk all seams and joints. Caulk all electrical boxes at the hole where the wire comes

> through, or else purchase gasketed boxes. Refer to *Division 16, Gasketed Electrical Boxes* for product information.

Acceptable Air Barriers

The following products generate little or no emissions and are suitable for air barriers.

- **Aluma-foil***: Foil laminated on two sides of kraft paper with nontoxic adhesive.
- **Cross-Tuff**: Cross-laminated polyethylene sheeting. If you specify "for a healthy house," the manufacturer will then incorporate two additional processes.
- **Denny Foil Vapor Barrier***: Virgin kraft paper with foil laminated to it on both sides using sodium silicate adhesive.
- **Reflectix**: Foil-faced and backed over plastic bubbles; especially designed to reflect heat.
- **Tu-Tuf 3 or Tu-Tuf 4**: High-density, cross-laminated polyethylene sheeting.
- **Tyvek HomeWrap**: Housewrap, vapor barrier.
- * Not suitable for areas that may get wet.

Roofing

A well-sloped roof with a sizable overhang is preferable to a flat or low-sloped roof for a healthy home, for the following reasons.

- The roof overhang plays an important role in protecting the walls and foundations from water damage by directing water away from the building.
- Inert roofing materials are readily available and are standard products for sloped roof construction, whereas they are an exception for flat or low-sloped residential roof construction.
- Sloped roofs shed water quickly, whereas water will puddle and linger on poorly constructed flat roofing.
- Flat roofs have a higher failure rate and shorter life expectancy, which may lead to devastating mold problems.
- Overhangs can be sized to suit the solar conditions in your region to provide shade in the summer while allowing maximum heat entry in the winter.

Northern New Mexico style straw bale building with metal roofing. Architect: Baker-Laporte and Associates; Builder: Living Structures; Photo: Paula Baker-Laport.

Sloped Roofing Materials

Asphalt-based rolled roofing and shingles will offgas when heated by the sun and should be avoided. Clay tile, concrete tile, metal, and slate are all healthy, long-lasting slope roof solutions. Wood shingles can be a good roofing material where fire danger is low and if rot-resistant woods such as cedar are used. Zinc or copper strip applied at the ridge will wash wood shingles with preservatives every time it rains. Availability of these roofing materials varies from region to region.

In many cases, roofers will want to install an asphalt-based felt paper over the roof sheathing. If you are unable to locate an experienced roofer who will warranty the work without this liner, then it is important to seal the roofing material from the structure by using a suitable air barrier on the inside, as discussed above.

Membrane Roofing

Membranes for flat roofing are more problematic. These roofs are more accurately described as having a very low slope, usually $1/4"$ per foot or less. Tile shingles and most metal applications, which depend on rapid water runoff, will not hold up under standing water conditions and are not suitable for low-slope roofs.

Built-up tar-and-gravel roofing is the most common and least expensive material available for flat roof applications, but we do not recommend it. A tar-and-gravel roof will emit volatile organic compounds (VOCs) from asphalt, benzene, polynuclear aromatics, toluene, and xylene. It will continually outgas when heated by the sun. Some of these vapors will inevitably find their way into

The Problem: A leak in a flat roof has resulted in fungal growth on the underside of the roof sheathing.
Recommendation: Roofs should be inspected regularly. Roof leaks shuld be repaired immediately and rapid drying should be performed to prevent fungal growth.
Photo: Restoration Consultants.

the living space and degrade air quality. Eventually the roof will outgas to the point where it does not adversely affect indoor air quality, but soon after that it will need to be replaced. The average tar-and-gravel roof is guaranteed for only two to five years and will require replacement in less than ten years. Since most people are not in a position to move out for several weeks when their roof is replaced, they will be exposed to high levels of toxic fumes every time the roof is repaired or replaced. Chemically sensitive individuals often have difficulty tolerating a tar-and-gravel roof that is less than one or two years old.

Toxicity is not the only health concern that should be considered when choosing a product. Many unhealthy and persistent mold and mildew infestations begin with an undetected roof leak. No type of roofing installation is foolproof, but the use of high-quality roofing materials and skilled installers will reduce the risk of leakage.

Although other solutions are typically more expensive than tar-and-gravel, you must carefully weigh both life cycle and health costs when making a roofing choice. Single-ply membranes such as **Brae Roof** contain asphalt and will outgas to a certain extent when heat is applied to fuse the membrane during application, but they are fairly stable once installed. They also carry a longer warranty period. They can be applied by heat-welding the seams, which is the least odorous method, or by sticking the seams together with an application of hot tar, which we do not recommend. Base courses under the Brae can be glued down over a layer of hot mopped tar, which we do not recommend, or mechanically fastened.

Certain single-ply membranes can be repaired by welding patches onto the existing roof, thereby extending the roof life for many years. There are also roll-on paint applications that do not require roofing contractors for application or repair.

It is especially important with roofing materials that the manufacturer's instructions for installation and warranty criteria be carefully followed. Following are some more benign alternatives to tar-and-gravel roofing for flat roof applications.

- **AFM Safecoat DynoFlex**: Low-toxic roof coating to replace tar-and-gravel. Can be walked on and remains flexible.
- **Brae Roof**: Specify torch-down application; otherwise the roof may be attached using hot tar, which will outgas indefinitely when reheated by the sun.
- **Mirrorseal**: A single-ply, fluid-applied roofing system.
- **Resource Conservation Technologies, Inc.**: An acrylic polymer paint- or roll-on system that uses titanium dioxide with propylene glycol and contains no toxic dispersants or tints.
- **Stevens EP**: A heat-weldable, scrim-reinforced, single-ply roofing membrane made of ethylene propylene.
- **Thermomaterials**: Paint-on roofing.

Joint Sealants

Many solvent-based caulking compounds contain hazardous solvents such as acetone, methyl ethyl acetone, toluene, and xylene. They are moderately toxic to handle and may offgas for extended periods of time. The following are suggested options for exterior use.

- **100% Pure Silicone Caulk**: Aquarium grade, of any brand. Be sure to read content labels because some products are presented as "pure silicone," but contain other ingredients.
- **100% Silicone Sealant**: Clear sealant.
- **AFM Safecoat Caulking Compound**: Water-based elastic emulsion.
- **Cord Caulk**: This is an acrylic yarn that has been saturated with an adhesive wax polymer. Apply according to manufacturer's directions around all

openings, such as doors, windows, below exterior door thresholds, and wherever necessary to obtain a complete weathertight, exterior building seal.

- **Silicone Plus**: Paintable, water-soluble silicone sealant.
- **Extend, Pro-Series**: A low-VOC exterior/interior urethane acrylic sealant.
- **GE 012**: Clear silicone sealant.
- **GE 5091**: Silicone paintable sealant.
- **Lithoseal Building Caulk**: Urethane-modified polymer that is inert once cured.
- **Phenoseal**: Line of water-based sealants and caulks.
- **Weatherall UV Guard Premium Caulking**: A professional strength acrylic-based sealant designed for use in a wide variety of construction applications.

Further Reading

Lafavore, Michael. *Radon: The Invisible Threat*. Rodale Press, 1987.

Lstibureck, Joe. *EEBA Builder's Guides*. Available through Energy Efficient Building Association, 10740 Lyndale Avenue South, Suite 10W, Bloomington, MN 55420. Phone: (952) 881·3048; Internet: www.eeba.org. A series of climate-based field guides with explanations, details, and techniques to effectively implement energy- and resource-efficient residential construction.

Lstibureck, Joseph and John Carmody. *Moisture Control Handbook: Principles and Practices for Residential and Small Commercial Buildings*. Van Nostrand Reinhold, 1993.

U.S. Environmental Protection Agency. *A Citizen's Guide to Radon*. Second Edition. Washington, DC: U.S. Government Printing Office, EPA 402-K-92-001, May 1992.

U.S. Environmental Protection Agency. *Consumer's Guide to Radon Reduction*. Washington, DC: U.S. Government Printing Office, EPA 402-K-92-003, May 1992.

U.S. Environmental Protection Agency. *Indoor Radon and Radon Decay Reduction Measurement Device Protocols*. Washington, DC: U.S. Government Printing Office, EPA 402-R-92-004, July 1992.

U.S. Environmental Protection Agency. *Model Standards and Techniques for Control of Radon in New Residential Buildings*. Washington, DC: U.S. Government Printing Office, EPA 402-R-94-009, March 1994.

U.S. Environmental Protection Agency. *Radon Contractor Proficiency (RCP) Program*. Washington, DC: U.S. Government Printing Office, EPA 402-B-94-002, September 1994.

Resource List

Product	Description	Manufacturer/Distributor
100% Silicone Sealant	Clear sealant.	DAP/Dow Corning Products 855 North 3rd Street Tip City, OH 45371 (800) 634•8382 Available at many hardware chains including Home Depot, Ace Hardware, Hacienda Homecenters, and Builders Square.
AFM Safecoat Caulking Compound	Water-based, elastic-emulsion caulking compound designed to replace traditional caulk and putty for windows, cracks, and maintenance. Limited distribution.	AFM (American Formulating and Manufacturing) 3251–3rd Avenue San Diego, CA 92103 (800) 239•0321, (619) 239•0321 www.afmsafecoat.com Also available from: The Living Source P.O. Box 20155, Waco, TX 76702 (254) 776•4878
AFM Safecoat DynoFlex	Available in sprayable form to use as topcoat over DynoSeal.	Same
AFM Safecoat DynoSeal	Flexible, low-odor, waterproof, vaporproof barrier.	Same
AirChek Radon Land Test Kit	The open land sampler is a one-day test device mailed to the lab for reading.	AirChek, Inc. Box 2000 Naples, NC 28760 (800) 247•2435 www.radon.com
Air Krete	Cementitious foam insulation made of magnesium oxide, calcium, and silicate. R value equals 3.9/inch.	Nordic Builders 162 North Sierra Court Gilbert, AZ 85234 (480) 892•0603 www.nontoxicinsulation.com Also available through: Palmer Industries, Inc. 10611 Old Annapolis Road, Frederick, MD 21701 (800) 545•7383 www.palmerindustriesinc.com
Aluma-foil	Air barrier of foil laminated on two sides of kraft paper with nontoxic adhesive.	Advanced Foil Systems, Inc. 820 South Rockefeller Avenue, Suite A Ontario, CA 91761 (800) 421•5947, (909) 390•5125 www.afs-foil.com
Brae Roof	Modified bitumen roofing.	For local certified applicators call US Intec, Inc. P.O. Box 2845 Port Arthur, TX 77643 (800) 624•6832, (800) 331•5228 www.usintec.com
Celbar	Spray-in or loose-fill cellulose insulation treated with a borate compound as a fire retardant. Loose-fill insulation can be ordered without recycled newspaper content.	International Cellulose Corporation P.O. Box 450006 12315 Robin Boulevard Houston, TX 77245 (800) 444•1252, (713) 433•6701 www.celbar.com
CertainTeed	Manufacturer of undyed, unbacked, fiberglass batt insulation.	CertainTeed Corporation 750 East Swedesford Valley Forge, PA 19482 (800) 274•8530 for closest distributor call (800) 441•9850 www.certainteed.com

Product	Description	Manufacturer/Distributor
Climate Pro	Blown-in blanket system fiberglass insulation without chemicals and with inert binders.	Johns Manville Insulation Group P.O. Box 5108 Denver CO 80217-5108 (800) 654•3103
ComfortTherm	A white fiberglass batt insulation with a polyethylene wrap.	Same
Cord Caulk	Acrylic yarn saturated with adhesive wax polymers for sealing around doors, windows, and sills.	Delta Products, Inc. 26 Arnold Road North Quincy, MA 02171-3002 (617) 471•7477 Available through the following mail-order houses: Brookstone Company (800) 846•3000 Real Goods (800) 762•7325
Cross-Tuff	Cross-laminated polyethylene air barrier and under-slab radon barrier.	Manufactured Plastics and Distribution, Inc. 10367 West Centennial Road Littleton, CO 80127 (303) 972•0123, (719) 488•2143 www.mpdplastics.com
Denny Foil Vapor Barrier	Virgin kraft paper with foil laminated to it on both sides using sodium silicate adhesive.	Denny Wholesale Services, Inc. 3500 Gateway Drive Pompano Beach, FL 33069 (800) 327•6616, (954) 971•3100 www.dennywholesale.com
Extend, Pro-Series	A low-VOC exterior/interior urethane acrylic sealant.	OSI Sealants, Inc. 7405 Production Drive Mentor, OH 44060 (800) 321•3578 www.osisealants.com
GE 012	Clear silicone sealant.	GE 260 Hudson River Road Waterford, NY 12100 Technical service: (800) 255•8886 www.gesilicones.com Available through the following retail outlets: True Value, Ace Hardware, Home Base.
GE 5091	Silicone paintable sealant.	Same
Great Stuff	Expanding foam sealant that is free of CFCs, HCFCs, and formaldehyde.	Insta Foam, Division of Dow Chemical Co. 1881 West Oak Parkway Marietta, GA 30062 (800) 366•4740, (888) 868•1183 (technical support) www.flexibleproducts.com
Icynene Insulation System	A modified low-density urethane sprayed-on foam insulation. Good performance and extremely low outgassing make this product acceptable for many with chemical sensitivities.	Icynene, Inc. 5805 Whittle Road, Unit 110 Mississauga, Ontario, Canada L4Z 2J1 (800) 946•7325, (905) 890•7325, (888) 946•7325 www.icynene.com
InstaSeal Eco Blend	Builders' line of expanding foam sealant that is free of CFCs, HCFCs, and formaldehyde.	Insta Foam, Division of Dow Chemical Co. 1881 West Oak Parkway Marietta, GA 30062 (800) 366•4740, (888) 868•1183 (technical support) www.flexibleproducts.com

Product	Description	Manufacturer/Distributor
InsulSafe III	Blown-in blanket system fiberglass insulation without chemicals and with inert binders.	CertainTeed Corporation 750 East Swedesford Valley Forge, PA 19482 (800) 274•8530 for closest distributor call (800) 441•9850 www.certainteed.com
Lithoseal Building Caulk	High-quality urethane modified polymer. Inert once cured.	LM Scofield Company P.O. Box 1525 Los Angeles, CA 90040 (800) 800•9900, (323) 723•5285 www.scofield.com
Miraflex	Less-toxic, undyed, fiberglass insulation material. The modified fibers are "safer," according to the manufacturer.	Owens Corning One Owens Corning Parkway Toledo, OH 43659 (800) 438•7465 www.owenscorning.com
Mirrorseal	Nonpetroleum-based polymer, fluid-applied roofing system. Can be applied and repaired by unskilled labor without specialized tools.	Innovative Formulation 670 West 33rd Street Tucson, AZ 85713 (800) 346•7265, (602) 628•1553 www.mirrorseal.com
Optima	Blown-in blanket system fiberglass insulation without chemicals and with inert binders.	CertainTeed Corporation 750 East Swedesford Valley Forge, PA 19482 (800) 274•8530 for closest distributor call (800) 441•9850 www.certainteed.com
Phenoseal	Water-based, nontoxic, nonflammable caulks and sealants available in translucent and 15 colors.	Gloucester Company, Inc. P.O. Box 428 Franklin, MA 02038 (800) 343•4963, (508) 528•2200 www.phenoseal.com
Polyken Tape +337	Aluminum tape that forms an effective air barrier.	Tyco Adhesives 1400 Providence Highway Norwood, MA 02062 (800) 248•0147 www.tycoadhesives.com
Professional Discount Supply	Radon mitigation supplies and technical support.	Professional Discount Supply 1029 South Sierra Madre, Suite B Colorado Springs, CO 80903 (719) 444•0646 www.radonpds.com
Reflectix	Foil-faced and backed over plastic bubbles; especially designed to reflect heat.	Reflectix, Inc. PO Box 108 Markleville, IN 46056 (800) 21•9063, (765) 533•4332 www.reflectixinc.com Available at Home Depot, Home Base, Furrows, Ace, True Value.
Resource Conservation Technologies, Inc.	Acrylic polymer roll-on paint roofing without toxic dispersants or tints.	Resource Conservation Technologies, Inc. 2633 North Calvert Street Baltimore, MD 21218 (410) 366•1146
Rub-R-Wall	Rubber polymer foundation waterproofing membrane containing no asphalt. Spray-on application. Manufacturer claims product is nontoxic once dry.	Rubber Polymer Corporation 1135 West Portage Trail Extension Akron, OH 44313•8283 (800) 860•7721 www.rpcInfo.com

Product	Description	Manufacturer/Distributor
Silicone Plus	Paintable, water-soluble silicone sealant.	DAP/Dow Corning Products 855 North 3rd Street Tip City, OH 45371 (800) 634·8382 Available at many hardware chains including Home Depot, Ace Hardware, Hacienda Homecenters, and Builders Square.
Soil Gas Collector Matting	Used alongside perimeter at top of stem wall along with "T" risers and piping. Effectively removes radon gas before it enters building.	Professional Discount Supply 1029 South Sierra Madre, Suite B Colorado Springs, CO 80903 (800) 688·5776, (719) 444·0646 www.radonpds.com
Stevens EP	Low-odor, ethylene propylene, heat-weldable roofing membrane.	Stevens Roofing Products 9 Sullivan Road Holyoke, MA 01040 (800) 621·7663, (413) 533·8100
Thermal Shield Free	An unfaced, formaldehyde-free fiberglass.	Johns Manville Insulation Group P.O. Box 5108 Denver, CO 80217-5108 (800) 654·3103
Thoroseal Foundation Coating	Cementitious waterproofing for concrete surfaces.	Thoro Systems Products 8570 Phillips Highway, Suite 101 Jacksonville, FL 32256-8208 (800) 433·9517, (904) 828·4900 www.chemrex.com
Touch'n Foam	Expanding foam sealant that is free of CFCs, HCFCs, and formaldehyde.	Convenience Products 866 Horan Drive Fenton, MO 63026 (800) 325·6180, (636) 349·5855 www.convenienceproducts.com
Tu-Tuf 3	High-density, cross-laminated polyethelene, puncture-resistant air barrier.	Stocote Products, Inc. Drawer 310 Richmond, IL 60071 (800) 435·2621, (815) 675·6713; (262) 279·6000
Tu-Tuf 4	Tu-Tuf 4 is thicker than Tu-Tuf 3 and can be effectively used under concrete.	Same
Tyvek HomeWrap	Housewrap, vapor barrier.	DuPont Co. 1007 Market Street Wilmington, DE 19898 (800) 44TYVEK, (800) 441·7515 www.dupont.com
Ultra-Touch	Recycled fiber insulation.	Bonded Logic 411 East Ray Road Chandler, AZ 85225 (480) 812·9114 www.bondedlogic.com
Volclay	4' x 4' corrugated kraft panels filled with bentonite clay that expand when wet to form a waterproof barrier.	Cetco 1500 West Shure Drive Arlington Heights, IL 60004-1440 (800) 426·5564, (800) 527·9948, (847)392·5800 www.cetco.com
Weatherall UV Guard Premium Caulking	A professional strength acrylic-based sealant designed for use in a wide variety of construction applications.	Weatherall Co., Inc. 106 Industrial Way Charlestown, IN 47111 (800) 367·7068, (303) 697·1680
Xypex	EPA-approved for concrete potable water containers. Protects concrete against spalling, effervescence, and other damage caused by weathering and bleeding of salt.	Xypex Chemical Corporation 13731 Mayfield Place Richmond, BC, Canada V6V 2G9 (800) 961·4477, (604) 273·5265 www.xypex.com

Division 8: Openings

Wood Doors

Standard Manufactured Doors

Wood doors, both solid and paneled, are typically treated with biocides and manufactured with toxic glues. Paneled doors use less glue than solid veneered doors and will therefore outgas less. The face veneer used on flush wood doors is Luan, a mahogany that is commonly imported from the Philippines or Thailand, where it is obtained through environmentally damaging forestry practices. Interior fire-rated doors and hollow-core doors often contain a particleboard core, which will continuously offgas formaldehyde fumes. Standard manufactured doors should be sealed to lock in harmful vapors. We recommend the following specifications when using standard manufactured doors.

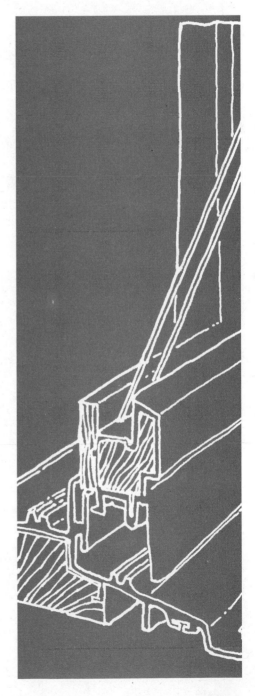

- All doors shall be thoroughly sealed on all six surfaces.
- For a clear finish, seal doors with one of the vapor-barrier sealants listed in *Division 9, Clear Vapor-barrier Sealants for Wood.* Follow the manufacturer's instructions.
- For a painted finish, prime all six sides with one of the primer paints that seal in VOCs listed in *Division 9, Paints.*

Custom Wood Doors

Choosing custom doors allows you the opportunity to select style, type of wood, and finishes. Some custom door manufacturers will work with you to create a healthier product by using benign glues and less-toxic shop finishes. You can also purchase doors unfinished and have the contractor finish the doors according to your own specifications. Although most custom doors are more expensive, some custom door companies have production or builder lines, which are almost cost-competitive with manufactured doors. Paula's chemically sensitive clients, who wish to have the warmth and beauty of wood without the turpene emissions of pine doors, will often order doors made of harder, less odorous woods such as maple or poplar. For custom doors, specify the following items.

The owner of this ranch home wanted the warmth of wood windows and doors but is extremely sensitive to pesticides. In order to avoid the use of pesticide treated wood all windows and doors were custom made by a local craftsman.
Architect: Baker-Laporte and Associates;
Builder: Living Structures;
Photo: Paula Baker-Laporte.

- Doors shall be glued with a solvent-free glue such as **Titebond Solvent Free Construction Adhesive, Elmer's Carpenter's Glue, AFM Almighty Adhesive,** or **Envirotec Health Guard Adhesive #2101.**
- Doors shall be finished using the specified low-toxic finish (refer to *Division 9* for choices) or with an approved shop-applied finish. Submit dated sample, MSDS, and product literature of any proposed shop finishes for owner's approval.

Sources for Custom Doors

- **Santa Fe Heritage Door Company:** This company uses **Titebond** glues upon request and will either supply doors unfinished or work with your specified finishes.
- **Spanish Pueblo Doors:** Owner Will Ott uses solvent-free glues and will work with the client to create custom finishes using low-VOC products.

Window and Door Screens

Windows and sliding glass doors generally come with removable screens. Screen doors for French doors or glass swinging doors are not usually provided by the manufacturer and must be custom made. Aluminum screening was standard in the past. Aluminum screening has been almost completely replaced with fiberglass or nylon mesh. These materials are more flexible than aluminum, more transparent, do not dent, and are easy to replace. Unfortunately, screening made from fiberglass or nylon mesh can also be more odorous, especially if they have been treated. When windows arrive onsite, the screens should be unwrapped and stacked in a protected environment so they have an opportunity to air out prior to installation in the completed home. If after a substantial airing the screens still have an objectionable odor, they can be exchanged for aluminum or copper at a custom screening company. **Andersen Windows** still use aluminum mesh as their standard screening material, and **Marvin Windows** can be ordered with aluminum screening.

Screens on crank-out casement or awning windows will have more impact on the indoor air quality because they are placed on the inside of the glass. Occupants will be exposed to these screens even when the windows are closed.

Windows

Moisture Problems Associated with Windows

By far the biggest health problem involving windows occurs when they fail to do their job properly. This job is to let in natural light and allow for ventilation while keeping water out. Windows have drainage channels that are designed to shed water away from the building; if these are not working properly they can channel water into the building cavity, causing serious water damage. A simple testing procedure can determine if the windows themselves are shedding water properly (refer to *Division 13, Window Testing*). Windows can be faulty due to manufacturing defects, mishandling during transport, or improper installation.

Windows have a structural weak point where the sill is screwed into the jamb. The seal can break during handling, and the tiny gaps can go undetected. Some window manufacturers have added a neoprene gasket at this juncture to make it more secure. If the juncture between the window and the wall contains gaps due to incomplete or incorrect application of sealing, then air will travel through the gaps. When that air sheds moisture due to temperature differentials, condensation can accumulate. Proper sealing around windows and doors is discussed in *Division 7, Insulation around Windows and Doors*.

Improper sill flashing can also result in water finding its way into the wall cavity. These water intrusions, which are not readily detectable in the completed building, can eventually lead to structural deterioration and mold problems. In *Division 13, Waterproof Testing,* we discuss a test that can help determine if there are any installation faults that will lead to future water damage. This test can be performed at a time in the construction process when faults can still be easily and inexpensively corrected. All of these potential problems regarding windows are exacerbated if the wall cavity does not have a means of drying out once it gets wet.

Because the quality control testing procedures that we have referred to are not standard for most residential construction companies, it is unlikely that they will be executed unless you specify them in your construction documents. These measures will take a little extra time but can potentially extend the life of a building for many years and prevent potential mold problems that could be devastating to your health.

Wood Window Frames

Wood windows are routinely dipped in a waterborne fungicide. While wood doors are often custom made, it is usually cost-prohibitive to have operable windows custom made. Chemically sensitive individuals will often choose steel or aluminum windows with a baked-on enamel finish to avoid exposure to the fungicide and to the turpenes from pine frames. Wood windows should be sealed to avoid exposure to the fungicide. You may wish to specify the following.

> • All windows shall be thoroughly sealed on all surfaces exposed to the interior.
> • Use a clear vapor-barrier sealant, as specified in *Division 9, Clear Vapor-barrier Sealants for Wood,* where a clear finish is scheduled, or primed with one of the primer paints that seal in VOCs, listed in *Division 9, Paints,* where a painted finish is scheduled.

Most wood window manufacturers also produce clad windows, which contain wood on the inside and aluminum, steel, or fiberglass coating on the outside for weather protection. This provides UV protection so that it is unnecessary to apply protective coatings on the window exterior. If unclad windows are used, you will need to do yearly maintenance, including staining and sealing, in order to protect them from the elements.

You can use the following products for the exterior preservation of wood window frames and doors. They do not contain many of the toxic substances found in exterior wood finishing products, though they can be more difficult to apply than standard products. It may be advisable to sample a small area first if the person applying the exterior finish has no previous experience with the products.

- **AFM Safecoat DuroStain**: Wood stain.
- **Auro No. 131 Natural Resin Oil Glaze**: Transparent, tintable finish.
- **Bio Shield Penetrating Oil Primer #81**: Undercoat. Use finish coat of **Livos Kaldet Stain** or **Livos Vindo Enamel Paint**.
- **Bio Shield Transparent Wood Glaze**: Wood finish with ultraviolet protection.
- **OS/Color One Coat Only**: Weather- and UV-resistant, water-repellant, semi-transparent wood stains.
- **Weather Pro**: Water-based, water-repellant wood stain.

Weather Stripping

Weather stripping is used around doors to make them airtight and resistant to water leakage. Weather stripping can also be specified around interior doors where noise or odor control is desired. Most available weather strips are made of synthetics, including silicone, urethane foam, polypropylene nylon, and neoprene. Some will outgas. Neoprene, for example, can have a strong odor. Brass and stainless steel are also available at many hardware stores. Choose the least odorous weather stripping that accomplishes the job.

Weather Stripping at Garage and Mechanical Doors

When planning a healthy home, the garage and mechanical room should be designed so they do not open directly to the interior, because they will introduce harmful by-products of combustion and odors to the home. A simple breezeway can provide weather protection between a detached garage and the home. However, doors leading directly from the garage, and common walls shared by the garage and living area, are found in almost all new housing because many people find a detached garage to be an unacceptable inconvenience. Where a door to the garage or mechanical room opens into the living space, it is important to specify that these doors have a sealed threshold, using a silicone or other acceptable sealant. The doors should be fully weather stripped in order to prevent harmful fumes from entering the living space. In fact, the entire common wall between the home and garage should be made airtight so that fumes do not seep from the garage, through the wall, into the home.

Resource List

Product	Description	Manufacturer/Distributor
AFM Almighty Adhesive	Zero-VOC clamping adhesive for gluing wood and wood laminates. This product is available only through special order at a 50-gallon minimum.	AFM (American Formulating and Manufacturing) 3251–3rd Avenue San Diego, CA 92103 (800) 239•0321, (619) 239•0321 www.afmsafecoat.com
AFM Safecoat DuroStain	Interior/exterior, water-based, semi-transparent wood stains in seven different earth pigments.	Same
Andersen Windows	Wood clad windows that come with aluminum screens.	Andersen Windows 100–4th Avenue North P.O. Box 12 Bayport, MN 55003-1096 (800) 426•7691 www.andersenwindows.com
Auro No. 131 Natural Resin Oil Glaze	Transparent, tintable finish for exterior porous wood protection. Note: This product is made with natural plant and mineral derivatives in a process called plant chemistry. Some sensitive individuals may have severe reactions to the natural turpenes, citrus derivatives, and oils.	Sinan Company P.O. Box 857 Davis, CA 95617 (530) 753•3104 www.dcn.davis.ca.us/go/sinan
BIN Shellac	White shellac/sealer used to create an effective air barrier.	Wm. Zinsser & Company 173 Belmont Drive Somerset, NJ 08875 (732) 469•8100 www.zinsser.com
Bio Shield Penetrating Oil Primer #81	Sealer, undercoat, and primer for absorbent surfaces of wood, cork, stone, slate, and brick.	Eco Design/Natural Choice 1365 Rufina Circle Santa Fe, NM 87505 (800) 621•2591, (505) 438•3448 www.bioshieldpaint.com
Bio Shield Transparent Wood Glaze	Interior/exterior wood finish with ultraviolet protection.	Same
Elmer's Carpenter's Glue	Solvent-free glue.	Borden, Inc. 180 Broad Street Columbus, OH 43215 (800) 426•7336, (800) 848•9400 www.elmers.com Available in many retail outlets.
Envirotec Health Guard Adhesive #2101	Zero-VOC, solvent-free adhesive without alcohol, glycol, ammonia, or carcinogens.	W.F. Taylor Company, Inc. 11545 Pacific Avenue Fontana, CA 92337 (800) 397•4583, (909) 360•6677 www.wftaylor.com

Product	Description	Manufacturer/Distributor
Livos Kaldet Stain	Stain and finish oil in 12 colors for interior and exterior surfaces made of wood, clay, or stone. Note: Livos products are made from plant and mineral derivatives. As with many natural products, some chemically sensitive individuals may not tolerate turpenes, oils, and citrus-based or other aromatic components found in these formulations.	Building for Health-Materials Center P.O. Box 113 Carbondale, CO 81623 (970) 963•0437, (800) 292•4838 www.buildingforhealth.com
Livos Vindo Enamel Paint	Wood finish coat.	Same
Marvin Windows and Doors	Wood clad windows that can be ordered with aluminum screens	Marvin Windows and Doors P.O. Box 100 Warroad, MN 56763 (800) 346•5128 www.marvin.com
OS/Color One Coat Only	Twelve different stain colors in base of vegetable oils. Interior/exterior use. No preservatives or biocides.	Environmental Home Center 1724–4th Avenue South Seattle, WA 98134 (800) 281•9785, (206) 682•7332 www.enviresource.com
Santa Fe Heritage Door Company	Custom wood doors.	Santa Fe Heritage Door Company 418 Montezuma Avenue Santa Fe, NM 87501 (800) 684•2981, (505) 988•3328
Spanish Pueblo Doors	Custom wood doors and cabinets.	Spanish Pueblo Doors P.O. Box 2517 Santa Fe, NM 87504 (505) 473•0464 www.spdoors.com
Titebond Solvent Free Construction Adhesive	Solvent-free adhesive.	Franklin International 2020 Bruck Street Columbus, OH 43207 (800) 347•4583 www.titebond.com
Weather Pro	Water-based, water-repellant wood stain for interior/exterior. VOC compliant.	Okon, Inc. 4725 Leyden Street, Unit A Denver, CO 80216 (800) 237•0565, (303) 377•7800 www.okoninc.com

Division 9: Finishes

Introduction

Finishes include all surface materials and treatments in the home. They are what is seen on a daily basis and, along with furnishings, constitute the personal signature of the owner. Finishes are the predominant source of odors in a new home. They can introduce a multitude of toxic volatile organic compounds into the air and will continue to volatilize, or outgas, for years after the home is completed. However, when chosen carefully, finishes can enhance health and well-being, as well as add to the aesthetic value of the home.

Until recently, nonpolluting finishing products were considered specialty items. Fortunately, healthier solutions are now regularly appearing on the market. Many of these items are easily accessible, cost-competitive, and comparable in performance to their more toxic counterparts. Some even have the ability to seal in toxins that may be present in underlying materials, thereby improving air quality.

In some regions traditional nontoxic finish materials are widely available and used. For example, in the Southwest, tiles, stones, natural woods, and plasters are commonplace, whereas in many regions of the country they have been replaced by wall-to-wall carpeting, vinyl wall coatings, laminate cabinetry, and other synthetic substitutes, even in custom homes. When you build a healthy home, we encourage you to take full advantage of the traditional materials native to your region.

Plaster and Gypsum Board

Plaster

Plaster generally provides a healthful interior wall finish. Because of the labor and skill involved in its application, it is a more expensive finish, but because of its beauty, it is often specified. Plaster has the ability to block VOCs present in small quantities in the gypsum lath and taped joints, which comprise its base in frame construction. Although the dense material works well as an air barrier, plaster will develop gaps due to shrinkage and will on occasion develop minor cracks. In order to maintain a good barrier, these gaps should be filled with an acceptable sealant.

Case Study 9.1:

Formaldehyde Exposure: Immune dysfunction related to formaldehyde exposure in the home

P.F. is a 51-year-old woman who was in good health until 1981, when she moved into a new mobile home. Shortly thereafter she developed a digestive disorder with gas and bloating, severe insomnia, and a chronic cough with frequent episodes of bronchitis. By the following year she was suffering from persistent fatigue and frequent respiratory infections, including her first case of pneumonia. She became sensitive to most products containing formaldehyde, especially pressboard. She noted that she experienced "brain fog" while shopping at the local mall. Her symptoms continued to worsen and now included allergies, hypoglycemia, and lethargy.

P.F. consulted with several health care practitioners, including a pulmonary specialist, psychiatrist, hypnotist, nutritionist, acupuncturist, and many more. None of them ever questioned her about the air quality in her home. Eventually a physician with similar symptoms diagnosed her as having multiple chemical sensitivity, and she was finally educated as to the underlying cause of her health problems. In 1992 P.F. moved into a house that contained low formaldehyde levels, which alleviated some of her symptoms. Her house contained several healthful features, such as radiant heat in concrete floors, and the absence of pressboard and particleboard in its construction.

However, further modifications were necessary before her health could be stabilized and improved. All gas appliances were removed, filtration was installed for both air and water, and the mechanical room was vented to the outside. By 1996 P.F. had regained her health. However, as is typical in such cases, she still becomes symptomatic upon re-exposure to toxic fumes and must diligently maintain a "safe" environment for herself.

Discussion

Indoor formaldehyde is gaining recognition as a severe health hazard for occupants of homes and office buildings where chronic exposure occurs. Several organizations, such as the American Lung Association, have recommended that formaldehyde levels not exceed 0.1 parts per million (ppm). People who have already become sensitized to formaldehyde will have reactions at levels as low as 0.02 ppm. Approximately 50% of the population is exposed on a daily basis in the workplace to levels that exceed the 0.1 ppm limit. Mobile homes are notorious for causing health problems due to the extremely high levels of formaldehyde emitted from the plywood and particleboard used in construction.[1]

Individuals who develop permanent health problems associated with formaldehyde exposure often relate the onset of their symptoms to a flu-like illness, which is diagnosed as a viral infection. However, the affected individual usually does not totally recover from this so-called flu and is left with general malaise, fatigue, and depression. Other symptoms can include rashes, eye irritation, frequent sore throats, hoarse voice, repeated sinus infections, nasal congestion, chronic cough, chest pains, palpitations, muscle spasms and joint pains, numbness and tingling of the extremities, colitis and other digestive disorders, severe headaches, dizziness, loss of memory, inability to recall words and names, and disorientation. Formaldehyde is an immune-system sensitizer, which means that chronic exposure can lead to multiple allergies and sensitivities to substances that are entirely unrelated to formaldehyde. This is known as the "spreading phenomenon."

P.F. is typical of people whose multiple chemical sensitivities stem from formaldehyde exposure in that she consulted numerous physicians and specialists in an attempt to obtain a diagnosis for her chronic ill health. Physical examinations and standard testing usually fail to identify the cause of such health problems. Sometimes it is suggested that the patient is a hypochondriac or in need of psychiatric evaluation. When asked if there might be a connection between the symptoms and formaldehyde, most physicians either do not know or are of the opinion that formaldehyde merely causes irritation. As a result, the patient's health continues to deteriorate due to continued exposure.

Most of this movement will take place over the first 18 months, so it makes sense to wait to do these minor repairs. In pumice-crete, straw-clay, and adobe construction (refer to Division 4), the plaster may be applied directly to the wall material.

Although most plasters are inert, some contain polyvinyl additives subject to outgassing. These additives should be avoided. Any additives in plaster should be clearly marked on the packaging. Nevertheless, it is best to verify the presence of additives with the manufacturer prior to purchase.

One potential health hazard associated with plaster lies in the method by which it is dried. Because new plaster releases a significant amount of moisture, it is necessary to dry it out quickly so that other building materials are not adversely affected. This is especially problematic in the winter months, when the cold temperatures and lack of ventilation slow down the rate of evaporation. The standard solution is to use gasoline or kerosene heaters. The by-products of combustion generated by this machinery are readily absorbed into the plaster and other building materials, and they create unhealthy air quality for the workers exposed to their fumes. We do not recommend this practice. Electric heaters tend to be more expensive to run, with far less BTU output. We recommend a combination of careful scheduling (so that the plasterwork is done during a warm dry period) and the use of dehumidifiers when necessary. Although heat may be required for the comfort of the construction team, it is far less significant to the proper drying process of wet building materials than dehumidification is. In summary we suggest that the following instructions be included in your specifications.

- Plaster shall be free of additives.
- The use of gas- or kerosene-generated heaters within the building envelope is prohibited.
- Turbo high-velocity heaters, other electric heaters, and blow-in heaters with respective combustion sources outside the building envelope are acceptable for adding heat to a building during cold weather construction.
- If plaster is applied when weather conditions do not permit the building to remain open and well-ventilated, electric dehumidification should be used. At temperatures under 70 degrees Fahrenheit, moisture levels should be maintained at approximately 45% relative air humidity using electric dehumidification until the building is dry enough that this range can be consistently maintained without the use of dehumidification equipment. Interior surface temperatures shall remain above 50 degrees.

Plaster Finish

Because of the porous nature of plaster, it will stain and show fingerprints if left unfinished. Plaster walls, which were the norm before the advent of gypsum board or sheetrock, were commonly painted or covered with wallpaper. Recently plaster has become a more prestigious finish material. Most people prefer to apply a clear finish over it to protect and enhance its natural beauty.

Natural beeswax finishes will protect the wall while maintaining its "breathability." Traditionally, beeswax was applied with a hot knife and troweled on the wall. There are very few craftsmen who know this art form today. However, we have found a natural beeswax furniture polish (**Livos Glievo Liquid Wax**), which can simply be applied with a cloth and buffed. (As with all plant chemistry products, chemically sensitive individuals may find the scent objectionable and should test a small sample first.) Some synthetic finishes will create a more impervious seal and are less expensive, easier to apply, and more enduring, though they should be carefully evaluated for suitability. Some may be toxic or increase problems with static electricity. Since most make the surface nonporous, they may encourage mold growth on the paper backing of the gypsum lathing behind the plaster if moisture becomes trapped. So, as with gypsum board, if a water accident occurs it should be quickly dried. We have successfully used the following finishes:

This Santa Fe Style interior combines hard trowelled plaster wall finishes with brick flooring and stone detailing to create a healthy interior.
Architect: Baker-Laporte and Associates;
Builder: Prull and Associates;
Photo: Lisl Dennis.

+ **Livos Glievo Liquid Wax:** Apply a thin coat and buff by hand.
+ **Okon Seal and Finish:** For satin gloss.

Gypsum Board

Gypsum board, also known as gypboard, sheet rock, or drywall, is the most common form of interior wall sheathing in modern residential construction. It is considerably less expensive than plaster. The 4' × 8' sheets are attached to the studs, then taped, sealed, textured, and painted.

Gypsum board is composed of natural gypsum sandwiched between two sheets of cardboard that are made from recycled newsprint. This cardboard

Stone floor tile, natural plasters and solid wood furniture featured in the Baker-Laporte Residence. Builder: Econest Building Co.; Photo: Lisl Dennis.

backing creates problems when water damage occurs because it is a nutrient that encourages mold growth. In his mold investigation work, John Banta has seen many cases where mold has begun to grow less than 72 hours after water damage occurs. Getting immediate help from a remediation specialist who has know-how and the proper drying equipment is often the key to saving money and health when a water disaster occurs. A skilled specialist will know how to remove mold safely while isolating it so that no further contamination occurs.

The installation of gypsum board in standard practice may negatively affect indoor air quality for the following reasons.

- Dust and debris within wall cavities are often enclosed and concealed by the gypboard. If dust and debris are not cleaned out, they can cause problems over time. Dust can eventually work its way back into the living space and become a maintenance problem as well as an air pollutant, and other construction debris can become a breeding ground for mold if it becomes wet.
- The gypboard itself will outgas because of the inks remaining in the recycled newspaper. In order to seal in the small quantity of undesirable VOCs that are generated by the surfacing board, the walls may be primed with a specialty paint or primer as specified below.
- The standard premixed joint compounds may contain several undesirable chemicals, including formaldehyde.

- Like plaster, gypboard is highly absorbent. In standard practice, gas and kerosene heaters may be used to dry the joint compounds. The by-products of combustion are absorbed into the walls and will outgas into the building envelope of the completed home.

- Special gypsum boards are made for use in areas that get wet such as showers, tub surrounds, and countertops. When walls using these products in wet areas are disassembled after several years, the water-resistant papers are often moldy, especially at the joints between boards. Cementitious boards without paper backing are also made to be used as backer board in wet locations and do not have the same mold problems that are associated with the paper-backed products.

In order to avoid these problems, include the following specifications.

- All wall cavities shall be thoroughly vacuumed and free of debris prior to installation of the gypboard.
- Joint compound shall be a powdered joint cement and texture compound such as **Murco M-100 Hi-Po** or approved equal that is formulated with inert fillers and without formaldehyde or preservatives.
- Heaters fueled by gasoline or kerosene are prohibited.
- If relative humidity rises above 55%, electric dehumidification should be applied until relative humidity remains consistently between 45% and 55% without additional dehumidification. Interior surface temperatures shall remain above 50 degrees.
- The joint compound must be completely dry before the application of primer.
- In order to seal in VOCs that are generated by the surfacing board, all gypboard walls must be primed with a paint that will seal the board. Walls shall be primed with one of the primers listed in *Vapor Retardant Primer Paints* in the paint section of this *Division* or approved equal.
- In wet areas such as showers, tub surrounds, and sink counters, cementitous backer board shall be used. The backer board shall not have paper backing. **Cemroc**, **Durock**, **PermaBase**, or approved equal may be used for this purpose.

Creating an Air Barrier with Gypsum Board

From the standpoint of indoor air quality there are often undesirable emissions from materials used in the building envelope in stud wall construction. Even when you take the greatest care in choosing materials, there may not be completely inert, cost-effective products available, so it often makes sense to create an airtight barrier on the inside face of the building envelope to block the entry of undesirable substances from within the wall cavity itself. This also makes great sense from the standpoint of moisture control and energy efficiency. A tightly sealed and taped gypsum board wall, in combination with gasketed or foamed sill and top plates, and thorough sealing around all openings (windows, electrical outlets, plumbing penetrations, and recessed lighting), will create an airtight barrier that can perform the same function as an air barrier made out of carefully joined plastic sheeting as described in *Division 7, Air Barrier*. This type of airtight assembly will prevent airborne moisture from pouring through cracks into the wall, but will allow a small amount of moisture to be carried through by diffusion. In climatic conditions where the building tends to dry to the inside (i.e., when the inside temperature of the building is cooler than the outside temperature), the gypsum board assembly will also allow moderate amounts of moisture in the wall cavity to dry out instead of remaining trapped. Because gypsum board allows some water vapor to move through it, this is a superior solution for blocking chemical gases out of living spaces where air conditioning (cooling) is used and moisture would tend to condense on a layer of impermeable plastic sheeting (if one were present) and remain trapped in the wall cavity.

Gypsum board can store limited amounts of moisture before it begins to mold, and it will not stand up to large amounts of wetting. In hot, humid climates where mechanical cooling is used, there must be sufficient vapor barrier on the exterior of the building to prevent excessive moisture from penetrating the wall from the outside and causing the cardboard on the gypsum board to mold. Similarly, when a home is heated, it may be necessary to retard some of the water vapor that would naturally diffuse through the gypsum board by using a paint or primer with a low permeability rating. **86001 Seal** is a primer that has a low enough perm rating to serve as a vapor retardant.

Gypsum board can be purchased with foil backing. Although foil is an excellent vapor blocker, we do not recommend it because it is problematic if water damage occurs. The foil prevents a moisture meter from taking accurate readings so assessment is hampered. It is also more difficult to dry out a flooded wall cavity when foil-backed gypsum board has been used.

To summarize, using the gypsum board in an airtight manner on stud frame construction makes sense in all climatic conditions. However, this only takes care of one piece of the moisture control strategy. Developing an overall strategy for the control of moisture in any building must take into account the climatic conditions of the site. The best solution will be different for different locations. A full discussion of moisture movement and best solutions is beyond the scope of this book, yet an understanding of moisture movement is essential for the ongoing success of a health-enhancing building in all but the most forgiving dry climates. To this end, we highly recommend the *EEBA Builder's Guides*, listed in the bibliography at the end of *Section 1*.

Tile

Tile is generally an inert and healthful floor, wall, and counter surfacing material. We recommend factory-finished tiles that require no further finishing on site. Many attractive and reasonably priced tiles are rated for commercial and exterior use. This rating almost guarantees a low-maintenance, long-wearing product that will not require onsite refinishing.

The following concerns must be addressed in order to achieve a healthful installation.

- In standard construction, tile is often laid over an unacceptable backing such as particleboard, which contains high formaldehyde levels.
- In wet areas, tile may be laid over green board, which will eventually lead to mold problems.
- Certain imported tiles contain lead-based glazes or asbestos fillers. Lead content can be simply verified by a lead swab test (refer to the *Division 13 Resource List*).
- Certain glazes, primarily imports, have been found to be radioactive, especially cobalt blues and burnt oranges.
- Many tile-sealing products contain harmful chemicals and high levels of VOCs. Selecting tiles with commercially rated finishes and glazes will bypass the need to use tile sealers on the construction site.
- Some standard tile adhesives and mortars contain harmful chemicals.
- Standard grouts usually contain fungicides and latex additives.

Ceramic tile slate and glass create this shower enclosure that brings views of the beautiful surroundings into this bathroom. Architect: Baker-Laporte and Associates; Builder: Prull and Associates; Photo: Julie Dean.

+ Grouts are porous and can harbor mold and mildew. They should be sealed where exposed to water.

Underlayment for Ceramic Tile

The following are acceptable underlayments for ceramic tile.

+ A clean, level, concrete slab or gypcrete base that has been fully cured.
+ Exterior grade plywood that has been aired out and sealed. Use only where a cementitious underlayment is unavailable. This method will require mastic adhesive and is not recommended for areas that get wet.
+ **Medex:** A nonstructural, formaldehyde-free, medium-density fiberboard. Tile application will require mastic adhesive. The board is not waterproof and will require either a waterproof sealer such as **AFM Safecoat Safe Seal** or sufficient time to dry out completely prior to application of grout. Not recommended for areas that get wet.
+ A lightweight, strong, noncombustible, highly water-resistant cementitious board such as **Cemroc**, **Durock**, **Hardibacker Board**, or **PermaBase**.

Tile Installation

The three basic methods for installing tiles are thicksetting, thinsetting, and adhesion with organic mastics.

Thickset Method

This is the tried and true, old-fashioned way of adhering tiles, prevalent prior to the invention of additives. A thick reinforced bed of mortar consisting of

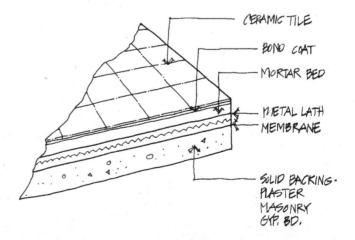

CERAMIC TILE
BOND COAT
MORTAR BED
METAL LATH
MEMBRANE
SOLID BACKING·
PLASTER
MASONRY
GYP. BD.

Thick-set tile installation

Portland cement sand and, in some cases, lime is floated. While the base is still plastic, a thin layer of Portland cement paste, known as the bond coat, is spread over it; the tile is adhered to the bond coat and allowed to cure for several days before the tile is grouted.

This method will create the strongest, most durable tile installation available without the use of chemical additives. The following should be specified for this type of installation.

- Use only additive-free Portland cement, clean sand, lime where required, and potable water. Use the recommended reinforcing and specified cleavage membrane.
- For walls, ceiling, and floor installations, follow the method covered by ANSI A108.1 and set the tiles on the mortar bed while it is still plastic.
- The cleavage membrane shall be non-asphalt-impregnated, 4 mm polyethylene such as **Tu-Tuff**, **Cross-Tuff**, or an approved equivalent.

It is not always possible to use a thickset installation. The $1^1/4$" depth required for thicksetting may not be available unless carefully planned from the outset. Tile setters skilled in this method are sometimes difficult to locate. This method is labor-intensive and will be more costly than other installation methods.

Thinset Method

Thinset mortars are powdered sand and cement products, mixed with liquid, and spread to approximately $1/8$" to $3/8$" thickness. Once dried, they are unaffected by water and can be used in wet applications.

A variety of thinsets are available. Most thinset mortars contain various chemical additives to enhance workability, flexibility, and bonding strength, thus expanding the range of application. Water-mixed thinsets consist of powdered sand and cement, are available with or without powdered latex and acrylic additives, and are mixed onsite with water. Latex and acrylic thinsets consist of powdered sand and cement mixed with liquid latexes and acrylics instead of water. They have higher bond and compressive strength and improved flexibility compared to thinsets mixed with water. Epoxy thinsets develop bonds more quickly than other thinsets. The epoxies emit noxious fumes while curing, and these fumes can be absorbed by porous surfaces. The use of epoxies is almost always unnecessary in residential construction. If epoxies are used, workers should wear protective vapor respirators during application.

The actual additive ingredients used in these thinset mixtures are proprietary and not disclosed on the label. When selecting a thinset product, choose one that can do the job at hand and that has the smallest amount of chemical additives and the least odor.

Thinsets without Synthetic Additives

The following water-mixed thinsets are available without synthetic additives. They gain their strength through the use of high-quality Portland cement, but are generally considered to be less flexible and more prone to cracking than thinsets with latex additives. They may be used successfully over clean concrete slabs, properly supported cementitious boards, and mortar beds.

- **C-Cure Floor Mix 900, Wall Mix 901,** and **Thinset 911** (dual purpose): These products constitute the "economy" line of C-Cure Mortars, which contain no additives other than mineral salts.
- **Laticrete Additive Free Thinset**

Low-Odor Thinsets with Vinyl Polymer Additives

The following water-mixed thinsets contain vinyl polymers, which give them greater strength and range of application. They have little odor and are virtually odorless once cured. Anyone with sensitivities to vinyl polymer additives, however, is advised to test these products prior to using them.

- **C-Cure Permabond 902:** A dry-set mortar with Portland cement, sand, and additives for use over cementitious substrates.
- **C-Cure Multi-Cure 905:** A latex-enhanced, dry-set mortar with added bonding strength and flexibility for use over cementitious and plywood substrates.

Organic Mastics

Organic mastics are either water- or petroleum-based adhesives that consist of a bonding agent and a liquid vehicle. For petroleum-based mastics, the vehicle is a solvent, usually toluene. These formulations are both highly toxic and flammable and are not recommended for use in a healthy home.

Organic mastics enjoy widespread popularity because they are inexpensive, stickier than thinsets, and allow the quickest installations. However, they do not have the strength, flexibility, or water resistance of thinset or thickset applications. Because they are applied very thinly, they do not have leveling capabilities and they are only suitable for application over flat surfaces such as plywood or drywall. When you are using them over concrete, check the vapor emission rate and pH of the slab to ensure compatibility with the mastic. The mastic can break down if too much moisture is emitted from the slab. If the slab is too alkaline, adverse pH reactions in the mastic can result in a persistent odor that is strong and unpleasant. Refer to *Division 13, Calcium Chloride Moisture Testing and pH Testing for Concrete Slabs*. Most mastics are not recommended for areas that get wet. Where mastic applications are appropriate, you may wish to specify one of the following water-based products:

- **AFM Safecoat 3 in 1 Adhesive:** Low-odor, low-VOC, water-based mastic for hard-composition wall and floor tiles.
- **CHAPCO Safe-Set 69, 75, and 90 Floor Tile Adhesives:** Solvent-free, nonflammable, freeze/thaw-stable, and almost odor-free ceramic floor tile adhesives.
- **Envirobond #801:** Water-based latex mastic that can be used in wet areas. The product is VOC compliant, containing no toluene, hexane, or benzene. Allow it to cure prior to grouting.
- **Envirobond #901 Odyssey Type I Premium Ceramic Tile Adhesive:** An adhesive for ceramic floor and wall tile adhesion. (More readily available than Envirobond # 801.)

Grouts

As with tile-setting mortars, there are a number of additives that may be used in commercial grouts to impart certain performance characteristics such as improved strength and flexibility, increased water or stain resistance, and improved freeze-thaw stability. Some of these additives, such as epoxies, are quite noxious. In grout applications, they will be exposed to the living space and will continue to outgas until completely cured. Homemade grouts can be mixed onsite by combining Portland cement, sand, lime (optional), and water. They can be colored with the same pigments used to color concrete (refer to *Division 3*). It is important that the person mixing the grout know the proper proportions and sand size for the particular tile application. These applications should be damp-cured for three days. The following commercially available grouts are free of latex additives.

Additive-free Grouts

- **C-Cure AR Grout:** A sanded grout available in a limited selection of colors.
- **C-Cure Supreme 925 Grout:** An unsanded grout for joints less than $1/8$" and for use with tiles that are easily scratched, such as marble.
- **Mapei $2^1/_2$" to 1:** For large grout joints greater than $3/8$".
- **Summitville-700 SummitChromes:** Sanded grout without polymer additives, available in 32 colors.

Grout Sealers

Sealing grouts will make grout joints easier to clean and more resistant to water penetration and staining. When water penetrates grout joints, it makes them susceptible to mold and bacteria growth. Even grouts containing mildewcides can eventually become moldy. Besides sealing grouts in wet areas, the key to mold-free grout is maintenance. Bathrooms should be kept dry by using exhaust fans, and grout joints should be cleaned regularly. We do not recommend the commercially available grouts enhanced with additives. We have found the following sealing methods to be generally well-tolerated by chemically sensitive individuals.

- **AFM Safecoat Safe Seal:** An odorless, zero-VOC, water-based, low-gloss sealer for highly porous surfaces. Can be diluted in a 50:50 ratio with water, then mixed into the dry grout to form an integral grout sealer.
- **Sodium Silicate:** Also known as water glass, this clear liquid sealer can be painted over grout joints. Make sure that grout joints are clean, dry, and free of additives or soap scum.

Tile Sealers

If you have used unsealed tiles, it is important to specify sealants that are free of harmful chemicals. Many of the commercially available tile sealers are solvent-based, highly toxic products that will emit noxious fumes for a long time after application. If they are used to cover a large floor area, the negative impact can be significant. Consider specifying the following specially formulated products.

- **AFM Safecoat MexeSeal** over **AFM Safecoat Paver Seal .003**: For sealing previously unsealed tile floors.
- **Pace Crystal Shield**: Odorless once dry; available in velvet or gloss finish.
- **ZipGuard Environmental Water Base Urethane**: Can be used to seal very clean, previously unsealed tile floors.

Stone

While stone is generally a healthful and beautiful choice for flooring and decorative accents, it raises the same concerns about proper installation as ceramic tile does. The specifications we have outlined for ceramic tile also apply to stone. We have tested several stone products for radiation and radon content and found a range of readings from very low to high levels. Although uranium content in construction materials is not usually considered to be a serious concern, John's experience, as shared in *Case Study 9.2*, leads us to conclude that stone can contribute significantly to ambient radon levels in a home. We recommend that stone, especially granite, be screened for radon prior to installation, even though the Granite Institute has issued a scientific report concluding that granite countertops do not emit radioactivity into the home. Tests are easily performed, as described in *Division 13*.

Stone Installation

Refer to *Thickset Method* in the *Tile Installation* section. Refer also to the section on stone countertops in *Division 6*.

Sealers for Stone

The following finishes are free of petroleum-based solvents and can be used for most stone flooring, shelving, and countertops.

- **AFM Safecoat MexeSeal**: A durable sealer providing water and oil repellency, applied over **AFM Safecoat Paver Seal .003**, an undersealer for porous materials.
- **Livos Meldos Hard Oil** and **Livos Bilo Floor Wax**: A penetrating oil sealer and a clear, mar-resistant finish wax, respectively. These products can be odorous when first applied and should be carefully tested prior to use by a chemically sensitive individual.

Case Study 9.2:

Radon: A very hot bed

Prior to purchasing a home, a family contacted a consultant to conduct radon testing with electronic monitors, following the EPA's protocol. Closed house conditions were established 12 hours prior to the start of testing and were maintained throughout the tests. During the testing, one of the electronic monitors located in the dining room indicated 12.5 pico-curies of radon per liter (pCi/L) of air, while another monitor elsewhere showed close to normal levels. The client was advised that the electronic readings were suspicious and that additional testing was necessary. As the investigation proceeded, it became clear that there was a radon source at one end of the home. In fact, the radon results for a test conducted on a night table in the guest bedroom were 27.0 pCi/L, while the family room a short way down the hall was 7.0 pCi/L. The further the monitors had been placed from the guest bedroom, the lower the radon value.

Upon visual examination of the guest bedroom, the tester noted that the headboards for the two beds were made of rock that appeared to be granite. The headboards were later measured with a small Geiger counter. While normal radioactive background levels away from the headboards were approximately 12 radioactive counts per minute, the counts close to the headboards were over 300. It was clear that the headboards were at least one source of radon in the room.

The headboards were in fact a decorative granite rock imported from Italy. Each headboard weighed several hundred pounds. The floors and walls had been especially constructed to hold the extra weight. It took six strong men to remove each of the headboards to a detached garage. The radon tests were repeated throughout the home, with all values now under 1.0 pCi/L. The home was given a radon clearance, contingent upon the proper disposal of the headboards.

This was the first home John inspected in which a radon source was a building material or furnishing. Although radon from the soil is the most common cause of elevated radiation levels in a home, there are many other possible sources. Since granite rock is sometimes high in uranium, it must be considered a potential source of radon when used in construction. Rock can be a superb building material, but it should always be tested prior to use for the rare possibility of radiation.

• **Naturel Cleaner and Sealer:** Water-soluble flakes that clean, protect, and finish stone surfaces.

Flooring

Flooring Installations Over Concrete

Flooring materials such as wood, carpeting. and resilient flooring are often laid over a concrete slab. If the concrete slab has high moisture content due to inadequate curing time or a high water table, then the perfect conditions for mold growth occur—an environment that is dark, moist, still, and nutritious. Flooring manufacturers publish recommended maximum vapor-emission levels that their products can withstand when installed over concrete slab. When these levels are exceeded, the warranty is void. Unfortunately, slabs are rarely measured for vapor emissions.

Where finish flooring, especially wood flooring, is laid over concrete slab with radiant heat tubing in it, we have encountered an additional problem. A slab that appears to be fully cured will have unacceptably high vapor emissions when the heat is first turned on. Often the heat is turned on only after floor finishes have been applied and the construction is complete.

We consider these to be important quality-control issues and suggest the following specifications.

> • Prior to the installation of flooring or subflooring over a concrete slab, a Calcium Chloride Vapor Emissions test shall be performed in order to verify that the slab meets manufacturer's maximum vapor-emissions criteria. Testing shall be performed at a rate of one test per every 500 ft. and at a minimum of once per concrete pour area.
> • Where adhesives are used to apply wood floor directly over concrete slab, the slab should be tested to determine if the pH level in the concrete will be compatible with the adhesive.
> • Where radiant heat tubing is installed in a concrete slab, heat should be circulated in the floor for two weeks prior to performing a Calcium Chloride Emissions test.

Wood Flooring

Wood is a healthy choice for flooring provided that the subflooring, adhesives (if used), and finishes are carefully chosen to be healthful as well. In standard construction, unfinished wood floors are commonly nailed to formaldehyde-emitting underlayment, then finished with solvent-based finishes that will outgas for many months. Noxious glues may also be used in the installation process.

There are several prefinished, engineered flooring systems available. These can be applied directly over concrete in a floating floor installation method. When considering a prefinished floor, be sure you have a dated sample sent along with product literature and MSDS. Manufacturers will publish their underlayment requirements. Most require a vapor barrier of some sort between the underlayment and the flooring product, and they will state allowable maximum vapor emissions from the subfloor.

Most factory finishes have, in our experience, proven to be far more durable then any of the more benign finishes that are available for job-site application. Furthermore, when a wood floor must be finished onsite, the required sanding is a very dusty process. The dust levels can be reduced if you specify that a "dustless" process be used. For "dustless" sanding, a double-filter vacuum called a DCS unit is attached to the floor sander. It can contain up to 90% of the dust, making the process less dusty but by no means "dustless."

Each wood floor application must be carefully analyzed in terms of all individual components, from underlayment to finish. If you can examine both new and older installations that are similar to your proposed application, then you will be able to carefully evaluate what the product smells like when it is new and how well it wears over time.

Prefinished Engineered Wood Flooring Systems

The following wood flooring systems meet stringent European emissions standards.

- **Admont Natural Floors:** Preengineered flooring available in spruce, larch, beech, oak, ash, maple, or recycled pine. Available in two thicknesses for floating or fixed installation. Bonded with waterproof adhesives that the manufacturer claims are "free from all harmful substances." Available unfinished or prefinished with a "chemical and toxin-free" hard wax surface.
- **Junckers:** A solid wood, engineered flooring system from Denmark that can be applied directly over concrete. Factory UV-cured urethane finish comes in a variety of woods, with trim pieces. Wood comes from source with managed forestry practices.
- **Kahrs:** A solid wood, engineered flooring system from Sweden. Factory-applied UV-cured, multilayered acrylic finish. Wear layer is solid $1/8$" plain sawn and available in 11 wood species.

+ **Rappgo:** A Swedish system, manufactured to meet German DIN emissions standards, that contains a central layer of low-emissions plywood sandwiched between a top and bottom layer of solid wood. Distinctive in that the top wood has long plank length and that the flooring holds up well in very dry conditions. It comes with a durable factory-processed UV-cured acrylic finish that is fully cured by the time it reaches the job site.

Underlayment for Wood Flooring

Interior grade plywood or particleboard is most commonly used for wood floor underlayment, but should not be used anywhere in a healthy house. The following underlayments are acceptable.

+ 1" or 2" tongue-and-groove wood or rough-sawn lumber laid diagonally.
+ Exterior grade plywood (CDX), if used for underlayment, should be stickered to air out onsite. When used for chemically sensitive persons, it should be sealed with an acceptable vapor-barrier sealant, as specified in this *Division*.

Adhesives for Wood Flooring

Use only solvent-free adhesives or 100% silicone. Refer to the adhesives section in *Division 6*.

Finishes for Wood Flooring

When finishing or refinishing a wood floor onsite, it is advisable to specify "dustless" sanding. As explained above, this technique will help lower the amount of dust generated, but a thorough vacuuming with a true HEPA (High Efficiency Particulate Accumulator) vacuum will still be required.

There are a wide variety of floor-finishing products available. Some of them have very toxic ingredients. Because the floor is usually one of the last things to be finished, these emissions can be readily absorbed into other porous finishes and may continue to outgas for weeks or months before fully cured. It is therefore important to apply a product that is free of harsh, solvent-based chemicals.

Water-based Sealers for Wood Flooring
+ **AFM Safecoat Hard Seal** over **AFM Safecoat Lock-In New Wood Sanding Sealer** for medium gloss.

- **AFM Safecoat Polyureseal** or **Polyureseal BP** over **AFM Safecoat Lock-In New Wood Sanding Sealer.**
- **Pace Crystal Shield:** Clear, durable seal for hardwood floors. It has a history of being well-tolerated by chemically sensitive individuals once cured, but is quite odorous when first applied. Use copious amounts of ventilation until it is cured.
- **Zip Guard Environmental Water Base Urethane.** Clear finish.

Natural Sealers, Waxes, and Oils for Wood Flooring

Most naturally derived products have a scent associated with them that many people find to be pleasant, but which may be intolerable to others. It is important to test the following prior to application.

- **Bio Shield Penetrating Oil Sealer #5:** By itself or as an undercoat with **Bio Shield Hard Oil #9**, or as an undercoat with a topcoat of **Bio Shield Natural Resin Floor Finish #92.**
- **Livos Ardvos Wood Oil** or **Livos Meldos Hard Oil:** Medium to high gloss.
- **Livos Bilo Floor Wax** or **Livos Glievo Liquid Wax:** Plant chemistry or beeswax products.
- **OS/Color Hard Wax/Oil:** A satin-matt oil or wax finish.

Bamboo Flooring

Bamboo flooring has now become a cost-competitive and aesthetic rival to wood flooring. Bamboo can grow to a height of 40 feet in five years, and a bamboo forest will continually renew itself. The bamboo is split into strips and then kiln dried. It is more dimensionally stable than wood flooring and is 12% harder than rock maple! Bamboo flooring is available through the following sources:

- **Bamboo Flooring International:** Three-ply solid bamboo tongue-and-groove floor planking and accessories. Available in vertical or flat grain and in natural blonde color or carbonized to a brown color. (The carbonization process reduces the strength so it is comparable to that of walnut.) It comes in a UV-cured acrylic polyurethane finish. Processing and finishing occur in China, and MSDS is not available.
- **Plyboo:** Plyboo is grown in managed forests in Asia and harvested by hand. Planks are 3" wide tongue-and-groove and come in natural or amber color. Accessories, paneling, and veneer are also available. Plyboo comes unfinished

or with an acrylic polyurethane finish. Processing occurs in Asia, and MSDS is not available.

- **TimberGrass:** Available unfinished in vertical or flat grain in 12" wide panels or 4" wide tongue-and-groove planks for flooring. A variety of milled trim accessories are also available. Sustainably harvested and grown without the use of pesticides, fertilizers, or irrigation. TimberGrass will soon be available with a durable German-made, 100% solid, UV-catalyzed, factory-applied urethane finish.

Resilient Flooring

Easy cleanup, economy, and a soft walking surface have made sheet vinyl a popular flooring for kitchen and utility areas, yet vinyl flooring is associated with health hazards. Vinyl chloride fumes emitted from the vinyl flooring are a known carcinogen. In addition, in hot or humid climates requiring air conditioning, the vinyl will trap moisture, which can promote delamination and mold growth or rot. We do not recommend vinyl in the healthy home.

Natural linoleum, also known as battleship linoleum, is made from linseed oil, pine resins, wood powder, and jute. It is free of synthetic chemicals. This flooring does have a noticeable odor when it is newly installed, which some people do not tolerate.

Cork tile is another natural choice for resilient flooring. The natural smell of the cork is also evident at first unless it is presealed. Both cork and linoleum are available with factory-applied acrylic finishes. In hot and humid climates these finishes may impede vapor permeability, causing moisture to be trapped under the surface.

Sources for Natural Cork and Linoleum Flooring

- **Bangor Cork Company:** Cork tiles and sheet flooring and linoleum.
- **DLW Linoleums:** Natural linoleums in a variety of colors with natural jute backing.
- **Dodge-Regupol, Inc.:** Cork tile available unfinished, waxed, or with polyurethane matt or gloss finishes.
- **Eco Design/Natural Choice:** Cork floor tiles and adhesives.
- **Forbo Industries:** Natural linoleum flooring products.
- **Hendricksen Naturlich:** Cork, natural linoleum, and other natural floor coverings and adhesives.
- **Natural Cork Co.:** Offers cork in a variety of colors, patterns, and finishes.

Adhesives for Natural Cork and Linoleum Flooring
  + AFM Safecoat 3 in 1 Adhesive
  + Auro No. 383 Natural Linoleum Glue
  + Bio Shield Cork Adhesive
  + Envirotec Health Guard Adhesive #2027

Carpeting

Carpeting has been associated with a growing number of health problems. In a typical carpet, toxic chemicals may be found in the fiber bonding material, dyes, backing glues, fire retardant, latex binder, fungicide, and antistatic and stain-resistant treatments. In 1992, during a congressional hearing on the potential risk of carpets, the U.S. Environmental Protection Agency stated that a typical carpet sample contains at least 120 chemicals, many of which are known to be neurotoxic. Outgassing from new carpeting can persist at significantly high levels for up to three years after installation. Once discarded, carpet is neither renewable nor biodegradable. In major cities, discarded carpeting accounts for 7% of the landfill mass.

The most common carpet backing—synthetic latex—contains approximately 100 different gases, which contribute to the unpleasant and harmful "new carpet smell." Most underpads are made of foamed plastic or synthetic rubber and contain petroleum products, which cause pollution in every stage of production and continue to pollute once installed. Felt backings are generally less polluting. We have specified safer carpet backings below. Typically, brands labeled "hypoallergenic" will be odorless.

Carpet Installation

There are two ways to install wall-to-wall carpeting: tack down or glue down. Tack-down installations are preferable because they do not destroy the floor surface, the carpet is easier to remove, and the carpeting can be partially recycled. Tacking strips are nailed, screwed, or glued down around the perimeter of the room. If the tacking strips are glued, it is important that they are attached with a low-toxic glue. The carpet and underpad are then stretched, and the edges are folded with the underside tacked down.

Most standard adhesives for carpet installation are solvent based and contain harmful chemicals. Where a glue-down installation is required, avoid solvent-based adhesives. We have specified several healthier options below. In either

Division 9: Finishes

Case Study 9.3:

Carpeting: Toddler made severely ill by carpet

B.J. is a six-year-old boy who was in excellent health until the age of 10 months, at which time he suddenly developed seizures. These episodes of rigidity and tremors occurred up to 40 or 50 times a day. Many different specialists subjected the baby to a series of invasive diagnostic evaluations. The blood tests, brain scans, and electroencephalograms revealed no apparent cause of the seizures. The baby was placed on medication to suppress the central nervous system. The seizures persisted, although their intensity declined.

The baby's grandfather, a building contractor, suggested that the culprit might be the expensive new carpet installed shortly before the onset of the seizures. The parents contacted a representative from the carpet industry, who denied any similar complaints of neurological problems from customers. The parents suspected that this information was incorrect. They sent samples of the carpet to the independent Anderson Labs in Vermont for testing. Air was blown across the carpet samples into the cages of mice, whose symptoms were then observed and documented. After a short period of time, the mice developed tremors, rigidity, and seizures. The parents were horrified by the report. It was clear that their beautiful new carpet had essentially poisoned their son. The carpet and pad were immediately removed from the home, the adhesive scraped off, and the house aired out. The seizures stopped. The child is now off all medication and doing much better, although blood testing shows immune-system damage consistent with chemical injury.

installation procedure, seaming tapes will be required to fasten sections of carpeting together. Safer seaming tapes are also specified below.

There are several untreated natural fibers available for wall-to-wall installations, including wool, coir, and sisal. When these are installed with low- or nontoxic backing and either tack-down or low-toxic glue installation, they will provide a safer solution than most standard installations. **WARNING:** Wool carpets are often treated with highly toxic mothproofing pesticides. Therefore, an expensive 100% wool carpet does not necessarily mean a safer carpet.

Wall-to-wall carpeting, whether standard or natural, serves as a reservoir for dirt, dust, mold, bacterial growth, and toxins tracked in from outside, even when regularly vacuumed and shampooed. It is also highly absorbent and will readily acquire odors. Typical cleaning agents for wall-to-wall carpets contain harmful ingredients, including perfumes, chemical soil removers, brighteners, and antibacterial agents.

Although we strongly recommend the use of throw rugs of natural fibers, which can be removed and cleaned, instead of wall-to-wall carpeting, we offer the following guidelines for selecting the least-toxic carpeting for those who choose to use it.

- Verify with manufacturer that wool carpets have not been mothproofed.
- Of the synthetic carpets, 100% nylon is considered to be one of the safest.
- Choose carpeting that has little or no odor. Even the slightest odor on a small sample will be magnified many times in a fully carpeted room and can result in a very prominent, unpleasant, and unhealthy smell.
- Choose your carpeting as early as possible so it will have the most time to air out prior to installation. Also, buy carpeting from a supplier who will warehouse the carpet for you. This means that the carpet will be unrolled and aired out in the warehouse prior to shipping.
- Avoid carpeting that contains antimicrobial agents such as fungicides and mildewcides.
- Avoid carpeting containing permanent-stain-resistance treatment.
- Avoid carpeting or pads containing styrene-butadiene rubber.
- Carpeting with woven backing is preferable to rubberized backing.
- Follow underpad and installation recommendations in these specifications.
- Use nontoxic and odor-free shampoos, and maintain carpets regularly to prevent mold, bacteria, dust, and pesticide buildup.
- Vacuum the carpets on a regular basis, moving furniture if necessary to reach all areas where larvae may hide, in order to prevent moth infestations in untreated wool carpets. A vacuum cleaner that is equipped with a true HEPA (High Efficiency Particulate Accumulator) is a must if you have carpet. It is the only type that collects the very tiny particles, like dust mite feces and mold spores. Portable vacuums that are not equipped with HEPA filtration will spew dust into circulation, often leaving a room with more ambient dust than was there prior to cleaning.
- Establish a no-shoes policy for your home.
- If the carpet or pad gets wet, dry it as quickly as possible to prevent microbial growth.
- **WARNING**: Never use wall-to-wall carpet in bathrooms, kitchens, laundry rooms, or mechanical rooms. Carpeting in these areas inevitably becomes damp, inviting mold and bacteria infestation.

Case Study 9.4:

Carpeting: EPA takes a "stand" on the carpet controversy

In October 1987 the EPA began carpet installation at its headquarters in Washington, D.C. A total of 1,141 complaints were received regarding adverse health effects related to the new carpet.[2] These complaints included decreased short-term memory, loss of concentration, confusion, anxiety, headaches, joint and muscle pains, rashes, digestive disorders, reproductive abnormalities, asthma, insomnia, chronic fatigue, and multiple chemical sensitivities. Dozens of workers remained permanently disabled. After the EPA investigated these carpet complaints, it published a report showing a positive correlation between the EPA worker complaints and the new carpet.[3]

Despite the results of its own study, and the removal of 27,000 square yards of carpet from the headquarters building in 1989, the EPA published a public information brochure that states, "Limited research to date has found no links between adverse health effects and the levels of chemicals emitted by new carpet."[4]

The EPA's Director of Health and Safety told the *Washington Times* that "the freshly manufactured carpet clearly caused the initial illness." Within a few weeks of making that statement he was removed from his job. EPA management expressed concern that testing and regulation of carpet emissions could potentially cost the carpet industry billions of dollars.[5]

Discussion

The Consumer Product Safety Commission (CPSC) has received hundreds of complaints about carpets causing respiratory and neurological problems.[6] Toxic emissions from carpets include fumes from formaldehyde, benzene, xylene, toluene, butadiene, styrene, and 4-phenyl-cyclo-hexene (4PC). These chemicals can potentially cause cancer, birth defects, reproductive disorders, respiratory problems, and neurological damage such as anxiety, depression, inability to concentrate, confusion, short-term memory loss, and seizures. The carpet industry has consistently denied the adverse health effects of carpeting in spite of overwhelming evidence to the contrary.

In 1992, in response to public concern, the carpet industry announced its Green Tag program, which has lured consumers into a false sense of safety. The program tests a small sampling of carpets once a year. The testing is based only on volatile organic compound emissions, not biological health effects.[7] In fact, some carpets from the Green Tag program tested at the Anderson Labs have caused mice exposed to the fumes to die.[8]

In new construction, homeowners are typically given an allowance and asked to choose the carpeting. This allowance can also be used towards the purchase of healthier floor coverings.

175

The following carpet installation products contain fewer harmful chemicals.

Sources for Nontoxic Underpadding

- **Endurance II:** Synthetic jute pad in 20- or 32-ounce weights.
- **Hartex Carpet Cushion:** Available in three weights.
- **Hendricksen Naturlich:** Recycled felt underpadding, heat bonded with no chemical additives.
- **Ultra Touch:** 29 oz. carpet cushion of recycled fibers

Adhesives and Seaming Tapes for Carpet Installation

- **AFM Safecoat Almighty Adhesive:** Available by special order only.
- **AFM Safecoat 3 in 1 Adhesive**
- **Auro No. 385 Natural Carpet Glue**
- **CHAPCO Safe-Set 3 Premium Fast Grab Carpet Adhesive**
- **Envirotec Health Guard Adhesives #2027, 2045, 2054, 2055, 2060, 2070, 2080**
- **Envirotec Health Guard Seaming Tapes #3070, 3080, 3090, 3093, 3094**
- **Hendricksen Naturlich Manufacturer's Adhesive**

Carpet Treatment

The following carpet treatment will help remove pesticides, formaldehyde, and other chemicals from the carpeting and pad, and will also seal in chemicals to prevent outgassing. The treatment is not suitable for carpets with a large wool or cotton content because the wet application can cause shrinkage.

- **AFM SafeChoice Carpet Shampoo, AFM SafeChoice Carpet Guard**, and **AFM SafeChoice Carpet Lock-Out:** Follow manufacturer's instructions. Test a small sample of carpet with these products for shrinkage and color fastness prior to full application.

Wet-applied Finish Materials

Paints, stains, and sealers are all wet-applied finishing materials that will have the greatest impact on indoor air quality as they are drying. Once thoroughly cured they will no longer release VOCs. While some materials will have very low odor and/or will dry almost instantly, others may be odorous for months. Because of the large surface area that these materials cover, their impact can be significant and they must be carefully chosen. Consider the following:

1. **Performance**: A product that is more durable will not need to be reapplied as often. A product that is more odorous initially, but that has time to cure completely during the construction period, may be well worth considering if it is more durable than the alternatives. However, you must include adequate ventilation for the construction team during the curing period in this strategy.

2. **Application Procedure**: Manufacturer's instructions must be strictly followed. If applications are not sufficiently dried between coatings, they may remain tacky and odorous indefinitely. This same problem can occur if underlying joint compounds or plasters are not sufficiently cured.

3. **Construction Protocol**: Good ventilation during the application of wet products will not only speed drying time, but will also (along with the use of recommended safety gear) help assure the well-being of the construction team. Furthermore, good ventilation at the time of application will reduce the impact of these odors on porous materials that can acquire odor easily. Planning for and specifying a flush-out period at the end of all construction is a good way to allow offgassing prior to occupancy. Where weather permits, use fans with open windows to speed this process. Air filters and ventilation equipment may help during inclement weather.

4. **Factory-applied Finishes**: Some materials come with an optional factory-applied prefinish. Wood, bamboo, and cork flooring and ceramic tiles are some examples of materials that are commonly offered prefinished or unfinished. Factories often have facilities for safely and fully curing the finishes before the products are shipped out. These factory-applied finishes are often more durable than the lower-VOC finishes that would be suitable for onsite application. Prior to approving a factory-applied finish, it is prudent to have a dated sample sent to you to examine along with MSDS sheets. On occasion, samples may still have persistent odors and MSDS sheets may reveal the use of unacceptable toxins.

Paints

Because paints cover such large surface areas, careful selection is crucial. Paints are commonly a source of indoor air pollution. Certain paints and coatings, on the other hand, can improve indoor air quality by sealing odors in subsurfaces so that they do not offgas into the living space.

All paints and wet-applied coatings have three major components: pigment, binder, and carrier, also known as the vehicle. Water-based (latex) paints use water as the carrier, whereas oil-based (alkyd) paints use a variety of much more volatile solvents. In the past, oil-based paints were considered to be more enduring than latex paints. However, with recent improvements in latex paint technology, oil-based paints can be entirely eliminated from residential construction.

Amongst the thousands of latex paints available, there is a wide range in terms of volatility, toxicity, and performance. Since the first edition of this book was published, many more low- to zero-VOC water-base paints are being offered by commercial manufacturers. In addition, some of the original commercial "environmental paint" efforts have been reformulated for higher performance in the areas of hideability, wearability, and scrubability.

Low VOC is not the only measure of a paint's effect on human health. Both synthetic binders and various additives can cause negative reactions for some people, and paints often contain substances that are environmentally undesirable. Finding out about the presence of these ingredients can be challenging. Additives such as biocides are often proprietary or present in such low quantities that they will not be listed on an MSDS sheet. Several independent not-for-profit organizations have arisen internationally in order to set environmental standards for consumer products. **Green Seal** is a U.S.-based organization that has created evaluation standards for architectural coatings that include low VOC emissions and the exclusion of 5 heavy metals and 21 toxic organic compounds. The commercially available paints listed below have, according to the manufacturers, met these Green Seal criteria. A more extensive list can be obtained through Green Seal.

Individuals with chemical sensitivities should test paints to determine the best choice for them. Our experience has shown that sensitive individuals will react to some paints and be fine with others, and that none of the paints have a perfect track record with everyone. **Note:** In some cases paints with acrylic rather than vinyl or vinyl acrylic binders have been better tolerated.

Following are several of the lowest VOC content paints that you may wish to consider for your project.

Commercially Available Interior Zero- and Low-VOC Paints from Conventional Manufacturers
The following paint lines have met the Green Seal criteria. Please note that the product names shown in bold type are the paint lines being recommended for the

specific manufacturer. These manufacturers also make paint lines that we do not recommend.

- **Air Care Odorless Solvent Free** Eggshell and Flat by Coronado Paints
- **Enviro-Cote** paints by Kelly-Moore
- **Genesis Odor Free** paints by Duron
- **HealthSpec** paints by Sherwin Williams
- **Lifemaster 2000** paints by ICI Dulux/Glidden
- **Pristine Eco Spec** paints by Benjamin Moore

Specially Formulated Paints from Alternative Manufacturers

Although generally more expensive, the following paints have been specially formulated and often better meet the needs of chemically sensitive individuals.

- **AFM SafeCoat Enamel Low VOC and Safecoat Zero VOC:** These paints are formulated with propylene glycol instead of ethylene glycol, and are free of ammonia, acetone, formaldehyde, and masking agents.
- **EarthTech Paints:** Zero-VOC, low-odor paints for interior and exterior use. Paint does not contain preservatives, biocides, or ethylene glycol.
- **Ecological/Canary Paints:** Odorless, formaldehyde-free, water-based terpolymer paint.
- **Enviro Safe Paints:** Contain no fungicides and are low biocide, custom mixed to order.
- **Miller LBNF:** A specialty paint with low biocide and no fungicide.
- **Murco GF1000 and Murco LE1000:** Contain no fungicides and only "in-can" preservatives, which enhance the shelf life, but which become entombed in the dry paint.

Paints Derived from Natural Sources

The following paints, which are derived from natural sources, contain few or no chemically derived ingredients and may be more environmentally sound choices. Some may not be suitable for the chemically sensitive. Products that contain d-Limonene may have vapors that are more toxic than those of petroleum distillates or turpentine and should be used with proper ventilation.[9] They are often harder to work with, but when skillfully executed can render a more lively wall surface.

- **Auro Natural Paints:** Made exclusively from natural sources by Sinan Co., a company that makes an effort to support ecological diversity.

- **Bio Shield Solvent Free Wall Paint** and **Bio Shield Casein "Milk" Paint:** Made from naturally or minimally toxic synthetic materials and contain very low VOCs.
- **Livos Naturals:** Low-toxic paints, all ingredients listed on label, many organically grown, both water- and oil-based products available.
- **Milk Paint:** Made from milk protein, lime, earth pigments, and clay, this petrochemical-free, biodegradable, nontoxic paint is odorless when dry. Not recommended for damp locations because it is susceptible to mildew. Milk paint can sour in liquid form. Comes in 16 colors; sold in powder form by **Old-Fashioned Milk Paint Co. Clear Coat** is a recommended topcoat.

Vapor Retardant Paints

The following paints are vapor retarders. They can be used to block unwanted vapors found in a material from offgassing.

- **86001 Seal:** A clear, water-reducible primer sealer and vapor retarder.
- **AFM Safecoat New Wallboard Primecoat HPV:** Especially formulated to cover the uneven porosity of new gypsum board and other surfaces with a high recycled content.
- **AFM Safecoat Primer Undercoater:** For use on drywall, wood, and masonite. Seals and reduces outgassing.
- **BIN Primer Sealer:** A white-pigmented shellac sealer that is used as an undercoat, primer, and sealer. It is free of biocides. It will effectively seal in odors from drywall. It should be used in a well-ventilated space since the alcohol base has a strong smell during application. It is available through most paint and hardware stores.

Stains and Transparent Finishes

Most standard sealers for wood are solvent based and contain several highly toxic chemicals that outgas for long periods of time after application. Recently, several more healthful, water-based products have come on the market. Since water-based products tend to raise the grain on wood or absorb unevenly, many installers inexperienced with their use have been disappointed by the results. We have found several good installers who have overcome their initial reluctance and now insist on using less-toxic, water-based products, knowing that in doing so they are safeguarding themselves, their employees, and their clients. Natural, more healthful oils, lacquers, shellacs, and waxes are also available.

Clear-seal, Water-reducible Wood Finishes

- **AFM Safecoat Hard Seal:** Used in conjunction with **AFM Safecoat Lock-In New Wood Sanding Sealer.**
- **Aqua-Zar:** Water-based nonyellowing polyurethane in satin or gloss finish.
- **EarthTech Finishes:** Non-yellowing, quick-drying, water-based finishes in satin or gloss for interior and exterior finishes.
- **Hydroshield Plus:** Water-based polyurethane for interior and exterior use.
- **Pace Crystal Shield:** Clear sealant for flooring and woodwork; odorous when wet, odor-free once dry.
- **Zip Guard Environmental Water Base Urethane:** Clear finish for interior woodwork. **Note:** The same company makes a product called "Zip Guard," which is solvent based.

Natural Oil, Lacquer, and Shellac Wood Finishes

- **Auro No. 131 Natural Resin Oil Glaze:** Transparent, tintable oil varnish. For exterior use.
- **Auro No. 213 Clear Semi-Gloss Shellac:** Semi-gloss, interior wood lacquer.
- **Auro No. 235 Natural Resin Oil Top Coat:** White, semi-gloss oil lacquer for interior and exterior use.
- **Auro No. 240 Natural Resin Oil Top Coat:** Interior and exterior in eight colors.

Wood Stains

- **AFM Safecoat DuroStain:** Interior and exterior.
- **Bio Shield Earth Pigments #88**
- **Hydrocote Danish Oil Finish:** Stain that colors and protects in one step.
- **Livos Kaldet Stain, Resin, and Oil Finish:** Satin, semi-flat, water-resistant finish for interior and exterior with strong surface-hardening capacity for wood cabinets, doors, and windows.
- **Old Growth:** Two-step process using minerals and hydrogen peroxide. Gives an aged patina to wood.
- **OS/Color One Coat Only:** Natural oil-based stains.

Clear Vapor-barrier Sealants for Wood

These products are used to help lock in noxious fumes so that they do not escape into the air. In fact, since no seal is ever perfect, vapor-barrier sealants generally serve to decrease the amount of outgassing at any one time, while increasing the overall time it takes for any substance to completely volatilize. We recommend that all efforts be made to speed up outgassing before you apply vapor-barrier sealants.

Outgassing can be accelerated by airing outdoors where protected from the weather, or by using filtration or "adsorbers" indoors. VOCs readily release noxious vapors in heat. Harmful chemicals can thus be dissipated more quickly if they are exposed to elevated temperatures. This can work well in controlled factory conditions but is not recommended for products in-situ in the home. Adsorbers are substances such as zeolite or aluminum silicate to which VOCs adhere. When adsorbers are placed in a room, they help remove VOCs from the ambient air.

Although most coatings seal to some degree and will be more effective when applied in several layers, the following products are advertised by their respective manufacturers as recommended specifically for the purpose of locking in noxious fumes.

- **AFM Safecoat Hard Seal:** Clear sealer for low-moisture areas.
- **AFM Safecoat Safe Seal:** Clear sealer for porous surfaces; also an effective primer.
- **Pace Crystal Shield:** Replaces lacquers, varathanes, and urethanes.

Manufacturer's instructions for application must be followed in order to achieve an optimum seal.

Endnotes

[1] Jack Thrasher and Alan Broughton, *The Poisoning of Our Homes and Workplaces* (Seadora, Inc., 1989), 50–72.

[2] Bill Hirzy, EPA Senior Scientist, President of EPA Union Local 2050, "Chronology: EPA and Its Professionals, Union Involvement with Carpet," 1992. Cited in "Carpet: Trouble Underfoot," *Informed Consent* (November/December 1993), 31.

[3] Environmental Protection Agency, "Indoor Air Quality and New Carpet: What You Should Know" (Washington, DC: U.S. Government Printing Office, EPA/560/2-91/003, March 1992), Pamphlet.

[4] Hirzy, 31.

[5] Memorandum by Susan E. Womble, Project Manager, Consumer Products Safety Commission (CPSC) Chemical Hazards Program, "Evaluation of Complaints Associated with the Installation of New Carpet," August 13, 1990.

[6] Ibid.

[7] Carpet and Rug Institute (Dalton, GA) press release, "Carpet Industry Program Steps Out Front on Indoor Air Quality: Labeling for Consumers Now Underway," July 17, 1992.

[8] Anderson Laboratories (Hartford, VT) press release, "Carpet Off-gassing and Lethal Effects on Mice," August 18, 1992.

[9] Monona Rossol, "Acts Facts," Vol. 4. No. 7 (*Arts, Crafts and Theater Safety*, July 1990, updated 11-18-1994).

Further Reading and Services

Anderson Labs., P.O. Box 323, West Hartford, VT 05064. Phone: (802) 295-7344. Provides evaluation of toxic effects of selected carpets, insulation, and other building materials through testing on mice. Consultations are available by phone for a fee.

Carpet and Indoor Air: What You Should Know. June 1993. Available free of charge from New York State Attorney General, 120 Broadway, New York, NY 10271.

Environmental Access Research Network (EARN), 315 West 7th Avenue, Sisserton, SD 59645. For a list of carpet-related articles, studies, and reports available from EARN's photocopying service, send $1.00 and request "Carpet List."

Thrasher, Jack and Alan Broughton. *The Poisoning of Our Homes and Workplaces: The Truth about the Indoor Formaldehyde Crisis*. Seadora, Inc., 1989.

Resource List

Product	Description	Manufacturer/Distributor
86001 Seal	Clear, water-reducible sealer and primer for gypsum board.	Palmer Industries, Inc. 10611 Old Annapolis Road. Frederick, MD 21701 (800) 545•7383, (301) 898•7848 www.palmerindustriesinc.com
Admont Natural Floors	Pre-engineered flooring available in spruce, larch, beech, oak, ash, maple, or recycled pine.	Distributed by: Planetary Solutions 2030–17th Street Boulder, CO 80302 (303) 442•6228 www.planetearth.com
AFM SafeChoice Carpet Guard	Sealer designed to help prevent outgassing of harmful chemicals from carpet backing and adhesives.	AFM (American Formulating and Manufacturing) 3251–3rd Avenue San Diego, CA 92103 (800) 239•0321, (619) 239•0321 www.afmsafecoat.com
AFM SafeChoice Carpet Lock-Out	A final spray application that seals harmful chemicals in carpet and repels dirt and stains.	Same
AFM SafeChoice Carpet Shampoo	Odorless carpet shampoo that helps remove chemicals such as pesticides and formaldehyde from new carpet.	Same
AFM Safecoat Acrylacq	High-gloss, clear, water-based wood finishes replacing conventional lacquer.	Same
AFM Safecoat Almighty Adhesive	Zero-VOC clamping adhesive for gluing wood and wood laminates. This product is available only through special order at a 50-gallon minimum.	Same
AFM Safecoat DuroStain	Interior/exterior, water-based, semi-transparent wood stains in seven different earth pigments.	Same
AFM Safecoat Enamel	Comes in flat, eggshell, semi-gloss, and gloss water-based paints without extenders, drying agents, or formaldehyde.	Same
AFM Safecoat Hard Seal	Water-based, general-purpose clear sealer for vinyl, porous tile, concrete, plastics, and particleboard plywood. Not recommended where exposed to heavy moisture or standing water.	Same
AFM Safecoat Lock-In New Wood Sanding Sealer	Sandable sealer helps raise grain on new woods in preparation for sanding prior to finish coat.	Same
AFM Safecoat MexeSeal	Topcoat used over Paver Seal .003 undercoat. Very durable sealer providing water and oil repellency for use on Mexican clay tile, stone, granite, concrete, and stone pavers. Glossy when multiple coats are applied.	Same
AFM Safecoat New Wallboard Primecoat HPV	Water-reducible, one-coat coverage primer for new gypboard, green board, and high-recycled-content material.	Same
AFM Safecoat Paver Seal .003	Undersurface sealer for new or unsealed porous tile, concrete, and grout. Used with MexeSeal topcoat.	Same
AFM Safecoat Polyureseal	Clear gloss wood finish replaces conventional solvent- and water-based polyurethanes for low-traffic interior wood floor and furniture applications.	Same
AFM Safecoat Polyureseal BP	As above for high-traffic situations, high durability, and abrasion resistance.	Same

Product	Description	Manufacturer/Distributor
AFM Safecoat Primer Undercoater	Primer for use on drywall, wood, and masonite with excellent sealing properties; reduces outgassing.	Same
AFM Safecoat Safe Seal	Clear sealer for porous surfaces; effective in blocking outgassing from processed woods. Improves adhesion of finish coats.	Same
AFM Safecoat 3 in 1 Adhesive	Adhesive for ceramic, vinyl, parquet, Formica, slate, and carpet.	Same
AFM Safecoat Zero VOC Paint	Flat and semi-gloss paint. No VOCs, formaldehyde, ammonia, or masking agents.	Same
Air Care Odorless Paints	Acrylic paints that are zero to low VOC.	Coronado Paint Co. 308 Old Country Road Edgewater, FL 32132 (800) 883•4193, (904) 428•6461
Aqua-Zar	Water-based, non-yellowing polyurethane in satin or semi-gloss finishes.	United Gilsonite Laboratories P.O. Box 70 Scranton, PA 18501-0070 (800) 845•5227, (717) 344•1202 www.ugl.com
Auro Natural Paints	Made exclusively from natural sources, with an effort to support ecological diversity. Packaged in powder form. Note: This and the following Auro products are made with natural plant and mineral derivatives in a process called plant chemistry. Some sensitive individuals may have severe reactions to the natural turpenes, citrus derivatives, and oils.	Sinan Company P.O. Box 857 Davis, CA 95617 (530) 753•3104 www.dcn.davis.ca.us/go/sinan
Auro No. 131 Natural Resin Oil Glaze	Transparent, tintable finish for exterior porous wood protection.	Same
Auro No. 211–215 Shellacs	Various natural shellacs with different degrees of gloss.	Same
Auro No. 235 & 240 Natural Resin Oil Top Coat	Indoor/outdoor enamels in white and eight colors.	Same
Auro No. 383 Natural Linoleum Glue	Adhesive for linoleum flooring.	Same
Auro No. 385 Natural Carpet Glue	Organic binder that remains permanently elastic.	Same
Bamboo Flooring International	Bamboo flooring and accessories.	Bamboo Flooring International 20950 Currier Road Walnut CA 91789 (800) 827•9261, (909) 594•4189 www.bamboo-flooring.com
Bangor Cork Company	Natural cork "carpeting" and battleship linoleum flooring.	Bangor Cork Company William and D Streets Pen Argyl, PA 18072-1025 (610) 863•9041
BIN Primer Sealer	White, paint-on, vapor-barrier sealer for use as prime coat on gypboard and wherever an opaque sealer is desired.	Wm. Zinsser & Company 173 Belmont Drive Somerset, NJ 08875 (732) 469•8100 www.zinsser.com
Bio Shield Casein "Milk" Paint #10	A very low-VOC paint made from naturally or minimally toxic synthetic materials. This and the following Bio Shield products make up a line of oil finishes free of formaldehyde, lead and other heavy metals, and fungicides. As with many natural products, some chemically sensitive individuals may not tolerate turpenes, oils, or citrus-based and other aromatic components found in these formulations.	Eco Design/Natural Choice 1365 Rufina Circle Santa Fe, NM 87505 (800) 621•2591, (505) 438•3448 www.bioshieldpaint.com

Product	Description	Manufacturer/Distributor
Bio Shield Cork Adhesive	Water-based elastic glue for cork, linoleum, or wool with jute backing. Adheres to concrete, wood, or plywood.	Same
Bio Shield Earth Pigments #88	Fine pigment powders extracted from earth or rock containing little or no heavy metals. Can be used with Bio Shield oil finishes.	Same
Bio Shield Hard Oil #9	For use on hardwood and softwood floors and stone in areas exposed to moisture. Use over surfaces primed with Bio Shield Penetrating Oil Sealer #8 or Bio Shield Penetrating Oil Sealer #5.	Same
Bio Shield Natural Resin Floor Finish #92	Finish for hardwood and softwood floors primed with Bio Shield Penetrating Oil Sealer #8 or Bio Shield Penetrating Oil Sealer #5.	Same
Bio Shield Penetrating Oil Sealer #5	A sealer, undercoat, and primer for absorbent surfaces of wood, cork, stone, slate, or brick.	Same
Bio Shield Penetrating Oil Sealer #8	A thinner oil for priming less-absorbent woods.	Same
Bio Shield Solvent Free Wall Paint #18	A very low VOC paint made from naturally or minimally toxic synthetic materials.	Same
C-Cure AR Grout	Portland cement, lime, earth pigment, and sand, without latex modifiers. Available in 40 colors.	C-Cure Corporation 13001 Seal Beach Boulevard Seal Beach, CA 90740 (800) 895•2874, (562) 598•8808 www.custombuildingproducts.com; www.c-cure.com
C-Cure Floor Mix 900	Dry-set mortar used for floor and wall installations of absorptive, semi-vitreous, and vitreous tiles.	Same
C-Cure Multi-Cure 905	Latex-cement mortar used for setting all types of ceramic tile; used on dry interior walls and exterior grade plywood.	Same
C-Cure PermaBond 902	For low-odor tile setting.	Same
C-Cure Supreme 925 Grout	Dry tile grout with exceptional working qualities and a permanent joint life; nonshrinking, nontoxic, odorless, inhibits fungal growth.	Same
C-Cure ThinSet 911	Dry-set mortar used for installation of low absorptive tiles (less than 7%).	Same
C-Cure Wall Mix 901	Dry-set mortar used for the installation of absorptive tiles (more than 7%).	Same
Cemroc	A lightweight, strong, noncombustible, highly water-resistant board that can be used as a backer for ceramic tile installations in wet areas in place of green board.	Cemplank P.O. Box 99 Blandon, PA 19510 (888) 327•0723, (610) 926•5533 www.cemplank.com
CHAPCO Safe-Set 3	A zero-VOC adhesive for carpet installation.	Chicago Adhesive Products Company 1165 Arbor Drive Romeoville, IL 60446 (800) 621•0220 www.chapco-adhesive.com
CHAPCO Safe-Set 69, 75, and 90	Solvent-free, nonflammable, freeze/thaw stable, and almost odor-free ceramic floor tile adhesives.	Same
Coronado Supreme Collection	Zero-VOC latex paint; dries to highly washable surface.	Coronado Paint Co. 308 Old Country Road Edgewater, FL 32132 (800) 883•4193, (904) 428•6461
Cross-Tuff	Cross-laminated polyethylene air barrier and under-slab radon barrier.	Manufactured Plastics and Distribution, Inc. 10367 W. Centennial Road Littleton, CO 80127 (303) 972•0123, (719) 488•2143 www.mpdplastics.com

Product	Description	Manufacturer/Distributor
DLW Linoleums	Manufactured from all natural products (linseed oil, cork, wood flour, resin binders, gum, and pigments) with natural jute backing.	Armstrong World Industries P.O. Box 3001 Lancaster, PA 17604 (717) 397·0611
Dodge-Regupol, Inc.	Cork tile available unfinished, waxed, or with polyurethane matt or gloss finishes.	Dodge-Regupol, Inc. P.O. Box 989 Lancaster, PA 17608-0989 (800) 322·1923, (717) 295·3400 www.regupol.com
Durock	A rigid cementitious substrate that is suitable for use in wet areas.	U.S. Gypsum 14643 Dallas Parkway, Suite 575, LB#78 Dallas, TX 75240 (800) 527·5193 (Southwest), (800) 274·9778 (East)
EarthTech Paints and Finishes	Low-odor, zero-VOC paints for interior and exterior use. Low-VOC gloss and satin interior and exterior finishes.	EarthTech Paints and Finishes P.O. Box 1325 Arvada, CO 80001 (303) 465·1537 www.earthtechinc.com
Eco Design/Natural Choice	Source for cork floors and other natural building products.	Eco Design/Nautral Choice 1365 Rufina Circle Santa Fe, NM 87505 (800) 621·2591, (505) 438·3448 www.bioshieldpaint.com
Ecological/Canary Paints	Water-based, resin terpolymer paint; odorless, formaldehyde-free. Also carries Canary line of paints, which are biocide- and fungicide-free.	Innovative Formulations 1810 South 6th Avenue Tucson, AZ 85713 (800) 346·7265, (520) 628·1553 www.mirrorseal.com
Endurance II	Synthetic jute pad; odorless, hypoallergenic.	Distributed through: Statements 1441 Paseo de Peralta Santa Fe, NM 87501 (505) 988·4440
Envirobond #801 and #901	Water-based organic mastic; VOC compliant.	W.F. Taylor Company, Inc. 11545 Pacific Avenue Fontana, CA 92337 (800) 397·4583, (909) 360·6677 www.wftaylor.com
Enviro-Cote	Zero-VOC paint in flat, satin, or semi-gloss finish.	Kelly-Moore Paint Co. 1015 Commercial Street San Carlos, CA 94070 (888) 677·2468 www.kellymoore.com
Enviro Safe Paints	No-fungicide, low-biocide paints mixed to order. Low-toxic, naturally derived preservative. Has only one-year shelf life.	Chem Safe P.O. Box 33023 San Antonio, TX 78265 (210) 657·5321 www.environproducts.com
Envirotec Health Guard Adhesives and Seaming Tapes	A line of zero-VOC, solvent-free adhesives and seaming tapes without alcohol, glycol, ammonia, or carcinogens. Call distributor to find best product for a particular installation.	W.F. Taylor Company, Inc. 11545 Pacific Avenue Fontana, CA 92337 (800) 397·4583, (909) 360·6677 www.wftaylor.com
Forbo Industries	Natural linoleum and cork flooring.	Forbo Industries P.O. Box 667 Hazelton, PA 18201 (800) 233·0475, (570) 459-0771, (800) 842·7839 www.forbo-industries.com

Product	Description	Manufacturer/Distributor
Genesis Odor Free Paint	Zero-VOC vinyl acrylic paints.	Duron Paints 10406 Tucker Street Beltsville, MD 20705 (800) 723•8766 www.duron.com
Green Seal	A national, independent, nonprofit, environmental labeling and consumer education organization. Issues a seal of approval to consumer products that meet rigorous environmental standards.	Green Seal 1001 Connecticut Avenue NW, Suite 827 Washington, DC 20036-5525 (202) 872•6400 www.greenseal.org
Hardibacker Board	Cementitious tile backer board for use in moist/wet applications.	James Hardie Building Company 26300 La Alameda, Suite 250 Mission Viejo, CA 92691 (800) 426•4051, (909) 356•6300, (949) 348•1800; www.jameshardie.com
Hartex Carpet Cushion	Odorless, synthetic jute underpadding for carpet.	Leggett & Platt 1100 S. McKinney Street Mexia, TX 76667 (800) 880•6092, (254) 562•2814
HealthSpec	Low-odor, vinyl acrylic, interior latex paint. More durable but a bit more odorous than other commercially available low-/no-odor paints.	The Sherwin Williams Company 101 Prospect Avenue NW Cleveland, OH 44115 (800) 524•5979, (216) 566•2902 www.sherwin-williams.com Sold at Sherwin Williams paint stores throughout the country.
Hendricksen Naturlich	Supplier of cork, natural linoleum, wool carpeting, other natural fiber carpeting, felt underpads, and adhesives.	Hendricksen Naturlich P.O. Box 1677 Sebastopol, CA 95473 (707) 824•0914 www.naturalhomeproducts.com
Hydrocote Danish Oil Finish	Nontoxic penetrating oil. One-step stain and seal in nine wood tones.	The Hydrocote Company, Inc. 61 Berry Street Somerset, NJ 08873 (800) 229•4937 www.hydrocote.com
Hydroshield Plus	Clear coat available in gloss or satin sheen. Water-based polyurethane giving impact and weather resistance for interior or exterior.	Same
Junckers	A solid wood, prefinished, engineered flooring system.	Junckers Hardwood, Inc. 4920 East Landon Drive Anaheim, CA 92807 (800) 878•9663, (714) 777•6430 www.junckershardwood.com
Kahrs	A solid wood, prefinished, engineered floor system.	Kahrs Intenational 951 Mariners Island, Suite 630 San Mateo, CA 94404 (650) 341•8400 www.kahrs.com
Laticrete Additive-Free Thinset	For use over concrete, cement backer board, or wire-reinforced mud. Contains Portland cement and sand.	Laticrete 1 Laticrete Park North Bethany, CT 06524-3498 (203) 393•0010 www.laticrete.com
Lifemaster 2000	Replaces Spred 2000, formerly by Glidden. Has better performance, zero VOC and is solvent-free.	ICI Dulux Paints 925 Euclid Avenue Cleveland, OH 44115 (800) 984•5444 www.iciduluxpaints.com

Product	Description	Manufacturer/Distributor
Living Source	Source of nontoxic carpets and adhesives.	For consultation, contact: Living Source P.O. Box 20155 Waco, TX 76702 (800) 662·8787, (254) 776·4878 www.livingsource.com
Livos Ardvos Wood Oil	Penetrating oil primer and finish for interior hardwoods. May be topcoated with Livos Bilo Floor Wax. This and the following four items are a line of plant chemistry products made from plant and mineral derivatives. As with many natural products, some chemically sensitive individuals may not tolerate turpenes, oils, or citrus-based and other aromatic components found in these formulations.	Building for Health—Materials Center P.O. Box 113 Carbondale, CO 81623 (970) 963·0437, (800) 292·4838 (Orders only) www.buildingforhealth.com
Livos Bilo Floor Wax	A clear, mar-resistant finish for wood, stone, terra cotta, and linoleum.	Same
Livos Glievo Liquid Wax	Clean, apply, and buff furniture and floor wax. We have also applied this product to plastered walls.	Same
Livos Kaldet Stain	A stain and finish oil in 12 colors for interior and exterior surfaces made of wood, clay, or stone.	Same
Livos Meldos Hard Oil	A penetrating oil sealer and finish for interior absorbent surfaces made of wood, cork, porous stone, terra cotta tiles, and brick.	Same
Livos Naturals	Low-toxic paints, all ingredients listed on label, many organically grown, water- and oil-based products available.	Same
Mapei 2-1/2 to 1	An additive-free grout for joints larger than 3/8".	Mapei, Inc. 1501 Wall Street Garland, TX 75041 (800) 992·6273
Medex	Formaldehyde-free, exterior grade, medium-density fiberboard.	Medite Corporation P.O. Box 4040 Medford, OR 97501 (800) 676·3339, (916) 772·3422, (541) 773·2522 www.sierrapine.com
Medite 11	Formaldehyde-free, interior grade, medium-density fiberboard.	Same
Milk Paint	Made from milk protein, lime, earth pigments, and clay, this petrochemical-free, biodegradeable, nontoxic paint is odorless when dry. Comes in 16 colors. Sold in powder form.	Old-Fashioned Milk Paint Company 436 Main Street Groton, MA 01450 (978) 448·6336 www.milkpaint.com
Miller LBNF	The LBNF line of paints has low biocide content and no fungicides. Solvent-free. Flat, satin, and semi-gloss.	Miller Paint Company 317 SE Grand Avenue Portland, OR 97214 (800) 852·3254, (503) 233·4491 www.millerpaint.com
Murco GF1000	Flat wall paint. Odorless when dry. Preservatives are entombed in dry paint. No slow-releasing compounds or airborne fungicides.	Murco Wall Products 2032 North Commerce Fort Worth, TX 76117 (800) 446·7124, (817) 626·1987 www.murcowall.com
Murco LE1000	Higher gloss paint, formulated as above, for use where latex enamels are recommended.	Same
Murco M-100 Hi-Po	Powdered all-purpose joint cement, a texture compound formulated with inert fillers and natural binders only. No preservatives.	Same

Product	Description	Manufacturer/Distributor
Natural Cork Co.	Natural cork flooring in a variety of colors and finishes.	Natural Cork Co Ltd. 1710 North Leg Court Augusta, GA 30909 (800) 404·2675 www.naturalcork.com
Naturel Cleaner and Sealer	Nontoxic, biodegradable, water-soluble flakes that clean, protect, and finish stone surfaces.	Available from Building for Health—Materials Center P.O. Box 113 Carbondale, CO 81623 (970) 963·0437, (800) 292·4838 (Orders only) www.buildingforhealth.com
Okon Seal & Finish	A satin or gloss clear sealer that can be used to seal plaster.	Okon, Inc. 4725 Leyden Street, Unit A Denver, CO 80216 (800) 237·0565, (303) 377·7800 www.okoninc.com
Old Growth Aging and Staining Solutions for Wood	Wood is treated with a nontoxic mineral compound and then with a nontoxic catalyst that binds the natural mineral colors to cellulose, creating an aged patina. It imparts antimicrobial and antifungal properties to the wood, while the pigments provide UV protection.	Old Growth Co. P.O. Box 1371 Santa Fe, NM 87504-1371 (505) 983·6877 www.olgrowth.com
OS/Color Hard Wax/Oil	A satin-matt oil/wax finish for interior wood floor and cork. Water repellant, easy to refinish. Odorous until dry.	Environmental Home Center 1724–4th Avenue South Seattle, WA 98134 (800) 281·9785, (206) 682·7332 www.enviresource.com
OS/Color One Coat Only	Twelve different stain colors in a base of vegetable oils. Interior/exterior use. No preservatives or biocides.	Same
Pace Crystal Shield	Replaces lacquers, varathanes, and urethanes. Clear seal strong enough for hardwood floors. Can be used as sealant to block formaldehyde and other chemical emissions from manufactured wood products. Can be used to seal tile flooring.	Pace Chem Industries 3050 Westwood Drive, B10 Las Vegas, NV 89109 (800) 350·2912, (702) 369·1424 www.pacechemusa.com
PermaBase	A rigid cementitious substrate that is suitable for use in wet areas.	Unifix, Inc. National Gypsum Co./Gold Bond 2001 Rexford Road Charlotte, NC 28211 (800) 628·4662, (704) 365·7300 www.national-gypsum.com
Plyboo	Bamboo flooring and accessories.	Smith & Fong Company 601 Grandview Drive South San Francisco, CA 94080 (650) 872·1184 www.plyboo.com
Pristine Eco Spec	Commercially available acrylic latex paint without VOCs. Available in several finishes.	Benjamin Moore & Company 51 Chestnut Ridge Road Montvale, NJ 07645 (800) 344·0400, (201) 573·9600 www.benjaminmoore.com
Rappgo	Prefinished engineered wood flooring system from Sweden with very low emissions.	Distributed in the U.S. by: Plaza Hardwood, Inc. 219 West Manhattan Avenue Santa Fe NM 87501 (800) 662·6306, (505) 992·3260 www.plzfloor.com

Product	Description	Manufacturer/Distributor
Sodium Silicate	Clear sealer for concrete floors. Widely distributed in hardware and ceramic supply stores.	Ashland Chemical, Inc. 5200 Blazer Parkway Dublin, OH 43017 (800) 258•0711, (614) 889•3333 www.gotoashland.com
Spectra-Tone Paints	Zero-VOC, solvent-free, latex paint; cost-competitive with standard quality latex.	Spectra-Tone Paint Corporation 1595 East San Bernardino Avenue San Bernardino, CA 92408-2946 (800) 272•4687, (909) 478•3485 www.spectra-tone.com
Summitville-700 SummitChromes	Sanded grout without polymer additives, available in 32 colors.	Summitville Tiles, Inc. Summitville, OH 43962 (330) 223•1511 www.summitville.com
TimberGrass	Bamboo flooring and accessories.	TimberGrass LLC 9790 NE Murden Cove Drive Bainbridge Island, WA 98110 (800) 929•6333, (206) 842•9477 www.timbergrass.com
Tu-Tuf 3	High-density, cross-laminated polyethylene, puncture-resistant air barrier.	Stocote Products, Inc. Drawer 310 Richmond, IL 60071 (800) 435•2621, (262) 279•6000
Ultra Touch	29 oz. carpet cushion of recycled fibers.	Bonded Logic 411 East Ray Road Chandler, AZ 85225 (480) 812•9114 www.bondedlogic.com
Zip Guard Environmental Water Base Urethane	Clear finish for interior woodwork.	Star Bronze Co., Inc. P.O. Box 2206 Alliance, OH 44601 (800) 321•9870, (330) 823•1550 www.starbronze.com

Division 10: Specialties

Integrated Pest Management and New Construction

All creatures have their rightful place in nature. For most, this place is not within the walls of human habitations. Hence the need for humans to exercise pest control. While many pest control companies advocate regular prophylactic spraying of homes with toxic chemicals, this approach can have devastating consequences for the health of all living beings, including the occupants of the home. Although pests are effectively killed, the underlying structural problems that created inviting conditions for them have not been addressed, so they eventually return.

Integrated pest management (IPM) offers a holistic approach to controlling pests. It differs from standard pest management in that it emphasizes prevention and the least toxic methods of pest control. The goal is to work effectively with nature to alter conditions without creating harm to the environment. IPM precepts can be summarized as follows:

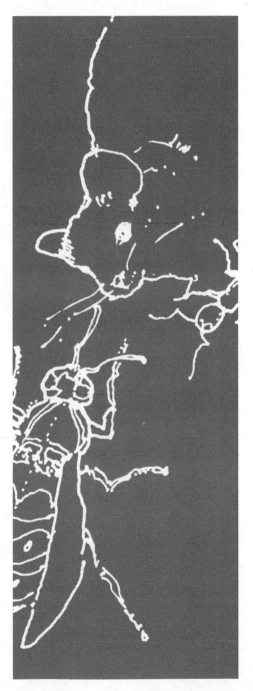

- Accurate identification or "naming" of a pest is necessary so that its modus operandi may be understood and incorporated into a pest management plan.
- Careful consideration is given as to whether any action is required at all. "Entomophobia" is rampant in our culture. For many, the first reaction upon seeing an insect is to kill it. Pesticide commercials persuade us that panic and lightning-speed action are necessary. In contrast, IPM encourages an attitude of tolerance to creatures that do no harm. It also encourages rational determination as to when intervention will be necessary.
- If a pest must be eliminated, the first step is to see if its current access to nourishment and habitat can be limited. In the case of ants, for example, this might mean cleaning up crumbs from the floor and counters, and caulking the cracks.
- If a pest must be trapped or killed, the most environmentally benign methods are considered first. Least toxic chemicals are employed as a last resort.
- If a chemical must be used, then toxicity, risk, and exposure must be carefully evaluated. (The Northwest Coalition for Alternatives to Pesticides (NCAP) produces fact sheets on the various pesticides—see the Further Reading and Resources list at the end of this Division.)

• Careful observation and record keeping are an essential part of an integrated pest management program.

In new home construction you have the opportunity and responsibility to prevent infestations before they occur. An integrated approach to pest management in new construction would include the following items.

• Identification of potential pests found in the building site area.
• Research on identified pests, including eating habits, reproductive cycles, habitat, and common routes of entry into the home.
• Use of strategies in home construction that will create inhospitable and inaccessible conditions for pests.

In general, a well-constructed home will also be pest resistant, incorporating the following features:

• Weathertightness
• Appropriate grading and drainage
• Provisions for the prevention of excess moisture buildup from within, including extraction fans and windows that allow cross ventilation
• Dry wood without rot or infestation used in construction
• Exterior wood appropriately treated for prevailing climatic conditions
• Screening on all openings such as basement and soffit vents
• Removal of all ground cover, leaves, chip and wood piles, and other potential insect habitats from around the building

Throughout the book we have specified techniques for preventing pest infestations where appropriate. If you are building in an area with a particularly difficult pest problem, then you may need to take measures above and beyond the scope of this book. For example, if your home is next to a shipyard or close to a row of poorly constructed grain elevators, then you may wish to incorporate more rat control techniques into your construction than would generally be specified. We heartily recommend *Common Sense Pest Control* by Olkowski, et al., as a comprehensive guide to specific pest problems. *Chart 10.1* provides an overview of major household pests and construction techniques that discourage them.

Chart 10.1: Common Pests and Management Strategies

Pest	Types of damage	Modus operandi	Recommendations
Termites (subterranean)	• Structural damage • Tunnels created in wood	• Require moist conditions • Must be able to get from the soil into wood structure via earthen tubes; these insects do not live in wood	• Control moisture • Seal wood from ground contact • Use termite shielding, sand barriers, and/or termite-resistant sill plates
Termites (drywood)	• Structural damage • Tunnels created in wood	• Can access house through walls • Live in wood	• Tight construction • Caulked joints • Boric acid in framing
Rats	• Unaesthetic • Carry disease • Destroy food supply • Breed quickly	• Require hole $1/2$" wide to enter	• Screen all points of entry including openings along pipes and wires • Make home weathertight • Ground floors should be elevated 18" above ground • Subterranean concrete floors should be at least 2" thick • Use wire mesh under wood floors • Use noncombustible cement stops between floor joists
Mice	• Chew through electrical wires causing fire hazard • Transmit pathogens • Breed quickly	• Require dime-size openings • Feed on dry foods, grains, clothing, paper • Usually inhabit buildings when outdoor climatic conditions become severe	• Seal all holes and crevices, especially where pipes and wires protrude through surfaces
Ants (carpenter)	• Create nests inside walls and ceilings, under siding, and where wood and soil are in contact near foundations • Infest both hard and softwood	• Require wood with high moisture content (minimum 15%)	• Use kiln- or air-dried lumber and keep it dry • Prevent structural wood and earth from coming into contact with each other • Allow for proper ventilation of damp areas

Prescriptions for a Healthy House

Pest	Types of damage	Modus operandi	Recommendations
Bees (carpenter)	• Chew on wood • Burrow into structural members and exposed wood elements	• Enjoy untreated exposed wood (especially softwoods)	• Paint or varnish exposed wood (sills, trim, etc.) • Fill in holes and indentations in wood
Beetles (wood-boring)	• Bore through wood	• Require moisture content in wood to be 10 to 20%	• Prevent moisture changes and temperature fluctuations • Allow for good ventilation in attic spaces • Keep roof frame and sheathing dry • Use air- or kiln-dried lumber • Seal wood
Cockroaches	• Invade food storage areas such as kitchens and cupboards • Can carry disease-causing organisms	• Most species prefer warm, moist areas	• Avoid moisture and decayed organic buildup around home • Use boric acid in framing in areas prone to infestation • Use screens on vents and windows
Fungi (wood decay)	• Attacks and weakens wood leaving it susceptible to invasion by wood-boring and -eating insects	• Grows best at temperatures between 50 and 95 degrees F • Requires a minimum of 20% moisture	• Allow for proper roof insulation and ventilation to prevent condensation • Seal wood joints at corners, edges, and intersections • Prevent moisture accumulation near pipes, vents, and ducts • Do not use wood containing mold in construction • Seal all wood exposed to the elements • Control moisture buildup through proper ventilation • Use building products and procedures that allow moisture vapor to escape rather than being trapped

Further Reading and Resources

Books

Moses, Marion. *Designer Poisons: How to Protect Your Health and Home from Toxic Pesticides*. San Francisco, CA: Pesticide Education Center, 1995. A sobering expose about specific pesticides and the chronic health effects that can result from their use; provides useful information on safer alternatives.

Olkowski, William, Sheila Daar, and Helga Olkowski. *Common Sense Pest Control: Least-Toxic Solutions for Your Home, Garden, Pets, and Community*. Newtown, CT: Taunton Press, 1991. Comprehensive, well-documented information on integrated pest management and least-toxic pest control for all kinds of pests.

Schultz, Warren. *The Chemical-Free Lawn: The Newest Varieties and Techniques to Grow Lush, Hardy Grass*. Rodale Press, 1989. Techniques for growing lush and hardy grass without using pesticides, herbicides, or chemical fertilizers.

Organizations

Biointegral Resource Center (BIRC), P.O. Box 7414, Berkeley, CA 94707. Phone: (510) 524•2567. Useful source of pesticide information and alternative pest treatments.

National Coalition Against Misuse of Pesticides, 701 E Street SE, Suite 200, Washington, DC 20003. Phone: (202) 543•5450; Internet: info@beyond pesticides.org. Provides useful information about pesticides and nontoxic alternatives.

Northwest Coalition for Alternatives to Pesticides (NCAP), P.O. Box 1393, Eugene, OR 97440. Phone: (541) 344•5044. Provides a comprehensive information service on the hazards of pesticides and alternatives to their use. The NCAP maintains an extensive library of over 8,000 articles, government documents, videos, and other reference materials, and offers information packets, fact sheets, and the quarterly *Journal of Pesticide Reform*.

Product

Spotcheck Pesticide Testing Kit. Instant pesticide-checking kit based on technology developed for U.S. military applications. Ships with supplies to carry out four tests of soil, water, food, or surfaces. Pesticides that the user can test for include Sevin, Dursban, Diazinon, Malathion, and Parathion. Available through The Cutting Edge Catalog, P.O. Box 5034, Southhampton, NY 11969. Phone: (800) 497•9516.

Division 11: Equipment

Water Treatment Equipment

Water Purification in Standard Construction

Poor indoor air quality is not the only form of pollution that affects human health. The water supply has also become increasingly polluted. Whether you are on a well or a municipal water system, you may be receiving water that is unfit to drink, as indicated by the following interesting facts.

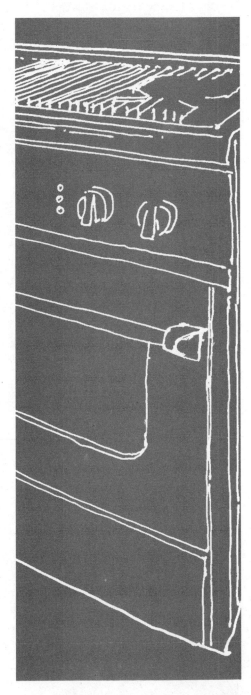

- Of the over 2,000 contaminants found in potable water, the U.S. Environmental Protection Agency (EPA) has established standards for only 82.[1]
- Municipal water treatment is primarily set up for disinfection rather than water purification. Only 50 of the more than 60,000 water treatment facilities in the United States have modern equipment that can effectively remove toxic chemicals.[2]
- Over half of community water systems fail to comply with federal testing requirements.[3]
- When an adult takes a 15-minute bath in water that contains chlorine or other VOCs, as many toxins will enter that person's body as would be ingested by drinking two gallons of the same water. The absorption levels are even higher in children.[4]
- In the United States alone, 42 million people are drinking water contaminated at dangerously high levels.[5]
- One in six people drinks water containing excessive amounts of lead, which can impair cognitive function, especially in children.[6]
- Over the past two decades, reports containing warnings about water pollution have been issued by the American Chemical Society, the National Academy of Science, the Natural Resources Defense Council, the American Petroleum Institute, and the Office of Technology Assessment.[7]

If you are receiving municipal water, laws have been passed to help determine what is in your water and how best to protect your household. The Safe Drinking

Water Act of 1974, as amended in 1996, requires public water utilities to reveal to the public the following facts.

+ Where your water comes from
+ How the water is treated
+ The nature of water quality tests, or what the water is tested for
+ How people are notified when violations occur
+ A history of the utility's water problems

Since 1998 the EPA has required water suppliers to provide customers with annual drinking water quality reports, called "Consumer Confidence Reports," which include levels of contaminants found in the water and phone numbers for additional information. You can obtain this information by contacting your local water utility company. Remember, however, that the water leaving the treatment plant may be further contaminated by the time it reaches your tap. During its journey, treated water can pick up lead from solder and copper from metal pipes. Pipes made of PVC, the most common type of new piping, release chlorinated compounds and other chemicals into the water. Pipes that have breaks can suck in mud and silt.

Municipally treated water is usually low in biological contaminants, but it is not well-screened for industrial and hazardous waste (see the list of common contaminants in *Chart 11.1*). The chlorine with which almost all municipal water has been treated often reacts with naturally occurring organic compounds, creating potentially harmful organochlorides and trihaliomethanes. Water experts in your area will know the range of contaminants found in your municipal system and the best strategies for eliminating them.

In contrast, well water must be tested on a case by case basis. Two wells side by side can have very different water quality. Well water is free of added chlorine, but is consequently more susceptible to biological contamination. Testing for all possible contaminants is not financially feasible or necessary. Local experts will be able to advise you as to which tests are most appropriate in your area.

Water purification is not standard in home construction, and unless you specify that water testing and purification are to be done, they will not be included. Although water purification is usually considered an "extra," whole-house systems are best planned for and installed at the time of construction.

Chart 11.1: Common Contaminants Found in Water Supplies

Contaminant	Health effects*	Cause	Solution	Comments
Biological contaminants				
Bacteria and viruses	Flu-like symptoms, muscle aches, fatigue	Naturally occurring	Ultraviolet sterilization, ozonation, pasteurization, reverse osmosis (R/O) with TFC (thin film composite) membrane will remove small amounts of bacteria from well water	Not all solutions are equally effective for all biological contaminants. Consult a water treatment specialist.
Parasites	Gastrointestinal upset, diarrhea	Naturally occurring	Same	Same
Amoebae	Nausea, vomiting, dysentery	Naturally occurring	Same	Same
Molds		Naturally occurring	Same	Same
Algae		Naturally occurring	Same	Same
Organic contaminants				
Petroleum hydrocarbons	Cancer	Leaks from service stations, oil refineries, gasoline spills	Activated carbon block removes many organic compounds. KDF (kinetic degradation fluxation) filters are only effective for the removal of free chlorine	Carbon filters must be changed regularly to be effective.
Benzene	Immune-system sensitizer	By-product of gasoline use	Same	Same
Chlorobenzene	Cancer		Same	Same
Pesticides	Cancer, neurotoxicity	Agricultural runoff	Same	Same
Chlorinated compounds	Cancer, respiratory problems, chronic skin irritation	By-product of chlorination, released from PVC pipe	Same	Same
Trihalomethanes	Cancer	By-products of chlorination	Aeration or use of proprietary carbon blend	Same

Prescriptions for a Healthy House

Contaminant	Health effects*	Cause	Solution	Comments
Inorganic contaminants				
Nitrates	Break down to form carcinogens. Interfere with ability of red blood cells to transfer oxygen.	Nitrogen combines with soil bacteria to form naturally occurring nitrates. Nitrates from agricultural fertilizers leach into ground water. In non-farming areas, septic systems and cesspools are the most common sources of nitrates.	Ion exchange, R/O, distillation	Particularly dangerous to infants. Has been linked to miscarriage. The presence of nitrates can be an indicator of other contaminants.
Arsenic	Poison, carcinogen, can cause diabetes and cardiovascular disease.	Natural occurrence, pesticides, industrial pollutants.	R/O, distillation, anion-exchange carbon.	New EPA regulations have recently created stricter standards.
Asbestos		Asbestos-reinforced supply pipe.	R/O, distillation, carbon block.	Your utility company will know if asbestos-reinforced supply pipe is used in your area.
Heavy metals (cadmium, chromium, selenium, mercury, lead, barium, aluminum, fluoride)	Gastrointestinal cancer. Health effects are specific to metal and include: kidney damage, cancer, impairment of nervous system, behavioral disorders, lowering of IQ in children, Alzheimer's disease.	Naturally occurring, plumbing pipes and solder, automobile exhaust, industrial waste, fertilizers, pesticides, brass fixtures, older water coolers.	R/O, carbon block, distillation, resins formulated to remove specific metals. KDF can be effective if Total Dissolved Solids in water are high and the pH is in correct range.	Carbon block is only effective when filter is relatively unclogged and water is continually tested. If concentrations are high enough, there may be no filtration system that will produce safe, potable water.
Radon gas	Lung cancer, immune dysfunction	Radioactive gases permeate groundwater and become airborne through household use	Specially designed activated-carbon filters for levels below 5,000 pCi/L; aeration for levels above 5,000 pCi/L	
Radium and uranium	Bone cancer, leukemia, thyroid cancer	Water dissolving radio-logicals in soil or rock	Specialized R/O filters, ion exchanger	Very common in areas with granite

Types of Water Purification Systems

We recommend a whole-house water purification system as an essential feature of the healthy home for most locations. Choosing the proper system will depend on several factors including location, budget, water use, and taste preference (see *Chart 11.2* for a summary of different systems). No single filtration medium can remove all contaminants from all water. Because water quality and individual needs vary, no single combination of systems will provide a universal solution.

Choosing a system can be a complex and confusing process. The average homeowner typically does not know the right questions to ask in order to get accurate information. Water filtration systems have become popular network market items. Many people selling the filter devices are not much more knowledgeable about the range of needs and possibilities than potential clients. We recommend that you consult with an individual who possesses the following credentials:

- A broad-based, longstanding experience with water quality in your area
- A wide variety of equipment from several manufacturers
- Ability to provide you with several options at various prices
- Ability to explain the pros and cons of each system

Chart 11.2: Summary of Water Filtration Methods

Type of system	How it works	What's eliminated	What's not eliminated	Comments
Carbon filters:				
There are over 500 varieties of carbon filters. The two most commonly used filters in water purification are described here. Generally, the carbon filter works like a honeycomb, with acres of surface area that absorb contaminants. These filters are not bacteriostatic and will become contaminated with use. Inexpensive sediment prefilters will extend their life. Inexpensive chlorine tests can indicate when to change the filter if it's used with chlorinated water. These filters can become a source of pollution if not changed often enough. Locate the tank away from inhabited areas when it is used to filter radon.				
GAC (granulated activated carbon)	Carbon is steam-treated so that the surface becomes pitted, thereby increasing surface area and adsorption capacity	Trihalomethanes, dissolved gases including chlorines, most pesticides, many chemical pollutants, radon gas	Heavy metals, sediment, fluoride, viruses and bacteriologicals, dissolved solids, particulates including radioactive particulate matter	Requires that water have sufficient contact time with filter. As GAC can breed bacteriologicals, it is most effective when used with treated municipal water.
Carbon block	Powdered carbon is glued together to form a matrix structure that adsorbs contaminants	As above for GAC, particulate matter, can be used for heavy metal under some limited conditions	Fluoride, nitrates, viruses, and bacteriologicals	Considered more effective than GAC if water conditions are within certain parameters. Will only remove heavy metals for a limited time period. Periodic testing is essential. Not recommended for most heavy metal removal. Glue content is a concern. Whole house or point source available. Limited gallonage.
Reverse Osmosis:				
Most often comes with sediment prefilter and carbon postfilter. Plastic bodies can be a problem for individuals with petrochemical sensitivities.				
City membrane CTA (cellulose triacetate)	Water is forced under pressure through a fine membrane that screens out dissolved solids	Dissolved solids (60 to 90%), heavy metals, asbestos, radioactive particles, some bacteria	Dissolved gases, some biological contaminants, sediment	Most suitable for pretreated municipal water in which biological contaminants are

Type of system	How it works	What's eliminated	What's not eliminated	Comments
City membrane CTA (cellulose triacetate) – *cont.*				already low. Filter requires chlorinated water supply to prevent bacteriological decay.
Well membrane TFC (thin film composite)	Same as above	Dissolved solids (60 to 98%), heavy metals, asbestos, radioactive particles, some bacteria, limited amount of biological contaminants	Dissolved gases, sediment	Cannot be used with chlorinated supply water unless prefiltered with carbon.

Sterilization:

Type of system	How it works	What's eliminated	What's not eliminated	Comments
Ultraviolet purification	Ultraviolet ray penetrates membrane of microbe and inactivates it	Biological contaminants	Dissolved gases, sediment	Does not provide residual disinfection. Sediments, hardness, iron, manganese, or turbidity will make system ineffective.
Oxidation with ozone, hydrogen peroxide, chlorine, or injected air	Oxidation "burns" contaminants	Clarifies, deodorizes, precipitates metals, oxidizes, eliminates bacteria, viruses, and organic matter	VOC's, pesticides, chlorine; does not remove anything from water	Use of chlorine as oxidizing agent not recommended from ecological and health standpoints.

Others:

Type of system	How it works	What's eliminated	What's not eliminated	Comments
KDF (kinetic degradation fluxation)	Chemical transformation of contaminants as they pass through KDF, which disrupts metabolic function of bacteria	Controls bacterial growth; removes some heavy metals, chlorine, biological contaminants	Trihaliomethanes, bacteria	Very effective when used as prefilter, followed by carbon filter and then reverse osmosis. Does not work well in all pH conditions, requires 150 ppm of Total Dissolved Solids in order to be effective. Suitable for water with very low bacteriological count. Is bacteriostatic but not a bacteriocide. Works best

Prescriptions for a Healthy House

Type of system	How it works	What's eliminated	What's not eliminated	Comments
KDF – *cont.*				on hot water. Testing after installation advised.
Shower head filters	Small filter/shower heads screw into existing plumbing	Chlorine	Radiologicals, pesticides, gasoline, bacteriologicals; does not remove trihaliomethanes, pesticides or VOC's due to lack of contact time	Very inexpensive. Does not require plumber to install.
Distillation	Water is turned to vapor, condensed, and then collected	Dissolved solids, microorganisms, nitrates, heavy metals, sediment, radioactive particulate matter	VOCs, dissolved gases including chlorine	Effective when used with carbon postfilter. High maintenance, low production. Flat taste. Metal-bodied distillers may add aluminum or other heavy metals to water. May leach necessary minerals from the body.
Sediment filters	Can be settlement tank where water is siphoned off top after particulate sinks; can be a filter medium	Particulate matter, sand, dirt	Only removes particles	Most often used as a prefilter for other systems. Back-flushing models are self-cleaning.
Aeration	Water is run over a series of plates where it is depressurized and blown with a fan so that gases and odors can escape. It is then repressurized.	Radon, odors, dissolved gases	Bacteria, solids, heavy metals	Aeration is EPA preferred method for radon removal. It is very expensive.

Water Conditioning

Water conditioners are used to improve water's color, corrosiveness, clarity, and hardness. They eliminate aesthetically undesirable substances from the water, such as calcium and magnesium, which precipitate on fixtures, laundry, hot-water heaters, dishwashers, shower stalls, sinks, and skin. Water conditioners can also be effective in removing certain metals, such as iron and low levels of manganese, both of which can cause stains. The conditioned water is often referred to as "soft water."

Water conditioners use a process of ion exchange, exchanging a calcium or magnesium ion for either sodium or potassium. Sodium has traditionally been the exchange regenerate. When sodium is used in a conditioning system, we strongly recommend using separate piping from the water supply entry point of the home to all potable water distribution points and hose bibs. The elevated levels of sodium that occur in water softened this way are not desirable for human or plant consumption. In fact, water softened with sodium contains levels high enough to be considered an environmental hazard, harmful to groundwater when the sodium eventually works its way back to the water table.

Potassium has more recently been introduced as a regenerate for water conditioning. It is a healthier and more ecologically sound choice. Potassium is essentially refined potash, and when returned to the groundwater it can serve as a fertilizer for many plants. Most people have a shortage of potassium in their diets. The small amount ingested daily from water conditioned with potassium is about equivalent to what you'd gain by eating half a banana, so potassium-conditioned water can actually be a positive addition to your diet.

Note: If your water is extremely hard, it might require potassium levels that are too high to be safely ingested, necessitating a split distribution system as described above for systems using sodium as a regenerate. For those who have a medical condition affecting electrolyte balance, blood pressure, or kidney function, we suggest you consult a physician before you consider purchasing a water-conditioning system. Potash, from which potassium is derived, can occasionally contain radioactive uranium. Potassium derived from a radioactive source is not acceptable in water systems.

Flow rate is affected by both the size and design of the water softener and must be appropriately specified on an individual basis. Water-conditioning systems can also be designed to remove sediment, chlorine, odor from hydrogen sulfide, and elevated levels of iron.

Case Study 11.1:

Water Purification: Bath water found to be culprit in copper toxicity case

F.W. is a 67-year-old woman who was seen by Dr. Elliott for a chronic vaginal discharge that persisted for five years. Several health care practitioners had previously evaluated her regarding this problem. Although her gynecologist was unable to find evidence of a yeast or bacterial infection, she was nevertheless placed on a variety of antibiotics, which seemed to exacerbate the problem.

During the interview, Dr. Elliott discovered that the patient's symptoms seemed to improve when she traveled. F.W. went on to disclose that a rash she had throughout her body also improved while she was away from home. She concluded that her symptoms were probably related to stress, although there were no obvious new stressors in her life that could have accounted for this peculiar reaction. When questioned about events that took place around the time of onset of her symptoms, the patient remembered that she had moved into a new home approximately five years earlier. Dr. Elliott suspected that the source of the patient's problem was the bath water, since water was the only substance in contact with her vagina.

A water sample was sent to a laboratory for analysis. The results showed extremely high copper levels. Upon further inquiry, it was discovered that many water samples from the same part of town were showing high copper levels. Apparently the carbon dioxide in the water created an environment acidic enough to dissolve the copper in the water supply piping.

The patient decided to install a whole-house water filtration system that could be customized to remove carbon dioxide in the household water. Within a few days after installation, her rash and vaginitis disappeared. Because of evidence of excess copper stored in her body, the patient underwent a program of heavy metal chelation and vitamin and mineral supplementation. She is currently doing well and is without complaints. In a follow-up visit, she revealed that the greenish ring that had been present on the bathroom fixtures had disappeared.

Discussion

While the need for filtering the household drinking water may be obvious, this case study illustrates that an unrecognized source of toxic exposure may be bath water. Because skin is a large surface area, it allows for significant absorption of substances into the body from bath water. We do not suggest that you avoid tub bathing, which can be both pleasurable and therapeutic. Instead, we recommend that your water be filtered at the point of entry into the house.

Filtration systems are most effective when they are customized to fit both the homeowner's personal needs as well as local water conditions. These conditions can vary greatly from one location to another. Whether or not you decide to install a whole-house water filtration system, we recommend that you have your water tested periodically.

Residential Equipment

Much has been written about the energy efficiency of appliances. Appliances account for as much as 30% of household energy usage. Thus, choosing wisely can greatly reduce energy consumption. Because many sources of information are available on appliance energy values, we have limited discussion in this book to health issues related to appliance selection. (See the *Further Reading and Resources* section at the end of this *Division* for books about reducing appliance energy consumption.)

Appliances and Magnetic Fields

All motorized equipment found in homes will generate magnetic fields when in operation. Some epidemiological studies have linked exposure to these magnetic fields with increased incidence of cancer, Alzheimer's disease, and miscarriage. Magnetic fields from properly wired appliances drop off very quickly in an exponential relationship to the distance you are standing from them. These fields can be easily measured with a small handheld instrument called a gaussmeter, which allows the user to determine the safe distance from an appliance.

The U.S. government has not yet set reasonable standards for safe exposure levels, nor has it taken a strong position regarding health effects of magnetic fields. However, various government documents state that if you are concerned, you can practice "prudent avoidance" of these fields. Recommended safe exposure limits set by U.S. experts range from 0.5 milligauss to 1,000 milligauss. The Swedish National Energy Administration has recommended that children should not be subjected to magnetic field levels greater than 3 milligauss. We suggest that "prudent avoidance" translates to avoiding prolonged exposure to fields greater than 1 milligauss.

In *Division 16* we include recommended specifications and information for designing and building a home in which magnetic fields transmitted by household wiring do not surpass 0.5 milligauss. You can follow the simple guidelines listed below to limit your exposure to magnetic fields from appliances.

- Design your home so that major appliances are located at a safe distance from sitting and sleeping areas. In doing so, remember that magnetic fields travel with ease through walls made of common building materials, and that areas located out of sight behind an appliance are also exposed. For example, placing a refrigerator back to back with a bed, even though they are separated by a wall, will expose the sleeping person continually to an elevated magnetic field.

- Duration of exposure may be a factor, as well as strength. A low-level exposure for long periods of time may be more harmful than brief high-level exposures. For this reason, pay particular attention to fields that may be generated around sleeping areas.
- We suggest that you buy and learn to use a gaussmeter. With this device you can determine low-field distances from all appliances. For more information on choosing and operating a gaussmeter, see *Division 16*.
- Check your home and appliances regularly with the gaussmeter to determine whether field levels have increased. Elevated fields can sometimes indicate that an appliance has developed dangerous ground faults or that it is about to fail. Early detection of these fields will also decrease the risk of fire or electrocution.

Appliances and Electric Fields

Whereas magnetic fields exist only when appliances are being used, electric fields are present as long as the appliance is plugged in. Unfortunately, few appliances are manufactured in a manner that results in low electric fields. It is possible to rewire appliances so that they operate with reduced electric fields, but this requires the services of an electrician familiar with electric field shielding. Electric fields from appliances are relatively easy to control by following the suggestions listed below.

- Keep appliances unplugged when they are not in use, especially in the bedroom. Not only will this eliminate the electric field, but it will also reduce the risk of fire. Although this practice is much more common in Europe, the American Association of Home Appliances and Underwriters Laboratories has also issued a warning stating that small appliances should be unplugged as a fire prevention measure.
- Avoid using extension cords around beds or areas where your family spends a lot of time. They tend to emit high electric fields when they are plugged in.
- Use a battery-operated or windup clock next to the bed.
- Wire your bedroom so that the circuitry can be conveniently shut off when you go to sleep, thus eliminating electric fields altogether. Refer to *Division 16* for details.

Appliance Selection

Microwave Ovens

Microwave ovens are high electromagnetic field (EMF) emitters. They are designed to heat food by creating enough microwave energy to vibrate molecules in the food until heat is produced. When they are in use, magnetic fields extend up to 12 feet. The actual microwaves produced during operation are supposed to be contained in the oven by internal shielding, but leaks can occur. If you decide to use a microwave oven, the following suggestions will make using it safer.

- Maintain a distance of 4 to 12 feet from the microwave oven while it is in use. This is especially important for children, who might enjoy watching the food as it is cooking.
- Have your appliance professionally checked for microwave leakage on an annual basis. You can check for yourself on a more frequent basis with a less precise do-it-yourself tester. (One is available through **Professional Equipment**, a mail-order catalog.) Any detected leakage is unacceptable. Microwave leakage standards in the United States are much less stringent than in some parts of Europe. Unfortunately, differences in the power supply prevent the use of European microwave ovens in North America.
- Do not use a microwave that appears to be malfunctioning. Signs of this include sparks flying, funny noises, fires, or the unit turning on or cycling when the door is open. If any of these occur, evacuate the area immediately. Do not take time to try to unplug the unit. Instead, shut off the circuit breaker to the microwave. If you do not know which one it is, shut them all off. Only then is it safe to return to the room to unplug the microwave oven.
- The shielding on a microwave is delicate. A very small amount of damage can cause a complete shielding failure. Even a paper towel stuck in the door is enough to cause the microwave shielding to fail.
- Do not microwave food in plastic containers. Chemicals from the plastic can leach into the food. Some of these chemicals are known to disrupt the endocrine system.

Trash Compactors

Trash compactors are now commonplace in new homes. They can be convenient, but they can also be difficult to clean. When choosing a trash compactor, examine it carefully to be sure you will be able to reach into it easily for cleaning. Verify that accidental liquid spills inside the unit will be contained and not run under or behind the unit. You may want to have the trash compactor installed in such a way that it can be easily removed for cleaning.

Some trash compactors come with a deodorizer chamber. With the exceptions of baking soda and zeolyte, most deodorizers contain phenols, formaldehyde, or paradichlorobenzene, all of which should be avoided.

Refrigerators and Freezers

There are many styles of refrigeration units available. The self-defrosting models have a drip pan located somewhere under the unit. Some units have drip pans located in the back or mounted internally where they are inaccessible. When purchasing a unit, make sure the drip pan is easily accessible from the front and has adequate clearance underneath for ease in cleaning. The pan should be cleaned monthly to prevent odors or the growth of microorganisms. It is also important to keep the cooling coils clean so that they do not become coated with dust. Not only will this improve your air quality, but the unit will not have to work as hard to stay cold, which, in turn, will save energy.

Cook Tops, Ovens, and Ranges

All electric cook tops, ovens, and ranges produce elevated magnetic fields. Surprisingly, it is frequently the built-in electric clock that is the largest source of fields, regardless of whether the equipment is gas or electric. Use a gaussmeter to determine the distance of the field.

The act of cooking generates significant amounts of indoor air pollution in the form of vapors and airborne particulate matter such as grease. In addition, food particles left on burners are incinerated and release combustion by-products.

Gas-fueled appliances are a significant source of indoor air pollution and can release carbon monoxide, carbon dioxide, nitrogen dioxide, nitrous oxides, and aldehydes into the air. In his book *Why Your House May Endanger Your Health*, Dr. Alfred Zamm describes how gas kitchen ranges have been the hidden culprit in many cases of "housewives' malaise." According to Zamm, "A gas oven operating at 350°F for one hour, because of the inevitable incomplete combustion, can cause kitchen air pollution, even with an exhaust fan in operation, comparable to a heavy Los Angeles smog. Without the fan, levels of carbon monoxide and nitrogen dioxide can zoom to three or more times that."

For chemically sensitive individuals, any combustion appliance may be undesirable, and we recommend electric over gas for choice of range/oven.

However, many cooks prefer to cook with gas because it allows for better timing and temperature control. If you choose a gas range, the following measures will help reduce the amount of pollution it emits.

- Choose an appliance with electronic ignition instead of pilot lights. Any model built in the United States after 1991 will be equipped with electronic ignition.
- Have flames adjusted to burn correctly. They should burn blue. A yellow flame indicates incomplete combustion and the subsequent production of carbon monoxide.
- Follow the guidelines for proper ventilation discussed below.

If your preference is to cook with gas, consider purchasing a gas-fired range top with an electric oven. It is not necessary or even desirable from a chef's standpoint for the oven to be a combustion appliance.

Various smooth cook-top surfaces are available, including magnetic induction and halogen units. Because they are much easier to clean than coiled elements, they produce less pollution caused by the burning of trapped food particles. These units should be tested with a gaussmeter to determine the extent of their magnetic fields while in operation.

Oven cleaning is another source of pollution generated in the kitchen. Continuous-cleaning ovens contain wall coatings that continuously offgas noxious fumes. Self-cleaning ovens produce polynuclear aromatic hydrocarbons, which are a source of air pollution. Most brand-name oven cleaners are toxic. The safest way to clean an oven is with baking soda and elbow grease. If baking soda is poured over the spill shortly after it occurs, it can easily be cleaned up after the oven has cooled.

Kitchen Ventilation

Because the kitchen generates significant indoor pollution, the ventilation of this room should be given special consideration above and beyond general home ventilation.

Range hoods must be vented to the outside. There are models available that simply circulate the air through a carbon filter and back into the room. These do not remove kitchen pollution sufficiently but, unfortunately, many kitchens come equipped with this type of unit because it is inexpensive and does not require a roof penetration.

We recommend the largest range hood available, with variable speed control so that you can adjust speed according to your requirements. Some models come equipped with remote fans that are quieter when operating. When ventilation fans are in operation, and especially when operating at higher speeds, it is important that makeup air be supplied. If a home is not equipped with a whole-house air supply system, then you should open a window to supply makeup air. If a clean source of air intake is not provided by design, the exhausting of air can create enough negative pressure that air will be sucked into the house through the path of least resistance. This path could be through a chimney flue for a furnace or water heater, causing dangerous backdrafting of air many times more polluted than that which it is replacing.

Laundry Appliances

Washers and dryers with porcelain-on-steel or stainless steel interiors are preferable to those with plastic interiors. Although gas dryers are more energy efficient than electric dryers, they cause the same pollution problems as gas ranges. By planning a laundry room with easy access to a drying yard, you can take advantage of the most energy efficient of all dryers: the sun.

Dryers should be vented directly to the outdoors. Some heat recovery devices are available that recirculate the hot air from the dryer back into the house. We do not recommend these because they do not sufficiently filter fine particles, and if a gas dryer is being used, combustion gases can be released into the indoor air instead of being vented outdoors.

Vacuum Cleaners

Conventional portable vacuum cleaners suck air through a filter bag and then pump the "cleaned" air back into the room. The air that is returned is only as clean as the filtering mechanism is efficient. In fact, conventional vacuuming can stir up dust and pollen to such an extent that the ambient air is more polluted with small particulate matter than it was before the cleaning. Several brands of HEPA vacuums are available and are far superior to conventional vacuum cleaners. Their "high efficiency particulate air filter" effectively traps microscopic particulate matter.

Water-filter vacuums were popular before the availability of HEPA vacuums. They can become a reservoir for mold and bacteria unless thoroughly dried after each use.

If you are building a new home, you have the opportunity to install a central vacuum system. Because the motor and dirt receptacles are located far from living

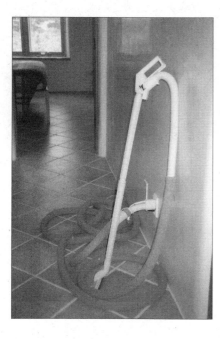

A central vacuum system is convenient and dust free.
Photo: Paula Baker-Laporte.

areas in a basement, garage, or utility room, central vacuums avoid the pollution problems associated with most portable models. Although more expensive than conventional portables, they cost only slightly more than a good HEPA or water-filter model. They are convenient and easy to operate. The hose is simply plugged into a wall receptacle and there is no machinery to lug around. We recommend central vacuums that exhaust air directly to the outdoors, as this will prevent any small particles missed by the collection bag being exhausted back into the home.

Endnotes

[1] EPA Safe Drinking Water Act, as amended in 1996.

[2] Debra Lynn Dadd, *Nontoxic, Natural, and Earthwise* (Tarcher/Perigee, 1990), 41.

[3] Ibid.

[4] Halina Szeinwald-Brown, PhD, Donna R. Bishop, MPH, and Carol A. Rowan, MSPH, "The Role of Skin Absorption as a Route of Exposure for Volatile Organic Compunds in Drinking Water," *American Journal of Public Health* Vol 74, No. 5.

[5] Maury M. Breecher and Shirley Lynde, *Healthy Homes in a Toxic World: Preventing, Identifying, and Eliminating Hidden Health Hazards in Your Home* (John Wiley & Sons, 1992), 121.

[6] Ibid., 142.

[7] Ibid.

Further Reading and Resources

Books

American Institute of Architecture, Denver Chapter. *Sustainable Design Resource Guide.* ADPSR Colorado, OEC Colorado, 1994. For information about energy efficiency and appliances.

Bower, Lynn Marie. *The Healthy Household.* Healthy House Institute, 1995. This book contains a useful section on household cleansers.

Conacher, Duff. *Troubled Waters on Tap: Organic Chemicals in Public Drinking Water Systems and the Failure of Regulation.* Center for Study of Responsive Law, January 1988.

Goldbeck, David. *The Smart Kitchen: How to Create a Comfortable, Safe, Energy-Efficient, and Environment Friendly Workplace.* Ceres Press, 1994.

Ingram, Colin. *The Drinking Water Book: A Complete Guide to Safe Drinking Water*. Ten Speed Press, 1991. A guide for safe drinking water.

Lono Kahuna Kapua A'o. *Don't Drink the Water: The Essential Guide to Our Contaminated Drinking Water and What You Can Do About It*. Kali Press, 1996.

Zamm, Alfred. *Why Your House May Endanger Your Health*. Simon and Schuster, 1980.

Resources

EPA Safe Drinking Water Hot Line. Phone: (800) 426·4791; Internet: www.epa.gov/safewater.

The Good Water Company, owned by Greg Friedman, 2778 Agua Fria, Building. C, Suite B, Santa Fe, NM 87501. Phone: (800) 471·9036, (505) 471·9036; Internet: www.goodwaterglobal.com. Water filtration and consultation.

Hague Quality Water International, 4343 South Hamilton Road, Groveport, OH 43125-9332. Phone: (614) 836·2115. Excellent whole-house water purification system.

National Testing Laboratories, Inc., 6555 Wilson Mills Road, Cleveland, OH 44143. Phone: (800) 458·3330; Internet: www.watercheck.com. Comprehensive water testing.

Nigra Enterprises, owned by Jim Nigra, 5699 Kanan Road, Agoura, CA 91301-3328. Phone: (818) 889·6877; Internet: www.nigra.org. Broker for high-quality air and water filtration, vacuum cleaners, paints, sealants, saunas, and heaters. Free consultation available.

Ozark Water Services and Air Quality, 114 Spring Street, Sulphur Springs, AR 72768. For air and water testing, and consultation regarding toxic gases, molds, asbestos, VOCs, pesticides, gas leaks, EMFs, and radon.

Professional Equipment, 90 Plant Avenue, Suite 3, Hauppauge, NY 11788-3813. Phone: (800) 334·9291; Internet: www.professionalequipment.com. Mail-order catalog with various testing devices.

Division 12: Furnishings

Introduction

Residential furniture is rarely included in the construction contract. The owner will typically select the furniture and have it installed on her or his own or with the guidance of an architect or interior designer. Nevertheless, we are including some guidelines and resources for the selection of healthful furniture because new furnishings can have a major impact on indoor air quality.

Most standard furniture is built like most standard housing. It is mass-produced with little or no thought about the health of the buyer. For those of you who have gone to great effort to create a healthy home, shopping wisely for healthy furnishings is the next logical step. Once again, you will find yourself in the role of a pioneer. Most furniture salespeople will not understand what you mean when you speak of healthy furniture. Yet formaldehyde and other chemical levels can soar when new furnishings are brought into the home. The furniture can continue to pollute the environment throughout its life.

As with the production of building materials, there are many broader environmental concerns pertaining to the manufacture of furniture. These include the use of endangered wood species, toxic waste produced at the manufacturing facility, factory workers' exposure to hazardous chemicals, wasteful packaging, and the exploitation of exporting countries. These factors are discussed in depth in other publications. We will concentrate on health concerns related to the homeowner.

Wood Furniture

Most newly constructed wood furniture is actually veneered wood attached to a core of particleboard or plywood. These manufactured sheetgoods are bound with urea-formaldehyde glues, which will offgas for many years. Even so-called solid wood pieces may contain hidden plywood or particleboard components in order to save on production costs. When selecting wood furnishings, keep the following recommendations in mind.

Interiors of Daryl Stanton Residence, owner of "Healthy Interiors," features solid wood antique furniture, custom made organic cotton and wool upholstered furniture and area rugs. Kitchen has solid wood cabinets and open shelving.
Architect: Baker-laporte Associates;
Builder: Econest Building Co.;
Photo: David Hoptman.

• Purchase solid wood furniture that does not make use of veneers or sheetgoods. Hardwoods are preferable because they emit fewer terpenes than softer woods. Numerous farmed hardwoods are available. Old-growth forest need not be destroyed by virtue of your furniture selection. Although the initial purchase price for solid wood furniture may be more expensive, you will be investing in heirloom quality. Mail-order catalogs for several manufacturers of solid wood furniture are listed in the *Division 12, Resource List.*

• If veneered wood is all that your budget will allow, then consider sealing all surfaces and edges with one of the low-VOC vapor-barrier sealants listed in *Division 9*. In addition, consider other materials such as wrought iron and glass for tables, and wicker or rattan for seating. **Note:** Examine cane furniture prior to purchase to make sure that it is free of mildew and mold. Furniture imported from tropical countries is often sprayed with pesticides while in transit.

• Veneered furniture imported from Denmark is constructed with low-emission sheetgoods to meet that country's more stringent standards.

Finishes on Wood Furniture

Durability, not health, is the criterion used by manufacturers when choosing finishes for wood furniture. The majority of commercial wood sealers are solvent based and will outgas harmful chemicals. We offer the following suggestions:

- Look for furniture with low-VOC, water-based natural oil or wax finishes.
- Buy unfinished furniture and finish with low-VOC finishes.
- If you purchase furniture with a standard finish, air it out before placing it in your living space. Finishes will eventually offgas.

Upholstery

Most commercially available upholstered furniture is stuffed with synthetic foam or latex. Many foams will initially have a strong odor. They will break down over time and emit fine particles of chemical dust into the air. Polyurethane foams are extremely hazardous when burned.

Furniture stuffing can be made with natural ingredients such as wool, down, kapok, and organic cotton batting. Although these alternatives are not widely available in readymade form, you may find an upholsterer in your vicinity who is willing to work with you. A hardwood frame made for a futon, or solid hardwood benches, can be turned into healthy couches with the addition of custom-made pillows. **Furnature, Inc.**, offers natural, organic, upholstered furniture by mail order. **Note:** Down and kapok stuffings can be allergens for some people.

Upholstery textiles are often synthetic and treated with toxic chemicals to improve stain resistance. Look for natural, untreated upholstery fabrics such as organic cotton, wool, or silk. Selected sources appear in the *Resource List*. **AFM Safechoice Carpet Lock-Out** (in the *Division 9, Resource List*) can be used on some fabrics to help repel dirt and stains. Test materials for shrink resistance and color fastness before using this product.

Window Dressings

Most window dressings are made of synthetic fabrics treated with chemicals to make them wrinkle resistant. The recommended dry-cleaning process further contributes to the chemical load. Natural fabrics can also be problematic because ultraviolet light breaks down the fabric, creating dust and the need for frequent replacements.

Naturally finished wood shutters, louvers, metallic venetian blinds, or bamboo rolldowns can be attractive solutions that avoid the problems associated with fabric window dressings. **Pella Corporation** produces a line of windows that come with retractable shades sandwiched between double windowpanes.

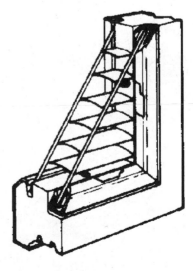

Cutaway view of narrow slat blinds between window panes.
Credit: Pella Corporation

Shower Curtains and Liners

New PVC liners and shower curtains have strong odors from offgassing toxins. Many shower curtains are treated with harmful chemicals to create mildew resistance.

Cotton duck cloth curtains are naturally water repellant, wrinkle resistant, and attractive, but they take a long time to dry and must be treated in order to resist mildew growth. They can be machine washed and dried. They are available through several mail-order companies including **Harmony** and **Heart of Vermont**. Natural hemp curtains are now available through **Real Goods**. A glass shower enclosure, although more expensive to install, will be a permanent, low-maintenance and healthy solution.

Beds and Bedding

The most important furniture choice with regard to health is bedding. We spend approximately a third of our lives in bed. Infants and children spend even more time there. While we are asleep, our noses are in close contact with bedding.

Standard mattresses are made of synthetic fabrics and padding, and treated with petrochemical fire retardants. Permanent-press bedding is treated with formaldehyde, which remains in the fabric after washing. Wool blankets may be mothproofed with harmful chemicals. Even pure cottons, unless organically grown, are heavily sprayed with pesticides.

A bed that promotes health should have many of the same characteristics as a home that promotes health. The bed should be:

+ Nontoxic
+ Able to absorb and dispel moisture without supporting mold or mildew growth
+ Easy to clean and sanitize
+ Nonconductive of electricity (free of metal)
+ Highly insulative

The following futon bedding system fulfills these characteristics. The mattress is made of layers. One or more layers of 1" to 4" thick, untreated, organic cotton futon are topped with a 1" to 3" wool futon. The layers rest on a slatted frame that is raised above the floor at a comfortable seating height.

The cotton futon provides firm back support while the wool futon, placed on top, adds resilience. Varying thickness and numbers of layers will accommodate

Case Study 12.1:

The bedroom as sanctuary

J.D. is a 55-year-old man who came to see Dr. Elliott complaining of insomnia, asthma, and fatigue. After she took an exhaustive environmental history, it became clear that J.D.'s symptoms began during the time he lived downwind from a location where aerial spraying was carried out seasonally for pest control. It appeared that the repeated pesticide exposures had left the patient feeling debilitated, without his usual zest for life and with multiple medical problems, including allergies and sensitivities to a wide range of substances.

As part of his treatment program, J.D. was advised to reduce his exposure to toxins in his home. Since he was on a limited budget owing to his decreased earning capacity, he concentrated his cleanup efforts primarily on the bedroom. At a later date he intended to focus on the rest of the house.

Given the amount of time he spent in bed, J.D. realized that his bedroom should be the healthiest place in the house. He had recently purchased a mattress made of artificial foam. The synthetic fibers were emitting formaldehyde fumes as the mattress aged, which probably contributed to the tight feeling in his chest upon waking. Fortunately, J.D. was able to sell his box-spring mattress and purchase an organic cotton futon, which he placed in an untreated wooden frame. He exchanged his formaldehyde-impregnated, wrinkle-free sheets and polyester bedding for 100% organic cotton pillows, sheets, and blankets. Because of his concern about possible dust mites in the mattress, he used an organic cotton barrier cloth, woven so tightly that these insects could not penetrate it. He laundered his bedding frequently in unscented, nonchlorinated detergent.

After J.D. recovered financially from replacing his bedding, his next project was to pull up the old carpet in the bedroom. Although the carpet was several years old and no longer outgassed toxic fumes, it was still a reservoir for dust, dirt, and microorganisms, in spite of frequent vacuuming. J.D. wanted a floor that was attractive, health enhancing, and easy to clean. He chose to install presealed cork flooring because it resembled wood, yet felt soft to the bare foot. On the floor he placed two untreated wool scatter rugs, which could be easily taken up and cleaned.

The heating system in J.D.'s house was forced air. The ductwork had been cleaned on a regular basis, and electrostatic air filters were used on the return air ducts. Nevertheless, J.D. decided to close off the vents to his bedroom and use an electric ceramic heater. In addition, he bought a portable air filter for the bedroom, which contained an HEPA filter for dust, mold spores, and pollens, and a charcoal filter for fumes. The electric motor in the air filter was sealed to avoid toxic emissions, and the unit itself was housed in a metal box.

J.D. did not know whether he was sensitive to electromagnetic fields. Since there would be little time or expense involved, he decided to take the necessary measures to reduce the EMFs. He discarded his electric blanket, substituted a battery-operated unit for his digital alarm clock, moved his telephone into an adjacent room, and plugged his television into the other side of the room so that the screen was more than eight feet from his head.

He replaced the curtains on the windows with naturally finished wooden louvers, which were handsome and easy to clean. He cleaned the room once a week with a simple solution of vinegar and water and was careful not to introduce toxic odors such as air fresheners, fabric softeners, colognes, and other artificially scented household products. When he needed to dry-clean his clothes, he left them in a closet outside the bedroom. And he was careful to remove his shoes before entering his sanctuary.

J.D.'s efforts paid off. He noted a definite improvement in his overall health. He was now able to get a full night of uninterrupted sleep and awoke feeling refreshed, without the tight sensation in his chest. His energy increased and he was able to think more clearly. J.D. gradually regained his enthusiasm for life and and has become a great proponent of the benefits of bedroom sanctuaries.

Discussion

We spend an average of eight hours a day in our bedrooms. Sleep is an important time for rest and recovery for all of us, whether we are sick or in the best of health. Designing our bedrooms with special care can create a healing environment where our bodies can mend from the daily barrage of exposures that we all experience to varying degrees.

different firmness preferences. To properly maintain a futon, it should be aired weekly in sunlight to sanitize it, then fluffed, rotated, and replaced so it will wear evenly. A thin futon has an advantage over thicker mattress arrangements because the layers can be easily lifted and carried.

It is important that air be allowed to circulate under the futon. This facilitates evaporation of moisture, thereby preventing mold or mildew growth. A slatted platform will hold the futon firmly in place and permit air circulation around it.

Another metal-free bedding system that has gained popularity is natural latex/wool/organic cotton mattresses. This combination system conforms to the body's shape and comes in a variety of firmnesses offering good support and absorbency in a chemical-free environment. Untreated wool will repel dust mites, mold, and mildew. The mattress base consists of a European-style wood-slat foundation that gives the same height and look as a conventional box spring. **Samina, Crown/The Natural Bedroom**, and **Oasis/Sleeptek** all manufacture this type of mattress. People with sensitivities to natural latex would need to test this type of bed before making a costly purchase. Most bedding is nonreturnable.

Several companies are now offering more conventional mattress and box spring setups that are free of chemicals and made of natural cotton or cotton-wool combinations. **Crown/The Natural Bedroom** and **Oasis/Sleeptek** both offer this type of system.

This bedroom, found in Arizona, provides its owner with an abundance of fresh air! Photo: Robert Laporte.

Healthy choices for bedding include organic cotton, silk, or linen sheets; organic cotton flannel sheets; and down, silk, wool, or organic cotton comforters, duvets, and blankets. Some of the specialty mail-order suppliers listed in the *Division 12, Resource List* carry these items.

There is some confusion about the various terms used to describe cotton products. According to the Pesticide Action Network, conventionally grown cotton accounts for nearly 25% of the world's insecticide use. Organic cotton is grown without the use of synthetic pesticides or fertilizers and with farming practices that increase soil fertility. "Natural" or "Green" cotton products use conventionally grown cotton but are free of harsh chemical bleaches, dyes, and sizing elements such as formaldehyde. 100% cotton labeling indicates that no other fibers have been used in the fabric, but does not mean that the fabric is organic or naturally processed.

Further Reading

Leclair, Kim and David Rousseau. *Environmental by Design*. Hartley and Marks, 1992.
   Overview of larger environmental concerns related to furniture manufacturing.

Resource List

Manufacturer/Catalog	Products	Contact Points
Allergy Relief Shop, Inc.	Organic cotton mattresses, futons, sheets, and blankets.	Allergy Relief Shop, Inc. 3360 Andersonville Highway Andersonville, TN 37705 (800) 626•2810, (865) 494•4100 www.allergyreliefshop.com
Bright Futures Futons	Many styles of futons and couch beds.	Bright Futures Futons 3120 Central SE Albuquerque, NM 87106 (888) 645•4452, (505) 268•9738 www.organiccottonalts.com
Coyuchi	Organic cotton bedding.	Coyuchi 11101 State Route One, #201 P.O. Box 845 Pointe Reyes Station, CA 94956 (415) 663•8077 www.coyuchiorganic.com
Crate and Barrel	Solid wood, glass, and metal furnishings and accessories.	Crate and Barrel P.O. Box 3210 Naperville, Il 60566-7210 (800) 323•5461 www.crateandbarrel.com
Crown/The Natural Bedroom (formerly Janz Design)	Natural bedroom furniture and bedding.	Crown/The Natural Bedroom 11134 Rush Street South El Monte, CA 91733 (626) 452•8617
Environmental Home Center	Natural and organic wool and cotton bedding, natural mattresses and box springs.	Environmental Home Center 1724–4th Avenue South Seattle, WA 98134 (800) 281•9785, (206) 682•7332 www.enviresource.com
Furnature, Inc.	Chemical-free upholstered sofas, chairs, and mattresses using 100% organically grown ingredients.	Furnature, Inc. 319 Washington Street Brighton, MA 02135 (877) 877•8020, (617) 787•2888 www.furnature.com
Harmony (formerly Seventh Generation)	Organic bedding, towels, and shower curtains.	Gaiam, Inc. 360 Interlocken Boulevard, Suite 300 Broomfield CO 80021 (800) 869•3446 www.gaiam.com
Healthy Interiors	Consultant and retail source for beds, bedding, linens, furniture, and custom upholstery. Knowledgeable service and reasonable pricing.	Healthy Interiors P.O. Box 9001 Santa Fe NM 87504 (505) 820•7634 www.healthyhomeinteriors.com
Heart of Vermont	Bedding and other "products for the chemically sensitive and environmentally concerned."	Heart of Vermont 131 South Main Street P.O. Box 612 Barre VT 05641 (800) 639•4123 www.heartofvermont.com
Homespun Fabrics and Draperies	Handwoven, 100% cotton fabrics without finishes or chemicals.	Homespun Fabrics and Draperies 1865 El Monte Drive P.O. Box 4315 Thousand Oaks, CA 91359 www.homespunfabrics.com

Manufacturer/Catalog	Products	Contact Points
Janice Corporation	Cotton mattresses and bedding.	Janice Corporation 198 Route 46 Budd Lake, NJ 07828 (800) 526•4237, (973) 691•2979 www.janices.com
Natural Home	Natural beds, bedding.	Naturlich-Natural Home P.O. Box 1677 Sebastopol, CA 95473-1677 (707) 824•0914 www.naturalhomeproducts.com
Nigra Enterprises	Air filtration systems.	Nigra Enterprises 5699 Kanan Road Agoura, CA 91301-3328 (818) 889•6877 www.nigra.org
Nirvana Safe Haven	Organic cotton and wool mattresses and bedding.	Nirvana Safe Haven 3441 Golden Rain Road, Suite 3 Walnut Creek, CA 94595 (800) 968•9355 www.nontoxic.com
Oasis/Sleeptek	Manufacturers of organic cotton and cotton-and-latex box springs and mattresses.	Contact through Furnature or Healthy Interiors.
Pacific Rim	Makers of handcrafted solid maple furniture using maple grown in managed forests from U.S. sources. Call for your nearest distributor.	Pacific Rim P.O. Box 2844 Eugene, OR 97402 (541) 342•4508
Pella Corporation	Windows come with optional "Slimshade" blinds between the two layers of glass; the blinds never require cleaning.	Pella Corporation 102 Main Street Pella, IA 50219 (800) 547•3552 www.pella.com
Pottery Barn	Solid wood furniture, glass and metal furniture and accessories, cotton window dressings.	Pottery Barn P.O. Box 7044 San Francisco, CA 94120-7044 (800) 922•5507 www.potterybarn.com
Real Goods	Catalog sales for natural and organic mattresses, bedding, shower curtains, and towels.	Real Goods 200 Clara Avenue Ukiah CA 95482•4004 (800) 762•7325 www.realgoods.com
Samina	Manufacturers of organic cotton, wool, and latex mattress systems.	Samina USA Rohorn, Inc. 1530 Northern Boulevard Manhasset, NY 11030 (516) 869•6005 www.samina.com
Smith and Hawken	A variety of sustainably harvested teak and cedar solid wood furniture.	Smith and Hawken Two Arbor Lane, Box 6900 Florence, KY 41022-6900 (800) 776•3336 www.SmithandHawken.com

Division 13: Special Construction

Swimming Pools and Hot Tubs

If you wish to include a swimming pool or hot tub inside your home, the two major health concerns to consider are water sterilization and humidity-related mold infestation.

The standard disinfectants used to kill microbes and algae in swimming pools are chlorine or other halogenated compounds, which are easily absorbed through the swimmer's skin as well as inhaled into the lungs. There are several alternatives to chlorination. Ozonation is a popular method used in Europe for sterilizing water (see the *Division 13 Resource List, Swimming Pool Purificaion Systems*). Other methods include electrolysis, ultraviolet light, and filtration through charcoal and pesticide-free diatomaceous earth. Pools using these alternate methods need to be frequently monitored for the presence of bacteria. Occasionally a small amount of harsher chemicals may be required.

Enclosing a large body of heated water within a living space will create a humid microclimate, which is an invitation for mold growth and can result in damage from condensation. Design measures can prevent both these problems. The following strategies should be integrated into the design.

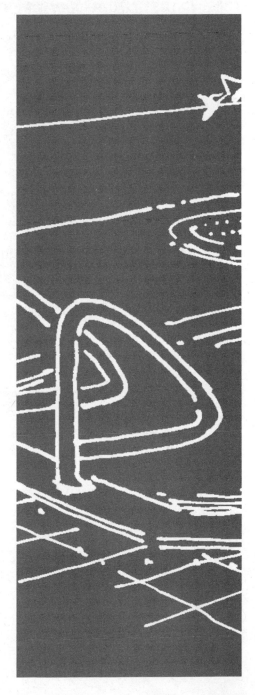

- Adequate mechanical ventilation and dehumidification
- Fitted covers that remain in place when the pool or hot tub is unoccupied in order to prevent evaporation
- Watertight enclosure around the pool area that retards vapor diffusion in order to prevent water damage to the surrounding structure
- Surface finishes that are impervious to water and easily cleaned
- Rigorous maintenance program to remove condensation and mold growth as soon as it appears

There can be advantages to having a large body of heated water inside the home. The water acts as a reservoir for solar heat storage and humidification. Strategies for taking advantage of these benefits should be considered in the initial design process.

Case Study 13.1:

Asthma from chlorinated swimming pool

B.W. is a nine-year-old boy who came with his parents to consult with Dr. Elliott regarding his asthma. The most recent flare-up had occurred during a school field trip to the local swimming pool. Upon further questioning, a pattern emerged that revealed a relationship between water and the triggering of asthma in the child. Dr. Elliott suspected that the chlorine in the water was acting as an irritant to the boy's airways. She suggested to the family that they swim in one of the public pools that had switched to ozone for water purification. In that particular pool, chlorine was used as a supplement, but only in very small quantities. The family was happy to note that their son could now swim comfortably with his friends without having difficulty breathing. The family went on to purchase filters for their shower heads, which effectively removed chlorine from the showers. They also removed all chlorinated cleaning products from their home. Now that there was one less triggering agent for the asthma, Dr. Elliott could more effectively focus on strengthening the boy's lungs.

Discussion

Chlorine is a poison used to kill bacteria in the water. It is absorbed through skin, inhaled into the lungs, and ingested. At room temperature, chlorine is a gas with a pungent smell. It is very reactive, combining readily with most elements to form compounds, many of which are known to be carcinogenic, such as chloroform, trihalomethanes, and organochlorines.

Symptoms commonly seen after swimming in chlorinated water include runny nose, red eyes, cough, asthma, joint pains, swelling, nausea, urinary discomfort, rashes, and hives. We suggest that you use a less toxic disinfectant for your pool.

However, due to the intensive upkeep required to maintain a pool or spa so that it does not negatively impact indoor air quality, we do not readily recommend including an enclosed body of water inside a healthy home.

Environmental Testing

It may be desirable to conduct diverse quality-control tests or checks throughout the process of construction and selection of materials. This testing can help ensure that materials and installations are as specified. We recommend you plan for many of these tests in advance. Waiting until the last minute will result in costly construction delays since many of these procedures will require that you order test kits, hire specialists, or wait for laboratory results.

Material Testing

In choosing healthy materials, you and your architect will base decisions on information supplied by the manufacturer, such as product literature and MSDS sheets, as well as on the appearance and smell of the products. While certain hazardous substances, such as lead, asbestos, mercury, and polychlorinated biphenyls (PCBs), are no longer a concern for products manufactured in the United States, precautions may be required if you are using recycled or imported materials. Available tests for lead and asbestos are included in the *Division 13, Resource List*. You may want to consider doing the materials tests discussed below.

pH Testing for Concrete Slabs

It is essential that concrete be properly cured to ensure its strength and durability. Improperly cured concrete may exhibit strongly alkaline pH. This can cause adverse chemical reactions when the concrete comes in contact with certain adhesives and flooring materials. The pH of cured concrete must be under 9 to be considered acceptable. You perform a pH test by dampening an area of concrete with distilled or deionized water, then test the dampened area with pH paper or with a special pH test pencil from the **Sinak Corporation**. The color of the paper or pencil marks indicate the pH level.

Formaldehyde Testing

Although many manufacturers are now using less formaldehyde than they once were, it is still a common additive in many products. The cumulative effect of several products containing only moderate amounts of formaldehyde can cause severe health consequences. Our approach is to avoid this chemical whenever formaldehyde-free substitutes can be located.

A simple, do-it-yourself spot check can be used to ensure that you do not have products containing formaldehyde. Place a drop of test solution on the material in question and allow it to stand for two minutes. If the drop's color changes from clear to purple, formaldehyde or other harmful aldehydes are present. The shade of purple will range from a faint pink to a dark plum depending on the concentration of formaldehyde. The test must be read at exactly two minutes, because the drop will eventually turn purple even if no aldehydes are present. The solution leaves a purple stain on porous materials and should be used in a place where it is not visible.

Surface Sampling for Fungus

Materials damaged by mold growth should be rejected, but not all stains are from mold. Laboratory analysis will probably be required to determine if mold is a problem, but there are three do-it-yourself methods for collecting mold samples.

Bulk Sampling

Collect a small amount of the material in question in a doubled plastic bag and send it to the laboratory. A teaspoonful of the suspected material is probably enough.

Tape Sampling

Press a piece of clear cellophane tape onto the surface to be tested. The best place for sampling is at the edge between the stained area and the clean area. Then stick the tape to a plastic bag or glass slide and ship it to the laboratory. The lab technicians will stain the tape sample to make the fungal growth easier to view, then examine it under a microscope.

Culture Collection

Special moist, sterile swabs called "culturettes" are good for this type of sampling. The culturette is presterilized and comes with a fluid-filled glass ampule to provide just the right amount of moisture. The glass ampule and swab are housed in a sterile plastic tube.

About one minute before collecting the sample, squeeze the area of the tube over the glass ampule to break the ampule and release the fluid, which then soaks the cotton swab. Slide the moistened swab from its sterile tube and use it to wipe one square inch of the material to be tested. Then insert the swab back into the sterile plastic tube for shipment to the lab. Since this method uses liquid, the fungal spores will be hydrated and begin to colonize. It is important to ship the specimen to the lab via overnight delivery service; otherwise the test may be invalid.

The practice of testing for molds using culture dishes is becoming less common. Certain harmful molds, such as aspergillus and penicillium, are very light and have a tendency not to settle on culture dishes. They are therefore underrepresented in the analysis.

Other methods of testing for airborne fungal spores and contaminated materials are available, but require a trained technician with sophisticated equipment.

Radioactivity

Although radioactivity in building materials is rare, John Banta's home inspections have revealed radioactive stone and tile glazes. Highly radioactive materials can be tested simply by holding a radiation detector next to the material.

For lower levels of radiation, measurements of longer duration should be performed. Place at least one pound of the material in question in a glass container with an instrument for measuring radioactivity. A useful instrument designed for this purpose is **Rad Alert**, whose small size allows it to fit easily inside a one-gallon glass pickle jar, along with the material to be tested. The meter should be set for total counts and left to measure for a timed period of 12 to 24 hours. As a control, the test must also be performed in the same way, in the same location, but with the jar empty. Repeat both tests several times to be sure a radiation-emitting solar flare or short-term cosmic event did not interfere with the results. The total number of counts recorded for each test should be divided by the total number of minutes the test ran in order to provide an average count per minute. A substance that measures less than 10% higher than the control test is considered to be free of radiation. Readings more than 20% higher than the control test are considered to be significant.

Moisture Testing

Ensuring that materials are dry is essential in healthy building. Building materials can be ruined by moisture damage. The following four building practices can be responsible for warpage, deterioration of materials, and microbial growth.

- Application of finish flooring materials over insufficiently cured concrete slabs
- Failure to quickly and thoroughly dry out precipitation that enters an unfinished structure
- Installation of wood members with a moisture content greater than 17%
- Enclosure of walls containing wet applied insulation systems, such as cellulose or spray foams, before they are properly cured

It is not always possible to detect by visual inspection if a material is wet. A variety of test procedures have been developed to assist in determining if a material is dry.

Moisture Meters

There are two general types of moisture meters. The first uses sharp pin probes that are pushed into the material to be tested. The pin probe meter detects moisture by electrical conductivity, since wet materials conduct greater amounts of electricity than dry materials. This meter leaves pin holes in the materials being tested.

The second type of meter sends an electronic signal into the material. The degree of moisture determines how the meter will register the returning signal.

Both types of moisture meters are battery operated and can be used repeatedly. The meters range in cost from about $200 to over $1,000 and can require some technical experience. For example, damp wood is measured with a different setting and scale than damp concrete or brick. Companies that specialize in fire-and-flood damage restoration are likely to have this equipment and be experienced in its use. If you do decide to purchase or borrow a moisture meter, plan on spending some time becoming familiar with it and thoroughly read the owner's manual and instructions. Keep in mind that hidden metals or salt deposits may falsely indicate that materials are wet when in fact they are dry.

Waterproof Testing

All homes are supposed to be weathertight, but many are not. One simple method for testing is to literally water the house. You can specify that the exterior of the house shall be weathertight before any interior construction begins. Once the exterior is complete and the doors and windows are installed and caulked, spray the house with a hose so that every part of the house gets soaked for at least 15 minutes. Then inspect all areas inside the house for leaks. A moisture meter will be useful for this task.

This test should only be performed prior to the installation of interior sheathing or insulation so that leaks can be easily detected, dried out, and remedied. The test will be much more effective if you can create a negative pressure in the house while the test is being performed, as this will more accurately simulate pressure conditions that exist during a storm. A blower door is an excellent way to create a known negative pressure for this test (see below).

Window Testing

Water infiltration caused by faulty windows or installation procedure is a common form of building failure leading to mold infestation and water damage. Because water will often leak directly into the wall cavity, a problem can go undetected for a long time, and once it is discovered, the damage is often extensive. Such problems can be avoided if proper testing protocol is carried out at the time of installation. Some windows are designed with drainage channels and weep holes that allow water to drain to the outside of the building and not into the wall. One way to test the effectiveness of a window's drainage capacity is to temporarily block the weep holes with putty and then fill the drainage channel with water. If the window is properly manufactured and installed, the water should not drain out of the drainage channel when the weep holes are plugged. This test should be performed on each window for a minimum of 15 minutes. Remove the putty from the weep holes when the test is complete.

Humidity/Temperature Testing

Generally, newly constructed buildings have higher humidity levels due to moisture inherent in building materials and processes. It is important that enclosed buildings are quickly dried out to levels that will not support mold growth. You should verify that acceptable levels have been reached and are maintained. Humidity should be monitored and controlled from the time the building is enclosed until all wet finish materials have been applied and dried. Humidity controls are especially important in humid climates, or when massive wet materials such as concrete or plaster are used. Inexpensive meters for determining temperature and relative humidity, called "thermohygrometers," can be purchased at most electronics and hardware stores.

Relative humidity (RH) varies depending on temperature. Warmer air will have a lower RH than colder air with the same amount of water vapor. Using a special chart called a "psychrometric table," you can convert readings from the thermohygrometer to determine the actual amount of water in the air or at surfaces at various temperatures. Use these figures to determine if a structure is dry enough. At 70 degrees Fahrenheit, mold will not grow at an RH level of under 60% measured at the surface. One way to measure the surface humidity is to affix the meter to the surface with a sheet of plastic sealed over it. After a few minutes the meter will stabilize and the RH can be read. If you determine that humidity levels are too high, we recommend electric dehumidification.

Certified water-loss technicians are trained and equipped to measure and dry buildings that have excessive levels of moisture. There are two associations that certify technicians and that can help you locate qualified technicians in your vicinity. These are **ASCR Water Loss Institute** and **IICRC. Hint:** If you can see condensation on the windows for two days in a row, then the building probably has areas that are wet enough to support microbial growth.

Calcium Chloride Moisture Testing

Large quantities of water are present in cement, gypcrete, aircrete, and other poured masonry materials. These materials must be adequately dried before finishes are applied. It is common in new construction for a carpet or other floor finish to be laid on a slab before the slab is thoroughly dry. Further drying is inhibited, allowing microbial spore levels to climb as mold invades these damp areas.

A kit for testing moisture in masonry is available. It uses calcium chloride salts, which absorb moisture from the air at a known rate. The kit contains a plate that holds the calcium chloride salt, a plastic dome, and an adhesive material. Weigh the calcium chloride to the nearest hundredth of a gram (you can find scales for measuring the salts at your local pharmacy), then place the calcium chloride test on the floor area to be tested and cover it with the plastic dome, which is sealed to the slab with the adhesive material. After 60 to 72 hours, remove the plastic dome and reweigh the calcium chloride. Based on the weight gain and the number of hours that have passed, you can determine the material's water vapor emissions rate. The kit instructions also contain a chart that will help you determine when the slab is dry enough for the application of various finishing materials. If a scale is unavailable, the sealed exposed kit can be shipped back to the manufacturer for weighing and calculations.

Energy Efficiency and Airflow Testing

Blower Doors

Blower doors consist of a sophisticated fan set in an adjustable frame. They are used to test airflow and pressure in a home. There are many uses for blower doors, such as detection of leaks in the walls and in heating, ventilation, and air conditioning (HVAC) system ductwork. You can also determine if the ventilation is adequate and identify the location of energy leaks in the structure.

The equipment requires extensive training to use. We recommend that you hire a technician to carry out blower door testing. For most new homes this testing will cost several hundred dollars. Dollars saved in energy conservation from identified and corrected leaks may soon offset the cost of testing.

Theatrical Fog Machine

Certain parts of the home, such as garages, attics, and crawl spaces, should be completely sealed from the rest of the house in order to prevent the passage of contaminated air into living spaces. One easy way to test for leaking airflow is to use a theatrical fog machine. This is the same equipment used on stage and in movies to create fog for special effects. It can be rented from most theatrical supply companies. Place the unit in the area to be tested and turn it on so it fills the space with fog, then observe the adjoining areas for signs of the fog. Leaks can be easily pinpointed and sealed.

When testing the garage, you need to seal the door and open vents with tape and plastic to prevent the fog from escaping. The same is true of attic and crawl-space vents and intentional openings to the outdoors. Common air-infiltration points revealed by the fog test include electrical outlets, the juncture where the sheetrock meets the floor, and poorly sealed plumbing, electrical, and ductwork penetrations. Theatrical fog testing is especially helpful when performed in conjunction with a blower door. This will allow simulation of a variety of adverse weather conditions, which may create unusual indoor air-quality problems during inclement weather.

Be sure to notify the fire department before you begin this type of test; otherwise a well-meaning neighbor who sees the smoke might dial 911 and set the fire trucks in motion.

Air Leakage in Air Distribution System Testing

You can test for air leakage in air distribution systems in a similar manner to blower door testing for a whole house. This testing should be done while the ductwork is still accessible, before it is covered with finishing materials. Seal off

The Problem: This furnace ductwork, located in an attic, was not firmly connected to the supply register. As a result heat is being lost in the living space and insulation fibers are being blown into the air resulting in poor indoor air quality. Recommendation: ductworks must be well sealed and tested for air leakage. Photo: Restoration Consultants.

supply and return registers so that the system can be depressurized using a blower door or calibrated fan. The combined airflow through all leakage openings can then be determined. Ideally, leakage should be less than 3%. If a small amount of excess leakage is revealed, use a theatrical fog machine to trace the sources. If leakage is extensive you will need to examine all junctures and reseal as appropriate prior to retesting.

Radon Testing

In *Division 7* we discussed radon gas and mitigation. There are several acceptable methods currently being used to measure radon in the air and in the water. Test kits are listed in the Resource List at the end of this *Division*. Some are available from local hardware stores. It is important to follow the manufacturer's instructions precisely.

Radon Testing in an Existing Structure

General principles that should be followed for radon air testing, regardless of the type of kit used, are listed below.

- Close the home for a minimum of 12 hours before beginning the test and keep it closed throughout the testing period. It's permissible to enter and leave the house as long as the doors are not left open.
- Place the sampler about 30 inches above the floor and at least two feet away from the wall in the area being tested. Keep the sampler away from doors, windows, fireplaces, outside walls, corners, and any other places where drafts or stagnant air may exist. These precautions are necessary to ensure that the sampler is exposed to a representative sample of air.
- Accurately record the starting and stopping time. You must include this information with the sample, along with the date, when it is returned to the lab. Without precise recording information, the results cannot be considered valid.

A typical radon test kit costs less than $25. After each individual test, the kit must be returned to a laboratory for analysis. Multiple testing or continuous monitoring can be carried out with electronic radon monitors.

Radon Soil Testing

Radon mitigation is most effective and least costly when it is incorporated into the construction of the home. If you are building a new home and there is reason to suspect a radon problem, then a soil test is advisable. Although the test will not provide definitive results as to what the radon levels will ultimately be in the finished home, it is nevertheless an indicator that can help you decide whether mitigation measures should be included in your construction plans.

The test kit available for measuring radon in the soil involves placing a special collection box with its open side over the soil to be tested. Soil is mounded around the lip of the box to form a tight seal and keep the box in place. Radon gas is trapped and concentrated in a carbon medium, which can then be measured by a testing apparatus. The starting time and date are recorded. After the prescribed period of time, usually 48 hours, the soil is pushed away and the tester retrieved and returned to its foil pouch. The stop time is recorded and sent with the other information and materials to the lab for analysis.

Radon Testing for Water

Radon found in water poses a health threat when the radon is released into the air and inhaled. Hot steamy baths or showers with water that has a high radon content can be a serious source of exposure. It is only necessary to test well water, because the EPA requires municipal water suppliers to screen for radon. Small amounts of radon can be removed with special carbon filters. A high content of radon in water (5,000 pCi/L or greater) is more difficult and costly to remove.

Testing for Chemical Fumes

A barrage of chemical smells often assaults new homeowners as they enter their home, and even though they might not consider themselves to be chemically sensitive, they may be bothered or made ill by the fumes in their homes. Sniffing finishing materials, such as upholstery, carpets, and paint, before they are installed will reveal important information. However, even if a building product or material passes the sniff test when sampled, the odor can become unbearable once the product is installed in the home. This is because chemical fumes accumulate inside the house and are emitted from a much larger surface area than that of the sample.

If you are unsure about how you will tolerate a product once it is applied or installed in your house, we recommend that you test the product before purchase in a manner that will simulate the level of concentration in the home. One method of testing is to place a sample of the product in question in a large glass jar with the top screwed on tightly to allow fumes to accumulate. The following day, open the jar and sniff the contents for unacceptable fumes. If the sample is too large to be placed inside a container, place it next to your pillow while you sleep. Pillow testing should only be done if you are reasonably sure that you will not have a severe reaction after prolonged exposure.

It is important that some samples be new. For example, a carpet swatch that has been in a showroom for three years will not provide an accurate indication of what a freshly unrolled carpet will smell like in your home. Other samples—such as wet applied finishes like paints, sealers, and adhesives—should be applied to an inert surface such as glass or foil and then be allowed to air out in an uncontaminated location for a few weeks, better simulating the cured or semi-cured state that the product will be in on "move-in day."

This type of testing, although somewhat helpful, has obvious limitations. While the test gives information about the particular product in question, it does not indicate cumulative nor synergistic effects when combined over time with other chemicals. Since you cannot predict these effects in advance, the goal is to choose products with the least amount of odor and toxic emissions.

Further Reading

Floor Seal Technology, Inc. *Concrete Vapor Emissions and Alkalinity Control.* Toll free: (800) 572•2344, or (800) 295•0221.

IICRC. *S 500 Standard & Reference Guide for Professional Water Damage Restoration.* Second Editon. Institute of Inspection, Cleaning and Restoration Certification, 2715 East Mill Plain Boulevard, Vancouver, WA 98661. Toll free: (800) 835•4624; Phone: (360) 693•5675; Internet: www.iicrc.org.

Resource List

Manufacturer	Product	Contact Points

Swimming Pool Purification Systems

Manufacturer	Product	Contact Points
ClearWater Tech, Inc.	Ozone generators for many different uses.	ClearWater Tech, Inc. P.O. Box 15330 San Luis Obispo, CA 93406 (805) 549•9724 www.cwtozone.com
DEL Industries	Water ozonation systems for pools, wells, and spas.	DEL Industries 3428 Bullock Lane San Luis Obispo, CA 93401 (800) 676•1335, (805) 541•1601 www.delozone.com
Real Goods	Source of "Floatron," a solar-powered pool purifier, combining solar electric power with mineral ionization. Reduces chlorine usage up to 80%.	Real Goods 200 Clara Avenue Ukiah, CA 95482-4004 (800) 762•7325 www.realgoods.com

Test Kits

Manufacturer	Product	Contact Points
AirChek, Inc.	Sells a variety of home test kits for radon, formaldehyde, and microwaves.	AirChek, Inc. Box 2000 Naples, NC 28760 (800) 247•2435 www.radon.com
Formaldehyde spot test kit	A colorimetric test that indicates if any object contains more than 10 ppm of formaldehyde. Each kit tests more than 100 objects.	Prestige Publishing P.O. Box 3068 Syracuse, NY 13220 (800) 846•6687, (325) 454•8119 www.prestigepublishing.com
Indoor air quality (IAQ) test kit	One kit tests total VOC level, formaldehyde level, and mold in surface samples.	Air Quality Sciences, Inc. Capitol Circle Atlanta, GA 30067 (800) 789•0419, (770) 993•0638 www.aqs.com
Lead check swabs—Item #K910	Lead check swabs turn pink if lead is present. Can be used on ceramics, paint, soil, and solder.	Professional Equipment 90 Plant Avenue, Suite 3 Hauppauge, NY 11788-3813 (800) 334•9291 www.professionalequipment.com
Mold and microbiology testing kits	Mail-order catalog from microbiology lab for culturing mold and other microorganisms.	The Allergy Relief Shop 3360 Andersonville Highway Andersonville, TN 37705 (800) 626•2810, (865) 494•4100 www.allergyreliefshop.com
Mold survey service	Mold test.	Prestige Publishing P.O. Box 3068 Syracuse, NY 13220 (800) 846•6687, (325) 454•8119 www.prestigepublishing.com
Mold test kit	Easy-to-use mold-testing kits for the home. $60 for kit and analysis.	Environmental Health Center 8345 Walnut Hill Lane, Suite 220 Dallas, TX 75231 (214) 373•5149 www.ehcd.com

Manufacturer	Product	Contact Points

Test Kits – continued:

Manufacturer	Product	Contact Points
Mold test kit—Item #K200	Easy-to-use mold-testing kits.	Professional Equipment 90 Plant Avenue, Suite 3 Hauppauge, NY 11788-3813 (800) 334•9291 www.professionalequipment.com
pH testing	A pH test pencil for measuring the alkalinity of concrete slabs.	Sinak Corp. 861 Sixth Avenue, Suite 411 San Diego, CA 92101 (800) 523•3147 www.sinakcorp.com
pH testing	A combined moisture and alkali test kit for concrete slabs.	Taylor Tools www.taylorflooringtools.com
Rad Alert	Device for measuring radioactivity.	International Med Com. 7497 Kennedy Road Sebastopol, CA 95472 (707) 823•0336 www.medcom.com
Radon test cannisters—Item #K550	Test kits for radon in air. Minimum order of 10 canisters.	Professional Equipment 90 Plant Avenue, Suite 3 Hauppauge, NY 11788-3813 (800) 334•9291 www.professionalequipment.com
Radon test kits	Test kits for radon in water and long- and short-term radon test kits for air.	Professional Discount Supply 1029 South Sierra Madre, Suite B Colorado Springs, CO 80903 (719) 444•0646 www.radonpds.com
Spotcheck pesticide testing kit	Instant pesticide-checking kit based on technology developed by the U.S. military. Ships with supplies to carry out four tests of soil, water, food, or surfaces. Some of the pesticides that can be tested for include Sevin, Dursban, Diazinon, Malathion, and Parathion.	The Cutting Edge Catalog P.O. Box 5034 Southhampton, NY 11969 (800) 497•9516 www.cutcat.com
Vapor emissions testing	A reusable calcium chloride dome test that won't mar or damage concrete surfaces.	Sinak Corp. 861 Sixth Avenue, Suite 411 San Diego, CA 92101 (800) 523•3147 www.sinakcorp.com
Vapor emissions testing	A calcium chloride vapor emissions testing kit for concrete slabs.	Taylor Tools www.taylorflooringtools.com
Vaprecision	A calcium chloride vapor emissions testing kit for concrete slabs.	Professional Vapor Emission Testing System P.O. Box 1396 Costa Mesa, CA 92628-1396 (800) 449•6194, (714) 754•6141 www.vaportest.com

Manufacturer	Product	Contact Points

Testing Consultants

Manufacturer	Product	Contact Points
ASCR-Water Loss Institute	Provides water-loss specialist technician certification and referrals.	ASCR-Water Loss Institute 8229 Cloverleaf Drive, #460 Millersville, MD 21108 (800) 272•7012, (410) 729•9900 www.ASCR.org
Environmental Testing and Technology	Wide variety of indoor air-quality testing services and consultation.	Peter H Sierck 1106 Second Street, Suite 102 Encinitas, CA 92024 (800) 811•5991, (760) 436•5990
Indoor Environmental Technologies, Inc.	Wide variety of indoor air-quality testing services and consultation.	William H. Spates III 1403 Cleveland Street Clearwater, FL 33755 (727) 446•7717
Institute for Bau-Biologie and Ecology	Referrals to certified bau-biologie home inspectors and consultants.	Institute for Bau-Biologie and Ecology P.O. Box 387 Clearwater, FL 33757 (727) 461•4371 www.bau-biologieusa.com
IICRC	Provides certification and referrals for water-damage restoration technicians and companies.	Institute of Inspection, Cleaning and Restoration Certification 2715 East Mill Plain Boulevard Vancouver, WA 98661 (800) 835•4624, (360) 693•5675 www.iicrc.org
Ozark Water Service and Air Services	For air and water testing, and consultation regarding toxic gases, molds, asbestos, VOCs, pesticides, gas leaks, EMFs, and radon.	Ozark Water Service and Air Services 114 Spring Street Sulphur Springs, AR 72768-0218 (800) 835•8908
Restoration Consultants	Years of experience with biological contamination of indoor environments, and restoration after fire and water damage.	Restoration Consultants 3463 Ramona Avenue, Suite 18 Sacramento, CA 95826 (916) 736•1100 www.restcon.com
Safe Environments	Consulting and testing for a wide range of indoor air-quality problems.	Safe Environments 1611 Merritt Drive Novato, CA 94949 (510) 549•969

Division 14: Conveying Systems

This division is not used in residential construction.

Division 15: Mechanical

Supply and Waste

Polyvinyl chloride (PVC) is the standard for residential supply and waste piping. PVC plastic piping has been shown to outgas diethyl phthalate, trimethylhexane, aliphatic hydrocarbons, and other harmful gases. It should not be used for water supply piping in a healthy home. We recommend seeking alternatives for waste lines as well, because of the pollution resulting from both the manufacture and disposal of PVC piping.

Water Supply Pipe

Although we can choose the type of supply pipe we want in our home, we have no control over how water is delivered to our property line. Well water is often delivered through PVC piping. Municipal water supply can be piped through a variety of unsavory piping including PVC and asbestos cement. In *Division 11* we recommended whole-house water purification. From the point at which water is purified, it makes sense to distribute it in piping that will not have an adverse affect on the water quality. Your specifications could include one of the following acceptable alternatives for supply piping.

> • **Type L or Type M copper:** Solder shall be lead-free silver solder. The system shall be flushed prior to occupancy to eliminate any flux from the soldering operation.
> • **Wirsbo Aquapex:** A cross-linked polyethylene that shall be installed by certified installer.

Waste Drain System

Waste drain systems do not have the same water quality concerns as supply piping does and are almost always plastic because it is most economical. We prefer to specify ABS piping because of the problems associated with the production and burning of PVC piping.

Pipe assembly glues are highly volatile and toxic, and their use on site should be carefully managed to reduce pollution. You may wish to specify the following.

> • Assemble pipes with the longest pieces possible to minimize the amount of glue or solder required.
> • When possible, glue waste pipe assembly outside the building envelope.
> • Wipe up excessive glues and protect all surfaces from glue drips and spills.
> • Whenever glue is being used inside the structure, provide adequate ventilation until all odors are dissipated.

Floor Drains

Appliances containing water, such as water heaters and washing machines, can malfunction and leak. You can avoid the subsequent water damage and mold if you plan for this possibility. By providing strategically located floor drains or drain pans, you will divert the water from accidental spills to the sewer line or to the outdoors. Drains that lead to the sewer line should be installed with a trap to prevent unwanted sewer gases from entering the home. It is important that the traps be "primed" or kept filled with water, which creates a physical barrier against the entry of sewer gases.

Plumbing Penetrations

Where plumbing penetrates walls and ceilings, the air space created around the opening must be completely sealed to prevent unwanted air infiltration. Consider specifying the following.

The Problem: Crawl space air was being drawn in to this home through plumbing penetrations before they were sealed Recommendation: Plumbing and other penetrations should be sealed to prevent infiltration.
Photo: Restoration Consultants.

> • Wherever plumbing penetrates the wall, apply 100% silicone caulking, aquarium grade, to create an airtight seal.

Backflow Protection

In some communities, sewage systems periodically back up and flow into homes, leading to devastating contamination. Backflow prevention devices installed on the home waste line will usually prevent this. The local planning department may be able to help you determine if backflow prevention devices are advisable. In many communities, claims for sewage damage will not be paid unless such devices were in place prior to the incident.

Residential Heating and Cooling

Methods of heating, cooling, and ventilating homes have many important health ramifications that will affect us long after the initial building materials have outgassed and reached a neutral state. Ideally, if we lived in a pristine natural environment with low humidity and mild temperatures, we would be able to condition our homes without mechanical assistance by means of solar gain, shading, and cross ventilation. Residents throughout most of North America do not have such luxury. Cold and cloudy winters, hot and humid summers, and polluted or pollen-filled air are realities from which homes must shelter occupants.

We have come to expect a level of comfort and temperature control in our homes undreamed of by our not-too-distant ancestors. Along with the increased comfort level, we have also unwittingly come to accept many health problems associated with heating and cooling systems. In fact, more than any other building system or component, heating and cooling methods can be a major cause of sick building syndrome. Some of the problems are listed below.

• Toxic fumes from gas, oil, or propane fuels that work their way into the building envelope through leaky supply lines, improperly ventilated or sealed mechanical rooms, and from open combustion appliances
• Backdrafting of hazardous and sometimes deadly gases into the living space from flues
• Infiltration of pollutants from outside the building envelope due to depressurization

- Fried dust resulting from hot surface temperatures on heating appliances
- Circulation of dust through unfiltered forced-air heating system
- Contamination due to mold growing in the ductwork and air-conditioning equipment
- Fiberglass fibers, originating in ductwork insulation, that circulate in the living space

Later in this Division we present options for heating and cooling that include guidelines for healthier installations, language for specifications, and maintenance suggestions that will help to eliminate some of the problems mentioned above. In the next section, we focus on ways to reduce the need for mechanical heating and cooling.

Reduction of Heating and Cooling Loads through Design Strategies

The application of a few simple design and planning principles can greatly reduce the amount of mechanical heating and cooling required to live comfortably, thereby improving health and lowering energy consumption. In designing the home for energy efficiency, consider the following suggestions.

Create an Energy-efficient Building Envelope

- Choose an exterior wall system with a high insulation value.
- Choose interior wall and floor systems with high levels of thermal mass to assist in keeping things cool in the summer and retaining heat in the winter.
- Seal cracks and joints to prevent unwanted infiltration and exfiltration.
- Choose a high insulation value for the ceiling. This measure will be especially cost-effective because most heat escapes through the roof.

Consider the Surrounding Site as an Extension of Your Climate Control Design

- Make use of deciduous trees to shade in the summer and allow solar gain in the winter.
- Observe prevailing wind patterns when planning for natural ventilation.
- Consider using trees as windbreaks to lower the heating load created by cold winter winds.
- Situate your home as far away from pollution sources as possible so that the site can provide a quality air supply for home ventilation.

Take Advantage of Solar Heat

+ Orient the home to take advantage of solar gain.
+ Plan fenestration (arrangement of doors and windows) for the desired amount of heat gain.
+ Make use of overhangs and sun angle information to prevent overheating in the summer.
+ Provide natural cross ventilation to facilitate natural air exchange and to provide natural cooling in the summer.
+ Use light colors to reflect heat and dark colors to absorb and store heat.
+ Provide thermal mass for heat storage.
+ Use thermal window-shading devices to control heat loss.
+ Use specialized window coatings to enhance solar gain where desired and to block unwanted heat gain.

Become a More Active Participant in Temperature Control

+ Open and close windows to control fresh air and temperature.
+ Open and close thermal shading devices to control heat gain and loss.
+ Use automated thermostat controls to economize on heating and cooling when you are absent or asleep
+ Be willing to add and subtract layers of clothing to allow for a greater range of acceptable temperatures.
+ Consciously temper your body to acclimatize to a broader comfort range.

This winter garden located in New Mexico provides a large portion of the homes heat in the winter. A small overhang prevents excessive solar gain from the high summer sun.
Architect: Paula Baker-Laporte;
Builder: Econest Building Co.;
Photo: Lisl Dennis.

Healthier Heating and Cooling

Each heating and cooling system has advantages and disadvantages that you must weigh carefully when choosing a system that best fits your needs and budget. Once you have made a choice, there are several design, construction, and maintenance considerations that will optimize performance and minimize the health risks of the system. In the preliminary design phase, you and your architect must consider certain factors, such as the location of the mechanical room. During the construction phase, the choice of materials and installation procedures can influence the ultimate outcome. For this reason we have provided specifications for the contractor where relevant. Finally, a regular cleaning and maintenance program is essential for optimal efficiency. This task will ultimately fall to the owner and may influence your choice of HVAC system.

Choice of Fuel Source

Gas and other combustion fuels can pollute the airstream if you do not plan carefully. Electric heat is often considered "cleaner" heat because combustion does not occur in the home. However, environmental pollution from electricity generation plants must be acknowledged. Moreover, electric heating appliances generate electromagnetic fields (EMFs), an invisible and often overlooked source of pollution. For many homeowners the higher cost of electric heat makes it unaffordable. Whatever your choice of fuel source, there are several strategies that can be employed in the mechanical room to will make heating healthier.

This "Tulikivi" brand masonry oven works on the principal of contra-flow design and mass storage capacity providing comfortable and energy efficient heat. Architect: Paula Baker-Laporte; Builder: Econest Building Co.; Photo: Lisl Dennis.

Mechanical Room Design

+ The mechanical room should be a dedicated room, insulated and isolated from the living space either by creating a separate building to house the equipment or by creating a well-sealed room that ventilates to the outside. It should be easily accessible because it must be regularly accessed for routine maintenance.
+ The equipment in the mechanical room may produce elevated levels of EMFs and should not be located adjacent to heavily occupied living spaces.
+ Ensure the supply of adequate combustion air to the mechanical room.
+ We recommend you have a fire alarm in the mechanical room.
+ If there is water in the mechanical room, there should also be a floor drain.

Heating and Cooling Appliances

We recommend the following guidelines for choosing, locating, and maintaining heating equipment.

+ Purchase equipment designed for backdraft prevention.
+ Use sealed combustion units to prevent transfer of combustion by-products into the airstream. This is especially important where the mechanical room must be accessed directly from the living space.
+ If you are using a forced-air system, we strongly recommend adding a good combination filtration system that will filter out both particulate matter and gas.
+ If possible, choose a heating system that does not run hot enough to fry dust. Hydronic systems and heat pumps meet this requirement (used mostly in mild climates).
+ Institute a regular maintenance program to clean components, purge mold or mildew growth, and change filters.

Heating and Cooling Options

Hydronic Heating

Hydronic heating, delivered through hot water, is usually a wall-mounted baseboard or radiant floor system.

Baseboard systems are usually copper tubes and aluminum radiating fins with painted steel covers. Baseboard radiators can be noisy if not maintained, and they can become traps for dust and dirt. Some baseboard units are subject to offgassing at first, when the factory-applied paint on them gets hot. Verify with the manufacturer if this will be a problem with the model that you are considering.

Hydronic radiant floor systems are usually plastic, rubber, or copper tubing installed in or under the floor. Hot water circulating through the tubing heats the floor mass, and then the heat rises through gentle convection. Radiant systems are silent and clean. The water running through the piping is not hot enough to fry dust. As well, because this form of heating heats feet, occupants are comfortable at lower operating temperatures. **Note:** Hydronic radiant floor heating should not be confused with radiant electric heating, in which the heat source is heated electrical wiring. We do not recommend this type of heating because it will distribute a magnetic field throughout the home when in operation.

At one time radiant floor heating used copper tubing almost exclusively, but the rising price of copper, combined with the introduction of plastic and rubber tubing, made this a less common option. Metal tubing, such as copper, can conduct EMFs through the structure if it becomes charged at any point along its route, and for this reason we do not recommend it.

Some infloor systems use very odorous rubber products. While this is not a problem where they are embedded in concrete, it can be a source of indoor pollution where the tubing is exposed at access points. We recommend **Wirsbo Hepex**, an odorless, cross-linked polyethylene tubing, for radiant floor heating.

The advantages of a hydronic system include slightly lower operating costs, even heating, quieter operation, ease of zoning, and independent room temperature control. Disadvantages of the hydronic system include slow response time and higher installation costs compared to forced air, due to the number of mechanical components.

Forced Air

Throughout most of the country, forced air is the most common form of heating and cooling in new construction. Besides quick response time, the main advantage of forced-air heating lies in the opportunity it gives the homeowner to commission modifications and additions to standard equipment so that it can become a healthy air-distribution system. A modified system can control humidity, filter air, and introduce fresh conditioned air from the outside. Disadvantages of forced-air systems may include greater operating costs, noisy operation, larger space requirements for equipment installation and ductwork housing, and the need for regular maintenance and cleaning of ductwork to prevent mold and dirt buildup. Disadvantages of a nonaugmented forced-air

Case Study 15.1:

Ductwork: A constant supply of warm dust

A retired couple contacted John Banta because they were experiencing eye irritation and difficulty breathing due to dust in their home. In spite of frequent vacuuming and dusting, an unusually heavy deposit of dust was noted on the furnishings during the house inspection. John suspected that the furnace system was the source of contamination because the heat registers in the home were lined with a fine dust, and the clients' symptoms worsened when the furnace was on.

John was puzzled, though, by the lack of dirt on the cold-air return filter and the absence of air movement. He opened the cold-air return and examined the inside wall to see if there were any visible obstructions. To his surprise, he found no duct at all. The cold-air return was a dummy and went nowhere.

Further investigation revealed that the furnace and duct system were located in the crawl space under the home. John inspected the crawl space, where he discovered that there was no connection between the cold-air return port on the furnace and the rest of the house. In fact, the furnace was taking cold air from the crawl space and blowing the unfiltered, contaminated air directly into the house. He recommended consultation with a heating and air-conditioning company to correct this construction defect.

Discussion

HVAC duct systems should always be leak tested to ensure that they meet specified standards. The stated industry standard for a sealed duct system is less than 3% leakage, which is rarely achieved. The furnace itself will account for much of the leakage since it is difficult to seal. The furnace should be mounted in a clean, easily accessible area like a mechanical room, and not in an attic or crawl space.

Leakage also occurs at unsealed joints where the metal ducts fit together. Since the return side of the furnace is sucking air back into the furnace, it will suck contaminants through leaks in the ductwork. If the unsealed ducts pass through walls or attics containing fiberglass, then these fiberglass particles are sucked into the ducts and blown into the house. If the unsealed ducts are in a crawl space under the home, then moldy, pesticide-laden, or dusty air can be sucked into the furnace system and blown into the house.

system can also include distribution of odors and particulate matter, and unwanted dehumidification. Forced-air heating, which heats air, is considered to be far less comfortable than radiant heating, which heats objects.

A forced-air system must be properly designed for appropriate balancing and distribution. Poor indoor air quality, energy inefficiency, and discomfort can result when system design is inadequate.

If forced air is your choice for heating and cooling (in much of the country this may be the only cost-effective choice), then you can take advantage of the whole-house air distribution ducting that will already be in place, and improve air quality by implementing the following steps.

+ Use a fresh-air intake vent from the outside to the furnace in order to introduce and distribute fresh, tempered ventilation into your home. Locate the vent so that it receives "fresh" air; do not place the vent near trash storage areas or where auto exhaust and other pollutants could be brought inside the house.
+ Install enhanced filtration in your forced-air stream (see the *Air Filtration* section below).
+ Choose a furnace with sealed combustion to avoid the entry of combustion by-products into the airstream.

Design of Forced-air Ductwork

Care must be taken during the design, installation, and maintenance of forced-air ductwork because the means of air distribution is often the source of allergies and other health problems associated with forced-air heating and cooling.

Ductless air plenums are a common source of air contamination associated with HVAC systems. Joisted floors, and wall cavities without ductwork, act as pathways for contaminated attic or crawl-space air to enter into the building if air is forced through them. Fibers from wall and ceiling insulation are frequently sucked into the return side of the heating system and circulated throughout the building envelope. Furthermore, the plenums are inaccessible for cleaning and impossible to seal.

From a health standpoint, floor registers should be avoided because debris will inevitably accumulate in them, not only during construction, but in the course of occupancy as well. Supply and return registers should ideally be located on walls or ceilings.

Below-slab ductwork should be avoided because it can collect moisture and dirt, providing a breeding ground for microbes. Also avoid running ductwork through uninsulated spaces if at all possible. If this is unavoidable, the ductwork should be well insulated on its exterior.

Ductwork should be easily accessible for future inspection and maintenance. A good design should specify cleaning portals that will give access to all ductwork, especially points of probable condensation.

The Problem: Home investigation revealed that ductwork had not been sealed on the return side of this system causing contaminated air to be sucked in to the system and blown throughout the home. Recommendation: All duetwork should be throroughly sealed and tested for air leakage.
Photo: Restoration Consultants.

Sheet metal is preferable to plastic flex ducts because the flex ducts are difficult to keep clean and are easily damaged. Ductwork may be coated with undesirable oils from the manufacturing process and should be cleaned of all oil prior to installation.

Installation of Forced-air Ductwork

Quality control during the installation of a well-designed ductwork system will help ensure optimum efficiency and health. Ductwork should be well sealed with a nontoxic sealer. Ideally, an air distribution system should have a neutral effect on building pressurization.

A large amount of dust and debris is generated during the construction process, and it frequently finds its way into the ductwork, becoming a source of air contamination once the system is in operation unless measures are taken during construction to keep the ductwork clean. In order to achieve an optimal ductwork system installation, we suggest the following specifications.

- Metal ductwork shall be free of all oil residue prior to installation.
- Ductwork shall be well sealed with nontoxic compounds such as **RCD6, AFM Safecoat DynoFlex, United Duct Sealer (Waterbase), Uni-Mastic 181, Uni-Flex Duct Sealer,** or approved equal. Mastics shall be water resistant and water based, with a flame spread rating no higher than 25, and a maximum smoke developed rating of 50.
- During construction, the ends of any partially installed ductwork shall be sealed with plastic and duct tape to avoid the introduction of dust and debris from construction.
- All forced air must be ducted. The use of unducted plenum space for the transport of supply or conditioned air is prohibited.
- Cloth duct tape shall not be used. (It has a high failure rate that can result in undetected leakage.)
- Seal all joints, including premanufactured joints and longitudinal seams.
- Gaps greater than $1/8$" must be reinforced with fiber mesh.
- All ductwork running through uninsulated spaces shall be insulated to a minimum of R10 to prevent condensation problems and to save energy.
- Any ductwork requiring insulation should have the insulation located on the outside of the ducts. *...continued over*

> - Ductwork must be professionally cleaned prior to occupancy. The duct-cleaning vacuums should have true HEPA filtration or be exhausted to the outside. No chemicals shall be used in the process.
> - Prior to occupancy, the air distribution shall be tested for leakage by a qualified third party or in the presence of the owner or architect. Any leakage greater than 3% shall be remedied by the contractor at no additional expense to the owner.

Once the ducts are in place, a regular maintenance program is essential to maintaining a healthy system. Identify a professional maintenance company that uses high-powered duct cleaning equipment. Avoid the use of chemical cleaners.

Combined Heating and Cooling Systems

Heat pumps are far more energy efficient than electric resistance heat and can be used for both heating and cooling. Heat pumps extract heat from outside air or, in some cases, from a water source. Air-source heat pumps are most common in areas where winter temperatures seldom fall below 30 degrees Fahrenheit and where summer cooling loads are high. As temperatures fall below 30 degrees, the heat pump must rely on electric resistance heating to make up the difference, at which point it loses its economic advantage.

The main advantages of a heat pump are that heating and cooling needs are met by a single unit, humidity is not added to the air, and operation is quiet.

Cooling Systems

Common types of air conditioners include condensing or refrigerated air conditioners, electric heat pumps as discussed above, and evaporative coolers.

Condensing air conditioners are available either as small units designed to cool one area of a home, or as central air conditioners, which will cool an entire home via ductwork. Advantages of central air conditioners are out-of-the-way location, quiet operation, integration with the forced-air heating system, and greater cooling capacity and efficiency than portable models. However, these systems are expensive to operate and consume a lot of energy. They cost up to seven times more to operate than evaporative cooling systems.

It is important to choose an air-conditioning unit that continues to blow air across the cooling coils for a time after the cooler is turned off. This allows any moisture remaining on the coils to be dried off, thereby discouraging mold growth.

Room air conditioners are less expensive to install than central air conditioners. Since they only cool designated areas, they save money and energy. However, they do tend to be noisy.

Evaporative coolers are practical in very dry areas and are available either as a "direct model," which adds humidity to the home, or an "indirect model," which does not add humidity. The operating costs for evaporative coolers are significantly lower than those for condensing units, and evaporative units are fairly inexpensive to install. They bring fresh outdoor air into the living space and exhaust stale air. Evaporative coolers have a lower cooling capacity and work well only in low-humidity conditions, such as those found in the southwestern states. Another name for an evaporative cooler is "swamp" cooler. They must be kept clean or they truly become swamps, filled with microorganisms

When using mechanical air-conditioning, you can save energy and money by keeping the windows closed. One exception to this rule is in the case of evaporative coolers, which are more efficient when windows are left partially open. Air conditioners should be shut off and windows opened at night, when it is cool outside. Do not cool unoccupied rooms or homes. Insulate all exterior ducting. This can save you at least 10% of the energy costs of cooling. Maintain systems regularly, keeping coils and filters clean. Locate the cooler in a shaded area.

Chart 15.1: Heating and Cooling Systems Summary

Type of system	How it works	Advantages	Disadvantages	Comments
Heating Systems				
Forced air	A fan pulls air through a heating unit and distributes the air throughout the house via ducts.	• Can be easily adapted for filtration, humidification, and dehumidification. • Almost immediate response time. • Inexpensive to operate.	• Less comfortable than radiant heat. • Stirs up and fries dust. • Can exacerbate allergies. • Ductwork is architecturally cumbersome. • Leaky ducts can depressurize home. • Noisy. • Needs regular cleaning.	• Many of the disadvantages of forced air can be rectified by adding filtration to the system both at the furnace and where the air exits into the room.

Type of system	How it works	Advantages	Disadvantages	Comments
Forced air – *cont.*			• Metal ductwork grounds negative ions. • Fumes from gas or oil fuel can enter airstream. • Insulation particles can enter airstream.	
Radiant hydronic floor heat	Hot water is run through plastic or metal tubing in floor or under floor. Natural convection gently distributes heat.	• Even, comfortable heating. • Comfortable at lower temperatures. • Efficient. • Not hot enough to fry dust. • Silent. • Low maintenance. • Easy zonation. • Invisible.	• Slow response time. • Initial installation costly. • Does not filter air. • Not practical for cooling.	• Avoid metal tubing that can transmit EMFs.
Liquid-filled baseboard heaters	Hot liquid is circulated through fin tube baseboard units and radiates into room.	• Heats quickly. • Comfortable radiant heat. • Not hot enough to fry dust. • Less expensive than in-floor heating.	• Baseboard units are dust traps. • Limits furniture placement. • Can be hot to touch.	• Heated surfaces of baseboard units may offgas. • Leaks (other than water) may be toxic.
Electric radiant floor, wall, or ceiling heat	Electric current passes through resistant wiring imbedded in walls, floors, or ceilings.	• Even heating. • Comfortable, radiant heat.	• Expensive to run. • Can create high levels of EMFs. • Less-expensive systems run hotter and fry dust.	• Not recommended in a healthy home because of EMFs and high degree of energy consumption.
Electric baseboard heating	Individual units are plugged in.	• Initial installation is inexpensive and easy. • Does not require centralized machinery. • Puts heat only where required.	• Expensive to run. • Hot to touch. • Traps and fries dust. • Emits EMFs.	• Heated surfaces may offgas.

Type of system	How it works	Advantage	Disadvantages	Comments
Wood-burning stoves	Wood fire is contained in a noncombustible stove. Heat radiates into room.	• Radiant heat source. • No central equipment required. • Inexpensive to install and operate.	• Messy to run, requiring high maintenance. • Much higher rate of respiratory problems in children in homes using wood stoves reported. • Burn and fire hazard. • Chimney can be subject to backdrafting. • Burning wood produces more than 200 toxic by-products of combustion. • Most of heat escapes up the chimney.	• Not recommended in a healthy home. • Choose the most efficient models available, burn hardwoods, and clean flue often.
Masonry heater ("Kacheloffen")	Heat from wood fire travels through a series of masonry chambers, is stored in the masonry mass, and slowly radiates into the room.	• Very efficient use of fuel requires less tending than conventional wood stoves. • Burns cleaner. • Produces comfortable radiant heat; does not fry dust or burn people. • Inexpensive to operate, requires no further equipment. • Can incorporate cook stove or oven. • Can be an architectural feature.	• Initial installation is costly; few craftspeople in the United States know how to build. • Generates a small amount of combustion by-products.	• Less convenient than central heating systems. • Considered the most healthful way to heat according to bau-biologie.
Passive solar heating	Heat from the sun is captured through glazing and stored in building components with high thermal mass such as concrete and adobe walls and floors.	• No operation expenses. • Does not consume fossil fuels. • Does not fry or circulate dust.	• Dependent on the weather. • Requires a relatively high degree of human interaction. • Must be incorporated into architecture.	• For more information refer to "Further Reading" section.

Prescriptions for a Healthy House

Type of system	How it works	Advantage	Disadvantages	Comments
Heat pump	Heat or cold is extracted from outside air and transferred to inside air.	• Can be used for heating or cooling. • Cost-effective in mild climate. • Quiet.	• Not cost-effective where temperatures are frequently below 30°. • Uses freon as transfer medium. (Freon is an atmospheric ozone depleter.)	

Cooling Systems

Type of system	How it works	Advantage	Disadvantages	Comments
Central refrigerant coolers	Freon gas is passed through a condenser. Heat is transferred to the outdoors and the cool air is distributed throughout house via ductwork.	• Can also dehumidify air. • Will handle large cooling load. • Can be quiet to operate if condenser is remote. • Shares ductwork with central heating	• Expensive to operate. • High energy consumption. • Uses freon. • Requires maintenance to prevent mold.	• Drip pan must be inspected and cleaned regularly for mold-free operation.
Room refrigerant coolers	Freon gas is passed through a condenser. Heat is transferred to the outdoors and the cooled air is blown into the room.	• Inexpensive initial installation. • Cools only designated, occupied areas, so energy waste and expense are reduced.	• High consumption of energy. • Uses freon. • Requires maintenance to prevent mold. • Noisy.	
Evaporative (swamp) coolers	Air is passed over a wet medium. As evaporation occurs, air is cooled and then blown into home.	• Low cost initially and when in operation. • Uses no CFCs or HCFCs. • Requires 80% less energy than refrigerant coolers. • Works well in hot, dry climates.	• Subject to mold and other microorganism growth. • Not suitable in humid conditions. • Cannot take as large a load as refrigerant models. • Can be noisy. • Requires maintenance to keep mold-free and needs frost protection in cold winter climates.	• Should be drained and cleaned monthly.

Ventilation

Until the 1960s, ventilation in homes occurred naturally, obviating the need for intentional ventilation systems. Homes were loosely built, allowing enough outside air to make its way through the home to keep it fresh. By some accounts, this loose construction allowed as many as three or four air exchanges per hour. Currently, with energy-efficient construction, much of the unintentional air exchange has been eliminated. As well, while homes were built of more natural, nonpolluting materials in the past, in recent years indoor air has become at least five to ten times more polluted than outdoor air and is often too polluted for optimal health. Although minimum air-exchange rates are enforced for commercial structures, this is not the case for residential construction, except where exhaust fans are mandated.

Ventilation, like many other components essential to health, is, in standard construction, considered an "extra." The American Society for Heating, Refrigeration, and Air Conditioning Engineers (ASHRAE) has set a standard of .35 air exchanges per hour or 15 cubic feet per minute (cfm) per resident for residential ventilation. Although this may be sufficient to dispel pollutants created by human activity, it may not be enough to dispel the chemical pollution generated by standard construction or the thousands of other chemicals introduced into homes through furnishings, clothing, cleaning products, cosmetics, and other scented products. ASHRAE determines its requirements based on the level at which 80% of a test population feels comfortable. It should be noted that it is quite possible to feel comfortable in environments that are polluted enough to be detrimental to health. The human body has the ability to become accustomed to harmful chemicals, much like one might adapt over time to the toxic effects of tobacco smoke. Whether the ASHRAE standard is sufficient to meet health requirements is irrelevant, because in fact most homes are not equipped with ventilation other than spot exhaust fans and do not meet the ASHRAE recommendations.

Ventilation strategies are necessary even in a healthy home because with tight construction, air exchange is necessary to ensure fresh air and dispel odors from everyday living. Care should be taken to locate the fresh-air supply away from exhaust-air piping and in the most advantageous location for receiving an unpolluted airstream.

Chart 15.2: Residential Ventilation Strategies

Type	Purpose	How it works	Advantages	Disadvantages	Comments
Natural ventilation	To bring fresh air into the home and exhaust stale air.	Takes advantage of natural air patterns. Strategically placed openings encourage fresh air to move diagonally through the space, entering low and exiting high.	Quiet. Free. Maintenance-free. Does not require energy to operate.	Can be drafty and create greater heating/cooling load. Air cannot be filtered. Allows for minimal control.	This strategy works best in mild climates and can be enhanced through various roof ventilation techniques.
Exhaust fans	To remove localized pollution at the point of generation. Primarily used for kitchens and baths.	Stale and moisture-laden air is sucked out of house at the point of generation, using a powerful fan.	Pollution is quickly removed before the rest of the home is affected.	Can depressurize home, causing infiltration and possible backdrafting.	It is important to supply replacement air when fans are in operation. Exhaust fans are required by code in bath and laundry rooms without operable windows.
Supply fans	To provide fresh air.	A fan blows fresh outside air into the home, creating positive pressurization that forces stale air out.	Inexpensive. Pressurization of home prevents contaminants from infiltrating from outdoors.	Cold drafts around fan in winter. Pressurization can cause hidden moisture problems as humid air is forced through wall openings and then condenses.	Adequate and strategically placed vents are required to exhaust air. A good strategy for venting a basement. Supply fans are not suitable for dispelling kitchen- and bath-generated pollution.
Balanced mechanical ventilation	To provide fresh air and exhaust stale air while controlling pressurization.	A set of fans brings fresh air in through intake and distributes it, then exhausts stale air to the exterior.	Provides balanced pressurization. Comes equipped with, or can be adapted for, various filtration strategies.	Does not moderate temperature or humidity of incoming air. Can be noisy.	

Type	Purpose	How it works	Advantages	Disadvantages	Comments
Balanced mechanical ventilation – *cont.*				Relatively small fans are standard and are insufficient to handle large amounts of gas filtration.	
Air to air heat exchange or HRV (heat recovery ventilator)	As above. Also moderates the temperature of fresh supply air.	Incoming fresh air passes through a series of chambers adjacent to outgoing exhaust air. Heat, but not air, is transferred from one to the other.	Reduces heating and cooling costs by recovering 60 to 80% of heat.	Chambers can be made of paper that collect dirt, or of plastic, which can offgas. Choose one with metal chambers. More costly initially than other balanced ventilators. Causes condensation; must be maintained to remain mold-free.	Most effective for tight homes in cold climates. ERVs (energy recovery ventilators) also recover humidity.
Fresh-air intake incorporated into forced-air system	To provide fresh air when the central forced-air system is operating.	A 3" to 6" metal pipe with damper valve provides fresh air into the furnace supply stream.	Inexpensive to retrofit. Ventilation supply air is preheated or precooled. Makes use of existing ductwork for distribution. Creates slight positive pressurization and can compensate for air lost through leaky ducts.	Only operates during heating or cooling season. Depends on a well-maintained heating and cooling system to deliver good quality air.	Screen all intake pipes to prevent rodent infestation.

Air Filtration

The addition of filters to ventilation and forced-air heating and cooling systems allows for greater control of air quality. As discussed above, indoor air is often too polluted to properly nourish occupants. The first line of defense against such pollutants is to provide an ample supply of fresh outdoor air through ventilation. Unfortunately, "fresh" air, although considerably cleaner in most cases than indoor air, contains allergens in the form of molds and pollens and manufactured pollutants, including exhaust fumes, smoke, and pesticides. When your immediate surroundings are less than perfect, you may wish to incorporate some form of filtration into your home.

Home ventilation systems can easily be adapted to filter large particles like pollen and mold spores. However, most home ventilation systems are not equipped with very powerful fans and therefore cannot handle the air resistance created by some of the more efficient filtration methods, especially those designed to remove gases. Consequently, whole-house filtration is often more successfully combined with the forced-air distribution system. Standard filters used with most forced-air systems are designed primarily to prevent large particles from harming the motor and are insufficient to effectively filter out small particles injurious to human health. Most forced-air equipment must be adapted to receive additional filtration systems. A forced-air system, when equipped with good filters, will not only clean fresh intake air, but will continue to clean air as it recirculates.

Chart 15.3: Residential Filtration Strategies

Filter type	Purpose	How it works	Efficiency*	Advantages	Disadvantages	Comments
Standard furnace filters	Filters out large particulate matter to safeguard the motor, not inhabitants	A coarse, 1" thick filter traps large particles.	Removes 5% of particulate matter.	Inexpensive. Easy to change.	Indoor air quality is not significantly improved.	Can easily be replaced with 1" media filter, which will raise efficiency to 20%.
Medium-efficiency, extended-surface filter	Particulate filter	Air is strained through a pleated (extended surface area) filter that maintains airflow.	Removes 40%–50% of particulate matter.	Relatively inexpensive. Sufficient for most general filtration.	Filtration is inadequate for very polluted environments and/or very	Special adaptation required to work with HVAC. Media filters

Filter type	Purpose	How it works	Efficiency*	Advantages	Disadvantages	Comments
Medium-efficiency, extended-surface filter – *cont.*				Airflow resistance can be low enough to use with ventilator.	sensitive people. Does not filter out gaseous pollution.	become more efficient with time as pores become smaller, but air resistance increases.
HEPA (High Efficiency Particulate Air) filter	Particulate filter	Polyester or fiberglass fibers are bound with synthetic resins, creating a medium with extremely small pores.	Removes 97% + of particulate matter.	Can remove minute particles for extremely clean air. Can remove cigarette smoke.	High airflow resistance requires powerful fan. Expensive. May require custom design. Does not filter out gaseous pollution such as VOCs.	Not commonly used in residential filtration. A carbon postfilter will help eliminate odor generated by HEPA filter. An inexpensive, frequently changed prefilter will extend life of HEPA filter.
Electrostatic precipitator (Ionizer)	Particulate precipitator	Mechanism is mounted to ductwork, which statically charges dust. Dust is collected at oppositely charged plates in a filter.	Removes 90% of particulate matter when clean.	No resistance to airflow. Efficient when clean. Does not require replacement.	Must be adapted for residential use. Ozone produced as by-product of high voltage. Relatively expensive. Does not filter out gaseous pollution. Only efficient when clean. Generates EMFs.	Plates must be cleaned regularly.
Electrostatic air filter	Particulate filter	Electrostatic charge is generated by	Removes 10–15% of particulate matter.	Good for mold and pollen. No customization	Not efficient for capturing small particles.	A substitute for standard furnace filters.

265

Prescriptions for a Healthy House

Filter type	Purpose	How it works	Efficiency*	Advantages	Disadvantages	Comments
Electrostatic air filter – *cont.*		friction as air moves through special media.	required on some filters used with HVAC.	Inexpensive.	Limited efficiency. Does not filter out gaseous pollution.	An inexpensive way to relieve pollen and mold allergies.
TFP (Turbulent Flow Precipitator)	Particulate precipitator	Turbulent airstream "drops" particles into collection space where there is no airflow.	Manufacturer claims 100% for particulate matter.	No resistance to airflow. Can be used with ventilator. Very low maintenance.	Product is new on the residential market and does not have an established performance record. Does not filter gaseous pollution.	
Partial bypass filter	Absorption of gaseous pollutants.	Granules of absorptive material are held in place and separated by a metallic grid. Some air passes through medium and some flows past unrestricted.		Allows some air to flow through, thereby cutting down air resistance and requiring less-powerful fan.	Not suitable where air is highly polluted. Not suitable in ventilator.	Works in conjunction with HVAC where the same air is repeatedly run through the filter.
Activated carbon filter	Adsorption of gaseous pollutants.	Gases cling to many-faceted carbon granules.	Varies	Effectively removes gases with high molecular weight. Offered in standard furnace sizes for low-pollution situations.	Does not remove certain lightweight pollutants such as formaldehyde or carbon monoxide. Filters become contaminated with use and can release pollutants if not changed.	Can be treated to remove more gases. Must be changed regularly per manufacturer's recommendations.

Filter type	Purpose	How it works	Efficiency*	Advantages	Disadvantages	Comments
Activated alumina	Adsorption and transformation of gaseous pollutants.	Activated alumina is impregnated with potassium permanganate. It acts as a catalyst in changing the chemical composition of harmful gases and also acts through adsorption.		Will remove gases not removed by carbon, including formaldehyde. Lasts longer than carbon.	Not as adsorptive as carbon. More expensive than carbon.	Activated alumina changes color when depleted.

* Efficiency ratings for particulate filters are based on research by John Bower, published in *Understanding Ventilation: How to Design, Select and Install Residential Ventilation Systems* (Bloomington, IN: Healthy House Institute, 1995).

Further Reading

Bower, John. *Understanding Ventilation: How to Design, Select and Install Residential Ventilation Systems*. Bloomington, IN: The Healthy House Institute, 1995.

Mazria, Edward. *The Passive Solar Energy Book*. Rodale Press, 1979.

Resource List

Product	Description	Manufacturer/Distributor
AFM Safecoat DynoFlex	Used as a joint-sealant treatment for HVAC ducts to eliminate toxic outgassing from standard sealants.	AFM (American Formulating & Manufacturing) 3251–3rd Avenue San Diego, CA 92103 (619) 239•0321, (800) 239•0321 www.afmsafecoat.com
Energy Federation, Inc.	Various energy-saving products including foams, sealants, fans, light bulbs, ventilation systems.	Energy Federation, Inc. 40 Washington Street, Suite 3000 Westborough, MA 01581-1012 (800) 876•0660 www.efi.org

Prescriptions for a Healthy House

Product	Description	Manufacturer/Distributor
RCD6	Nontoxic water-based mastic for sealing ductwork and metal joints.	Positive Energy P.O. Box 7568 Boulder, CO 80306 (800) 488·4340, (303) 444·4340 www.positive-energy.com
United Duct Sealer (Waterbase)	Low-VOC, water-based duct mastic for residential use.	McGill AirSeal Corporation 2400 Fairwood Avenue Columbus, OH 43207-2700 (800) 624·5535
Uni-Mastic 181	Low-VOC, water-based duct mastic for residential use	Same
Uni-Flex Duct Sealer	Low-VOC, water-based duct mastic for residential use	Same
Wirsbo Aquapex	A cross-linked polyethylene nontoxic plumbing system.	Wirsbo 5925–148th Street W. Apple Valley, MN 55124-9928 (800) 321·4739 www.wirsbo.com
Wirsbo Hepex	Cross-linked polyethylene tubing for radiant floor heating.	Same

Sources for Portable Air Filtration & Heating Products

Allermed Corporation air filters	High-quality air filters with HEPA and charcoal.	Allermed Corporation 31 Steel Road Wylie, TX 75098 (972) 442·4898, (800) 213·6191 www.allermedcleanair.com
E.L. Foust Company air filters	High-quality air filters.	E.L. Foust Company, Inc. 754 Industrial Drive Elmhurst, IL 60126 (800) 225·9549 www.foustco.com
Nigra Enterprises	Broker for environmentally benign equipment and systems (e.g., air and water filtration, heaters, and vacuum cleaners). Free consultation.	Nigra Enterprises 5699 Kanan Road Agoura, CA 91301-3328 (818) 889·6877 www.nigra.org
Ozark Water Service and Air Services	For air and water testing, and consultation regarding toxic gases, molds, asbestos, VOCs, pesticides, gas leaks, EMFs, and radon.	Ozark Water Service and Air Services 114 Spring Street Sulphur Springs, AR 72768-0218 (800) 835·8908
Radiant heater	Low-temperature, long-wave, ceramic radiant heater designed for the chemically sensitive. No outgassing from heating elements, and no fans or blowers. Heats room quickly. Does not dry the air.	Radiant Heater Corp. P.O. Box 60 Greenport, NY 11944 (800) 331·6408
Van EE	Air to air heat exchanger.	Shelter Supply 17725 Juniper Path Lakeville, MN 55044 (800) 762·8399 www.sheltersupply.com

Division 16: Electrical

Introduction

Electric and magnetic fields are commonly discussed as if they were a single entity termed electromagnetic fields or EMFs. In fact, the two phenomena, although interrelated, are distinctly different, and each will be discussed separately in this *Division*. *Chart 16.1* presents a comparison of the two.

Magnetic Fields

Basic Home Wiring and Net Current

Although the relationship between human health and elevated magnetic fields remains controversial, there are definite safety concerns associated with wiring techniques that cause these fields. The National Electric Code, in recognition of such hazards, has mandated safer wiring.

Your electrician may be puzzled if you declare that you want a home free of all elevated magnetic fields. However, if you say that you wish to have a home in compliance with the electrical code and therefore free of net current, you are saying in effect the same thing in a language that electricians understand.

Most household wiring consists of 110-volt lines. If one were to peel back the outer insulating plastic on a piece of Romex, the most common wiring used, three strands would be revealed—one black, one white, and a third that is either green or bare copper. The black strand is referred to as the "hot" wire because it draws electricity from the breaker box or panel and delivers it to light fixtures and appliances. The white wire, called the neutral, returns the electricity to the panel after it is used. The green or bare copper wire is the ground wire. Under normal conditions it does not carry electricity. However, if a malfunction such as a short occurs, it serves as a fail-safe protective device, carrying power back to the ground until the breaker is tripped and the power to the faulty circuit is cut off, thereby helping to prevent shock and electrocution.

When the electrical system is functioning as it should, the amount of electricity flowing out to the appliance through the hot wire is equal to the amount of electricity flowing back through the neutral wire. This equal and opposite flow of

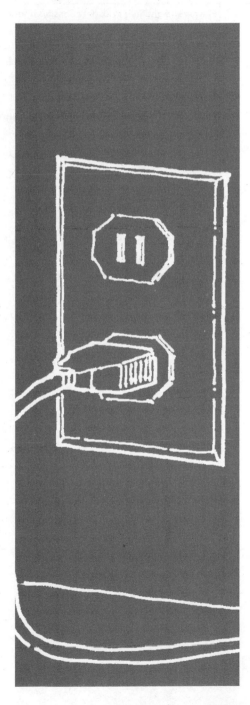

Chart 16.1: Electric fields versus magnetic fields

Electric fields	Magnetic fields
Flow in straight lines in all directions from source unless conductors attract them.	Radiate out from the source, flowing in loops.
Can be easily shielded.	Difficult and expensive to shield. (Even lead is not effective.)
Attracted by conductors such as metal or salt-water bodies, or people.	Penetrates all normal building materials.
Present whether switches for machinery are off or on.	Only occur when appliances are switched on and current is flowing.
Not widely recognized as a health threat in conventional circles at the time of this writing.	Safe exposure limits not regulated by the U.S. government. Sweden has set safe exposure limits.
Reportedly affect the nervous system and can cause insomnia, anxiety, depression, and aggressive behavior. Recently associated with higher risk of leukemia.[1]	Reportedly affect cellular function and have been statistically linked in some studies with increased cancer cell growth rate, Alzheimer's, miscarriage, and birth defects. Some sensitive individuals report physical reactions when in elevated magnetic fields.
Electrical code permits but does not mandate reduced electric field wiring.	Electrical code offers protection against exposure to magnetic fields produced by wiring in the structure, with some exceptions.
Proper use of electric field meters requires expertise.	Easily measured with a gaussmeter.

current through the wires creates a current of zero which is the desired condition. When, for various reasons, unequal supply and return currents are unable to cancel each other out, a net current is present and a magnetic field is automatically created.

A second condition that creates net current with associated magnetic fields occurs when the neutral and hot wires are separated by distance. When Romex wiring is used, the hot and neutral wires run adjacent to one another inside the plastic insulating sheathing, allowing them to cancel each other out. However, in an older wiring system known as "knob and tube," the hot and neutral wires were run on separate studs. The distance between the wires resulted in an uncancelled magnetic field. There was also no grounding. Although now prohibited by code, this dangerous system of wiring, along with its associated elevated magnetic fields, is still found in many older homes.

The National Electrical Code prohibits the production of net current, which should protect people from elevated magnetic fields as well. Unfortunately, subtle code violations resulting in the production of net current frequently occur, causing not only elevated magnetic fields, but also increased risk of fire and electrocution.

We have identified several commonly used wiring techniques that create very high magnetic fields. Although these techniques are considered to be code violations by most code interpreters because they create net current, they often go unnoticed by building inspectors. *Case Studies 16.1* and *16.2* are accounts of such occurrences. You should specify the following instructions for wiring techniques in order to detect and avoid conditions that create elevated magnetic fields.

- All wiring shall be performed in strict accordance with the National Electric Code.
- The ganging of neutral wires from different branch circuits is prohibited.
- Edison circuits are prohibited. (Edison circuits occur when three-wire Romex is used to create two 110-volt circuits and the single neutral wire is shared.)
- Bonding screws shall be removed from the neutral bus of all sub-panels per manufacturer's instructions.
- When wiring a $1/2$ switch outlet using two separate breakers for each half of the outlet, the two neutral wires must not make electrical contact. This is accomplished by breaking off the prescored conductive tabs between the two sections of the outlet per manufacturer's instructions.
- Neutral wires on $1/2$ switched outlets shall not be mixed. They shall remain paired with corresponding hot wire.
- When wiring enters an electrical box from more than one circuit, take care to ensure that the wires from the different circuits are isolated from one another so that electricity return paths are not shared. One good way to ensure that return paths are not shared is to install electrical wiring so that all wiring entering an electrical box is from the same circuit.
- At the time of the final electrical closeout, and in the presence of the general contractor, architect, or owner, the electrician shall apply a minimum load of three amps to the distal end of each electrical circuit. The home shall be inspected under load using a gaussmeter. Any elevated magnetic fields greater than .5 milligauss will indicate the presence of net current.
- It is the responsibility of the electrical contractor to locate and eliminate net current.

Magnetic Fields from Three- and Four-Way Switches

Lights switched from two different locations are called three-way switches. When lights are switched from three or more locations, they are called four-way switches. A correctly wired three- or four-way switch will not emit magnetic

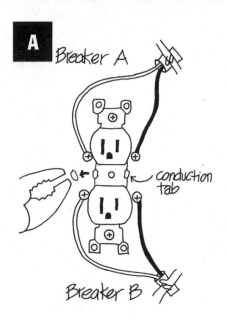

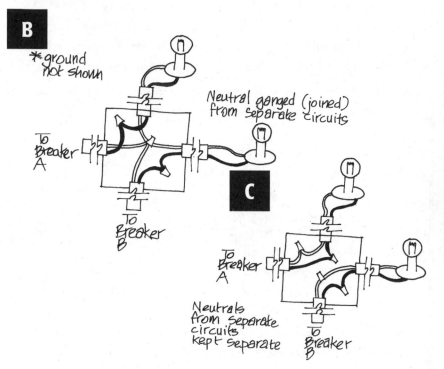

fields. However, these switches are often wired incorrectly and thus become a source of magnetic fields that can radiate throughout the entire room. To avoid improperly wired three- or four-way switches, specify the following items.

A above: 1/2 switched outlet. Both hot and neutral pre-scored conduction tabs must be snapped off when the upper and lower outlets are supplied by separate breakers.

B above right: Ganging Neutrals. This wiring will create net current and magnetic fields.

C far right: This diagram shows the correct configuration, which will not generate magnetic fields.

> - Three-wire Romex shall be used between the switches when wiring a three-way switch (see below). If alternate wire is used, it shall be twisted.
> - Each three- or four-way switch must be controlled by a single breaker.
> - All wiring for three- or four-way switches shall be contained in a single run of wire or a single metal conduit. All runs not in a conduit must be bundled.

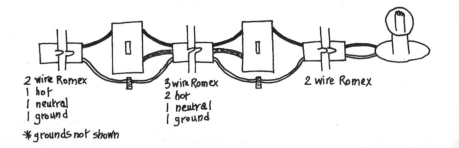

Properly wired 3-way switch

Dimmer Switches

Dimmer switches are a source of magnetic and radio frequency fields. If they are used, they should be located at a distance from seating and sleeping areas. The most expensive name-brand dimmers tend to emit smaller fields. Choose a model that emits no fields when it is all the way on or all the way off.

Magnetic Fields in Panels and Subpanels

Many electrical panels and subpanels emit substantially elevated magnetic fields. This problem arises because breaker and neutral bus bars are configured so that the neutral and hot wires are separated once fastened in place. As discussed earlier, this separation causes magnetic fields.

Some electrical panels are configured with the neutral bus bar split to run alongside the breakers. To cancel the fields, the hot and neutral wires would be the same length and installed beside one another. We recommend that such reduced field configuration panels and wiring be specified, as indicated below.

+ Panels and subpanels shall be configured so that hot and neutral field cancellation are possible.
+ The following panels and subpanels are acceptable: **Siemens EQIII**, standard load center electrical panels, and subpanels with split neutral.
+ Hot and neutral wires from the same run are to be installed adjacent to one another.
+ Wire lengths shall be equal.

Dielectric Unions

A dielectric union is a plastic joint that acts as an insulator, preventing the passage of electricity between conductive materials. In a typical home, conductive gas and water lines come into contact with appliances in several places. For example, water lines feed into refrigerators with icemakers, and gas lines feed into motorized furnaces. Should a fault occur in the appliance, wayward electricity will be distributed through the piping unless a dielectric union is used to isolate the appliance from the utility pipes. "Electrified" piping is undesirable for the reasons listed below.

+ Magnetic fields will radiate out from the pipes.
+ Net current in gas lines is an explosion hazard.

Case Study 16.1:

Magnetic field caused by wiring errors

John Banta was called to the home of a client who was concerned about the high magnetic field in the apartment she was renting. The living room, dining room, and kitchen showed a reading of around 16 milligauss. After carefully tracing the wires, John discovered the problem. The apartment had two light switches by the front door. One switch controlled the outdoor lights; the other, the living room lights. The two switches were controlled by different circuit breakers. When the switches were wired into the box, the neutral wires were joined together with a single electrical connector nut, a situation known in the trade as "ganged neutrals." The problem was easily remedied with the simple addition of a 14-cent electrical nut, which separated the two neutral wires. The magnetic fields throughout the house dropped to 0.5 milligauss, considered to be an acceptable level.

Discussion

This case study illustrates a simple code violation, which went unnoticed by the electrical inspector. Had the inspector used a gaussmeter, he would have easily detected it before final closeout. Surprisingly, this is not common practice. Had the tenant not used a gaussmeter, the code violation may never have been revealed.

• Pipes carrying net current can become an electrocution hazard.
• Electric current flowing through pipes causes electrolysis, which results in decomposition of the pipes.

The installation of dielectric unions is an inexpensive safeguard against a rarely occurring phenomenon, but one with potentially devastating results. We recommend specifying dielectric unions in healthy homes as follows.

• Metallic gas and water lines shall have dielectric unions installed wherever they enter into contact with any electrical appliance, when it is permitted by code.

Bonding and Grounding

As discussed in *Division 2*, it is important to choose a site that is free from elevated magnetic fields generated by overhead power lines. Magnetic fields caused by faulty wiring in a neighbor's home can also be transferred into your home through

Case Study 16.2:

Magnetic fields

A client sensitive to EMFs consulted with John Banta by telephone throughout the construction of her home, which was built according to specifications similar to those outlined in this book. After the client moved into her new home, she began experiencing symptoms—such as ringing in the ears and inability to concentrate—that occur when people are exposed to elevated magnetic fields. Using a gaussmeter, she discovered that about half of the home registered over 5.0 milligauss. She called John in a state of panic, convinced that her house was ruined and that she would never be able to live in it.

John contacted the client's electrician and offered to help him diagnose the problem over the telephone. Under John's guidance, the electrician conducted field testing with the client's gaussmeter. From the measurements, it became clear to John that the problem was located in the subpanel controlling a section of the house. At that point, the electrician realized what he had forgotten to do. Some panels and subpanels are interchangeable except for a single screw that must be removed from the neutral bus bar to electrically isolate it from the ground wires in the panel. Called a "bonding screw," it was causing net current in all circuits in the subpanel. The electrician simply removed the bond screw and the magnetic fields dropped in an instant to less than 0.2 milligauss.

This case study demonstrates the importance of checking the electrical installation under load with a gaussmeter before occupancy.

utility service lines. Because electricity will follow all available paths, metal plumbing, gas lines, cable TV lines, and telephone lines can become pathways for uninvited net current. Consequently, it is prudent to take simple precautions to prevent such an occurrence when site conditions allow.

Although the electrical code mandates grounding and bonding, it does not dictate the configuration of utilities entering residential structures. By grouping the entry point of all utilities and providing proper bonding, any net current traveling through public utility lines will be shunted back without ever entering the home. However, pathways of elevated magnetic fields may be created in your yard. These too can be blocked, but it will require the expertise of a knowledgeable consultant.

If site conditions do not allow for the grouping of all utilities, then it's a good precaution to use a gaussmeter to test for unwanted fields with the house power turned off, both during construction and periodically thereafter. If new magnetic fields are detected throughout the structure before it is energized, then it is reasonable to suspect that fields are entering from an outside source. At this point, consult an expert who can properly block the unwanted fields. Because neighborhood conditions may change over time, fields should be checked regularly.

Grouping the entry point of all utilities, along with the proper bonding and grounding, will also provide more protection against lightning damage. However, this is not a substitute for lightning rods, which are designed to take a direct lightning strike to the home.

The following are specifications for preventing the entry of magnetic fields through utility services.

> + All utilities, including telephone, cable TV, gas, and water, shall enter the building at approximately the same location, within a 4-foot radius.
> + All utilities entering the structure shall be properly bonded immediately prior to entry in accordance with the electrical code.
> + Bonds or grounds shall occur at only one point along each utility in accordance with the electrical code.
> + All utilities shall be tested with a gaussmeter when the house power is turned off. If magnetic fields are detected, inform owner or architect immediately.

Measuring Magnetic Fields

Magnetic fields are measured with a gaussmeter. A homeowner might consider purchasing a gaussmeter for one or more of the reasons listed below.

+ To determine safe distances from various household appliances
+ To help detect wiring errors that not only produce magnetic fields, but that may also be fire and electrocution hazards
+ As a periodic safety check to determine that no new problems have developed in household appliances
+ As a periodic safety check to ensure that no new magnetic fields are entering the home through utility lines

There are two basic types of gaussmeters: single and triple axis. Single-axis meters tend to be less expensive and are slightly more difficult for a novice to use because they must be rotated to align with the flow of the magnetic field in order

Case Study 16.3:

Net current in utilities

After purchasing a gaussmeter, an electrician was surprised to discover an elevated magnetic field throughout his entire driveway and a portion of his home. The field did not decline when he shut off the power to his home at the main breaker, so he concluded that the source of the field was net current in the gas line. A gas company technician visited the site and confirmed that the gas line was carrying electricity. There was no cause for concern, he said, because the amount of electricity was small. The electrician was not comforted by such reassurances.

As a specialist in complex wiring techniques for boats and marinas, he was familiar with the problems of electrolysis and galvanic action that result when electricity strays from its intended path. In fact, he had even seen boats at the local marina whose metal had gradually dissolved from exposure to net current. Thus, the electrician reasoned, the net current in his plumbing and gas lines would cause the lines to deteriorate at an accelerated rate. After informing a gas company representative that the galvanic action in the pipes was a liability for the company due to the possibility of an explosion, the electrician was finally able to persuade the company to take his complaint seriously.

to detect it. It is not necessary to point a triple-axis meter at a field in order to detect it, because this meter only needs to be positioned within the range of the field. Less-expensive gaussmeters will give false readings when measuring certain magnetic fields, such as those generated by computers and electrically ballasted fluorescent lights. The following table provides a comparison of widely available gaussmeters that are adequate for measuring household fields.

Chart 16.2: Gaussmeters

Brand name	Axis	Approximate cost	Accuracy for TV, fluorescents, computers
Dr. Gauss	Single	Under $20	May overestimate 60 Hz field due to interference from higher frequency fields
Tri-Field	Triple	$150	May overestimate 60 Hz field due to interference from higher frequency fields
MSI Magcheck	Single	$200	Accurate for 60 to 180 Hz field; does not measure higher frequency fields
EMF Field Tester	Single	$100	Accuracy unknown

Electric Fields

Wiring to Reduce Electric Fields

German bau-biologists have long been concerned about the negative health effects associated with exposure to electric fields. In the United States, mainstream science has given little credence to the notion that electric fields pose a health threat. However, we may soon see a change in the prevailing wisdom.

A 1996 study by the Ontario Hydroelectric Company indicated a sevenfold increase in cancers among workers exposed simultaneously to magnetic and electric fields.[2] The study suggests that the presence of electric fields potentiates the health impact of magnetic fields. Additional data published in 2000 supports the role of electric field exposure in leukemia.[3] These relatively new findings may shed light on why various studies of the impact on humans of magnetic fields alone have been inconclusive.

A certain proportion of the population appears to suffer from hypersensitivity to electric fields. These individuals react to exposure with immediate neurological symptoms such as insomnia, depression, and anxiety. One frequently reported symptom is feeling physically exhausted but too jittery to sleep, or "wired and tired."

Wiring for reduced electric fields is not required by the electrical code and can be costly. Electric fields generated by wiring can be shielded in metal conduit. This practice is standard in commercial construction, but rarely found in residential construction.

Even if metal conduit is used, electric fields will still be emitted by appliances or fixtures once they are plugged in, unless they have been specially wired or renovated. Typical electrical switches used for free-standing lamps and other appliances turn that equipment off by cutting the power on the hot wire (black wire). This does not cut off the electrical field as long as the equipment is plugged in. The entire run of wire up to the switch continues to radiate electric fields even when the switch is off.

For people with hypersensitivity to electric fields, special wiring may be a necessary expense. Techniques for this type of specialty wiring are beyond the scope of this book—you will need to consult with an expert. The following instructions may be specified to reduce electric fields generated by household wiring.

> - All household wiring shall be placed in MX, MC, or rigid metal conduit.
> - All electrical boxes and bushings shall be metal in order to shield electrical fields throughout the entire run to the panel.

A less-expensive approach would be to shield the wiring only in areas where occupants spend a great deal of time. A modified shielding plan might be specified as follows.

> - All wiring to bedrooms, den, family room, living room, and dining room shall be in MX, MC, or rigid metal conduit.
> - All other electrical runs shall be routed so as to avoid the abovementioned rooms to the greatest extent practical.
> - Avoid running wire under bed placement locations.

Wiring for Electric Field Reduction In the Bedroom with a Kill Switch

A third way to reduce electric fields in selected areas is to use a kill switch, which is designed to cut off the fields in any given run of wiring. Using a kill switch is especially applicable for bedrooms, where power isn't usually desired or necessary while one is asleep. You can turn off power to the bedroom just before you retire at night so that the bedroom becomes a field-free sanctuary. Because the presence of high electric fields is most commonly associated with sleep disturbances, we believe that such a device is an important feature in electric field reduction for the healthy bedroom.

The least expensive way to accomplish this is to install the switch in a convenient location along the run of electrical wire well before it enters the area of the home to be controlled. "Heavy duty" switches have a higher amperage limit rating and can perform this task, provided that the amperage on the circuit beyond the switch does not exceed the amperage limit rating of the switch. Combination electrical outlet and heavy-duty switch units are available. These contain an outlet and a switch in the same unit and can be installed in a typical outlet box. The switch is designed to cut off power to the adjoining outlet and to all outlets downstream from it. When the switch is on, electricity flows through the hot wire and anything plugged into the controlled electrical line will function normally. When the switch is off, the electrical wiring from the switch and

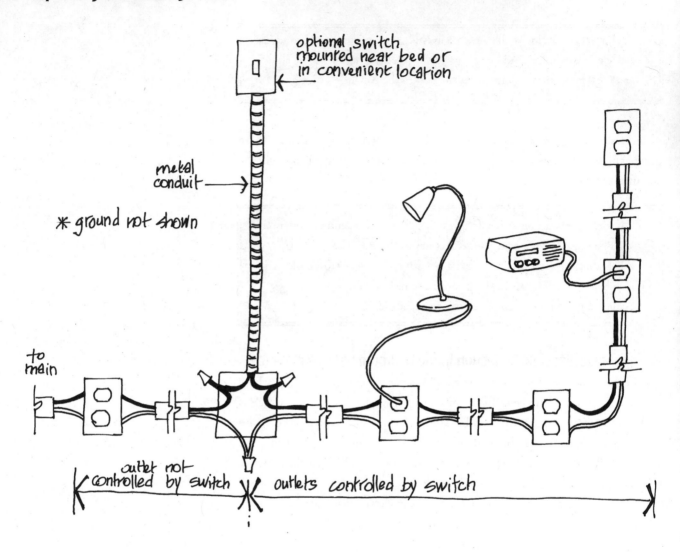

optional switch mounted near bed or in convenient location

metal conduit

* ground not shown

to main

outlet not controlled by switch

outlets controlled by switch

Kill Switch: The kill switch is used to eliminate electric and magnetic fields from plugged in appliances. When the kill switch is off the appliance is off and the fields are eliminated.

beyond is "dead" and no fields will be present in the rest of the circuit downstream from it.

This method of controlling fields may be inconvenient, since the switch must be turned off at a distance from the items to be controlled and it cannot be reached easily from the bedside. Kill switches can be wired into bedrooms and other chosen areas and placed more conveniently if the wires to the kill switch are run inside of grounded metal conduit. When wired in this manner, the switch can be placed so that it can be reached without having to get out of bed. The hot wire leading to the kill switch is still energized, but the field from it is shielded so that it does not escape the metal conduit. The room must be wired so that the kill switch is the first item on the circuit. When the switch is turned off, the fields are

Case Study 16.4:

Electric fields and insomnia

Several years ago John Banta was requested to investigate the house of a woman who claimed that she had not slept well since she moved into it. Upon inspecting the bedroom, John noted that the electrical fields registered over 5,000 millivolts on the meter. He explained that the goal for a healthy house is 20 millivolts or less. (These measurements are relative and are measured in the body using special equipment and techniques.)

The elevated electric fields were a result of the electrical wiring in and near the bedroom. The fields were being concentrated in the metallic bedsprings, which acted as an antenna, redirecting the electric field upward toward the client. John explained to the woman that the easiest way for an electrician to lower the electric fields in the bed would be to install a remote-controlled switch on the three circuit breakers in the basement that controlled the electrical wiring in and around the bedroom.

At that point in the conversation, the client's husband expressed his skepticism regarding the investigation and findings. He doubted that the presence of an electrical field could explain his wife's sleeplessness since he did not experience similar symptoms. He was reluctant to follow John's recommendations, so John suggested that the couple try an experiment to ensure that a remote switch would indeed be money well spent. He told them to turn off the three breakers in the basement every night before they went to bed to determine if the woman slept better. John reminded them that there would be no power in the bedroom and that they should have a battery-operated alarm clock and flashlight available.

A few weeks later the client contacted John to report that she was sleeping soundly for the first time in years and that both she and her husband were elated. She related to John what had transpired after he left the couple's home. When the time came to turn off the breakers on the first night, she could hear her husband grumbling with resentment and stomping loudly down the steps to the basement. That night she slept so long and soundly that she barely made it to the bathroom in time to empty her bladder the following morning. Her husband took note of her improvement and the second night went into the basement to shut off the breakers without saying a word. Again she slept soundly and awoke with the sun, feeling refreshed. By the third night she began to feel romantic, a feeling she had not experienced in a long time. By the fourth night her husband was whistling while he took the basement stairs two at a time. At this point the couple was eager to invest in a remote switching device.

Discussion

Because of standard wiring practices, readings of 1,000 millivolts or higher in a home are typical. Wiring homes for low electric fields is much easier and more cost-effective when this consideration is part of the initial building plans. Wiring paths, for example, can be situated in a way that limits the number of circuits involved, and high field emitters can be placed at a safe blocked and none of the electrical equipment plugged in along that run of wire will operate or produce fields.

Kill switches are most effectively used when wire runs are planned in advance. Electrical runs from adjoining areas need to be carefully considered so that their fields do not enter areas designated to be free of fields. It is also important that smoke detector and refrigerator/freezer circuits never be on a circuit with a kill switch that might turn them off. All equipment that must operate 24 hours a day should be specially shielded or positioned far enough away so as to prevent the fields from penetrating walls into the sleeping area. The electric fields generated by this type of household equipment generally do not extend more than 12 feet from the equipment.

Shielding Electrical Fields Emitted from Refrigerators

Because refrigerators generate large electric fields, we recommend that they be given a dedicated circuit and that the wiring be shielded with one of the recommended metal conduits. In addition, the metal refrigeration cabinet should be bonded to the electrical ground. Note that the compressor motor and defroster will still produce high magnetic fields. Consequently, the home should be designed so that the refrigerator is at least 12 feet away from living and sleeping areas.

Gasketed Electrical Boxes

As discussed in *Division 7, Air Barrier,* it is necessary to seal electrical boxes in order to make an exterior wall airtight. You may have felt the flow of air coming through an outlet on a cold day. This is due to the fact that the boxes are not installed in an airtight manner. It is necessary to stop air flowing into the living space from a wall cavity, not only for the sake of energy efficiency, but also to maintain optimal indoor air quality. The following gasketed electrical boxes are designed to create an airtight seal

+ Union Airtight Boxes
+ R & S Enviroseal
+ Lessco Air Vapor Barrier Boxes

Residential Lighting

Residential lighting types are typically incandescent, fluorescent, and low voltage. The following pointers concern residential lighting and EMFs.

+ Transformers of low-voltage lighting produce a magnetic field. If low-voltage lighting is used, choose remote transformers and locate them in closets at a distance from where occupants spend a lot of time.
+ Fluorescent lighting with ballasts emits magnetic fields that an inexpensive gaussmeter may not detect. Avoid using fluorescent lighting with ballasts in areas where occupants spend a lot of time. This kind of lighting should never be located on a ceiling below a bedroom.
+ If using recessed can lighting, specify airtight insulation contact (ATIC) cans. These types of cans save energy and prevent dust and attic gases from filtering into the cans.
+ If wiring is run through a metal conduit, the metal housing of the fixture must be in electrical contact with the metal conduit in order to shield the occupied space from electric fields.

Smoke Detectors

The two basic types of smoke detectors are ionizing and photoelectric. The ionization type contains a radioactive substance called Americium 241. Although the radioactive substance is shielded, we cannot recommend this type because there is no safe place for disposal once the smoke detector is discarded.

Smoke detectors are available for use with 9-volt batteries or for hardwiring into the 110-volt household wiring, with or without battery backup. We recommend a hardwired system with battery backup. Photoelectric smoke detectors with battery backup can be purchased through **BRK Electronics (First Alert)** and **MCS Referral & Resources.**

If you are wiring so that your bedroom circuitry can be shut off, it is important to put the smoke detector on a separate circuit so that it will always remain active. If this circuit is run through a metal conduit, the electric field will be minimal.

Carbon Monoxide Detectors

All gas-burning appliances to which occupants are exposed, such as gas ranges and dryers, should be tested for carbon monoxide (CO) emissions before the building is occupied. The installation of a simple monitoring device will insure that the occupants are alerted if a problem with carbon monoxide develops. The device should have battery backup and easy-to-read digital printout. The following CO monitors meet these criteria:

- **Nighthawk Carbon Monoxide Detector:** Contains a sensor that samples the air every 2.5 minutes and updates the digital readout.
- **Aim CO Monitor:** A portable unit with digital readout.
- **BRK Electronics (First Alert)**

Endnotes

[1] "Strong Electric Fields Implicated in Major Leukemia Risk for Workers" *Microwave News* (May-June 2000).

[2] Reported in *Microwave News* 5:4 (July-August 1996), 1, 5–7.

[3] "Strong Electric Fields Implicated in Major Leukemia Risk for Workers" *Microwave News* (May-June 2000).

Further Reading

Becker, Robert O. *Cross Currents: The Promise of Electromedicine, The Perils of Electropollution.* J.P. Tarcher, 1991. A timely and eloquent warning on the hazards of electronic pollution.

von Pohl, Gustav Freiherr. *Earth Currents: Causative Factor of Cancer and Other Diseases.* Stuttgart, Germany: Frech-Verlag, 1987

Resource List

Product/Services	Description	Manufacturer/Service Provider
Aim CO Monitor	Portable unit provides digital readout and has battery backup.	Available through: MCS Referral and Resources 2326 Pickwick Baltimore, MD 21207 (800) 466•9320, (410) 362•6400 www.mcsrr.org
BRK 2002 Line, First Alert	Line of photoelectric smoke detectors and carbon monoxide detectors with battery backup.	BRK Electronics (First Alert) 3901 Liberty Street Road Aurora, IL 60504 (800) 392•1395, (630) 851•7330 www.firstalert.com
EMF Field Tester	A reasonably priced, rugged, but lightweight single-axis gaussmeter.	Professional Equipment 90 Plant Avenue, Suite 3 Hauppauge, NY 11788-3813 (800) 334•9291 www.professionalequipment.com
Dr. Gauss	Gaussmeter.	Huntar Company, Inc. 473 Littlefield Avenue San Francisco, CA 94080 (800) 566•8686 www.learningmates.com
EMF reduction supplies	Various.	Healthy Home Center 1403-A Cleveland Street Clearwater, FL 33755 (727) 447•4454, (800) 583•9523 www.healthyhome.com
EMF reduction supplies	Various.	Less EMF, Inc. 26 Valley View Lane Ghent, NY 12075 (888) 537•7363 www.lessemf.com
Lessco Air Vapor Barrier Boxes	Airtight electrical boxes.	Shelter Supply, Inc. 17725 Juniper Path Lakeville, MN 55044-9482 (800) 762•8399 www.shelter-mn.com
MSI 95, Magcheck, and Bell 4080	Gaussmeters.	Magnetic Sciences International 367 Arlington Street Acton, MA 01720 (978) 266•9906, (800)749•9873 www.magneticsciences.com
Nighthawk Carbon Monoxide Detector	A portable unit with battery backup and digital readout.	Positive Energy Conservation Products P.O. Box 7568 Boulder, CO 80306 (800) 488•4340, (303) 444•4340 www.positive-energy.com
Photoelectric smoke detectors	Photoelectric smoke detectors with backup batteries.	MCS Referral & Resources 2326 Pickwick Baltimore, MD 21207 (410) 362•6400, (800) 466•9320 www.mcsrr.org
R & S Enviroseal	Airtight electrical boxes.	Available through: Shelter Supply, Inc. 17725 Juniper Path Lakeville, MN 55044-9482 (800) 762•8399 www.shelter-mn.com

Prescriptions for a Healthy House

Product/Services	Description	Manufacturer/Service Provider
Siemens EQ111	Standard load center electrical panels and subpanels with split neutral.	Siemens 2880 Sunrise Boulevard Rancho Cordova, CA 95742 (800) 964•4114 Widely distributed and available in many home improvement store chains, such as Home Depot.
Tri-Field Meter	Gaussmeter.	Alpha Labs, Inc. 1280 South, 300 West. Salt Lake City, UT 84101 (801) 487•9492, (800) 769•3754 www.trifield.com
Union Airtight Boxes	Airtight electrical boxes.	Available through: Minnesota Electric Supply North Highway 29 Alexandria, MN 56308 (320) 763•5131

EMF Consultants

Product/Services	Description	Manufacturer/Service Provider
Environmental Testing and Technology	EMF measurements and mitigation consultation, including household electric and magnetic fields, radio and microwave assessment.	Environmental Testing and Technology 1106 Second Street, Suite 102 Encinitas, CA 92024 (800) 811•5991, (760) 436•5990
IBE	Provides list of certified bau-biologie home inspectors for measuring magnetic and electric fields.	Institute for Bau-Biologie and Ecology P.O. Box 387 Clearwater, FL 33757 (727) 461•4371 www.bau-biologieusa.com
Indoor Environmental Technologies, Inc.	Wide variety of indoor air-quality testing services and consultation.	William H. Spates III 1403 Cleveland Street Clearwater, FL 33755 (727) 446•7717
National Electromagnetic Field Testing Association	Provides list of independent EMF consultants.	National Electromagnetic Field Testing Association 714 Laramie Glenview, IL 60025-3464 (847) 729•1532 www.theramp.net/nefta
Ozark Water Service and Air Services	For EMF testing and consultation.	Ozark Water Service and Air Services 114 Spring Street Sulphur Springs, AR 72768-0218 (800) 835•8908
Safe Environments	Consulting and testing for a wide range of indoor air-quality problems.	Safe Environments 1611 Merritt Drive Novato, CA 94949 (510) 549•9693

Appendix A: MCS: What is It?

Multiple Chemical Sensitivity/Environmental Illness

Multiple chemical sensitivity (MCS), often referred to as environmental illness, is an immune and nervous system disorder that involves severe reactions to many everyday chemicals and products. For some people MCS occurs with dramatic onset, precipitated by a major chemical exposure or industrial accident. But for most people the condition develops gradually as the result of the cumulative exposures of daily life.

The symptoms of MCS are diverse and unique to each person and can involve any organ of the body. Symptoms range from mild to disabling and sometimes life-threatening. These symptoms include headaches, fatigue, sleep disturbances, depression, panic attacks, emotional outbursts, difficulty concentrating, short-term memory loss, dizziness, heart palpitations, diarrhea, constipation, shortness of breath, asthma, rashes, flu-like symptoms, and seizures. Symptoms may be chronic or occur only when a person is exposed to certain substances. The particular organs affected depend on the individual's genetic background and prior history, as well as the specific chemicals involved in the exposure.

Symptoms are triggered by a wide range of substances found in the workplace and at home—solvents, paint, varnishes, adhesives, pesticides, and cleaning solutions are most frequently implicated. Other substances include new building materials and furnishings, formaldehyde in new clothes, artificial fragrances in cleaning compounds and personal care products, detergents, car exhaust, and copying machine and laser printer toner. Symptoms can occur after inhaling chemical vapors, after chemicals have touched the skin, or after ingestion. They are often triggered by very low levels of exposure, even lower than those established as permissible by government, and typically below the levels tolerated by most people. Sensitivity to a particular chemical can lead to sensitivity to an ever-widening range of other, often dissimilar, chemicals. This characteristic is known as the "spreading phenomenon."

It may be useful to think of MCS as one end of a spectrum that encompasses a wide range of chemical sensitivities. At one end are individuals who may suffer from mild symptoms, such as simple sinus congestion or headaches, which usually resolve when the triggering chemical agent is removed. At the other end of the spectrum are individuals with full-blown MCS, who suffer extremely debilitating symptoms that can last for months or years after exposure.

Why do some people contract MCS and others, with the same level of exposure, do not? Because of biochemical individuality, all humans manifest disease according to individual genetic makeup, past chemical exposure, and overall general state of health, which includes "total load." Total load refers to all stressors in a person's life, including chemical exposure, poor nutrition, emotional tension, allergies, infections, trauma, and physical stress.

Although the exact mechanism whereby chemicals create this phenomenon of heightened sensitivity has not yet been clearly elucidated, theories are emerging that we hope will lead to greater understanding and better treatment of MCS.

Recent studies have demonstrated how toxins, after gaining access to the brain via the olfactory nerve, can cause release of excitatory amino acids that result in swelling, dysregulation, and destruction of brain cells. The olfactory nerve is also the pathway to the limbic system, which is an area of the brain where the nervous, immune, and endocrine systems interact. The limbic system regulates an extremely wide variety of body functions. Many of the varied and seemingly bizarre symptoms reported by persons with MCS are actually consistent with symptoms known in the medical literature to occur when various parts of the limbic system are damaged by either chemicals or physical injury.

Toxic chemicals can also cause direct damage to specific tissues of the body—such as enzymes in the liver that are essential in the detoxification pathway. Because of inadequate amounts of detoxifying enzymes, the MCS person is less able to handle chemical loads. Also, recent data indicate that certain toxins in the environment, especially chlorinated compounds, mimic natural hormones, causing disruption of endocrine systems such as the thyroid, adrenal, and reproductive systems.

The first documented cases of environmental illness resulted from widespread chemical poisoning during World War I. The exposure to mustard gas had long-term consequences for soldiers, many of whom developed chronic symptoms of chemical sensitivities. More recently, thousands of veterans who fought in the Gulf War returned with symptoms that were similar to those found in patients diagnosed with MCS.

Since World War II the production of synthetic chemicals has increased significantly. In 1945, the estimated worldwide production of these chemicals was fewer than 10 million tons. Today it is over 110 million tons. As more and more synthetic chemicals are introduced into the environment, larger numbers of healthy people are becoming affected. Most people with MCS have not been through a war. They have become ill from ordinary day-to-day, low-level exposures to poor indoor air quality in their homes and workplaces. MCS sufferers often say that their role in society is like the canary in the coal mine. When the canary collapsed, the miners were warned that lethal gases were in the air.

Although MCS is a rapidly growing problem, sometimes called a silent epidemic, health care workers know little about the subject. Why? Chemical sensitivity is a relatively new field of medicine, controversial in nature, and not recognized or understood by most physicians. The illness does not fit neatly into the current medical model. And unlike diabetes or hypertension, there is no simple medical test that can be used to make the diagnosis. There are remarkably few individuals in medicine who have toxicology training and who are sensitive to the possible neurological, behavioral, and psychiatric problems resulting from chemical exposures. In addition, the chemical and insurance industries have played a major role in influencing the average person's perceptions about chemicals and their impact on living organisms.

One of the most important aspects of treatment of the chemically sensitive person is to avoid or reduce toxic chemical exposures as much as possible in order to allow the body to heal. A healthy home is a prerequisite for those who wish to regain their health. The person with MCS needs a sanctuary of peace and well-being amid a world saturated with toxic chemicals.

In spite of widespread ignorance and vested financial interests, the public is gradually gaining awareness of MCS as more and more people become ill. A small but growing number of physicians specializing in environmental medicine have focused on this serious problem for several years. If you would like information about a physician in your area who has expertise in the diagnosis and treatment of chemically related health problems, call the *American Academy of Environmental Medicine* in **New Hope, PA**, at Phone: **(215) 862-4544**.

Author Testimonials on MCS

Paula Baker-Laporte

If someone had told me in the early years of my career that I would be writing a technical "how to" book about healthy homes, I would have looked at them with total incredulity! I would have explained that, as an architect, my main concern was the creation of beautiful and interactive spatial forms, and that my aspirations were artistic rather than technical. It seems that fate had a different course for me. I joined the ranks of the chemically sensitive.

In retrospect, the roots of my illness can be traced back to formaldehyde overexposure that I suffered when, for a short period, I lived in a brand-new mobile home. Working in standard residential construction, my symptoms became severely aggravated whenever I visited a job site because of the prevalence of this toxic chemical in the materials that conventional homes are made of.

Erica Elliott, my friend and physician, diagnosed my condition and helped me to get back on my feet. It was through her that I first heard of healthy building. She told me of the alarming number of chronically ill patients consulting her who were diagnosed with MCS. For many, the primary cause of illness was exposure to multiple toxins in the home.

Even though I specialized in residential architecture, I had to admit that I knew little about the health implications of standard home construction. While working with Erica to design her home, I began intensive research into this new frontier in architecture and building. It was then that my personal and professional life took a new direction.

Once I learned the facts, I could never again allow certain products, techniques, or equipment to be used in any projects with which I was involved. I understood the health threat that they posed to my clients, other inhabitants, construction workers, and the planet.

In my efforts to learn everything I could about healthy building, I came across a body of information, translated from the original German, in the field of bau-biologie. Bau-biologie advocates an environmentally sustainable approach to healthy building, in part through the use of natural, unprocessed building materials.

I used these principles when I was designing a new home for my family, using a timber frame and straw-clay wall system. Robert Laporte, my husband and builder, introduced this building system to me when I first met him at a natural building workshop that he was leading. Our home has earth plasters and earth and stone floors, and is primarily heated by solar heat and a masonry oven. The electrical wiring is in metal conduit. My own health has improved steadily, partially as a result of the clean and vital environment afforded to me by our natural home and unpolluted surroundings. Although the bulk of my professional design work now incorporates alternative natural building systems, I realize that the majority of people planning a new home do not have access to these materials and methods of construction for numerous reasons. I also realize that for some chemically sensitive individuals, many natural materials can elicit symptoms as readily as synthetic ones do. For this reason the bulk of the information in this book is geared towards standard building practices.

A healthy home is far more than a home that is free of toxins. It must safeguard the residents on many other levels, described throughout this book. As a result of my research, my goals as an architect have grown. In order to truly nurture us, our buildings must not only be beautiful in a spatial sense; they must also be healthful and conceived with mindfulness of limited planetary resources. The same building can destroy human health or enhance vitality. The difference lies in the materials and methods of construction.

Erica Elliott

My involvement with indoor air quality issues began in 1991 when I went to work for a large medical corporation as a family physician. The building that housed the clinic was new and tightly sealed, with nonoperable windows and wall-to-wall carpeting. Previously in excellent health, a world-class mountaineer and marathon runner, I began to develop unexplainable fatigue. After several months, more symptoms developed, including rashes, burning eyes, chronic sore throat, and headaches. The symptoms subsided in the evenings after I left the workplace, only to return again when I re-entered the building.

By the second year of employment I had developed persistent migraine headaches, muscle and joint pains, insomnia, confusion, lack of coordination, memory loss, and mood swings. By then the symptoms had become permanent, even when I was away from the workplace on weekends. My physician colleagues were puzzled by my symptoms. Some felt I was suffering an unusual manifestation of depression and would benefit from antidepressant medication. These medicines were not helpful and only masked the problem. I finally had the good fortune to find a physician trained in environmental medicine who believed that I had nervous and immune system damage related to chronic, low-level exposure to poorly ventilated toxins in the workplace.

By the time I resigned my position on the staff of the clinic and the local hospital, I had a full-blown case of multiple chemical sensitivities, also known as environmental illness. Most synthetic chemicals commonly found in the modern world, even in minute amounts, caused me to have adverse reactions to such a degree that life became a painful ordeal. With diligent avoidance of toxins, abundant rest, detoxification therapies, and other measures, my life has begun to stabilize.

Since very few physicians are trained in toxicology and environmental medicine, I began immersing myself in this field of study, to help myself as well as others. It wasn't long before my practice consisted primarily of patients with immune dysfunction, including multiple chemical sensitivity, autoimmune disease, chronic fatigue syndrome, fibromyalgia, and severe allergies. I was struck by the number of patients who dated the onset of their symptoms to a move to a new home or to the remodeling of a school or office. They invariably had been to many doctors, who treated them for conditions such as allergies, asthma, sinusitis, and depression. The underlying causes were not identified. By the time the correct diagnosis was made, the patients' immune systems were often severely, sometimes irreversibly, damaged.

It was during my own recovery that I decided to build a home using nontoxic building materials. Paula Baker was my architect, patient, and neighbor. Together we began researching various available products and associated health effects. Shortly thereafter, we had the pleasure of meeting John Banta, the beginning of a fruitful collaboration.

John Banta

My introduction to the downside of indoor air quality occurred along with my introduction to fatherhood in 1980. Like many first-time parents, my wife and I wanted to welcome our newborn by decorating the nursery. We painted and carpeted the room in anticipation of our new arrival. The room smelled of chemicals; I noticed that I did not feel good in there. But it wasn't until our baby became ill that I realized what a serious problem we had created. By the time I made the connection between my daughter's medical condition and the toxins in the nursery, she had become sensitized to even minute amounts of toxic chemicals commonly found in the environment and was in severe distress. My wife and I decided to buy an old Victorian home that had not been remodeled in over 40 years. We proceeded to convert the building into a chemical-free sanctuary where our daughter could begin to heal from her devastating illness.

During that time I was working as a medical technician in a research lab where I was exposed to numerous toxic chemicals, including formaldehyde, benzene, toluene, xylene, and several disinfectants. Over the next four years I felt progressively worse while at work, yet I would feel better once I returned to our carefully remodeled home. My job-related health problems finally became so severe that I made the difficult decision to quit. Little did I know that a new and exciting career was awaiting me.

Because of my hands-on experience renovating my own healthy home, people began to ask me for advice. My wife urged me to begin consulting professionally, which I have done full-time since 1986.

Thousands of people have consulted me over the years about their homes. Typically, I am contacted in the middle of a disaster: "The walls are moldy," "The paint is causing headaches," or "The landlord sprayed pesticides to control insects." I am then hired to determine the cause and suggest a remedy for the problem. My job often includes educating a skeptical landlord or spouse about the causal relationship between the health of the occupant and the problem in the home.

The most rewarding work for me is consulting during the planning phase of new construction, when I can help my clients prevent problems before they occur. Although I do not design or build homes, I can troubleshoot and monitor to help ensure a nontoxic, healthful, and nurturing abode.

I have really enjoyed working with Paula and Erica in creating this book. For me, it offers a way to reach more people by providing them with the information they need to create a healthy home from the outset

Appendix B: Resource List

100% Silicone Sealant
Clear sealant.
DAP/Dow Corning
855 North 3rd Street
Tip City, OH 45371
(800) 634•8382
*Available at many hardware chains
including:*
Home Depot, Ace Hardware, Hacienda
Homecenters, Builders Square.

86001 Seal
Clear, water-reducible sealer and
primer for gypsum board
9400 W Impregnant
Solvent-free, water-repellant coating
that allows wood to breathe while
providing ultraviolet, mildew, and frost
protection.
Palmer Industries, Inc.
10611 Old Annapolis Road
Frederick, MD 21701
(800) 545•7383, (301) 898•7848;
www.palmerindustriesinc.com

ACQ Preserve
Pressure treatment for wood that uses
alkaline-copper-quat, which contains
no known carcinogens or EPA-listed
hazardous compounds. Not widely
distributed.
Chemical manufactured by:
Chemical Specialties, Inc.
One Woodlawn Green, Suite 250
Charlotte, NC 28217
(800) 421•8661
www.treatedwood.com
Treated wood manufactured by:
J.H. Baxter
1700 South El Camino Rael
San Mateo, CA 94402
(650) 349•0201, (800) 780•7073
www.jhbaxter.com

Admont Natural Floors
Pre engineered flooring available in
spruce, larch, beech, oak, ash, maple, or
recycled pine.
Distributed by:
Planetary Solutions
2030–17th Street
Boulder, CO 80302
(303) 442•6228
www.planetearth.com

AFM Coatings, Stains and Sealers
Products developed specifically for
chemically sensitive people in
consultation with environmental
medicine physicians.
AFM Safecoat Acrylacq
High-gloss, clear, water-based wood
finishes replacing conventional
lacquer.
AFM Safecoat DuroStain
Interior/exterior, water-based semi-
transparent wood stains in seven
different earth pigments.
AFM Safecoat DynoFlex
Available in sprayable form to use as
topcoat over DynoSeal. Also used as a
joint-sealant treatment for HVAC ducts
to eliminate toxic outgassing from
standard sealants. And useful as a low-
toxic roof coating to replace tar and
gravel. Can be walked on and remains
flexible.
AFM Safecoat DynoSeal
A flexible, low-odor, waterproof,
vaporproof barrier.
AFM Safecoat Enamel
Comes in flat, eggshell, semi-gloss, and
gloss water-based paints without
extenders, drying agents, or
formaldehyde.
AFM Safecoat Hard Seal
Water-based, general-purpose clear
sealer for vinyl, porous tile, concrete,
plastics, particleboard plywood. Not
recommended where exposed to
heavy moisture or standing water.
**AFM Safecoat Lock-In New Wood
Sanding Sealer**
Sandable sealer helps raise grain on
new woods in preparation for sanding
prior to finish coat.
AFM Safecoat MexeSeal
A satin-finish topcoat used over Paver
Seal .003 undercoat. Very durable sealer
providing water and oil repellency for
use on Mexican clay tile, stone, granite,
concrete, and stone pavers. Glossy
when multiple coats are applied.
**AFM Safecoat New Wallboard
Primecoat HPV**
Water-reducible, one-coat coverage
primer for new gypboard, green
board, and high-recycled-content
material.

AFM Safecoat Paver Seal .003
Undersurface sealer for new or
unsealed porous tile, concrete, and
grout. Fills up pores and preps slab for
topcoat. Used with MexeSeal topcoat.
AFM Safecoat Penetrating Waterstop
A satin-finish final coat that may be
used over MexeSeal to further
improve water repellence.
AFM Safecoat Polyureseal
Clear gloss wood finish replaces
conventional solvent- and water-
based polyurethanes for low-traffic
interior wood floor and furniture
applications.
AFM Safecoat Polyureseal BP
As above for high-traffic situations, high
durability, and abrasion resistance.
AFM Safecoat Primer Undercoater
Primer for use on drywall, wood, and
masonite with excellent sealing
properties; reduces outgassing.
AFM Safecoat Safe Seal
Clear sealer for porous surfaces;
effective in blocking outgassing from
processed woods. Improves adhesion
of finish coats.
AFM Safecoat Zero VOC Paint
Flat and semi-gloss paint. No VOCs,
formaldehyde, ammonia, or masking
agents.

AFM Cleaning and Maintenance
AFM SafeChoice Safety Clean
Industrial strength biodegradable
cleaner and degreaser for high
moisture areas.
AFM SafeChoice SuperClean
All-purpose, biodegradable
cleaner/degreaser.
AFM SafeChoice X158
Low-odor liquid surfactant coating for
prophylactic use where mold and
mildew are likely to appear.

AFM Carpet Maintenance System
AFM SafeChoice Carpet Guard
Sealer designed to help prevent
outgassing of harmful chemicals from
carpet backing and adhesives.
AFM SafeChoice Carpet Lock-Out
A final spray application seals in
harmful chemicals in carpet and repels
dirt and stains.

AFM SafeChoice Carpet Seal
Sealer designed to help prevent
outgassing of harmful chemicals from
carpet backing and adhesives.
AFM SafeChoice Carpet Shampoo
An odorless carpet shampoo that
helps remove chemicals such as
pesticides and formaldehyde from
new carpet.

AFM Other Products
AFM Safecoat 3 in 1 Adhesive
Adhesive for ceramic, vinyl, parquet,
Formica, slate, and carpet.
AFM Safecoat Almighty Adhesive
A low-odor, nontoxic, water-based
adhesive for gluing wood and wood
laminates. This product is available
only through special order at a 50-
gallon minimum.
AFM Safecoat Caulking Compound
Water-based, elastic-emulsion caulking
compound designed to replace
traditional caulk and putty for
windows, cracks, and maintenance.
Limited distribution.
AFM (American Formulating and
Manufacturing)
3251–3rd Avenue
San Diego, CA 92103
(619) 239•0321, (800) 239•0321
FAX: (619) 239•0565
www.afmsafecoat.com

Aim CO Monitor
A portable unit that provides digital
readout and has battery backup.
Available through:
MCS Referral and Resources
2326 Pickwick
Baltimore, MD 21207
(800) 466•9320, (410) 362•6400
www.mcsrr.org

Air Care Odorless Paints
Acrylic paints that are zero to low VOC.
Coronado Paint Co.
308 Old Country Road
Edgewater, FL 32132
(904) 428•6461, (800) 883•4193

AirChek, Inc.
The "Open Land Test Kits" sampler is a
one-day test device that is mailed

back to the lab for reading.
AirChek, Inc.
Box 2000
Naples, NC 28760
(800) 247•2435
www.radon.com

Air Krete
Cementitious foam insulation made of magnesium oxide, calcium, and silicate. High R value 3.9/inch.
Nordic Builders
162 North Sierra Court
Gilbert, AZ 85234
(480) 892•0603
www.nontoxicinsulation.com
Also available from:
Palmer Industries, Inc.
10611 Old Annapolis Road
Frederick, MD 21701
(800) 545•7383
www.palmerindustriesinc.com

The Allergy Relief Shop
Mail-order catalog offering supplies and building products for the allergy-free home.
The Allergy Relief Shop
3360 Andersonville Highway
Andersonville, TN 37705
(865) 494•4100, (800) 626•2810
www.allergyreliefshop.com

Allergy Resources
Nontoxic cleaning compounds and body care products.
Allergy Resources
301 East 57th Avenue, Unit D
Denver, CO 80216
(800) 873•3529, (303) 438•0600
www.catalogcity.com (under allergy related catalogs)
allergyresources@hotmail.com.

Allermed Corporation
High-quality air filters with HEPA and charcoal.
Allermed Corporation
31 Steel Road
Wylie, TX 75098
(972) 442•4898, (800) 213•6191
www.allermedcleanair.com

Allgreen MDF
A medium-density fiberboard made from 100% recovered wood fiber, containing no incremental formaldehyde emissions.
Available through:

Can Fibre
8 King Street East, Suite 1501
Toronto, Ontario, Canada M5C1B5
(416) 681•9990, (888) 355•4733
www.canfibre.com

Alpha Labs, Inc.
Tri-field meter, gaussmeter.
Alpha Labs, Inc.
1280 South, 300 West
Salt Lake City, UT 84101
(801) 487•9492, (800) 769•3754
www.trifield.com

Aluma-foil
Air barrier of foil laminated on two sides of kraft paper with nontoxic adhesive.
Advanced Foil Systems, Inc.
820 South Rockefeller Avenue, Suite A
Ontario, CA 91761
(800) 421•5947, (909) 390•5125
www.afs-foil.com

American Environmental Health Foundation
Sells a wide range of household, building, personal care, and medical products as well as organic clothing, books, and vitamins.
American Environmental Health Foundation
8345 Walnut Hill Lane, Suite 225
Dallas, TX 75231
(800) 428•2343, (214) 361•9515
www.aehf.com

Andersen Windows
Wood clad windows that come with aluminum screens.
Andersen Windows
100–4th Avenue North
P.O. Box 12
Bayport, MN 55003-1096
(800) 426•7691
www. Andersenwindows.com

Aubreys Organics
Over 200 hair, skin, and body care products made from herbs and vitamins, without synthetic chemicals.
Aubreys Organics
4419 North Manhattan Avenue
Tampa, FL 33614
(800) 282•7394
www.aubrey-organics.com

Aqua-Zar
Water-based, nonyellowing polyurethane in satin or semi-gloss finishes
United Gilsonite Laboratories
P.O. Box 70
Scranton, PA 18501-0070
(800) 845•5227, (717) 344•1202
www.ugl.com

Architectural Forest Enterprises
Hardwood plywood veneers from certified sources over a core of Medite II.
Architectural Forest Enterprises
3775 Bayshore Boulevard
Brisbane, CA 94005
(800) 483•6337, (415) 467•4800
www.ecoforeat.com

ASCR-Water Loss Institute
Provides water-loss specialist technician certification and referrals.
ASCR-Water Loss Institute
8229 Cloverleaf Drive, # 460
Millersville MD 21108
(800) 272•7012, (410) 729•9900
www.ASCR.org

Auro Products
Note: These products are made with natural plant and mineral derivatives in a process called plant chemistry. Some sensitive individuals may have severe reactions to the natural turpenes, citrus derivatives, and oils.
Auro Natural Paints
Made exclusively from natural sources, with an effort to support ecological diversity. Packaged in powder form.
Auro No. 131 Natural Resin Oil Glaze
Transparent, tintable finish for exterior porous wood protection.
Auro No. 211–215 Shellacs
Various natural shellacs with different degrees of gloss.
Auro No. 235 and 240 Natural Resin Oil Top Coat
Indoor/outdoor enamels in white and eight colors.
Auro No. 383 Natural Linoleum Glue
Adhesive for linoleum flooring.
Auro No. 385 Natural Carpet Glue
Organic binder that remains permanently elastic.
Sinan Company
P.O. Box 857
Davis, CA 95617
(530) 753•3104
www.dcn.davis.ca.us/go/sinan

Bamboo Flooring International
Bamboo flooring and accessories.
Bamboo Flooring International
20950 Currier Road
Walnut, CA 91789
(800) 827•9261, (909) 594•4189
www.bamboo-flooring.com

Bangor Cork Company
Natural cork "carpeting" and battleship linoleum flooring.
Bangor Cork Company
William and D Streets
Pen Argyl, PA 18072-1025
(610) 863•9041

BIN Primer Sealer
White, alcohol-based, paint-on, vapor-barrier sealer for use as prime coat on gypboard and wherever an opaque sealer is desired.

BIN Shellac
White shellac/sealer used to create an effective air barrier.
Wm. Zinsser & Company
173 Belmont Drive
Somerset, NJ 08875
(732) 469•8100
www.zinsser.com

Bio-Form
A very low odor, nontoxic spray-on application specifically designed for concrete form release.
Leahy-Wolf Company
1951 North 25th Avenue
Franklin Park, IL 60131
(888) 873•5327
www.leahywolf.com

Bio Shield Products
A line of environmental oil finishes that are free of formaldehyde, lead and other heavy metals, and fungicides. As with many natural products, some chemically sensitive individuals may not tolerate turpenes, oils, or citrus-based and other aromatic components found in these formulations.
Bio Shield Casein "Milk" Paint #10
A very low-VOC paint made from naturally or minimally toxic synthetic materials.
Bio Shield Cleaners
Biodegradable, soap-based household cleaning products.

295

Bio Shield Cork Adhesive

Water-based elastic glue for cork, linoleum, or wool with jute backing. Adheres to concrete, wood, or plywood.

Bio Shield Earth Pigments #88

Fine pigment powders extracted from earth or rock containing little or no heavy metals. Can be used with Bio Shield oil finishes.

Bio Shield Hard Oil #9

For use on hardwood and softwood floors and stone in areas exposed to moisture. Use over surfaces primed with Bio Shield Penetrating Oil Sealer #8 or Bio Shield Penetrating Oil Sealer #5.

Bio Shield Hardwood Penetrating Sealer

As Penetrating Oil Sealer, but a more dilute solution for use on hardwoods.

Bio Shield Natural Resin Floor Finish #92

Finish for hardwood and softwood floors that have been primed with Bio Shield Penetrating Oil Sealer #8 or Bio Shield Penetrating Oil Sealer #5.

Bio Shield Penetrating Oil Primer #81

A sealer, undercoat, and primer for absorbent surfaces of wood, cork, stone, slate, and brick.

Bio Shield Penetrating Oil Sealer

An undercoater for preserving wood, best used with a finishing stain for UV protection. Free of petroleum distillates and mineral spirits.

Bio Shield Penetrating Oil Sealer #5

A sealer, undercoat, and primer for absorbent surfaces of wood, cork, stone, slate, or brick.

Bio Shield Penetrating Oil Sealer #8

A thinner oil for priming less-absorbent woods.

Bio Shield Solvent Free Wall Paint #18

A very low VOC paint made from naturally or minimally toxic synthetic materials.

Bio Shield Transparent Wood Glaze

Interior/exterior wood finish with ultraviolet protection.

Eco Design/Natural Choice Catalog
1365 Rufina Circle
Santa Fe, NM 87505
(800) 621·2591, (505) 438·3448
www.bioshieldpaint.com

Bio-Wash Products

A line of safe products for cleaning, stripping, and protecting wood.

Bio-Wash Mill Glaze Away

Cleans and prepares wood for coating.

Bio-Wash Simple Wash

Powerful cleaner and brightener.

Bio Wash Wood Wash

Weathered wood restorer.

Bio-Wash Stripex

Wood stain stripper.

Bio-Wash Stripex-L

Varnish and latex stain stripper.

Bio-Wash Rinse or Peel

Water rinse paint stripper.

Bio-Wash Natural Deck Oil

Protective penetrating wood oil

Bio-Wash Supernatural

Protective wood finish system.

Bio-Wash Waste Paint Hardener

Gets rid of old latex paint and cleans up paint spills.

Bio-Wash Canada
101, 7156 Brown Street
Delta, BC, Canada V4G 1G8
(800) 858·5011
www.biowash.com
Distributed by:
Planetary Solutions
2030–17th Street
Boulder, CO 80302
(303) 442·6228
www.planetearth.com

Bon Ami Polishing Cleanser

Kitchen and bath scouring cleanser without perfumes, dyes, chlorines, or phosphates. Available in grocery and health food stores.

Faultless Starch/Bon Ami Company
Kansas City, MO 64101-1200

Bonsal

Sanded grouts without polymer additives in six colors.

Bonsal
P.O. Box 241148
Charlotte, NC 28224-1148
(704) 525·1621, (800) 738·1621

Bora-Care

Designed to penetrate and protect all types of wood from wood-boring insects. Contains disodium octaborate tetrahydrate in ethylene glycol carrier. Water-based solution requiring paint or sealer over it.

Nisus Corporation
215 Dunavunt Drive
Rockford, TN 37853
(865) 577·6119, (800) 264·0870
www.nisuscorp.com

Brae Roof

Modified bitumen roofing.
For local certified applicators call:
US Intec, Inc.
P.O. Box 2845
Port Arthur, TX 77643
(800) 624·6832, (800) 331·5228
www.usintec.com
Bright Futures Futons
Many styles of futons and couch beds.

Bright Futures Futons

3120 Central SE
Albuquerque, NM 87106
(888) 645·4452, (505) 268·9738
www.organiccottonalts.com

BRK/First Alert Products

BRK 2002 is a 120-volt photoelectric smoke detector with battery backup. BRK also carries photoelectric carbon monoxide detectors with battery backup.

BRK Electronics/First Alert
3901 Liberty Street Road
Aurora, IL 60504
(800) 392·1395, (630) 851·7330
www.firstalert.com

Building for Health—Materials Center

Distributor of a wide variety of healthy building products. The owner, Cedar Rose, is also a building contractor who has practical experience with most products sold by the Center.

Building for Health—Materials Center
P.O. Box 113
Carbondale, CO 81623
(970) 963·0437
For orders only: (800) 292·4838
www.buildingforhealth.com

C-Cure Products

C-Cure AR Grout

Portland cement, lime, earth pigment, and sand, without latex modifiers. Available in 40 colors.

C-Cure Floor Mix 900

Dry-set mortar used for floor and wall installations of absorptive, semi-vitreous, and vitreous tiles.

C-Cure MultiCure 905

Latex-cement mortar used for setting all types of ceramic tile; used on dry

interior walls and exterior grade plywood.

C-Cure PermaBond 902

For low-odor tile setting.

C-Cure Supreme 925 Grout

Dry tile grout with exceptional working qualities and a permanent joint life; nonshrinking, nontoxic, odorless, inhibits fungal growth.

C-Cure ThinSet 911

Dry-set mortar used for installation of low absorptive tiles (less than 7%).

C-Cure Wall Mix 901

Dry-set mortar used for the installation of absorptive tiles (more than 7%).

C-Cure Corporation
13001 Seal Beach Boulevard
Seal Beach, CA 90740
(800) 895·2874, (562) 598·8808
www.c-cure.com
www.custombuildingproducts.com

Celbar

Spray-in or loose-fill cellulose insulation treated with a borate compound as a fire retardant. Loose-fill insulation can be ordered without recycled newspaper content.

International Cellulose Corporation
P.O. Box 450006
12315 Robin Boulevard
Houston, TX 77245
(800) 444·1252, (713) 433·6701
www.celbar.com

Cemroc

A lightweight, strong, noncombustible, highly water-resistant board that can be used as a backer for ceramic tile installations in wet areas in place of green board

Cemplank
P.O. Box 99
Blandon, PA 19510
(888) 327·0723, (610) 926·5533
www.cemplank.com

CertainTeed Corporation

Manufacturer of undyed, unbacked fiberglass batt insulation.

CertainTeed Corporation
750 East Swedesford
Valley Forge, PA 19482
(800) 274·8530, (800) 441·9850
www.certainteed.com
For the closest distributor, call:
(800) 441·9850

Certified Forest Products Council
A nonprofit organization that actively promotes and facilitates the increased purchase, use, and sale of third-party, independently certified forest products.
Certified Forest Products Council
1478 SW Osprey Drive, Suite 285
Beaverton, OR 97007-8424
(503) 590•6600
www.certifiedwood.org

Cervitor
Metal kitchen cabinetry.
Cervitor Kitchens, Inc.
10775 Lower Azusa Road
El Monte, CA 91731-1351
(800) 523•2666, (626) 443•0184

CHAPCO Products
CHAPCO Safe-Set 3
A zero-VOC adhesive for carpet installation.
CHAPCO Safe-Set 69, 75, and 90
Solvent-free, nonflammable, freeze/thaw stable, and almost odor-free ceramic floor tile adhesives.
Chicago Adhesive Products Company
1165 Arbor Drive
Romeoville, IL 60446
(800) 621•0220
www.chapco-adhesive.com

Chromix Admixture and Lithochrome Color Hardener
Mineral pigments containing no chromium or other heavy metals; for use in concrete.
L.M. Scofield Company
P.O. Box 1525
Los Angeles, CA 90040
(800) 222•4100
www.scofield.com

ClearWater Tech, Inc.
Ozone generators for many purposes.
ClearWater Tech, Inc.
P.O. Box 15330
San Luis Obispo, CA 93406
(805) 549•9724
www.cwtozone.com

Climate Pro
Blown-in blanket system fiberglass insulation without chemicals and with inert binders.
Johns Manville Insulation Group
P.O. Box 5108
Denver CO 80217-5108
(800) 654•3103

ComfortTherm
A white fiberglass batt insulation with a polyethylene wrap
Johns Manville Insulation Group
P.O. Box 5108
Denver CO 80217-5108
(800) 654•3103

Cord Caulk
Acrylic yarn saturated with adhesive wax polymers for sealing around doors, windows and sills.
Delta Products, Inc.
26 Arnold Road
North Quincy, MA 02171-3002
(617) 471•7477, FAX (617) 773•4940
Available through the following mail-order houses:
Real Goods
200 Clara Avenue
Ukiah, CA 95482
(800) 762•7325
www.realgoods.com
Brookstone Company
(800) 846•3000

Coronado Supreme Collection
Zero-VOC latex paint; dries to highly washable surface.
Coronado Paint Co.
308 Old Country Road
Edgewater, FL 32132
(800) 883•4193, (904) 428•6461

Coyuchi
Organic cotton bedding.
Coyuchi
11101 State Route One, #201
P.O. Box 845
Pointe Reyes Station CA 94956
(415) 663•8077
www.coyuchiorganic.com

Crate and Barrel
Solid wood, glass, and metal furnishings and accessories.
Crate and Barrel
P.O. Box 3210
Naperville, IL 60566-7210
(800) 323•5461
www.crateandbarrel.com

Cross-Tuff
Cross-laminated polyethylene air barrier and under-slab radon barrier.
Manufactured Plastics and Distribution, Inc.
10367 W. Centennial Road
Littleton, CO 80127

(303) 972•0123, (719) 488•2143
www.mpdplastics.com

Crown/The Natural Bedroom
Formerly Janz Design. Natural bedroom furniture and bedding.
Crown/The Natural Bedroom
11134 Rush Street South
El Monte, CA 91733
(626) 452•8617

Dasun Company
Catalog sales of air- and water-purification products.
P.O. Box 668
Escondido, CA 92033
(800) 433•8929

Davis Colors
Mineral-based pigments for concrete.
Laporte Pigments/Davis Colors
3700 East Olympic Boulevard
Los Angeles, CA 90023
(800) 356•4848, (323) 269•7311
www.daviscolors.com

Dekswood
Cleaner and brightener for exterior wood.
The Flood Company
P.O. Box 2535
Hudson, OH 44236-0035
(800) 321•3444
www.floodco.com

DEL Industries
Water ozonation systems for pools, wells, and spas.
DEL Industries
3428 Bullock Lane
San Luis Obispo, CA 93401
(800) 676•1335, (805) 541•1601
www.delozone.com

Denny Foil Vapor Barrier
Virgin craft paper with foil laminated to it on both sides with sodium silicate adhesive.
Denny Wholesale Services, Inc.
3500 Gateway Drive
Pompano Beach, FL 33069
(800) 327•6616, (954) 971•3100
www.dennywholesale.com
Distributed by:
E.L. Foust Company
754 Industrial Drive
Elmhurst, IL 60126
(800) 225•9549
www.foustco.com

DLW Linoleums
Manufactured from all natural products (linseed oil, cork, wood flour, resin binders, gum, and pigments) with natural jute backing.
Armstrong World Industries
P.O. Box 3001
Lancaster, PA 17604
(717) 397•0611

Dodge-Regupol, Inc.
Cork tile.
Dodge-Regupol, Inc.
P.O. Box 989
Lancaster, PA 17608-0989
(717) 295•3400, (800) 322•1923
www.regupol.com

Durock
A rigid cementitious substrate that is suitable for use in wet areas.
U.S. Gypsum
14643 Dallas Parkway, Suite 575, LB#78
Dallas, TX 75240
(800) 527•5193 (Southwest)
(800) 274•9778 (East)

Earth Friendly Products
A complete line of domestic and institutional cleaning products.
Native Solutions
P.O. Box 3274
Lacey, WA 98509-3274
(888) 281•3524, (360) 491•0992
www.ecos.com

EarthTech Paints and Finishes
Low-odor, zero-VOC paints for interior and exterior use. Low-VOC gloss and satin interior and exterior finishes.
EarthTech
P.O. Box 1325
Arvada, CO 80001
(303) 465•1537
www.earthtechinc.com

ECO 2000
Multipurpose cleaner and degreaser meeting Green Seal standards.
KC Products
707 N.E. Broadway, Suite 210
Portland, OR 97232
(503) 287•4608, (888) 655•3772, (800) 927•9442
www.thomasregional.com/kcproducts
inc

Ecological/Canary Paints
Water-based, resin terpolymer paint that is odorless and formaldehyde-free. Also Canary line of paints that are biocide- and fungicide-free.
Innovative Formulations
1810 South 6th Avenue
Tucson, AZ 85713
(800) 346•7265, (520) 628•1553
www.mirrorseal.com

Eco Products, Inc.
Supplier of ecologically sound building products.
Eco Products, Inc.
3655 Frontier Ave
Boulder, CO 80301
(303) 449•1876
www.ecoproducts.com

E.L. Foust Company
High-quality air filters.
E.L. Foust Company
754 Industrial Drive
Elmhurst, IL 60126
(800) 225•9549
www.foustco.com

Elmer's Carpenter's Glue
Solvent-free glue.
Borden, Inc.
180 Borden Street
Columbus, OH 43215
(800) 426•7336, (800) 848•9400
www.elmers.com
Available in many retail outlets.

Endurance II
Synthetic jute pad; odorless, hypoallergenic.
Distributed through:
Statements
1441 Paseo de Peralta
Santa Fe, NM 87501
(505) 988•4440

Energy Federation, Inc.
Various energy-saving products including foams, sealants, fans, light bulbs, and ventilation systems.
Energy Federation, Inc.
40 Washington Street Suite 3000
Westborough, MA 01581-1012
(800) 876•0660
www.efi.org

Envirobond #801 and #901
Water-based latex mastics that can be used in wet areas.

W.F. Taylor Company, Inc.
11545 Pacific Avenue
Fontana, CA 92337
(800) 397•4583, (909) 360•6677
www.wftaylor.com

Enviro Care
Cleaning products for all washable surfaces: nontoxic, biodegradable, noncorrosive, and nonreactive.
Rochester Midland
1015 North Street
Omaha, NE 68102
(800) 283•4248, (402) 342•4248
www.rochestermidland.com

Enviro-Cote Paints
Low-odor, low- to zero-VOC, vinyl acrylic interior and exterior paints.
Kelly-Moore Paint Co.
1015 Commercial Street
San Carlos, CA 94070
(888) 677•2468
www.kellymoore.com

Environmental Health Center
Easy-to-use mold-testing kits for the home. $60 for kit and analysis.
Environmental Health Center
8345 Walnut Hill Lane, Suite 220
Dallas, TX 75231
(214) 373•5149
www.ehcd.com

Environmental Home Center
1724–4th Avenue South
Seattle, WA 98134
(800) 281•9785, (206) 682•7332
www.enviresource.com

Environmental Testing and Technology
Wide variety of indoor air-quality testing services and consultation.
Peter H Sierck
1106 Second Street, Suite 102
Encinitas, CA 92024
(800) 811•5991, (760) 436•5990

Enviro Safe Paints
No-fungicide, low-biocide paints mixed to order.
Chem Safe
P.O. Box 33023
San Antonio, TX 78265
(210) 657•5321
www.environproducts.com

EnviroSmart
"Natural Wonder" line of heavy duty cleaner, degreaser, and other household cleaning products.
EnviroSmart Products Company
555 West Arlington Place, Suite 502
Chicago, IL 60614
(773) 248•7089, (888)655•3772
www.espesp.com

Envirotec Health Guard Adhesive #2101
Envirotec Health Guard Seaming Tape
A line of zero-VOC, solvent-free adhesives without alcohol, glycol, ammonia, or carcinogens. Call distributor to find best product for a particular installation.
W.F. Taylor Company, Inc.
11545 Pacific Avenue
Fontana, CA 92337
(800) 397•4583, (909) 360•6677
www.wftaylor.com

Extend, Pro-Series
A low-VOC, exterior/interior, urethane acrylic sealant.
OSI Sealants, Inc.
7405 Production Drive
Mentor, OH 44060
(800) 321•3578, FAX (440) 255•1008
www.osisealants.com

Extra-Bond
A concentrated acrylic. Can be mixed with a first coat of Milk Paint to promote adhesion on surfaces other than bare wood. Nontoxic.
Old-Fashioned Milk Paint Company
436 Main Street
Groton, MA 01450
(978) 448•6336
www.milkpaint.com

Fiber-Lock
Polypropylene fiber additive reinforcement for concrete slabs.
Fiber-Lock Company
4308 Garland Drive
Fort Worth, TX 76117
(800) 852•8889, (817) 498•0042

Fibermesh
Fiberglass reinforcing for concrete slabs.
SI Geosolutions
P.O. Box 22788
Chattanooga, TN 37416
(800) 621•0444, (423) 899•0444
www.sixsoil.com

Fiberock
A reinforced gypsum sheathing used as a backer for exterior finishing.
U.S. Gypsum
14643 Dallas Parkway, Suite 575, LB#78
Dallas, TX 75240
(800) 527•5193 (Southwest)
(800) 274•9778 (East)

Forbo Industries
Natural linoleum flooring.
Forbo Industries
P.O. Box 667
Hazelton, PA 18201
(800) 233•0475, (570) 459•0771,
(800) 842•7839
www.forbo-industries.com

Formula G-510
Multipurpose cleaner meeting Green Seal standards.
20-10 Products, Inc.
P.O. Box 7609
Salem, OR 97303
www.2010products.com

Furnature, Inc.
Chemical-free upholstered sofas, chairs, and mattresses using 100% organically grown ingredients.
Furnature, Inc.
319 Washington Street
Brighton, MA 02135
(617) 787•2888, (877) 877•8020
www.furnature.com

GE 012
Clear silicone sealant.
GE 5091
Silicone paintable sealant.
GE
260 Hudson River Road
Waterford, NY 12100
(800) 255•8886 (Technical service)
www.gesilicones.com
Available through the following retail outlets:
True Value, Ace Hardware, Home Base.

Genesis Odor Free Paint
Zero-VOC, vinyl/acrylic paints.
Duron Paints
10406 Tucker Street
Beltsville, MD 20705
(800) 723•8766
www.duron.com

Great Stuff
Expanding foam sealant that is free of CFCs, HCFCs, and formaldehyde.
Insta Foam, Division of Dow Chemical Co.
1881 West Oak Parkway.
Marietta, GA 30062
(800) 366•4740, (888) 868•1183 (Technical support)
www.flexibleproducts.com
Available through the following retail outlets:
True Value, Ace Hardware, Home Depot

Green Seal
A national, independent, nonprofit, environmental labeling and consumer education organization. Issues a seal of approval to consumer products that meet rigorous environmental standards.
Green Seal
1001 Connecticut Avenue NW, Suite 827
Washington, DC 20036-5525
(202) 872•6400
www.greenseal.org

Greensoap
GNLD
P.O. Box 5012
Fremont, CA 9453
(800) 227•2926
www.gnld.com

Green Unikleen
An industrial strength, bio-degradable, water-soluble degreaser/cleaner formulated from synthetic surfactants.
IPAX Cleanogel, Inc.
8301 Lyndon Avenue
Detroit, MI 48238
(800) 930•4729, (313) 933•4211
www.ipax.com

Guardian
Borate-based wood preservative.
Perma-Chink Systems, Inc.
1605 Prosser Road
Knoxville, TN 37914
(800) 548•3554, (800) 548•1231
www.permachink.com

Hardibacker Board
Cementitious tile backer board for use in moist/wet applications.
James Hardie Building Company
26300 La Alameda, Suite 250

Mission Viejo, CA 92691
(800) 426•4051, (909) 356•6300, (949) 348•1800
www.jameshardie.com

Harmony
Formerly Seventh Generation. Organic bedding, towels, and shower curtains.
Gaiam, Inc.
360 Interlocken Boulevard, Suite 300
Broomfield, CO 80021
(800) 869•3446
www.gaiam.com

Hartex Carpet Cushion
Odorless, synthetic jute underpadding for carpet.
Leggett & Platt
1100 South McKinney Street
Mexia, TX 76667
(800) 880•6092, (254) 562•2814, (800) 660•2888 (New Mexico sales)

HealthSpec
Low-odor, vinyl acrylic, interior latex paint. It is more durable than some of the other commercially available low-/no-odor paints, but also has more odor.
The Sherwin Williams Company
101 Prospect Avenue NW
Cleveland, OH 44115
(800) 524•5979, (216) 566•2902
www.sherwin-williams.com
Sold at Sherwin Williams paint stores throughout the country.

Healthy Home Center
EMF reduction supplies and other healthy home products.
Healthy Home Center
1403-A Cleveland Street
Clearwater, FL 33755
(727) 447•4454, (800) 583•9523
www.healthyhome.com

Healthy Interiors
Consultant and retail source for beds, bedding, linens, furniture, and custom upholstery. Knowledgeable service and reasonable pricing.
Healthy Interiors
P.O. Box 9001
Santa Fe, NM 87504
(505) 820•7634
www.healthyhomeinteriors.com

Heart of Vermont
Bedding and other "products for the chemically sensitive and environmentally concerned."
Heart of Vermont
131 South Main Street
P.O. Box 612
Barre, VT 05641
(800) 639•4123
www.heartofvermont.com

Hendricksen Naturlich
Wool carpeting, other natural fiber carpeting, felt underpads, adhesives, and cork flooring.
Hendricksen Naturlich
P.O. Box 1677
Sebastopol, CA 95473
(707) 824•0914, FAX (800) 329•9398
www.naturalhomeproducts.com

Homespun Fabrics and Draperies
Handwoven, 100% cotton fabrics without finishes or chemicals.
Homespun Fabrics and Draperies
1865 El Monte Drive
P.O. Box 4315
Thousand Oaks, CA 91359
www.homespunfabrics.com

Huntar Company, Inc.
Dr. Gauss gaussmeter.
Huntar Company, Inc.
473 Littlefield Avenue
San Francisco, CA 94080
(800) 566•8686
www.learningmates.com

Hydrocote Products
Hydrocote Danish Oil Finish
A nontoxic penetrating oil. One-step stain and seal in nine wood tones.
Hydrocote Polyshield
A tough, super hard, nonyellowing polyurethane that is UV stabilized and UV stable. Use with **Hydrocote** stains. Can be used with **Hydrocote Ultraviolet Light Absorber Blocker** to increase UV resistance.
Hydroshield Plus
Clear coat available in gloss or satin sheen. Water-based polyurethane giving impact- and weather-resistance for interior or exterior.
The Hydrocote Company, Inc.
61 Berry Street
Somerset, NJ 08873
(800) 229•4937
www.hydrocote.com

Icynene Insulation System
A modified low-density urethane sprayed-on foam insulation. Good performance and extremely low outgassing make this product acceptable for many with chemical sensitivities.
Icynene, Inc.
5805 Whittle Road, Unit 110
Mississauga, Ontario, Canada L4Z 2J1
(800) 946•7325, (905) 890•7325, (888) 946•7325
www.icynene.com

Indoor Air Quality (IAQ) Test Kit.
One kit tests total VOC level, formaldehyde level, and mold in surface samples.
Air Quality Sciences, Inc.
Capitol Circle
Atlanta, GA 30067
(800) 789•0419, (770) 993•0638
www.aqs.com

Indoor Environmental Technologies, Inc.
Wide variety of indoor air-quality testing services and consultation.
William H. Spates III
1403 Cleveland Street
Clearwater, FL 33755
(727) 446•7717

InstaSeal Eco Blend
Builders line of expanding foam sealant that is free of CFCs, HCFCs, and formaldehyde.
Insta Foam, Division of Dow Chemical Co.
1881 West Oak Parkway
Marietta, GA 30062
(800) 366•4740
(888) 868•1183 (Technical support)
www.flexibleproducts.com

Institute for Bau-Biologie and Ecology
Referrals to certified bau-biologie home inspectors and consultants.
Institute for Bau-Biologie and Ecology
P.O. Box 387
Clearwater, FL 33757
(727) 461•4371
www.bau-biologieusa.com

IICRC
Provides certification and referrals for water-damage restoration technicians and companies.

Institute of Inspection, Cleaning and Restoration Certification
2715 East Mill Plain Boulevard
Vancouver, WA 98661
(800) 835•4624, (360) 693•5675
www.iicrc.org

InsulSafe III
Blown-in blanket system fiberglass insulation without chemicals and with inert binders.
CertainTeed Corporation
750 East Swedesford
Valley Forge, PA 19489
(800) 274•8530
For the closest distributor, call:
(800) 441•9850

Isobord
A medium-density fiberboard made from straw fiber, containing no incremental formaldehyde emissions.
Isobord Global Sales & Marketing Office
1300 SW Fifth Avenue, Suite 3030
Portland, OR 97201
(503) 242•7345
www.isobordenterprises.com

Janice Corporation
Supplier of natural and organic bedding and linens, as well as hypoallergenic and unscented personal care products.
Janice Corporation
198 Route 46
Budd Lake, NJ 07828
(800) 526•4237, (973) 691•2979
www.janices.com

Junckers
A solid wood, prefinished, engineered flooring system.
Junckers Hardwood, Inc.
4920 East Landon Drive
Anaheim, CA 92807
(800) 878•9663, (714) 777•6430
www.junckershardwood.com

Kahrs
A solid wood, prefinished, engineered floor system.
Kahrs Intenational
951 Mariners Island, Suite 630
San Mateo, CA 94404
(650) 341•8400
www.kahrs.com

Kelly-Moore Enviro-Cote Paint
Zero-VOC latex paint in flat, satin, and semi-gloss finishes.
Kelly-Moore Paint Co.
1015 Commercial Street
San Carlos, CA 94070
(800) 874•4436, (650) 592•8337
www.kellymorre.com

Kodiak FRP Rebar
Fiberglass reinforcing bars.
Seasafe, Inc.
209 Glaser Drive
Lafayette, LA 70508
(800) 326•8842, (337) 406•2345
www.seasafe.com

Laticrete Additive Free Thinset
For use over concrete, cement backer board, or wire-reinforced mud. Contains Portland cement and sand.
1 Laticrete Park North
Bethany, CT 06524-3498
(203) 393•0010
www.laticrete.com

Lessco Air Vapor Barrier Boxes
Airtight electrical boxes.
Available through:
Shelter Supply, Inc.
17725 Juniper Path
Lakeville, MN 55044-9482
(800) 762•8399
www.shelter-mn.com

Less EMF, Inc.
EMF reduction supplies.
Less EMF, Inc.
26 Valley View Lane
Ghent, NY 12075
(888) 537•7363
www.lessemf.com

Lifemaster 2000
Commercially available paint without petroleum-based solvents. Zero VOC.
ICI Dulux Paints
925 Euclid Avenue
Cleveland, OH 44115
(800) 984•5444
www.iciduluxpaints.com

LifeTime Wood Treatment
Wood preservative, stain and treatment.
Cedar Mountain Wood Products
143A Great Northern Road
Sault Suite Marie, Ontario, Canada
P6B 4Y9
(705) 941•9945

Lithochrome Color Hardener
See **Chromix Admixture**.

Lithoseal Building Caulk
High-quality urethane modified polymer. Inert once cured.
L.M. Scofield Company
P.O. Box 1525
Los Angeles, CA 90040
(800) 800•9900, (323) 723•5285
www.scofield.com

Living Source
Source of nontoxic carpets, adhesives, and "products for the environmentally aware and chemically sensitive."
P.O. Box 20155
Waco, TX 76702
(254) 776•4878, (800) 662•8787
www.livingsource.com

Livos Products
A line of plant chemistry products made from plant and mineral derivatives. As with many natural products, some chemically sensitive individuals may not tolerate turpenes, oils, or citrus-based and other aromatic components found in these formulations.
Livos Ardvos Wood Oil
Penetrating oil primer and finish for interior hardwoods. May be topcoated with Livos Bilo Floor Wax.
Livos Bilo Floor Wax
A clear, mar-resistant finish for wood, stone, terra cotta, and linoleum.
Livos Donnos Wood Pitch Impregnation
A penetrating preservative for exterior woodwork that is in contact with moisture. It is made of natural ingredients using plant chemistry.
Livos Dubno Primer Oil
A penetrating oil primer for use as an undercoat on exterior wood.
Livos Glievo Liquid Wax
Clear, apply, and buff furniture and floor wax. We have also applied this product to plastered walls.
Livos Kaldet Stain, Resin & Oil Finish
A stain and finish oil in 12 colors for interior and exterior surfaces made of wood, clay, or stone.
Livos Meldos Hard Oil
A penetrating oil sealer and finish for interior absorbent surfaces made of wood, cork, porous stone, terra cotta tiles, and brick.

Livos Naturals
Low-toxic paints, all ingredients listed on label, many organically grown, water- and oil-based products available.
Livos Vindo Enamel Paint
Wood finish coat.
Available in New Mexico through:
Building for Health—Materials Center
P.O. Box 113
Carbondale, CO 81623
(800) 292•4838 (Orders only), (970) 963•0437
www.buildingforhealth.com

Magnetic Sciences International
Has MSI 95, Magcheck, and Bell 4080 gaussmeters.
Magnetic Sciences International
367 Arlington Street
Acton, MA 01720
(978) 266•9906, (800) 749•9873
www.magneticsciences.com

Mapei 2 1/2 to 1
An additive-free grout for joints larger than 3/8".
Mapei, Inc.
1501 Wall Street
Garland, TX 75041
(800) 992•6273

Marvin Windows and Doors
Wood clad windows that can be ordered with aluminum screens
Marvin Windows and Doors
P.O. Box 100
Warroad, MN 56763
(800) 346•5128
www.marvin.com

MCS Referral & Resources
Photoelectric smoke detectors and electrochemical carbon monoxide alarms and monitors.
MCS Referral & Resources
2326 Pickwick
Baltimore, MD 21207
(800) 466•9320, (410) 362•6400
www.mcsrr.org

Medex
Formaldehyde-free, exterior grade, medium-density fiberboard
Medite II
Formaldehyde-free, interior grade, medium-density fiberboard
Medite Corporation
P.O. Box 4040

Medford, OR 97501
(800) 676•3339, (541) 773•2522
(916) 772•3422
www.sierrapine.com

Milk Paint
Made from milk protein, lime, earth pigments, and clay, this petrochemical-free, biodegradeable, nontoxic paint is odorless when dry. Comes in 16 colors. Sold in powder form.
Old-Fashioned Milk Paint Company
436 Main Street
Groton, MA 01450
(978) 448•6336
www.milkpaint.com

Miller LBNF
The LBNF line of paint has low-biocide content and no fungicides. Solvent-free. Flat, satin, semi-gloss.
Miller Paint Company
317 SE Grand Avenue
Portland, OR 97214
(800) 852•3254, (503) 233•4491
www.millerpaint.com

Miraflex
A less-toxic, undyed, fiberglass insulation material. The modified fibers are "safer," according to the manufacturer.
Owens Corning
One Owens Corning Parkway
Toledo, OH 43659
(800) 438•7465
www.owenscorning.com

Mirrorseal
A nonpetroleum-based polymer, fluid-applied roofing system. Can be applied and repaired by unskilled labor without specialized tools.
Innovative Formulation
670 West 33rd Street
Tuscon, AZ 85713
(800) 346•7265, (602) 628•1553
www.mirrorseal.com

Multi-core
Hardwood veneered plywood panels with low formaldehyde emissions. Suitable for cabinetry
Longlac Wood Industries
2000 Argentina Road
Mississauga, Ontario, Canada L5N 1P7
(905) 542•2700, (888) 566•4522
Available through:
Hardwoods Incorporated

1750–7th Street NW
Albuquerque, NM 87102
(505) 247•1000

Murco Products
Murco GF1000
Flat wall paint. Odorless when dry. In-can preservatives are entombed in dry paint. No slow-releasing compounds or airborne fungicides.
Murco LE1000
Higher gloss paint, formulated as above, for use where latex enamels are recommended.
Murco M-100 Hi-Po
Powdered all-purpose joint cement, a texture compound formulated with inert fillers and natural binders only. No preservatives.
Murco Wall Products
2032 North Commerce
Fort Worth, TX 76117
(800) 446•7124, (817) 626•1987
www.murcowall.com

Mystical
Odorless cleaner and deodorizer.
The Nontoxic Hot Line
3441 Golden Rain Road, #3
Walnut Creek, CA 94595
(800) 968•9355 (orders only),
(510) 472•8868
www.nontoxic.com

National Electromagnetic Field Testing Association
Provides list of independent EMF consultants.
National Electromagnetic Field Testing Association
714 Laramie
Glenview, IL 60025-3464
(847) 729•1532
www.theramp.net/nefta

Natural Choice
Source for cork floors, natural paints, stains, healthy home products, and other natural building products.
Eco Design/Natural Choice
1365 Rufina Circle
Santa Fe, NM 87505
(800) 621•2591, (505) 438•3448
www.bioshieldpaint.com

Natural Cork Co.
Natural cork flooring in a variety of colors and finishes.
Natural Cork Co. Ltd.

1710 North Leg Court
Augusta, GA 30909
(800) 404•2675
www.naturalcork.com

Natural Home
Natural beds, bedding
Naturlich-Natural Home
P.O. Box 1677
Sebastopol, CA 95473-1677
(707) 824•0914
www.naturalhomeproducts.com

Naturally Yours
A complete line of household cleaning products derived from pure, natural ingredients.
Naturally Yours
1926 South Glenstone Avenue, Suite 406
Springfield, MO 65804
(888) 801•7347, (417) 889•3995

Naturel Cleaner and Sealer
Nontoxic, biodegradable, water-soluble flakes that clean, protect, and finish stone surfaces.
Building for Health—Materials Center
P.O. Box 113
Carbondale, CO 81623
(800) 292•4838 (Orders only),
(970) 963•0437
www.buildingforhealth.com

NEEDS
Mail-order service offering a wide array of personal care products for the chemically sensitive.
NEEDS
6010 Drott Drive
East Syracuse, NY 13057
(800) 634•1380
www.needs.com
www.needs4u.com

Neff Cabinets
High-quality manufactured cabinets with low formaldehyde emissions. Boxes are made of phenolic glued plywoods. Solid wood doors can be ordered unfinished.
Neff Kitchen Manufacturers
6 Melanie Drive
Brampton, Ontario, Canada L6T 4K9
(800) 268•4527, (905) 791•7770
www.neffweb.com

Neil Kelly Cabinets
Cabinetry system designed to meet the needs of the chemically sensitive.
Neil Kelly Cabinets
804 North Alberta
Portland, OR 97217
(503) 335•9275
National Distributor:
Building for Health—Materials Center
P.O. Box 113
Carbondale, CO 81623
(800) 292•4838, (970) 963•0437
www.buildingforhealth.com

Nighthawk Carbon Monoxide Detector
A portable unit with battery backup and digital readout.
Positive Energy Conservation Products
P.O. Box 7568
Boulder. CO 80306
(800) 488•4340, (303) 444•4340
www.positive-energy.com

Nigra Enterprises
Air filtration systems
5699 Kanan Road
Agoura, CA 91301-3328
(818) 889•6877
www.nigra.org

Nirvana Safe Haven & The Nontoxic Hot Line
Catalog sales of products for achieving and maintaining indoor air quality and safety for homes, offices, and automobiles. Also organic cotton and wool mattresses and bedding
Nirvana Safe Haven
3441 Golden Rain Road, #3
Walnut Creek, CA 94595
For consultations: (510) 472•8868
Orders only: (800) 968•9355
www.nontoxic.com

Oasis/Sleeptek
Manufacturers of organic cotton and cotton-and-latex box springs and mattresses.
Contact: Furnature or Healthy Interiors.

Okon Seal & Finish
A satin or gloss clear sealer that can be used to seal plaster.
Okon, Inc.
4725 Leyden Street, Unit A
Denver, CO 80216
(800) 237•0565, (303) 377•7800
www.okoninc.com

Old Growth Aging and Staining Solutions for Wood
Wood is treated with a nontoxic mineral compound and then with a nontoxic catalyst that binds the natural mineral colors to cellulose, creating an aged patina. It imparts antimicrobial and antifungal properties to the wood, while the pigments provide UV protection.
Old Growth Co.
P.O. Box 1371
Santa Fe, NM 87504-1371
(505) 983•6877
www.olgrowth.com

Optima
Blown-in blanket system fiberglass insulation without chemicals and with inert binders.
CertainTeed Corporation
750 East Swedesford
Valley Forge, PA 19482
(800) 274•8530
www.certainteed.com
For the closest distributor, call:
(800) 441•9850

OS Products
OS/Color Hard Wax/Oil
A satin-matt oil/wax finish for interior wood floor and cork. Water repellent, easy to refinish.
OS/Color One Coat Only
Twelve different stain colors in a base of vegetable oils. Interior/exterior use. No preservatives or biocides.
OS Wood Protector
A penetrating, natural oil-based wood preservative with zinc oxide. For use on wood exposed to high humidity and moisture to prevent mold and mildew. Does not prevent insect infestation.
Environmental Home Center
1724–4th Avenue South
Seattle, WA 98134
(800) 281•9785, (206)682•7332
www.enviresource.com
Available in the Southwest through:
Planetary Solutions
2030–17th Street
Boulder, CO 80302
(303) 442•6228
www.planetearth.com
Building for Health—Materials Center
P.O. Box 113
Carbondale, CO 81623
(800) 292•4838 (orders only),

(970) 963•0437
www.buildingforhealth.com

Ozark Water Service and Air Services
For air and water testing, and consultation regarding toxic gases, molds, asbestos, VOCs, pesticides, gas leaks, EMFs, and radon.
Ozark Water Service and Air Services
114 Spring Street
Sulphur Springs, AR 72768-0218
(800) 835•8908

Pace Crystal Shield
Replaces lacquers, varathanes, and urethanes. Clear seal strong enough for hardwood floors. Can be used as sealant to block formaldehyde and other chemical emissions from manufactured wood products. Can be used to seal tile flooring.
Pace Chem Industries
3050 Westwood Drive, B10
Las Vegas, NV 89109
(800) 350•2912, (702) 369•1424
www.pacechemusa.com

Pacific Gold Board Products
Strawboard building materials made from annually renewable straw.

PGB
A rigid gypsum drywall alternative requiring no studs.

PGB3 (Baled Batt)
Strawboard building material used mainly as a decorative acoustical ceiling panel that resembles a thatched ceiling.
BioFab, LLC
P.O. Box 990556
Redding, CA 96099
www.strawboard.com
info@ricestraw.com

Pacific Rim
Makers of handcrafted solid maple furniture using maple grown in managed forests from U.S. sources.
Call for your nearest distributor:
Pacific Rim
P.O. Box 2844
Eugene, OR 97402
(541) 342•4508

Panolam
A melamine board thermally fused to a medex core.
Panolam
3030 SW Calapooia Street
Albany, OR 97321
(888) 726•6526, (541) 928•1942, (203) 925•1556
www.panolam.com

Pella Corporation
Windows come with optional "Slimshade" blinds between the two layers of glass; the blinds never require cleaning
Pella Corporation
102 Main Street
Pella, IA 50219
(800) 547•3552
www.pella.com

PermaBase
A rigid cementitious substrate that is suitable for use in wet areas.
Unifix, Inc.
National Gypsum Co./Gold Bond
2001 Rexford Road
Charlotte, NC 28211
(800) 628•4662, (704) 365•7300
www.national-gypsum.com

Perma-Zyme
A biodegradable and environmentally safe road stabilization enzyme that can be used in place of asphalt paving.
Idaho Enzymes, Inc.
1010 West Main
Jerome, ID 83338
(208) 324•3642

Phenoseal Products
Water-based, nontoxic, nonflammable caulks and sealants available in translucent and 15 colors.
Phenoseal "Surpass" Caulk and Sealant
Phenoseal Valve Seal
Phenoseal Vinyl Adhesive Caulk
Gloucester Company, Inc.
P.O. Box 428
Franklin, MA 02038
(800) 343•4963, (508) 528•2200
www.phenoseal.com

Planetary Solutions
Environmentally sound materials for interiors.
Planetary Solutions
2030–17th Street

P.O. Box 1049
Boulder, CO 80302
(303) 442•6228
www.planetearth.com

Plaza Hardwood, Inc.
Source for sustainably harvested and recycled wood.
Toni and Paul Fuge
219 W Manhattan Avenue
Santa Fe, NM 87501
(800) 662•6306, (505) 992•3260
www.plzfloor.com

Plyboo
Bamboo flooring and accessories.
Smith & Fong Company
601 Grandview Drive South
San Francisco, CA 94080
(650) 872•1184
www.plyboo.com
Available in the Southwest through:
Planetary Solutions
2030–17th Street
Boulder, CO 80302
(303) 442•6228
www.planetearth.com
Building for Health—Materials Center
P.O. Box 113
Carbondale, CO 81623
(800) 292•4838 (orders only), (970) 963•0437
www.buildingforhealth.com

Polyken Tape +337
Aluminum tape that forms an effective air barrier.
Tyco Adhesives
1400 Providence Highway
Norwood, MA 02062
(800) 248•0147
www.tycoadhesives.com
Polyken manufacturers representative:
Foster Sales Company
P.O. Box 1689
Las Cruces, NM 88004
(505) 523•7090

Pottery Barn
Solid wood furniture, glass and metal furniture and accessories, cotton window dressings.
Pottery Barn
P.O. Box 7044
San Francisco, CA 94120-7044
(800) 922•5507
www.potterybarn.com

Prestige Publishing
Formaldehyde Spot Test Kit
A colorimetric test that indicates if any object contains more than 10 ppm of formaldehyde. Each kit tests more than 100 objects.
Mold Survey Service
Mold tests
Prestige Publishing
P.O. Box 3068
Syracuse, NY 13220
(800) 846•6687, (325) 454•8119
www.prestigepublishing.com

Pristine Eco Spec
Commercially available acrylic latex paint without VOCs. Available in several finishes.
Benjamin Moore & Company
51 Chestnut Ridge Road
Montvale, NJ 07645
(800) 344•0400, (201) 573•9600
www.benjaminmoore.com

Professional Discount Supply
Radon mitigation supplies and technical support.
Professional Discount Supply
1029 S. Sierra Madre, Suite B
Colorado Springs, CO 80903
(719) 444•0646
www.radonpds.com

Professional Equipment
Various testing devices for radon, mold, lead, microwaves, and EMFs.
90 Plant Avenue, Suite 3
Hauppauge, NY 11788-3813
(800) 334•9291
www.professionalequipment.com

Quality Wood Products
Sustainably harvested wood.
Harry Morrison
Chama, NM 87520
(505) 756•2744

R & S Enviroseal
Airtight electrical boxes.
Available through:
Shelter Supply Product Catalogue
17725 Juniper Path
Lakeville, MN 55044-9482
(800) 762•8399, (612) 898•4500

Rad Alert
Device for measuring radioactivity.
International Med Com
7497 Kennedy Road

Sebastopol, CA 95472
(707) 823•0336
www.medcom.com

Radiant Heater Corp.
Low-temperature, long-wave, ceramic radiant heater designed for the chemically sensitive. No outgassing from heating elements, and no fans or blowers. Heats room quickly. Does not dry out the air.
Radiant Heater Corp.
P.O. Box 60
Greenport, NY 11944
(800) 331•6408

Rappgo
Prefinished engineered wood flooring system from Sweden with very low emissions.
Distributed in the USA by:
Plaza Hardwood, Inc.
219 West Manhattan Avenue
Santa Fe, NM 87501
(800) 662•6306, (505) 992•3260
www.plzfloor.com

RCD6
Nontoxic water-based mastic for sealing ductwork and metal joints.
Positive Energy
P.O. Box 7568
Boulder, CO 80306
(800) 488•4340, (303) 444•4340
www.positive-energy.com

Real Goods
Catalog sales for natural and organic mattresses, bedding, shower curtains, towels, and solar-powered pool purifier.
Real Goods
200 Clara Avenue
Ukiah, CA 95482-4004
(800) 762•7325
www.realgoods.com

Reflectix
Foil-faced, backed over plastic bubbles; especially designed to reflect heat.
Reflectix, Inc.
P.O. Box 108
Markleville, IN 46056
(765) 533•4332, (800) 218•9063
www.reflectixinc.com
Available in the Southwest through:
Home Depot, Home Base, Furrows, Ace True Value, and
Positive Energy Conservation Products
P.O. Box 7568

Boulder, CO 80306
(800) 488•4340
www.positive-energy.com

Resource Conservation Technologies, Inc.
Acrylic polymer roll-on paint roofing without toxic dispersants or tints.
Resource Conservation Technologies, Inc.
2633 North Calvert Street
Baltimore, MD 21218
(410) 366•1146

Restoration Consultants
Years of experience with biological contamination of indoor environments, and restoration after fire and water damage.
Restoration Consultants
3463 Ramona Avenue, Suite 18
Sacramento, CA 95826
(916) 736•1100
www.restcon.com

Road Oyl
An emulsion of natural tree resin that is combined with earth materials to create a high-strength pavement.
Distributed by:
Soil Stabilization Products Company, Inc.
P.O. Box 2779
Merced, CA 95344-0779
(800) 523•9992
www.sspco.org

Rub-R-Wall
Rubber polymer foundation waterproofing membrane containing no asphalt. Spray-on application. Manufacturer claims product is nontoxic once dry.
Rubber Polymer Corporation
1135 West Portage Trail Extension
Akron, OH 44313-8283
(800) 860•7721
www.rpcinfo.com

Safe Environments
Consulting and testing for a wide range of indoor air-quality problems.
Safe Environments
1611 Merritt Drive
Novato, CA 94949
(510) 549•9693

Samina
Manufacturers of organic cotton, wool, and latex mattress systems.

Samina USA Rohorn, Inc.
1530 Northern Boulevard
Manhasset, NY 11030
(516) 869•6005
www.samina.com

Santa Fe Heritage Door Company
Custom wood doors.
418 Montezuma Avenue
Santa Fe, NM 87501
(505) 988•3328, (800) 684•2981

Scientific Certification Systems
www.scs1.com

SDA 1600 (Spectracidal Disinfectant Agent)
Nontoxic germicide, EPA approved.
Apothecure, Inc.
13720 Midway Road, Suite 109
Dallas, TX 75244
(800) 969•6601
www.apothecure.com

Shellguard
Borate-based wood preservative.
Perma-Chink Systems, Inc.
1605 Prosser Road
Knoxville, TN 37914
(800) 548•3554, (800) 548•1231
www.permachink.com

Siemens EQIII
Standard load center electrical panels and subpanels with split neutral.
Siemens
2880 Sunrise Boulevard
Rancho Cordova, CA 95742
(800) 964•4114
Available in the Southwest through:
Home Depot

Sierra Paints
Acrylic copolymer interior/exterior paint available in primer, interior flat, interior eggshell enamel, interior semigloss enamel.
Dunn-Edwards Corp.
4885–East 52nd Place
Los Angeles, CA 90040
(888) 337•2468
Available in New Mexico through:
Wellborn/Dunn-Edwards Paints
Bill Santistevan
215 Rossmoor Road SW
Albuquerque, NM 87105
(505) 877•5050, (800) 228•0883, (800) 432•4069

Silicone Plus
Paintable silicone sealant, solvent in water.
DAP/Dow Corning
855 N. 3rd Street
Tip City, OH 45371
(800) 634•8382
Available at hardware chains including:
Home Depot, Ace Hardware, Hacienda Homecenters, Builders Square.

Sinak Corp.
pH Testing
A pH test pencil for measuring the alkalinity of concrete slabs.
Vapor emissions testing
A reusable calcium chloride dome test that won't mar or damage concrete surfaces
Sinak Corp.
861 Sixth Avenue, Suite 411
San Diego, CA 92101
(800) 523•3147
www.sinakcorp.com

Smart Wood Certification Program
www.smartwood.org

Smith and Hawken
A variety of sustainably harvested teak and cedar solid wood furniture.
Smith and Hawken
Two Arbor Lane, Box 6900
Florence, KY 41022-6900
(800) 776•3336
www.SmithandHawken.com

Sodium Silicate
Clear sealer for concrete floors. Widely distributed in hardware and ceramic supply stores.
Ashland Chemical, Inc.
5200 Blazer Parkway.
Dublin, OH 43017
(800) 258•0711, (614) 889•3333
www.gotoashland.com
Distributed by:
Copper Harbor
2250 Davis Street
San Leandro, CA 94577
(510) 639•4670
danw@copperharbor.com
(order by case of four 1-gallon packages.)

Soil Gas Collector Matting
Used alongside perimeter at top of stem wall along with "T" risers and piping. Effectively removes radon gas

before it enters building.
Professional Discount Supply
1029 South Sierra Madre, Suite B
Colorado Springs, CO 80903
(800) 688•5776, (719) 444•0646
www.radonpds.com

Spanish Pueblo Doors
Custom wood doors and cabinets.
Spanish Pueblo Doors
P.O. Box 2517
Santa Fe, NM 87504
(505) 473•0464
www.spdoors.com

Spectra-Tone Paints
Zero-VOC, solvent-free latex paint; cost-competitive with standard quality latex.
Spectra-Tone Paint Corporation
1595 E. San Bernardino Avenue
San Bernardino, CA 92408-2946
(800) 272•4687, (909) 478•3485
www.spectra-tone.com

Spotcheck Pesticide Testing Kit
Instant pesticide-checking kit based on technology developed by the U.S. military. Ships with supplies to carry out four tests of soil, water, food, or surfaces. Some of the pesticides that can be tested for include Sevin, Dursban, Diazinon, Malathion, and Parathion.
The Cutting Edge Catalog
P.O. Box 5034
Southhampton, NY 11969
(800) 497•9516
www.cutcat.com

Stabilizer
A colorless, odorless, psyllium-based additive for pathways, trails, and driveways.
Stabilizer Solutions, Inc.
205 South 28th Street
Phoenix, AZ 85034
(602) 225•5900, FAX (602) 225•5902, (800) 336•2468
stabilizersolutions.com
lphubbs@stabilizersolutions.com

Stevens EP
Low-odor, ethylene propylene, heat-weldable roofing membrane.
Stevens Roofing Products
9 Sullivan Road
Holyoke, MA 01040
(800) 621•7663, (413) 533•8100

Summitville-700 SummitChromes
Sanded grout without polymer additives, available in 32 colors.
Summitville Tiles, Inc.
Summitville, OH 43962
(330) 223•1511, FAX (330) 223•1414
www.summitville.com

Sure Seal Foam Tape
An adhesive-backed gasket that is extremely compressible and creates a tight seal. Must be mail ordered.
Denarco, Inc
301 Industrial Drive
Constantine, MI 49042
(616) 435•8404

Taylor Tools
pH Testing
A combined moisture and alkali test kit for concrete slabs.
Vapor emissions testing
A calcium chloride vapor emissions testing kit for concrete slabs
www.taylorflooringtools.com

The Natural
A complete line of cleaning and homecare products. Degreaser, Bath Tub & Tile Cleaner, and all-purpose products meet Green Seal standards.
The Clean Environment Co., Inc.
P.O. Box 4444
Lincoln, NE 68504
(402) 464•0988
www.safegreenclean.com

Thermal Shield Free
An unfaced, formaldahyde-free fiberglass.
Johns Manville Insulation Group
P.O. Box 5108
Denver, CO 80217-5108
(800) 654•3103

Thoroseal Foundation Coating
Cementitious waterproofing for concrete surfaces.
Thoro Systems Products
8570 Phillips Highway, Suite 101
Jacksonville, FL 32256-8208
(800) 433•9517, (904) 828•4900
www.chemrex.com

TimberGrass
Bamboo flooring and accessories.
TimberGrass LLC
9790 NE Murden Cove Drive
Bainbridge Island, WA 98110

(800) 929•6333, (206) 842•9477
www.timbergrass.com

Timberline 2051
Wood flooring adhesive for laminated plank and parquet flooring.
W.F. Taylor Company, Inc.
11545 Pacific Avenue
Fontana, CA 92337
(800) 397•4583, (909) 360•6677
www.wftaylor.com

Timber-Tek UV
An oil resin-based, waterborne penetrating oil.
Timber-Tek UV
13807 SE McLoughlin Bl., Suite 421
Milwaukie, OR 97222
(888) 888•6095
Distributed by:
Planetary Solutions
2030–17th Street
Boulder, CO 80302
(303) 442•6228
www.planetearth.com

Timbor
Disodium octaborate wood preservative protects against termites, fungus, and wood-boring beetles.
Nisus Corporation
215 Dunavunt Drive
Rockford, TN 37853
(800) 264•0870, (865) 577•6119
www.nisuscorp.com

Titebond Solvent Free Adhesives
Construction Adhesive
Subfloor Adhesive
A multi-purpose adhesive for a variety of porous surfaces, including plywood and wood paneling.
Franklin International
2020 Bruck Street
Columbus, OH 43207
(800) 347•4583
www.titebond.com

Touch'n Foam
Expanding foam sealant that is free of CFCs, HCFCs, and formaldehyde.
Convenience Products
866 Horan Drive
Fenton, MO 63026
(800) 325•6180, (636) 349•5855
www.convenienceproducts.com
Available through:
Walmart, Home Depot, and Ace True Value Hardware.

Truss Joist McMillan
Engineered wood joists.
6739 Academy Road NE, Suite 110
Albuquerque, NM 87109
(505) 764•0304, FAX (505) 764•0306

Tu-Tuf 3
High-density, cross-laminated
polyethylene, puncture-resistant air
barrier.

Tu-Tuf 4
Tu-Tuf 4 is thicker than Tu-Tuf 3 and
can be effectively used under concrete.
Stocote Products, Inc.
Drawer 310
Richmond, IL 60071
(800) 435•2621, (262) 279•6000

Tyvek HomeWrap
Housewrap, vapor barrier.
DuPont Co.
1007 Market Street
Wilmington, DE 19898
(800) 44TYVEK, (800) 441•7515
www.dupont.com

Ultra-Touch
29 oz. carpet cushion of recycled
fibers.
Bonded Logic
411 East Ray Road
Chandler, AZ 85225
(480) 812•9114
www.bondedlogic.com

Union Airtight Boxes
Airtight electrical boxes.
Available through:
Minnesota Electric Supply
North Highway 29
Alexandria, MN 56308
(320) 763•5131

**United Duct Sealer (Waterbase),
Uni-Mastic 181, Uni-Flex Duct Sealer
(Low VOC)**
Low-VOC, water-based duct mastics
for residential use.

McGill AirSeal Corporation
2400 Fairwood Avenue
Columbus, OH 43207-2700
(800) 624•5535

Van EE
Air to air heat exchanger.
Shelter Supply
17725 Juniper Path
Lakeville, MN 55044
(800) 762•8399
www.sheltersupply.com

Vaprecision
Vapor emissions testing. A calcium
chloride vapor emissions testing kit for
concrete slabs.
Professional Vapor Emission Testing
System
P.O. Box 1396
Costa Mesa, CA 92628-1396
(800) 449•6194, (714) 754•6141
www.vaportest.com

Vocomp-25
Water-based acrylic concrete sealer.
W.R. Meadows
P.O. Box 543
Elgin, IL 60121
(800) 342•5976
www.wrmeadows.com

Volclay
4' × 4' corrugted kraft panels filled with
bentonite clay that expand when wet
to form a waterproof barrier.
Cetco
1500 West Shure Drive
Arlington Heights, IL 60004-1440
(800) 426•5564, (800) 527•9948,
(847) 392•5800
www.cetco.com

Weatherall Products
Sealings, coating, adhesives.
Weatherall UV Guard
Exterior acrylic wood finish that
penetrates and seals, forming a
protective shield against UV, rot, and

decay. Comes in clear and semi-
transparent finishes.
**Weatherall UV Guard Premium
Caulking**
A professional strength acrylic-based
sealant designed for use in a wide
variety of construction applications.
Weatherall Co., Inc.
106 Industrial Way
Charlestown, IN 47111
(800) 367•7068, (303) 697•1680,
FAX (303) 697•1601

Weather-Bos Products
Stains and finishes for durable high
performance protection.
Masonry Boss Formula 9
Water-reducible sealer for all above-
grade concrete and masonry surfaces.
Helps reduce dusting, powdering,
efflorescence, spalling, cracking,
freeze-thaw damage.
The Boss
Four different formulas for protection
of exterior wood surfaces.
*Distributed and drop-shipped same day
by:*
Weather-Bos International
316 California Avenue, Suite 1082
Reno, NV 89509
(800) 664•3978, FAX (916) 272•8098
www.weatherbos.com
info@weatherbos.com

Weather Pro
A water-based, water-repellant wood
stain for interior/exterior. VOC
compliant.
Okon, Inc.
4725 Leyden Street, Unit A
Denver, CO 80216
(800) 237•0565, (303) 377•7800
www.okoninc.com

Wilsonart International
Solid surface (like Corian) material
called "Gibraltar." Wilsonart has put in
place some extensive "green"
manufacturing practices, and this

particular plastic offgases very little.
Wilsonart International
2400 Wilson Place
Temple, TX 76504
(800) 433•3222, FAX (254) 207•2474
www.wilsonart.com
Available through:
Wilsonart
30830 San Clemente Street
Hayward, CA 94544
(510) 489•9555, (800) 433•3222, FAX
(510) 489•7990

Wirsbo Aquapex
A cross-linked polyethylene nontoxic
plumbing system.
Wirsbo Hepex
Cross-linked polyethylene tubing for
radiant floor heating.
Wirsbo
5925–148th Street West
Apple Valley, MN 55124-9928
(800) 321•4739
www.wirsbo.com

Xypex
Concrete waterproofing by
crystallzation. EPA-approved for
potable water. Protects concrete
against spalding, efflorescence, and
other damage.
Xypex Chemical Corporation
13731 Mayfield Place
Richmond, BC, Canada V6V 2G9
(800) 961•4477, (604) 273•5265
www.xypex.com

**Zip Guard Environmental Water
Base Urethane**
Clear finish for interior woodwork.
Star Bronze Co., Inc.
P.O. Box 2206
Alliance, OH 44601
(800) 321•9870, (330) 823•1550
www.starbronze.com

If you have enjoyed *Prescriptions for a Healthy House* you might also enjoy other

BOOKS TO BUILD A NEW SOCIETY

Our books provide positive solutions for people who want to make a difference. We specialize in:

Sustainable Living ✦ Ecological Design and Planning ✦ Natural Building & Appropriate Technology

New Forestry ✦ Environment and Justice ✦ Conscientious Commerce ✦ Progressive Leadership

Educational and Parenting Resources ✦ Resistance and Community ✦ Nonviolence

For a full list of NSP's titles, please call 1-800-567-6772 or check out our web site at:

www.newsociety.com

New Society Publishers

ENVIRONMENTAL BENEFITS STATEMENT

New Society Publishers has chosen to produce this book on New Leaf EcoBook 100, recycled paper made with 100% post consumer waste, processed chlorine free, and old growth free.

For every 5,000 books printed, New Society saves the following resources:[1]

56	Trees
5,027	Pounds of Solid Waste
5,532	Gallons of Water
7,215	Kilowatt Hours of Electricity
9,139	Pounds of Greenhouse Gases
39	Pounds of HAPs, VOCs, and AOX Combined
14	Cubic Yards of Landfill Space

---

[1]Environmental benefits are calculated based on research done by the Environmental Defense Fund and other members of the Paper Task Force who study the environmental impacts of the paper industry.

For more information on this environmental benefits statement, or to inquire about environmentally friendly papers, please contact New Leaf Paper – info@newleafpaper.com Tel: 888 • 989 • 5323.

NEW SOCIETY PUBLISHERS